# MANAGING PRODUCTIVITY IN ORGANIZATIONS

## A PRACTICAL, PEOPLE-ORIENTED PERSPECTIVE

# McGraw-Hill Series in Management

Fred Luthans and Keith Davis, *Consulting Editors*

# MANAGING PRODUCTIVITY IN ORGANIZATIONS

## A PRACTICAL, PEOPLE-ORIENTED PERSPECTIVE

### Richard E. Kopelman

Baruch College
The City University of New York

**McGRAW-HILL BOOK COMPANY**

New York   St. Louis   San Francisco   Auckland   Bogotá
Hamburg   Johannesburg   London   Madrid   Mexico   Montreal   New Delhi
Panama   Paris   São Paulo   Singapore   Sydney   Tokyo   Toronto

89771

This book was set in Times Roman by University Graphics, Inc. (ECU).
The editors were John R. Meyer and Stephan O. Parnes;
the cover was designed by Cynthia Eyring;
the production supervisor was Marietta Breitwieser.
R. R. Donnelley & Sons Company was printer and binder.

**MANAGING PRODUCTIVITY IN ORGANIZATIONS: A
PRACTICAL, PEOPLE-ORIENTED PERSPECTIVE**

2 3 4 5 6 7 8 9 0  DOCDOC  8 9 8 7 6

ISBN 0-07-035329-8

Library of Congress Cataloging in Publication Data

Kopelman, Richard E.
    Managing productivity in organizations.

    (McGraw-Hill series in management)
    Includes indexes.
    1. Industrial productivity.   2. Organizational
effectiveness.   I. Title.   II. Series.
HD56.K66  1986      658.3′14      85-11640
ISBN 0-07-035329-8

The author gratefully acknowledges permission to reprint:

Excerpts from *Management: Tasks, Responsibilities, Practices* by Peter F. Drucker. Copyright
    © 1973, 1974 by Peter F. Drucker. Reprinted by permission of Harper & Row, Publishers,
    Inc.

Excerpts from *In Search of Excellence* by Thomas J. Peters and Robert H. Waterman.
    Copyright © 1982 by Thomas J. Peters and Robert H. Waterman. Reprinted by permission
    of Harper & Row, Publishers, Inc.

# CONTENTS

# PREFACE

This is a book about productivity. More specifically, it is about the effects of several behavioral science techniques (methods, approaches) that are widely believed to improve productivity in organizations.

A number of factors have contributed to my undertaking this effort. One is the growing skepticism I have noted among people in all walks of life as to whether the behavioral sciences offer any real, practical contributions to managing organizations. Increasingly, I have heard students complain that their textbooks are largely compilations of theories—and that the theories are often contradictory. Some students have apparently concluded that the major learnings from behavioral science courses consist of vagaries and platitudes such as "There is no one best way," "There are many ways to skin a cat," and "It all depends." Graduate students often arrive at the same conclusion but use more sophisticated terminology, for instance, "Results depend on contextual modifiers, boundary conditions, individual differences, situational factors, etc." In short, many students believe that there are no main effects, no reliable findings, no answers.

Many people in business and government have also apparently reached a similar conclusion. All too often, behavioral scientists are seen as producing uninterpretable mumbo jumbo, psychobabble, which even if it could be understood has little relationship to the practical problems of managing an organization.

For decades behavioral scientists themselves have warned their colleagues that the viability of their work depends, in the final analysis, on addressing and solving relevant problems. Yet while managers are interested in practical issues such as productivity, product quality, and personnel turnover, most (approximately 90 percent) of the academic literature has focused on scientific constructs largely related to such unobservable, intrapsychic phenomena as attitudes, perceptions, beliefs, intentions, values, and attributions. Managers, presumably, are supposed to make the leap of faith that attention to these latter phenomena will result in greater profits or help meet the payroll.

Aware that I was teaching behavioral science courses and that many people were skeptical about the practical value of such material, I was receptive to a request by Steven Markowitz, then of the Continental Group, Inc., to prepare a research report. He asked me to examine the results of prominent behavioral science approaches to improving productivity in organizations and to determine which approaches worked and which did not. After several years and major revisions, the result was this book.

Among other audiences, this book is intended for both graduate and advanced undergraduate students. Whereas many textbooks emphasize theories and prescriptions, this book focuses on descriptions and evaluations (What has been attempted? What has worked and what has not? Under what conditions?). Accordingly, it can supplement texts in courses such as organizational behavior, management, organizational psychology, human resource management, and organization development, or it can serve as the primary text in productivity management courses.

This book is also intended for managers and staff professionals, many of whom are continually bombarded with brochures making all sorts of claims about the efficacy of various productivity-improvement techniques. In the absence of a systematic, comprehensive examination of the evidence, it is difficult to judge the effectiveness of a particular human resource management technique; certainly, isolated success stories related by promoters of particular techniques should not be relied on too heavily.

As in all projects such as this, a debt is owed to many people. I would like to recognize and thank Paul H. Thompson and Gene W. Dalton, my teachers and mentors at the Harvard Business School, for showing me how to align theories with problems. A number of colleagues, past and present, at Baruch College have also been very helpful, most notably Gary A. Yukl, from whom I learned a lot, and Donald J. Vredenburgh, who provided a good deal of needed encouragement. I am particularly grateful to Benjamin S. Karan, a graduate student, for his excellent editorial comments. Thanks are also extended to Izhar Barlev, Dee Birnbaum, and Lynn S. Mullins for helping me track down articles, and to Terry Masiello for typing the first draft of the manuscript.

A number of readers provided many valuable substantive suggestions, and I would like to express my appreciation to: Wayne F. Cascio, University of Colorado, Denver; Nina Gupta, University of Arkansas; Richard A. Guzzo, New York University; F. Theodore Helmer, University of Hawaii at Manoa; R. Duane Ireland, Baylor University; Mariann Jelinek, Case Western Reserve University; G. Douglas Jenkins, Jr., University of Arkansas; Todd Jick, Harvard Business School; Leonard Sayles, Columbia University; Frank L. Schmidt, University of Iowa; Neal Schmitt, Michigan State University; Edward G. Siebert, Grumman Aerospace Corporation; Martin Starr, Columbia University; Paul E. Thomsen, Public Service Company of Colorado; Philip Van Auken, Baylor University; and Ray Zammuto, NCHEMS, University of Colorado, Denver.

My editors, Kathi A. Benson and John R. Meyer, and my consulting editor, Fred Luthans, have all been very patient, and I thank them for their confidence. Stephan O. Parnes, the editing supervisor for this book, also contributed importantly. Lastly, I would like to thank my entire family, especially my wife, Carol, and my sons, Joshua and Michael, for their continuing love and support.

*Richard E. Kopelman*

# PART ONE

# INTRODUCTION

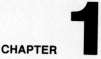

CHAPTER

# PRODUCTIVITY: AN OVERVIEW

What is meant by productivity, and why should we care about it? What factors influence the nation's productivity? These questions are central to a discussion of productivity; accordingly, this chapter addresses and attempts to answer them.

## THE MEANING OF PRODUCTIVITY

*"When I use a word," Humpty Dumpty said in a rather scornful tone, "it means just what I choose it to mean—neither more nor less."*

Lewis Carroll[1]

Productivity has become a popular term in recent years; indeed, it may be the number one buzzword of the 1980s. Yet many of those who use the term apparently (like Humpty Dumpty) have definitions in mind which are uniquely their own. Sample definitions include "getting more bang for the buck," "doing more with less," "the quality, timeliness, and cost-effectiveness with which an organization achieves its mission," "a state of mind—mind being confident that tomorrow can be better than today through one's own efforts."

Perhaps the most widely accepted definition of productivity is the physical process conceptualization used by many economists: *productivity* is the relationship between physical output and one or more of the associated physical inputs used in the production process. Broadly conceived, productivity is a

3

systems concept; it can apply to various entities, ranging from an individual or machine to a company, industry, or national economy. Physical process productivity, typically expressed as a ratio, reflects how efficiently resources are used in creating outputs. Frequently, partial productivity ratios are computed, showing the relationship between output and a single input, e.g., bushels of corn per acre, miles per gallon, units per labor hour.

Although partial productivity measures are most common, it is important to recognize that productivity is influenced by many factors, such as the amount and technical sophistication of capital equipment, the quality and availability of raw materials, the scale of operations, the skills, motivation and attitudes of employees, organizational work flow, and managerial competence. Notwithstanding the multiplicity of relevant inputs, productivity at the national level is typically measured solely in terms of output per hour of paid labor; organizations, too, frequently compute only labor productivity ratios. Several reasons have been advanced for the emphasis on labor productivity: (1) it is relatively easy to interpret, (2) it permits estimation of future labor requirements, and (3) it is related to unit labor costs.[2] Yet, partial productivity measures can be misleading. For example, suppose that the use of a higher-quality raw material by a manufacturing company increases labor productivity. Stockholders, employees, and consumers may all seek to distribute the gain in labor efficiency to themselves (via a dividend increase, higher wages, or lower prices, respectively). But the "gain" may previously have been distributed to suppliers in the form of higher raw material cost.[3]

Whereas physical process productivity pertains to the efficient use of resources, productivity can also be conceptualized in terms of value created. An organization, or any entity, can be highly *efficient* in producing goods or services, but this does not assure that the output is *effective* in satisfying needs and that it thus has value. The efficient manufacturer of buggy whips (or any output that is not demanded) is not likely to survive in a competitive economy: organizations must not only be efficient and "do things right," they must also be effective and "do the right things." Exclusive reliance on the efficiency criterion will likely discourage the investment needed to innovate and to create value over the long run. Accordingly, many organizational analysts recommend the computation of financial productivity (or "productiveness"). This measurement typically entails dividing value added (revenues minus goods and services purchased from others) by one or more physical inputs (e.g., labor hours, cubic feet of gas).

In a market economy, profitability is generally considered the best overall indicator of company performance. Profitability reflects the outcome of all managerial decisions: the products or services produced, marketing strategy, level of investment, and, of course, the underlying efficiency with which inputs are converted to outputs. When financial productivity is measured in terms of dollar value added and dollar (not physical) inputs, the resulting cost-effectiveness ratio is essentially a measure of profitability. Stated in another way,

$$\text{Profitability} = \frac{\text{output quantity}}{\text{input quantity}} \times \frac{\text{sales price}}{\text{cost price}}$$

$$= \text{physical process productivity} \times \text{price recovery}$$

$$= \frac{\text{output quantity} \times \text{sales price}}{\text{input quantity} \times \text{cost price}}$$

$$= \frac{\text{revenues}}{\text{expenses}}$$

In short, productivity as conventionally defined (physical process productivity), is a necessary, but not a sufficient, condition for economic success. Everything else being equal, the higher the level of physical process productivity, the greater the likelihood that an entity (individual, organization, etc.) will survive and prosper economically.[4] Of course, physical process productivity does not guarantee success, but guarantees are few and far between in any endeavor. The significance of productivity is discussed further, and in more concrete terms, in the next section.

## PRODUCTIVITY: WHY BOTHER?

Between 1947 and 1967 productivity increases in the private business sector averaged 3.2 percent per year; between 1967 and 1977 the average annual increase was 1.6 percent; and from 1977 to 1984 the average annual increase was 1.1 percent.[5] But why should we concern ourselves with productivity, a concept difficult to define and a phenomenon complex to measure? Because lagging productivity growth threatens our standard of living and national well-being in three ways.

*Real Income.* Growth in real income is dependent upon the production of more goods and the provision of more services, given available resources. We cannot, after all, consume more than we produce, unless we are willing to exhaust our savings and deplete capital.[6] Increased productivity, therefore, means more goods and services available for consumption (hence a higher standard of living) and/or increased capital formation, through greater savings.

*National Competitiveness.* In competitive markets, where prices reflect costs, scarcity, and values, productivity translates into jobs. If the United States fails to increase productivity as rapidly as other countries, domestically produced goods will become less and less competitive. Consequently, efficient foreign producers will win ever-increasing shares of domestic and foreign markets. Obviously, if we cannot sell, we cannot employ: the loss of competitiveness means loss of jobs.

*Quality of Life.* Increased productivity provides the means for an improved quality of life. Without productivity growth the economic pie is necessarily of fixed size, and attention naturally turns to divvying up the pie—i.e., the "zero-sum society" described by Lester Thurow.[7] One consequence is that various social programs (e.g., Social Security and Medicaid) must be contained or taxes increased. More generally, the result is a host of battles: between workers and retirees, between minorities and the majority, between city dwellers and suburbanites, between rich and poor, and on and on. But this need not be the case. Productivity growth creates the wherewithal to finance social programs, to improve education, to protect employees, consumers, and the environment, to support leisure-time pursuits—in short, to enhance the quality of life.

The relationship between productivity growth and real income, national competitiveness, and quality of life has been addressed in broad terms. A more detailed discussion follows.

### Real Income

There is much evidence that real income is tied to productivity. Figure 1-1 shows the strong correlation between real wages and productivity, and Figure 1-2 shows the other side of the coin, the correlation between labor costs and prices. As one commentator put it: Can a man run faster than his shadow? Of course, some industries have shown strong rates of productivity growth, while others have lagged far behind. Average annual productivity growth rates for selected industries are shown in Table 1-1. Not surprisingly, in industries with high productivity growth during the 1970s, real wages rose: 50 percent in

**FIGURE 1-1**
Real Earnings and Labor Productivity (output per hour) in the United States, 1947 to 1979 (1967 = 100). [*Reprinted with the permission of the Chamber of Commerce of the United States of America from Productivity, People and Public Policy (1981).*]

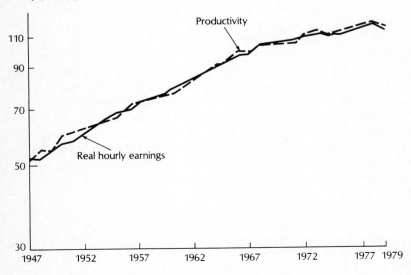

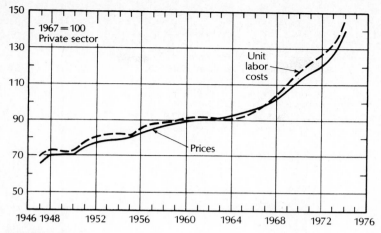

**FIGURE 1-2**
Prices and unit labor costs in the United States, 1947 to 1974 (1967 = 100). (*Warner & Swasey Company, in Business Week, 6 Dec.* 1976, p. 39.)

transportation and utilities and 25 percent in manufacturing. In industries with low productivity growth, real wages declined: 18 percent in service industries and 35 percent in retail trade.[8]

An examination of productivity growth rates across eleven industrialized countries reveals a similar relationship (see Table 1-2). Between 1970 and 1980

**TABLE 1-1**
AVERAGE ANNUAL GROWTH IN SELECTED U.S.
INDUSTRIES, 1970 TO 1980

| Industry | Percent average annual change in productivity (output per hour) |
|---|---|
| Synthetic fibers | 7.96 |
| Malt beverages | 7.05 |
| Telecommunications | 6.64 |
| Hosiery | 4.86 |
| Air transportation | 4.05 |
| Pharmaceuticals | 3.76 |
| Farm machinery | 2.44 |
| Steel | 1.62 |
| Concrete products | 0.26 |
| Footwear | 0.09 |
| Restaurants | −0.65 |
| Laundry and cleaning | −0.85 |
| Retail food stores | −0.96 |
| Coal mining | −2.24 |

*Source:* U.S. Department of Commerce, *Statistical Abstract of the United States* (Washington, D.C.: GPO, 1982–83), p. 399.

**TABLE 1-2**
AVERAGE ANNUAL GROWTH IN ELEVEN INDUSTRIALIZED
COUNTRIES, 1970 TO 1980

| Countries | Percent average annual increase | |
| --- | --- | --- |
| | Manufacturing productivity | Real hourly compensation |
| Japan | 7.40 | 4.14 |
| Belgium | 7.21 | 6.25 |
| Netherlands | 5.97 | 4.63 |
| Denmark | 5.79 | 3.95 |
| West Germany | 4.86 | 5.60 |
| Italy | 4.86 | 4.98 |
| France | 4.75 | 4.58 |
| Sweden | 3.30 | 3.58 |
| United Kingdom | 2.91 | 3.81 |
| Canada | 2.78 | 2.46 |
| United States | 2.54 | 0.84 |

*Source:* U.S. Department of Commerce, *Statistical Abstract of the United States* (Washington, D.C.: GPO, 1982–83), p. 874.

the U.S. productivity growth rate in manufacturing was 2.54 percent, far below the 4.86 percent median growth rate of the other countries. Concomitantly, the average annual increase in real hourly compensation was 0.84 percent in the United States, less than one-fifth of the 4.36 percent median increase in the other ten countries. And this finding is not an aberration. The four countries with the highest productivity growth rates experienced growth in real compensation that was 78 percent higher than that experienced by the four countries with the lowest productivity growth rates.[9]

Real wages are inherently linked to the value of goods and services produced per hour worked. Moreover, according to what is often called Bowley's law, the return to labor (wages and salaries) relative to the return to capital (rent, interest, profit) shows remarkable constancy, averaging 75 percent of the economic pie. In *A Century of Pay,* Brown and Browne reported that in five countries, labor's share of national income consistently averaged 75 percent between 1860 and 1960.[10] Had the United States maintained an average productivity growth rate of 3 percent during the 1970s, the average household would have had $4000 more personal income by 1980 and an estimated $7700 more by 1985.[11]

The relationship between productivity and standard of living has been known for some time. Seventy years ago Frederick W. Taylor observed:

There is fully twenty times the output per man now than there was three hundred years ago. That marks the increase in the real wealth of the world; that marks the increase in the happiness of the world, that gives us the opportunity for shorter hours, for better education, for amusement, for art, for music, for everything that is worthwhile in this world—goes right straight back to this increase in the output of the individual. . . . From what does the progress the world has made come? Simply from the increase in the output of the individual all over the world.[12]

The connection between productivity and numerous desiderata (a higher standard of living, lower inflation, increased investment, more jobs, greater leisure, etc.) is inexorable, regardless of the economic system. Consider the following: Labor productivity in East Germany in 1960 was 71 percent of that in West Germany, and the standard of living, 78 percent of that in West Germany; labor productivity in East Germany in 1980 was 46 percent of that in West Germany, and the standard of living, 43 percent of that in West Germany.[13]

Certainly the relationship between productivity and various social goals did not escape Yuri Andropov, the late Soviet leader. In his words (to factory workers):

> Miracles, as they say, don't happen. You understand yourselves that the Government can only give so many goods as are produced. The growth of wages—if it is not accompanied by needed wares, of good quality, if, finally, services are suffering— cannot give a real improvement in material well-being. . . . Everything we do and produce must be done and produced, to the degree possible, at minimum cost, high quality, quickly and durably. It is necessary to produce more goods, so shelves will not be empty any longer.[14]

### National Competitiveness

The evidence we have examined pertinent to real income growth across industrialized countries is, perhaps, disconcerting, but results are even grimmer in industries with low productivity (see Table 1-1). In steel, for example, or in footwear, we see the dramatic effects of low productivity growth on competitiveness, and the consequent loss of jobs. In 1970 the iron and steel industry employed 531,000 people and imports were 80 percent higher than exports. By 1981, employment had dropped to 391,000 and imports were 495 percent greater than exports. While net imports rose from 4 percent to 14 percent of domestic consumption, employment declined by 26 percent.[15] The decline in the footwear industry was even more pronounced: from 233,000 workers in 1965 to 144,000 workers in 1981, a reduction of 38 percent. During the same period, imports increased from $160 million to over $3 billion.[16] Of course, all U.S. industries have not fared as badly as the two cited, yet lagging productivity is certainly one of the reasons why imports have grown more rapidly than exports. Although many factors influence the merchandise balance of trade, clearly, economic competitiveness is contributory. In 1960, the United States showed a surplus of $5 billion, by 1981 a deficit of more than $25 billion.[17]

### Quality of Life

Besides raising the standard of living, productivity growth allows for alternative uses of all means of production: leisure in place of labor, consumption in place of capital formation, and conservation of natural resources in place of depletion.[18] Further, productivity growth allows for the transfer of income to insure that human wants do not go unmet. In this regard the United States has made admirable strides: expenditures on social programs increased from $62 billion in 1970 to almost $300 billion in 1982.[19] As Felix Rohatyn put it, "Fairness and wealth have to go hand in hand. . . . Without the capacity to create wealth, it is impossible to deal with the issue of fairness."[20] In the absence of productivity growth, society is faced with the painful dilemma of program cuts vs. tax increases.

Yet it should be recognized that although productivity creates the *means* to support social welfare efforts (including environmental, consumer, and employee protection), expenditures on such efforts are necessarily political decisions. In this regard, Daniel Bell has commented that postindustrial society is

> increasingly a communal society wherein public mechanisms rather than the market become the allocators of goods, and public choice, rather than individual demand, becomes the arbiter of services. A communal society by its very nature multiplies the definition of rights—the rights of children, of students, of the poor, of minorities—and translates them into claims of the community.[21]

Whereas the virtue of the marketplace, notes Bell, is that it "coordinates human interdependence in some optimal fashion, in accordance with the expressed preferences of buyers and sellers,"[22] there is no mechanism for determining the relative values of various social welfare programs or public services. Consider the following dialogue (from *The Wizard of Id*) between the King (K) and one of his constituents (C):[23]

*C:* I got potholes in front of my house!
*K:* How deep are your potholes?
*C:* About 40 votes deep.
*K:* [talking to his assistant] Duke! Take care of those [potholes] immediately!

Perhaps the most insightful and prescient summary statement regarding the significance of productivity was provided by Gordon Bloom. His comments about the 1970s are even more relevant today:

> The central domestic issue of the coming decade will be the need to accelerate the rate of improvement in our productivity. We shall come to recognize this basic fact as a nation, not by reason of a deep insight into the workings of our economic system, nor because of a clearer vision of the future perils which may result from the continuation of present policies. The recognition of the dominant importance of productivity will be brought home to us by default. We shall suddenly come to realize that nothing else will work without it. All of our ambitious national goals—to eliminate unemployment and pollution and the malaise of our cities—all will be rendered unattainable unless we can improve our productivity and scale down the tempo of inflation. . . .
>
> Once we have made a decision of national commitment to productivity, we come face to face with a surprising enigma. Productivity is a much more elusive and

intractable problem than pollution, or unemployment, or other social problems which have confronted us in recent years. Unlike pollution, government cannot pass a law and look forward to an improvement in productivity. Unlike unemployment, the expenditure of funds will not necessarily help productivity and may in fact deter it. The rate of growth in productivity may be affected by appropriate government policy but it cannot be turned on and off like a spigot.[24]

## FACTORS INFLUENCING PRODUCTIVITY

Four major factors have contributed to the declining growth rate in productivity: (1) declining capital intensity, (2) declining expenditures on research and development, (3) changes in the composition of the labor force and the economy, and (4) changing societal attitudes and values. These factors are considered in turn.

### Declining Capital Intensity

One way to measure capital intensity is in terms of capital outlays per worker. From 1950 to 1972 the average annual growth rate in capital outlays per worker was 2.9 percent; however, from 1972 to 1979 the average annual growth rate was 0.6 percent. Had the prior growth rate been maintained, the capital stock in 1979 would have been $200 billion larger. A second measure of capital intensity is in terms of gross national product (GNP). In 1980, expenditures on capital were approximately 10 percent of GNP, compared to roughly 20 percent in Japan.[25] At least six factors have contributed to the decline in capital intensity.

**Tax Policies** In 1969, capital gains taxes were nearly doubled, and they were raised again in 1976 to almost 50 percent. Consequently, if an asset appreciated by 40 percent, and one-half the increase were due to inflation, the capital gains tax equaled the entire noninflationary gain. Not surprisingly, between 1969 and 1978 (when capital gains taxes were lowered), some 6 million investors dropped out of the capital markets and new venture financing virtually disappeared.[26] The capital gains tax has since been reduced again, resulting (apparently) in the dramatic increase in capital commitments shown in Figure 1-3.

**Inflation** One impact of the inflationary environment of the 1970s was an increase in personal tax rates via "bracket creep"; concomitantly there was a decrease in personal savings.[27] Inflation did not merely reduce savings, it also affected investment choices: large sums were invested in passive hedges against inflation such as collectibles, e.g., precious metals, oriental rugs, stamps, vintage wines, and various other nonproductive assets.[28] Further, inflation caused corporate earnings to be overstated to the extent that inventory and depreciation expenses were less than current replacement costs. Capital investment, in effect, was taxed by inflation.

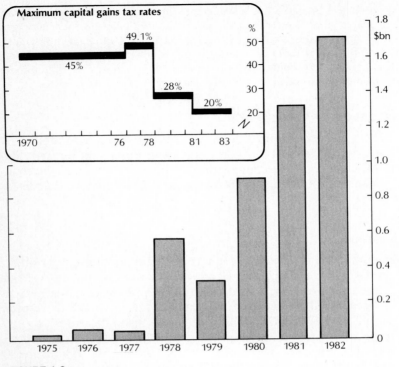

**FIGURE 1-3**
United States new capital commitments. (*Economist, 24 Dec. 1983, p. 65.*)

**Growth in the Public Sector** Evidence accumulated by the Hudson Institute Europe indicates that the larger an economy's public sector, the slower the rate of economic growth (see Figure 1-4). An independent study by David Smith found that the size of the public sector accounted for more than one-third of the variation in growth among nineteen nations.[29] Apparently, a larger public sector leads to slower economic growth through shrinking profits and declining capital investment—a "crowding-out" effect.

**Increased Energy Costs** It may not be mere coincidence that the sharp slowdown in productivity began in 1974, right after the energy crisis and the upsurge of inflation. Higher relative prices for energy very likely led to the substitution of labor for capital that became uneconomical with higher energy costs. There is evidence to support this view: From 1960 to 1972 labor productivity increased by 2.4 percent annually; however, from 1973 to 1980 labor productivity increased at a rate of only 0.3 percent. Almost the reverse pattern occurred with respect to energy. Energy productivity rose slightly in the early 1960s and was declining prior to the first OPEC price increase; however, from 1973 to 1980 energy productivity rose at the annual rate of 2 percent.[30] Higher

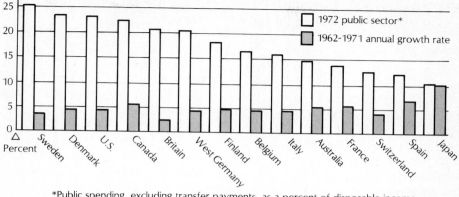

*Public spending, excluding transfer payments, as a percent of disposable income.
Data: Hudson Research Europe

**FIGURE 1-4**
The larger the public sector of an economy, the slower real growth. (*Reprinted from the
October 18, 1976 issue of Business Week by special permission, © 1976 by McGraw-Hill, Inc.*)

energy prices apparently induced firms to invest in capital that was cost-effective but not necessarily efficient regarding labor productivity.

    **Government Regulations**  In 1965 the number of regulatory agencies was 58; by 1976 the number was 455, employing 105,000 people, generating more than 9800 different types of forms, yielding an estimated 586 million responses.[31] The direct cost associated with completing the paperwork was approximately $5 billion in 1979.[32]

    Far greater than the paperwork costs are the indirect costs of complying with federal laws and regulations. The estimated total cost of regulations was $102.7 billion in 1979 and $150 billion in 1981.[33] Moreover, the opportunity costs associated with delays in introducing new products, deferred or cancelled new investments, and new workers not hired were excluded from these estimates.[34]

    **Aging Plant and Equipment**  Clearly, productivity depends not only on the unamortized amount of capital, but also on its technological up-to-dateness. In 1980, the average age of plants in the U.S. was 20 years; in West Germany it was 12 years, and in Japan 10 years.[35] In Japan, for example, the steel industry has been rebuilt several times since the war, and now incorporates the most modern technology; hence, higher productivity than among U.S. steelmakers.[36]

### Declining Expenditures on R&D

Historically, a large share of productivity improvement has resulted from new technology: the use of new production methods, materials, processes, and machinery. In recent years organized research and development (R&D) has been the primary source of technological advance. Some economists even treat R&D expenditures as a form of capital investment.[37]

Expenditures for R&D as a percentage of GNP reached a peak of 3.1 percent in 1964 and declined steadily to 2.2 percent in 1978. Since then R&D expenditures have risen slightly, reaching 2.4 percent in 1981.[38]

Another pertinent factor is engineering education, essential not only for R&D, but for implementing innovation. Although the federal education budget is quite substantial, only a small proportion is spent to further the education of engineers and scientists. Consider the following comparative data: In 1971 the United States produced 17,359 electrical engineering graduates and Japan produced 15,314. In 1977 the United States produced 14,290 electrical engineering graduates (a drop of 18 percent), whereas Japan produced 19,257 (an increase of 26 percent). Japan, a nation of 114 million people, produced 35 percent more electrical engineering graduates than the United States, a nation of 220 million people. Between 1971 and 1977 the Japanese economy grew at an annual rate of 3.9 percent; during the same period the U.S. economy contracted at a rate of 3.2 percent.[39]

Clearly, the extraordinary economic performance of Japan—a 7.4 percent annual growth rate in manufacturing productivity between 1970 and 1980—is due in part to rapidly implementing the fruits of R&D efforts. For example, recently a 7-year program was launched to introduce advanced machinery to companies too small to develop it independently.[40] And, as noted previously, the steel industry in Japan has continuously adopted the most modern technology.

### Changes in the Composition of the Labor Force and the Economy

An important factor contributing to declining U.S. productivity growth in the private sector has been the combined effects of changes in (1) the composition of the labor force and (2) the relative importance of different sectors of the economy. Each of these components is considered in turn.

**The Labor Force** Changing demographic characteristics of the labor force (in particular, age and sex) contributed importantly to declining U.S. productivity during the 1970s. The postwar baby boom resulted in a rapid increase in the proportion of younger workers in the work force during the 1970s. Also, during this period there was a dramatic expansion in the number of female employees, many without recent work experience, who entered the work force—(a Nielsen survey showed a 29 percent increase between 1973 and 1980).[41] With respect to these trends, Jerome Mark noted that "new entrants typically are less productive because they lack experience, and women, at least traditionally, are less productive because they are concentrated in less productive occupations"[42] (e.g., clerical or service jobs). Fortunately, these effects should diminish, and perhaps even be reversed, over time as the baby boom cohort gains experience, the increased participation of women centers more in the 25–44-year-old age group, and the proportion of semiskilled, skilled, and professional employees grows.[43]

**The Economy** The trend in overall private sector productivity reflects both changes in the productivity of component sectors and shifts in the relative sizes of these sectors. Three shifts have influenced the composite level of productivity: (1) from farm to nonfarm sectors, (2) from goods producing industries to service industries, and (3) from low-productivity energy producing industries to high-productivity energy producing industries.

Since the late 1940s there has been a marked shift from the farm sector to the nonfarm sectors of the economy. Because productivity has been relatively lower in farming, this shift has contributed substantially to the overall rise in productivity. In 1947, 19 percent of all hours worked in the private-business sector were in agriculture; however by 1966 only 7 percent of all hours were in agriculture. By 1977 the proportion was down to 5 percent.[44]

The shift from goods-producing industries to service industries is a second factor contributing to slower economic growth. Daniel Bell states that,

> The simple and obvious fact is that productivity and output grow much faster in goods than in services. . . . Productivity in services, because it is a relation between persons, rather than between man and machine, will inevitably be lower than it is in industry. . . . As William J. Baumol is fond of pointing out, a half-hour quintet calls for the expenditure of 2½ man hours in its performance, and there can be no increase in productivity when the musician's wage goes up.[45]

A third shift relates to energy-producing industries. There has been a slowing in the shift from less-productive energy industries (such as coal mining) to more-productive energy industries (such as oil and gas).

## Changes in Societal Attitudes and Values

During the past decade there have been accelerating changes in societal attitudes and values. Four changes, in particular, seem to bear on the declining productivity growth rate in the United States: (1) a decline in the work ethic, (2) a growing incidence of alcoholism and drug abuse, (3) a growing acceptance of the notion that justice means equality of results, and (4) growth in the subterranean economy.

**The Work Ethic** Data from various sources attest to a declining work ethic among large numbers of workers. Consider the following findings:

• In 1953 and 1976, large cross sections of Americans were asked, "If you were to get enough money to live comfortably, would you continue working?" In 1953, 20 percent of respondents said they would not continue working; in 1976 the proportion was 40 percent higher (28 percent).[46]

- In 1969, 58 percent of Americans believed that "hard work always pays off." By 1976, only 43 percent of Americans held this belief.[47]
- In the late 1960s, nearly 50 percent of all employed Americans saw their work as a source of personal fulfillment; however, by the late 1970s, the proportion dropped to under 25 percent.[48]
- In 1970, 34 percent of Americans agreed that "work is the center of my life." Only 13 percent agreed in 1978.[49]
- An extensive survey conducted in the late 1970s found that the work ethic was reasonably strong among older workers but was significantly weaker among younger workers. More specifically, pride in craftsmanship was less important to younger workers, who also reported that being of service was less desirable; on the other hand, having more leisure and free time were more important to younger workers, and for them it was more acceptable to do a poor job.[50]

In light of these trends it is not surprising that the average number of hours worked per week by full-time employees has fallen from 39.8 in 1950 to 38.8 in 1965, 36.2 in 1976, and 35.6 in 1980. Further, as of 1977 almost 14 percent of the pay package went to pay for time not worked.[51] This is significant because national productivity figures are based on the number of *paid* hours (including paid holidays, sick leave days, and vacation days), not the number of hours *worked*.

Moreover, not only has the workweek shrunk, so has the time spent working. For more than a decade, Robert Half International has collected data regarding paid work time spent not working—what they call "time theft": arriving late, overly long lunch hours, unreasonable socializing, reading magazines or attending to personal matters on company time, daydreaming, making numerous or long personal phone calls, and leaving early. Robert Half found that in 1970, 3½ hours per week were lost this way; however, their 1981 survey indicated that the loss had grown to 4 hours and 18 minutes.[52] If these data are accurate, and there is independent evidence that suggests that they are (see footnote 52), the loss in work time—roughly 2.5 percent of the workweek—corresponds closely to the drop in national productivity.

**Substance Abuse**   It has been estimated that between 5 and 10 percent of the employee population in the United States suffers from alcoholism and that between 3 and 7 percent use some form of illicit drug on a daily basis. Although the growth in substance abuse has gone virtually unchecked, a survey revealed that only 1.8 percent of executives from leading service-sector corporations believed that substance abuse was a "very serious problem."[53]

Yet the costs of substance abuse are very high. While the human cost in pain and suffering is immeasurable, the dollar costs for health care, days away from work, and lost productivity are known. "Employees with a drinking or drug problem are absent 16 times more than the average employee, have an accident rate that is 4 times greater, use a third more sickness benefits, and have 5 times more compensation claims while on the job."[54] All told, the costs associated with substance abuse approximate $70 billion; nearly half the amount—$30.1 billion—relates to lost productivity due to alcohol and drug abuse.[55]

### Equal Treatment Is Equitable

*Americans love the ideal of equality. In intellectual terms they may be confused as to what it implies, but emotionally they are not in doubt.*

John W. Gardner[56]

For most Americans the ideals of equality and justice are closely connected and derive, it would appear, from basic inalienable rights as codified in the Constitution of the United States.[57] Frequently, advocates of equality have argued that equality of opportunity is an inadequate means of achieving social justice; instead what is needed, they assert, is equality of treatment. Jencks, for example, has written that

> instead of trying to reduce people's capacity to gain a competitive advantage on one another, we [will] have to change the rules of the game so as to reduce the rewards of competitive success and the costs of failure. Instead of trying to make everyone equally lucky or equally good at his job, we [will] have to devise "insurance" systems which neutralize the effects of luck, and income sharing systems which break the link between vocational success and living standards.[58]

Similarly, Herbert Gans, in *More Equality,* has argued that new policies must aim for equality of results, so that people become more equal in income, education, quality of jobs, and political power.[59]

Along these lines, John Rawls has written in *A Theory of Justice* that the intent and effect of public policy must be to nullify the impact of "accidents of natural endowment and the contingencies of social circumstances."[60] He further asserts that "all social primary goods—liberty and opportunity, income and wealth, and the bases of self-respect—[should] be distributed equally unless an unequal distribution of any or all these goods is to the advantage of the less favored."[61]

It would appear that societal attitudes have drifted in the direction of equality of outcomes. But this trend may have some social costs. Hill and Dalton suggest that movement toward equality of results interferes with the use of incentives to improve productivity and output.[62] And Arthur Okun has written in *Equality and Efficiency: The Big Tradeoff* that in pursuing equality of results

> society would forgo any opportunity to use material rewards as incentives to production. And that would lead to inefficiencies that would be harmful to the welfare of the majority. Any insistence on carving the pie into equal shares would shrink the size of the pie. That fact poses the tradeoff between economic equality and economic efficiency.[63]

The assumption that equal treatment is equitable is philosophically antagonistic to the use of merit rewards. Yet there is abundant evidence, at the organizational level, that pay-for-performance plans increase labor productivity by approximately 30 percent compared to hourly pay plans (see Chapter 3). Even where measured outputs cannot be computed, evidence indicates that the merit reward approach increases overall levels of performance, compared to the "everyone gets the same" approach. Thus, to the extent that the connection between performance and rewards is attenuated (e.g., by paying merit raises ranging from 5 to 7 percent instead of from 2 to 10 percent), average productivity levels will likely fall.

**The Subterranean Economy**    Peter Gutmann estimated that in the United States in 1976 the subterranean economy—business that transactors did not want either recorded or taxed—generated a gross national product of $176 billion (a sum almost as large as the entire legal GNP in Canada that year).[64] More recently, Gutmann reported that the subterranean economy had grown at an accelerating rate, reaching $420 billion in 1982—a finding he attributed to high tax rates and onerous government regulations.[65] Of course, the subterranean economy is excluded from national income statistics; hence, to the extent that goods and services go unrecorded, official productivity measures may understate actual levels.

While societal attitudes and values have not been entirely supportive of productive growth, in recent years signs have emerged that views are becoming more favorable.[66] To be sure, the issue of productivity has received abundant attention in many forums. For example, one journalist has written that productivity "is neither conservative nor liberal. Increased productivity builds backyard tennis courts in Scarsdale, but it also pays for home pool tables in Bensonhurst and food stamps in Harlem."[67] In a similar vein, Walter Annenberg has noted that "the critical need for higher productivity already has been emphasized in a number of ways by various media. . . . What is also required is a continuing effort in print and, especially, in television to set forth again the common interest of Government and business and labor in increasing productivity, to make unmistakably clear the advantages of working together intelligently and equitably."[68]

## CONCLUSION

What is meant by productivity? Why should people care about it? What factors influence productivity at the national level? This chapter has addressed and has attempted to answer these questions. Whereas the focus in this chapter has been on productivity in terms of aggregate national and industry statistics (a macro perspective), the remainder of this book focuses on productivity in terms of the organization, department, work group, or individual (a micro perspective). The next chapter presents a conceptual framework of the determinants of productivity at the level of the organization; it also describes the method by which pertinent data have been obtained and analyzed.

# NOTES

1 Lewis Carroll, *Through the Looking Glass* (New York: Grosset & Dunlap, 1946), p. 238 (Ch. 6).

2 Leon Greenberg, *A Practical Guide to Productivity Measurement* (Washington, D.C.: BNA, 1973), p. 3.

3 Moreover, a partial productivity measure may increase while total productivity declines. Charles E. Craig and R. Clark Harris, "Total Productivity Measurement at the Firm Level," *Sloan Management Review,* 14 (Spring 1973), 13–28.

4 Additionally, in goods producing organizations (where physical output can be readily measured), it is useful to analyze the sources of changes in profitability. For example, an international steel company reported a profit increase of $120 million. Further analysis, however, revealed that improved price recovery added $170 million to profits, but lower physical process productivity reduced profits by $50 million. Although the net effect was positive, continuation of these trends could be detrimental in the long run, the result being decreased ability to compete coupled with heightened price competition. See Bazil J. van Loggerenberg and Stephen J. Cucchiaro, "Productivity Measurement and the Bottom Line," *National Productivity Review,* 1 (Winter 1981–82), 87–99.

5 Paradoxically, the dramatic slowdown in productivity growth in recent years may prove beneficial: surely there would currently be far less interest in productivity had increases continued at around 1.5 percent annually.

6 And, of course, capital is needed to replace and modernize plant and equipment, the nonhuman means of production.

7 Lester C. Thurow, *The Zero-Sum Society* (New York: Basic Books, 1980).

8 U.S. Department of Commerce, *Statistical Abstract of the United States* (Washington, D.C.: GPO, 1979), pp. 414, 420. These data pertain to real 1978 wages in constant 1967 dollars.

9 U.S. Department of Commerce, *Statistical Abstract of the United States* (Washington, D.C.: GPO, 1982–83), p. 874. It should be noted that U.S. productivity growth in manufacturing was higher than for the private business sector as a whole.

10 E. H. Phelps Brown and Margaret Browne, *A Century of Pay* (New York: St. Martin's Press, 1968).

11 *New York Times,* 23 Jan. 1980, p. D3.

12 Frederick W. Taylor, "The Principles of Scientific Management," *Advanced Management Journal* (Sept. 1963), p. 31; originally published in the Dec. 1916 *Bulletin of the Taylor Society,* based on an address given by Taylor in Mar. 1915.

13 Werner Obst, "Growing Economic Gap between the Two Germanies," *Wall Street Journal,* 10 Nov. 1982, p. 29.

14 *New York Times,* 1 Feb. 1983, pp. A1, 4. Copyright © 1983 by the New York Times Company. Reprinted by permission.

15 *Statistical Abstract of the United States,* (1982–83), pp. 724, 791. With respect to steel alone, imports amounted to 22 percent of domestic consumption by 1983, despite "voluntary restraints"—i.e., protectionist agreements, *Wall Street Journal,* 16 Feb. 1984, p. 34.

16 *Statistical Abstract of the United States* (1982–83), pp. 397, 843; also U.S. Department of Commerce, *Statistical Abstract of the United States* (Washington, D.C.: GPO, 1966), p. 224.

**17** U.S. Department of Commerce, *Statistical Abstract of the United States* (Washington, D.C.: GPO, 1982–83), p. 833.

**18** John W. Kendrick, *Understanding Productivity: An Introduction to the Dynamics of Productivity Change* (Baltimore: Johns Hopkins Univ. Press, 1977), pp. 6–7, 108.

**19** Daniel Yankelovich, *New Rules: Searching for Self-Fulfillment in a World Turned Upside Down* (New York: Bantam, 1982), p. 200.

**20** *The Economist,* 19 Sept. 1981, p. 32.

**21** Daniel Bell, *The Coming of Post-Industrial Society* (New York: Basic Books, 1973), p. 159. Reprinted by permission of the publisher.

**22** Ibid., p. 279. Reprinted by permission of the publisher.

**23** By permission of Johnny Hart and News Group Chicago, Inc.

**24** Gordon F. Bloom, *Productivity in the Food Service Industry: Problems and Potential* (Cambridge, Mass.: MIT Press, 1972), pp. 19, 21, 22. Copyright © 1972 by The Massachusetts Institute of Technology; reprinted by permission of the publisher.

**25** *Wall Street Journal,* 15 Apr. 1980, p. 24.

**26** *Wall Street Journal,* 22 Sept. 1978, p. 17 (regarding stockholders); National Center for Productivity and Quality of Working Life, *Productivity in the Changing World of the 1980's* (Washington, D.C.: GPO, 1978), p. 35 (regarding new venture underwritings). Commented Milton Friedman: "High marginal tax rates have diverted enterprise and ingenuity from the promotion of productive efficiency to the creation of tax shelters" (*Newsweek,* 8 Sept. 1980, p. 69).

**27** *New York Times,* 3 Feb. 1980, p. 9; also *American Business,* May 1980, p. 35. More specifically, the average savings rate during the period from 1970–1975 was 7.1 percent of disposable income; in 1979, the savings rate was 4.5 percent, the lowest level in more than 30 years.

**28** *New York Times,* 3 Feb. 1980, p. 8.

**29** *Business Week,* 18 Oct. 1976, p. 138.

**30** Thomas W. Synott III, "Energy and Productivity," *Business Economics,* 17 (Jan. 1982), 63.

**31** Paul Mali, *Improving Total Productivity* (New York: Wiley, 1978), p. 296.

**32** Murray L. Weidenbaum, "The High Cost of Government Regulation," *Challenge.* 22 (Nov.–Dec. 1979), p. 37. Lower estimates (for earlier years) were provided by Edward F. Denison, *Accounting for Slower Economic Growth: The United States in the 1970's* (Washington, D.C.: Brookings Institution, 1979), pp. 128–129.

**33** Murray L. Weidenbaum, "High Cost," p. 37 (1979 estimate); John S. McClenahen, "How Regulation Shackles Economic Growth," *Industry Week,* 1 June 1981, p. 64 (1981 estimate).

**34** In this regard, economist A. G. Shillings commented, "The uncertainty about what will come out of Washington has been the biggest negative on productivity. Today nobody in his right mind would build a steel mill, for example, because he wouldn't know if it could meet whatever the regulations are when it's completed" (*Newsweek* 8 Sept. 1980, p. 54).

**35** *New York Times,* 23 Jan. 1980, p. D3.

**36** National Center for Productivity and Quality of Working Life, *Changing World,* pp. 21–22. D. M. Roderick, chairman of U.S. Steel, noted that the steel industry alone will require nearly $7 billion of additional capital *per year* to remain competitive through the 1980s (*Newsweek,* 8 Sept. 1980, pp. 64–65).

**37** National Center for Productivity and Quality of Working Life, *Changing World,* p. 27.

**38** *Statistical Abstract of the United States* (1982–83), p. 596.

**39** Benjamin M. Rosen, "The Electrical Engineering Gap: The United States Versus Japan," Morgan Stanley *Electronics Letter,* 1980, p. 7. Interestingly, in 1971 the U.S. produced 17,421 new lawyers—almost identical in number to electrical engineering graduates. However, by 1979 the number of law school graduates doubled to approximately 34,000. According to Benjamin Rosen, what happened between 1971 and 1979 was that "our litigious society has created demands—and presumably rewards—for a veritable army of new lawyers each year." In contrast, Japan in 1979 managed to function with a total of only 15,000 lawyers whereas the U.S. then had 450,000, twenty times as many on a per capita basis. Comments Rosen, "Looked at another way, each year we graduate twice as many new lawyers as Japan has altogether in the country. Could this be one key to the difference in national productivity levels?" in "Where Are All the Engineers? (Probably in Law School)," Morgan Stanley *Electronics Letter,* Dec. 1979, pp. 2, 4. For a related discussion see *U.S. News & World Report,* 20 Dec. 1982, pp. 58–64. By 1984, there were 600,000 lawyers in the U.S. (see *Business Week,* 26 Nov. 1984, p. 15).

**40** National Center for Productivity and Quality of Working Life, *Changing World,* pp. 21–22.

**41** *Wall Street Journal,* 3 July 1980, p. 19. The increase in the proportion of female workers occurred, remarkably, as total U.S. employment increased by 24 percent during the 1970s (*Newsweek,* 8 Sept. 1980, p. 57).

**42** Jerome A. Mark, "Productivity Trends and Prospects," *Work in America: The Decade Ahead,* ed. Clark Kerr and Jerome M. Rosow (New York: Van Nostrand, 1979), p. 194.

**43** Ibid., pp. 194–195.

**44** Ibid., pp. 195–196.

**45** Daniel Bell, *The Coming of Post-Industrial Society* (New York: Basic Books, 1973), p. 155. Reprinted by permission of the publisher.

**46** Robert P. Vecchio, "The Function and Meaning of Work and the Job: Morse and Weiss (1955) Revisited," *Academy of Management Journal,* 23 (1980), 364.

**47** Daniel Yankelovich, "Yankelovich on Today's Workers: We Need New Motivational Tools," *Industry Week,* 6 Aug. 1979, p. 61.

**48** Ibid.

**49** Daniel Yankelovich, *New Rules: Searching for Self-Fulfillment in a World Turned Upside Down* (New York: Bantam, 1982), p. 92.

**50** David Cherrington, "The Values of Younger Workers," *Business Horizons,* 20 (1977), 20–30.

**51** Kent Sims, "Economic and Institutional Determinants of Total Compensation," *Proceedings, Western Regional Conference of the American Compensation Association* (1977), p. 111.

**52** *Great Neck Record,* 17 Dec. 1981, p. 1A. Adding to the confidence that can be placed in these estimates are the findings of the Time Use Surveys conducted by the Survey Research Center of the University of Michigan. Paid nonwork time was found to be 3½ hours in 1970 and 3 hours and 45 minutes in 1976 (compared to Half's finding of 4 hours and 18 minutes in 1981.) See Frank Stafford and Greg J. Duncan, "The Use of Time and Technology by Households in the United States," *Research in Labor Economics* (Greenwich, Ct.: JAI Press, 1980), III 344–348.

**53** Dan Quayle, "American Productivity: The Devastating Effect of Alcoholism and Drug Abuse," *American Psychologist,* 38 (1983), 456.

**54** Ibid., p. 455.

**55** Ibid.

**56** John W. Gardner, *Excellence: Can We Be Equal and Excellent Too?* (New York: Harper and Row, 1961), p. 11.

**57** Norman C. Hill and Gene W. Dalton, "Business and the New Egalitarianism," *Business Horizons,* 20 (1977), 5.

**58** Christopher Jencks, *Inequality: A Reassessment of the Effect of Family and Schooling in America* (New York: Basic Books, 1972), pp. 8–9. Reprinted by permission of the publisher.

**59** Herbert J. Gans, *More Equality* (New York: Pantheon Books, 1973), passim.

**60** John Rawls, *A Theory of Justice* (Cambridge, Mass.: Belknap Press, 1971), p. 15.

**61** Ibid., p. 303.

**62** Norman C. Hill and Gene W. Dalton, "Business and the New Egalitarianism," p. 9.

**63** Arthur M. Okun, *Equality and Efficiency: The Big Tradeoff* (Washington, D.C.: Brookings Institution, 1975), p. 48.

**64** Peter M. Gutmann, "The Subterranean Economy," *Financial Analysts Journal,* 33 (1977), 26–27, 34.

**65** Carol Sims, "Exploring the Underground Economy," PSC CUNY *Clarion,* Mar. 1982, p. 8. Recently other economists have issued estimates of the size of the underground economy. Vittorio Bonomo and J. Ernest Tanner, using assumptions similar to Gutmann's, concluded that the subterranean economy was $490 billion in 1980; but using what they considered to be more realistic assumptions, they estimated the size to be $588 billion in 1980. A still higher estimate was provided by Edward Feige of the University of Wisconsin. Feige calculated that the subterranean economy was $700 billion in 1978, and using his assumptions for 1980, the magnitude reached $950 billion, or 36 percent of measured GNP. See Vittorio Bonomo and J. Ernest Tanner, "The Underground Economy," *Executive,* 7, No. 3 (1981), 50–52. Aso see Adrian Perrachio, "The Underground Economy—The Poor Man's Tax Loophole," *Newsday,* 24 Aug. 1980, pp. 7, 86.

**66** See the survey by Roger Seasonwein Associates, *The Vital Consensus: American Attitudes on Economic Growth* (New York: Union Carbide Corporation, 1980), especially pp. 9, 17–19, 49.

**67** Peter Passell, "Arming the Productivity Weapon," *New York Times,* 19 Jan. 1979, p. A22.

**68** Walter H. Annenberg, "What's in It for Us?" *Wall Street Journal,* 14 July 1980, p. 9.

# CHAPTER 2

# PRODUCTIVITY IN ORGANIZATIONS: A CONCEPTUAL FRAMEWORK AND METHOD OF STUDY

*Theory without data is fantasy; but data without theory is chaos!*

Edward E. Lawler III[1]

There are two pillars on which rest the behavioral sciences, and science in general: logic and observation, deduction and induction, theory and fact. In the absence of theorizing, researchers can capitalize on chance findings, the result being "dust bowl empiricism." And the absence of evidence can render armchair philosophizing sterile and "academic." With these thoughts in mind, we present as the primary purpose of this chapter a conceptual framework for examining productivity in organizations. Such a framework provides a basis for organizing and interpreting, albeit broadly, the empirical evidence examined in Parts 2 and 3. A second objective of this chapter is to make explicit the method of study employed in this book.

## CONCEPTUAL FRAMEWORK

A good deal of theorizing in the behavioral sciences suggests that there are four primary determinants of organizational productivity: the environment, organizational characteristics, work characteristics, and individual characteristics.[2] A schematic representation of the conceptual framework used in this book is presented in Figure 2-1.

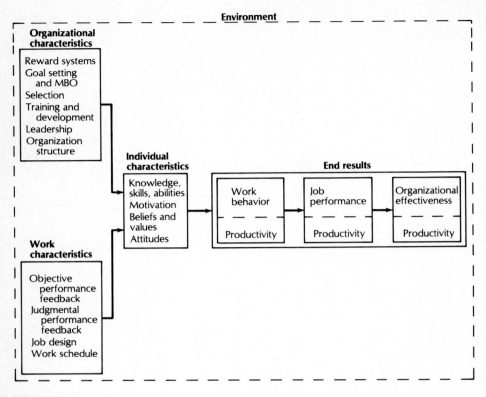

**FIGURE 2-1**
Conceptual framework of the determinants of productivity in organizations—a behavioral science approach.

### The Environment

Most of the variables discussed in Chapter 1 are largely uncontrollable by a given organization; for this reason these variables are viewed as comprising the environment. Environmental conditions can affect one or more of the controllable (to some extent) determinants of organizational productivity—organizational, work, and individual characteristics. Examples of the impact of environmental conditions on controllable factors include: (1) statutes, regulations, and court decisions which affect such organizational practices as recruitment, selection, promotion, training, and termination, (2) changing societal attitudes and values which influence individual characteristics such as worker attitudes, expectations, competencies, and values (e.g., job involvement, work motivation, organizational commitment, job satisfaction), and (3) changes in technology or changes in the relative costs of raw materials, energy, and capital which influence work characteristics (e.g., feedback, autonomy). Because environmental conditions are largely beyond the organization's control and the scope of this book, the focus now turns to those factors subject to organizational influence.

## Organizational Characteristics

Logic and abundant evidence indicate that numerous organizational characteristics or practices influence individuals, their work behavior, job performance, and organizational effectiveness. Yet all organizational practices, presumably, are not equal in their effects. In this book we consider seven types of organizational practices that are widely assumed to affect productivity. The practices and their intended effects are as follows:

- Reward systems to improve work motivation and job performance
- Goal setting programs to heighten worker motivation and enhance performance
- MBO programs to clarify and make more congruent organizational and individual objectives, thereby improving work planning and task motivation
- Selection procedures of various kinds to enhance the likelihood of hiring individuals whose aptitudes, knowledge, skills, and abilities better permit them to accomplish organizational goals
- Training and development programs to increase the knowledge and skills of employees, so that they can function more effectively
- Leadership changes or training programs to improve managerial effectiveness
- Organization structure changes to improve organizational effectiveness

## Work Characteristics

Another factor, largely controllable by management and pertinent to productivity in organizations, is the nature of the work performed. Relevant work characteristics include task variety, significance, identity, autonomy, and feedback. Additionally, with respect to technical professionals, highly relevant work characteristics include time pressure, work challenge, and frequency of change in technical assignments. Several managerial practices that have an impact on work characteristics include:

- Performance feedback to motivate and instruct employees
- Job design programs to enhance motivation and skills through job enrichment or to improve task-specific ability through work simplification
- Alternative work schedules, such as flexible work hours or the compressed workweek, to increase employee autonomy, decrease work-family conflict, and improve motivation and performance

## Individual Characteristics

Although organizational and work characteristics are often treated as causal variables, the fourth determinant of productivity in organizations—individual characteristics—is often viewed as an intervening variable in the causal network.[3] That is, organizational practices and work characteristics are translated into observable end results through their impact on unobservable individual attributes such as beliefs, values, attitudes, knowledge, goals, and intentions.

A number of relatively enduring properties of individuals (traits) as well as relatively transitory properties (states) have been found to be determinants of individual work behaviors, job performance, and organizational effectiveness, namely: (1) the degree to which personal satisfaction is experienced as a result of effective job performance (internal work motivation), (2) the degree to which effort expenditure is believed to lead to effective job performance and in turn to various outcomes (expectancies and instrumentalities) and the desirability of those outcomes (valences), (3) the degree of satisfaction experienced with the job in general or with particular job facets, (4) the relative importance of one's job in comparison to nonwork activities (job involvement), and of particular relevance to technical professionals, (5) the degree of professional and job up-to-dateness.

A few observations might be made in connection with individual characteristics. It is widely accepted that individual job performance (an end-result variable) is a multiplicative function of motivation and ability:[4] $P = f(M \times A)$. Thus, if either motivation or ability is absent, job performance will be low: a high level of ability does not compensate for a lack of motivation, and vice versa. Further, both motivation and ability are affected by organizational and work characteristics. With respect to motivation, organizational characteristics primarily influence *extrinsic* work motivation—i.e., the desire to perform effectively or be at work because of the external rewards (such as pay, benefits, perquisites, and power) which result. Work characteristics, in contrast, primarily influence *intrinsic* work motivation, which manifests itself in terms of either (1) internal work motivation (i.e., individuals desire to perform well because they like themselves better after doing a good job), or (2) inherent job enjoyableness (i.e., individuals desire to be at work because the job itself is pleasurable—work is play). Similarly, both organizational and work characteristics affect ability. Organizational practices regarding selection, training and development, and termination directly influence average levels of employee ability; task assignments can also influence ability.

Conversely, individual characteristics may influence work and organizational characteristics. People with high growth-need strength (i.e., the desire to grow and learn) are likely to seek out challenging task assignments, and people with a high need for security and a low tolerance for ambiguity are likely to seek out bureaucratic organizations in relatively stable environments.

### End-Result Variables

Three end-result variables are frequently identified in the organizational behavior literature: (1) work behavior—the specific observable activities the individual is engaged in, (2) job performance—the evaluated adequacy of an individual's accomplishment of a set of tasks, duties, and responsibilities, and

(3) organizational effectiveness—an index of organizational goal attainment. Work behavior is generally regarded as an antecedent of job performance, which in turn is an immediate antecedent of organizational effectiveness.[5] *Productivity, defined as a ratio of output to input, can be a criterion measure of all three end-result variables.* Productivity ratios can be computed with respect to specific work behaviors (e.g., telephone calls made per hour), individual job performance (e.g., sales per hour), or organizational effectiveness (e.g., value added per payroll dollar).

In practice, however, very few studies have actually measured productivity per se, computing productivity ratios. Rather, a number of behavioral indicators (e.g., grievances and absences), performance indicators (e.g., output and rated performance), and effectiveness indicators (e.g., costs and profits) have been used instead. For example, two comprehensive reviews of organizational productivity experiments, encompassing 207 field studies, categorized results in terms of 14 different criterion variables (e.g., output quantity). None of the criterion measures, however, was a true measure of productivity, i.e., an index of output divided by input.[6]

## METHOD OF STUDY

A primary purpose of this book is to examine the efficacy of ten prominent behavioral science approaches to productivity improvement. Apart from the claims and opinions of salespeople, consultants, and various advocates (e.g., the personnel manager responsible for selecting and implementing a given intervention), what does the evidence say, what are the facts? Toward this end, the next ten chapters review the results of hundreds of published and unpublished studies. The procedure by which studies were selected for inclusion, the manner of data analysis, and the requisite assumptions for this endeavor are discussed next.

### Selection Procedure

Of course, any review is limited by the contents of the existing literature. Unfortunately, although there are hundreds of studies relevant (in varying degrees) to productivity—indeed, a selected bibliography for 1976–1978 lists more than 1200 "productivity" studies—relatively few studies actually measure productivity. For example, an examination of the entire contents of the *Academy of Management Journal* for the years 1979–1983 reveals that only 3 percent of the 297 published articles dealt with measured outputs (quality or quantity), and only 7 percent pertained to either measured outputs or overt behaviors. Instead, the large majority focused on attitudes, perceptions, intentions, stress reactions, and so forth. Thus a decision had to be made regarding which types of studies to include in the present review. Clearly, limiting the present review to only those studies reporting actual productivity data would have been too restrictive; at the other extreme, including measures of attitudes, or even measures of rated performance, would have resulted in a great deal of criterion variability. Hence, a middle-ground solution was adopted: by and large, only those studies which reported results in terms of objective indicators (of work behaviors, job performance, or organizational effectiveness) were included.

Three additional delimitations should be noted. First, the present review does not examine all types of technologies which can affect productivity; rather only behavioral science interventions relevant to managing people at work are examined. Excluded, therefore, are interventions such as robotics, artificial intelligence, biomechanics (e.g., the design of office furniture), nutrition (e.g., vitamin therapy), and other approaches which might have important impacts on productivity. Second, not all behavioral science interventions are examined, rather only those approaches which have been most frequently tested. Excluded are several common but infrequently researched interventions (e.g., transactional analysis and Musak), as well as various esoteric potential approaches (e.g., biorhythms and transcendental meditation). Third, the present review focuses primarily on empirical (data-based) studies concerning permanent organizations—studies which are often published in rigorous academic and professional journals. Largely excluded are (1) inspirational narratives typically relying on anecdotal and impressionistic recollections rather than systematically collected quantitative data, and (2) laboratory experiments, which typically differ markedly from field interventions with respect to subjects, settings, and activities.[7]

## Data Analysis

The basic measure of effectiveness employed is the *percentage change* in a criterion variable; hence a decrease in the proportion of defective output from 12 to 9 percent is recorded as an improvement in performance quality of 25 percent. Although it is commonplace for researchers to describe results by comparing an initial score on a criterion measure (a baseline) with the score at the end of the experimental period, this method of analysis can overstate results. For example, the researcher may choose to end the experimental period on a "high note." Therefore, a more conservative approach was adopted: where possible, baseline scores have been compared to the *average* criterion score during the experimental period.

The average effect of a given productivity improvement approach was determined by using the median result. The median, rather than the mean, result was computed because a few of the productivity improvement approaches have been tested only a limited number of times. With a small number of tests a single extreme score can markedly influence (distort) the mean result.

## Requisite Assumptions

It should be noted that in aggregating results across studies it is necessary to assume that various differences from study to study, and from one type of intervention to the next, cancel each other out. However, at least nine possible confounding factors might be identified—factors which, in theory, might systematically suppress or distort results.[8] Hence, *ceteris paribus* needs to be coupled with caveat emptor.

**1** *Adequacy of criterion measure.* To the extent that a criterion measure is unreliable or invalid, results are likely to be inaccurate. Therefore, it must be assumed that criterion measures are of comparable adequacy across studies and types of interventions.

**2** *Duration of the observation period.* It has been demonstrated empirically that it takes time for an intervention to affect employee motivation and/or ability. Consequently, observation periods which are too short, or too long, may obscure the effects of an intervention.

**3** *Quality of execution.* Clearly, if an intervention is not carried out skillfully or, worse yet, is truly bungled, the results are not likely to be positive. After all, one should not fault the pencil if attempting to write with the eraser. Accordingly, it must be assumed that the quality of execution is not systematically related to the type of intervention.

**4** *Initial level of functioning.* Because of the regression-to-the-mean phenomenon, there will likely be an inverse relationship between the initial level of the criterion and the magnitude of productivity improvement. Colloquially speaking, if the initial situation is poor, then, "the only way to go is up—things can't get any worse." Moreover, the lower the initial level of functioning, the higher the probable receptivity to change. Thus, to the extent that a systematic relationship exists between the type of intervention attempted and the initial level of functioning, results may be confounded.

**5** *Extent of intervention.* It must be assumed that the various interventions are, on the average, implemented to roughly comparable degrees. Otherwise, we might be comparing extensive changes of one kind with minor changes of another kind.

**6** *Equality of publication rates.* Because most of the empirical evidence has been obtained from published sources, it must be assumed that publications are not systematically biased toward or against certain types of interventions. Presumably any such biases will cancel each other out across journals and over time (as editors change).

**7** *Quality of research design.* Rigorous research designs (e.g., those employing pre and post measures for experimental and control groups) are less likely to yield spurious results compared to more casual research designs.[9] Thus, it must be assumed that there is no systematic relationship between type of intervention and rigor of research design.

**8** *Relevant contingency variables.* Differences in organizational, work, and individual characteristics may affect the success of an intervention (e.g., top management support, employee trust, type of technology, employee needs). Accordingly, it must be assumed that these factors do not systematically interact with the experimental treatments across interventions.

**9** *Appropriateness of the intervention.* The assumption must be made that a given intervention is warranted in the situation where it is applied (e.g., that job enrichment is not attempted where jobs are already quite high in motivating potential). In brief, it must be assumed that across interventions, the "remedy fits the ailment" (or the punishment fits the crime).

## SUMMARY

This chapter has presented a conceptual framework for organizing and interpreting behavioral science approaches to productivity improvement. Broadly speaking, changes in organizational and work characteristics (causal variables) are seen as influencing various individual characteristics (intervening variables) which in turn affect three end-result variables: work behavior, job performance, and organizational effectiveness. Productivity indicators can meaningfully be computed for all three end-result variables.

A major objective of this book is to assess the efficacy of ten prominent behavioral science techniques used to improve productivity. In this quest, the next chapter examines the effects of reward systems.

## NOTES

1 Edward E. Lawler III, *Pay and Organizational Effectiveness: A Psychological View* (New York: McGraw-Hill, 1971), p. 205.
2 See, for example, John P. Campbell, Marvin D. Dunnette, Edward E. Lawler III, and Karl C. Weick, Jr., *Managerial Behavior, Performance, and Effectiveness* (New York: McGraw-Hill, 1970); see also Harold G. Kaufman, *Obsolescence and Professional Career Development* (New York: Amacom, 1974), and Keith Davis, *Human Behavior at Work,* 6th ed. (New York: McGraw-Hill, 1981).
3 Rensis Likert, *The Human Organization: Its Management and Value* (New York: McGraw-Hill, 1967).
4 Terence R. Mitchell, *People in Organizations: An Introduction to Organizational Behavior,* 2nd ed. (New York: McGraw-Hill, 1982); Victor H. Vroom, *Work and Motivation* (New York: Wiley, 1964).
5 John P. Campbell et al., pp. 474–478.
6 Raymond A. Katzell, Penney Bienstock, and Paul H. Faerstein, *A Guide to Worker Productivity Experiments in the United States 1971–75* (New York: New York University Press, 1977), pp. 176–177; also Richard A. Guzzo and Jeffrey S. Bondy, *A Guide to Worker Productivity Experiments in the United States 1976–81* (New York: Pergamon Press, 1983), p. 152. The authors of the more recent survey commented: "In studies of productivity, it is rare that changes in inputs *and* outputs are measured together; most report changes in either input or output following the implementation of some program and then assume that the observed changes actually reflect productivity. This assumption can be a tenuous one, although one which must be tolerated in light of the impracticalities—if not impossibilities—of precise, accurate productivity measurements" (p. 4).
7 It should be noted, however, that differences between laboratory experiments and field interventions do not automatically necessitate a lack of generalizability, i.e., that findings from the lab do not pertain to the "real world." Rather, the issue is largely an empirical one which only recently has begun to receive empirical attention. See E.

A. Locke, ed., *The Generalizability of Laboratory Experiments: An Inductive Survey* (Lexington, Mass.: Lexington Books, forthcoming).

8  Several of these assumptions have been noted by E. A. Locke, D. B. Feren, V. M. McCaleb, K. N. Shaw, and A. T. Denny, in "The Relative Effectiveness of Four Methods of Motivating Employee Performance," in *Changes in Working Life,* ed. K. D. Duncan, M. M. Gruneberg, and D. Wallis (Chichester, England: Wiley, Ltd., 1980), pp. 365–366.

9  In this regard, David Terpstra has reviewed 52 field experiments involving organizational improvement efforts. Among the 31 studies with the lowest methodological rigor, 84 percent reported uniformly positive results, and 16 percent reported mixed or nonsignificant results. In contrast, among the 21 most rigorous studies only 43 percent reported uniformly positive results, and 24 percent reported uniformly negative results. See David E. Terpstra, "Relationship between Methodological Rigor and Reported Outcomes in Organization Development Evaluation Research," *Journal of Applied Psychology,* 66 (1981), 541–543. Perhaps even more to the point, E. A. Locke et al., "Relative Effectiveness," found that productivity improvements were on the average 5 percentage points lower in studies employing rigorous compared to nonrigorous research designs (p. 376).

PART **TWO**

# IMPROVING
# PRODUCTIVITY:
# MODIFYING
# ORGANIZATIONAL
# CHARACTERISTICS

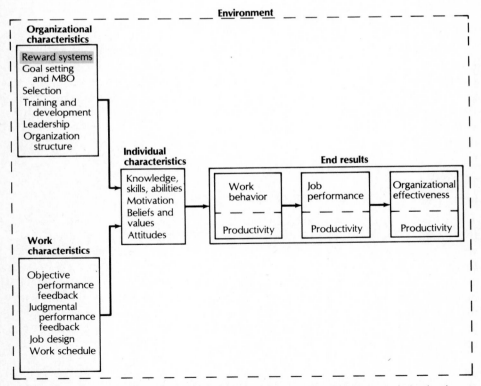

Conceptual framework of the determinants of productivity in organizations—a behavioral science approach.

# REWARD SYSTEMS

This chapter examines the many types of reward systems which have been used to influence work behavior, job performance, and organizational effectiveness.[1] The first two sections focus on individual output–based and group gainsharing systems; the third section reviews research and application related to judgmental reward systems; the fourth section reports on the use of reward systems to influence attendance behavior; the fifth section examines several miscellaneous reward systems; and the sixth and concluding section summarizes the discussion.

## INDIVIDUAL OUTPUT–BASED REWARD SYSTEMS

There is a long history to the practice of paying for measured output. During the reign of Nebuchadnezzar, king of Babylonia (ca. 600 B.C.), spinners and weavers were paid based on their production. The Chaldeans, during the fourth century B.C., also used piece-rate pay. And nearly 2000 years later, at the arsenal of Venice, piece-rate pay was the rule in the making of oars; day wages, however, were paid to those who fastened exposed timbers and planks.[2] The underlying logic was apparently that a defective oar was far less serious than a leaking boat—confirming the modern concept that piece-rate systems often foster high quantity at the expense of quality.[3]

Evidence concerning the effectiveness of output-based pay in comparison with time-based pay (e.g., an hourly wage) has been reviewed by Nash and Carroll in their book *The Management of Compensation*. They cited the results of five early surveys, encompassing more than 4700 cases. Average increases in productivity after switching from time-based to output-based pay ranged from 29 to 63 percent, the median increase being 34.5 percent.[4] Another survey of more than 400 industrial organizations showed that the institution of incentive wages increased productivity by an average of 42.9 percent.[5] More recently, an extensive literature review by Edwin Locke and his associates found that individual output-based pay plans produce a median performance improvement of 30 percent.[6]

Additionally, the 1977 and the 1983 publications entitled *A Guide to Worker Productivity Experiments* (hereafter cited as *WPE1* and *WPE2,* respectively) reported the results of eight studies that used individual incentives to improve job performance. In all cases results were positive: improvements ranged from 15 to 71.5 percent, the median increase being 32.1 percent.[7] One of the experiments, for example, involved individuals who trapped mountain beavers. Institution of a cash incentive, in addition to base pay, increased productivity by 41 percent. Taking into account the money spent on incentive payments, the cost of catching a "rat" declined by 23 percent.[8]

A number of field studies were not included in *WPE1* or *WPE2*. Hoerner Waldorf Corporation, a manufacturer of corrugated shipping containers, adopted a piece-rate plan for workers in 18 different operations. Increases in productivity were observed in 17 of the 18 operations; 16 of the increases were statistically significant. Overall, productivity rose by 58 percent after implementation of the piece-rate pay plan.[9]

Individual output–based pay plans have also been used in white-collar settings. In a billing department, the pay system was switched from a weekly salary to payment based on individual accomplishment (measured in terms of quantity and quality of work) with the following results: billing clerks earned 32 percent higher pay; productivity rose by 73 percent; billing errors "became virtually nonexistent"; and the first year's savings to the company was in excess of $375,000.[10]

Although most of the research on individual output–based reward systems has focused on the effects of going from time-based to output-based systems, three studies have examined the effects of going in the opposite direction. In one case, the removal of incentive pay for welders led to (1) an immediate drop in productivity of 23 percent, (2) a commensurate decline in employee earnings, and (3) greater variability in performance from week to week. After the change in pay plan, supervisors adopted some new practices: they showed graphs of performance to employees; they talked to employees about productivity; and they exhorted them to produce more. Consequently, the overall decline in productivity was limited to 10.5 percent over a 48-week observation period.[11]

In a second case, a large manufacturer of paper and paper products abandoned its performance-contingent pay plan in one of two virtually identical paper mills. The result was a dramatic and significant decline in performance in the plant that switched to hourly pay.[12] In the third case, a piece-rate system was discontinued in favor of an hourly wage. Subsequently, performance went down and turnover went up. However, 2 years later a plant-wide incentive system was installed. Suddenly, productivity rose by 45 percent and turnover dropped to a lower level than before the piece-rate plan was discontinued.[13]

Thus, there is abundant evidence that individual output–based reward systems tend to raise productivity in comparison with time-based pay systems. As John Miner has noted, whatever the motivational literature one reads, "the evidence of the motivating effects of contingent rewards is quite overwhelming."[14] One explanation for this phenomenon is the *law of effect:* Behavior that is reinforced is increasingly likely to be repeated; behavior that is punished is decreasingly likely to be repeated.[15] Further, it would appear that pay is a particularly salient reinforcer.[16] Comments Mitchell Fein, "By any measure pay tied to productivity is the most powerful motivator of improved work performance . . . it is undeniable that, from floor sweeper to president, all [employees] raise their productivity when their pay is tied to performance."[17] Somewhat ironically, for the past five decades many social scientists (for the most part academicians) have minimized or denied the efficacy of pay as a motivator and have emphasized the potency of nonfinancial rewards such as participation. Yet as Locke and his associates have concluded, "The results of research to date indicate that the opposite viewpoint would have been more accurate."[18]

While there is clear and consistent evidence that individual output–based incentive plans generally raise productivity, their use is not widespread. A recent large-scale survey, representative of all U.S. corporations with 100 or more employees, found that only 10 percent of the responding companies used piece-rate pay. As would be expected, the incidence of use varied by setting: 4 percent among nonmanufacturing corporations, 14 percent among manufacturing corporations, and 20 percent among large manufacturing corporations (10,000 or more employees).[19] Evidence also indicates that the use of wage incentives (piece-rate pay or group gainsharing plans) has declined steadily over time. Wage incentives were used by 75 percent of industrial organizations in 1935, by 52 percent in 1939, by 27 percent in 1958, and by 20 percent in 1982.[20] Further, among those corporations that had piece-rate pay plans in place in 1982, only 2 percent of the plans had been installed within the prior 2 years.[21]

A number of factors have contributed to the declining use of individual output–based reward systems. Such plans are best suited to jobs that are highly repetitive, that are employee-paced (rather than machine paced), that are performed on a relatively independent basis (i.e., "stand-alone" jobs), and that produce outputs that can be tested for quality and, if found acceptable, counted. Yet as Edward Lawler so aptly put it, today we are moving toward a "service-knowledge-information–high technology–based economy."[22] Indeed, during the past 30 years the U.S. economy has been transformed from a goods-producing economy to one in which the majority of workers produce, modify, or distribute information.[23] And as the complexity of work has increased, there has been a concomitant increase in technical, professional, and managerial jobs—jobs which typically do not yield uniform, countable outputs. As a result of these developments, the concept of pay for measured output may be seen as alien to many of today's new workers, given their high education levels and expectations for personal growth, participation, and professional career development. Further, the use of individual output–based reward systems may increase tensions (1) between workers and managers (e.g., disputes about standard output levels or about the quality of purchased materials) and (2) between direct and indirect labor, the former being paid based on output, the latter influencing output but being paid by the hour. Finally, administrative costs may be seen as outweighing gains in productivity (however, the use of real-time computerized systems may substantially reduce administrative costs in the future).[24]

## GROUP GAINSHARING PLANS

The three most prominent group gainsharing plans are the Scanlon, Rucker, and Improshare plans.[25] The Scanlon and Rucker plans share gains in economic productivity; the Improshare plan shares gains in physical process productivity. The sharing formula for the Scanlon plan is based on labor costs as a percentage of dollar sales. Reductions in labor costs (in relation to the "normal" ratio) are typically shared, with 75 percent going to (all) employees, 25 percent to ownership. The Rucker plan computes savings in terms of the ratio of labor costs to net value added (sales minus purchased goods and services). Consequently, with the Rucker plan, employees have an incentive to reduce scrap loss and to conserve materials, parts, and supplies. Most of the descriptive reports and effectiveness studies relating to economic productivity gainsharing plans, though, have focused on the Scanlon plan.

Although there is no such thing as *the* Scanlon Plan—applications vary considerably from one setting to the next—three commonalities can be identified: (1) a philosophy of management that entails a high degree of employee participation, (2) a set of structural arrangements that includes establishing employee-management committees to screen suggestions, implement changes, and monitor progress, and (3) a plantwide financial incentive plan that is based on labor cost savings.[26] Several positive outcomes have been reported as resulting from the implementation of a Scanlon plan:

**1** *An improved organizational climate.* Adversarial relationships between workers ("us") and managers ("them") may be replaced by a shared sense of mutual interest ("we").

**2** *Improved communications.* This will likely result from establishing employee-management committees and by disseminating information about monthly targets and operating results.

**3** *Employee training.* Technical skills may be broadened (if workers are cross-trained), and managerial skills may be developed via participation in employee-management committees.

**4** *Labor cost consciousness raising.* Employees may be motivated to reduce labor costs; there may even be a reluctance to replace people who have left the payroll.

**5** *Organization development.* A long-term, systems approach to organizational improvement may be fostered, rather than the all too common quickfix, fad-of-the-month approach.

On the other hand, a couple of possible problems have also been noted:

**1** *Management resistance.* Some managers, particularly those at lower levels in the hierarchy, may be threatened by the sharing of power with employees.

**2** *Lack of incentive.* At times there may be little motivation to work hard or offer suggestions, because the sharing formula is affected by many factors beyond the control of employees (e.g., market prices, resource costs, product mix, scale of operations).[27]

Notwithstanding the potential benefits and disadvantages, it is obviously important to examine the actual results. Overall, evidence indicates that roughly 80 percent of Scanlon plan interventions have been successful in improving labor efficiency.[28] A survey of effectiveness studies found the median performance improvement to have been 16 percent.[29]

Developed by Mitchell Fein, the Improshare plan—derived from "improving productivity through sharing"—was first implemented in 1974. As noted previously, the sharing formula is based on physical process productivity (the ratio of actual to standard labor hours used in producing a set of outputs), not economic productivity. Hence incentive earnings are relatively unaffected by economic factors beyond the control of workers, such as product prices and resource costs. Typically all gains resulting from improved productivity are shared fifty-fifty between employees and management; no attempt is made to pinpoint whether employees or management created the savings. Usually there is also an agreed-on ceiling to incentive earnings and a "buy back" provision that exchanges a cash payment for an increase in standard hours reflective of increased efficiency.[30] It might also be noted that because the plan is based on physical outputs, not dollar sales, it can be applied to work groups that are cost centers (e.g., a data processing department), not necesarily entire plants or profit centers.

To date, more than 100 organizations have implemented an Improshare plan, including Bell and Howell, General Electric, Firestone, and Phillips Petroleum.[31] A review of the evidence indicates a success rate of approximately 90 percent and a median productivity improvement of 20 percent.[32]

Consistent with the aforementioned evidence, a comprehensive review of various kinds of group gainsharing plans (researched by the U.S. General Accounting Office), reported an average labor savings of 16.9 percent.[33] Similarly, the review of group incentive plans by Locke and his associates found a median performance improvement of 18 percent.[34] In general, therefore, it would appear that group gainsharing plans are effective in raising productivity, but they tend to produce a smaller increase than individual output-based pay plans. Certainly this conclusion is in accord with the research finding that the size of the group sharing an incentive is inversely related to the motivational impact of the incentive plan.[35]

Yet, although group gainsharing plans may be a less powerful motivational technique than individual output–based incentive plans, they can often succeed in settings where it is not possible or cost-effective to measure individual outputs. Such settings include (1) those where functions are highly interdependent and competition between units can be dysfunctional[36] and (2) those where jobs require teamwork, making it difficult to isolate and measure the outputs of individuals. Given the general trend toward increasingly complex, interdependent jobs, group gainsharing plans will likely become increasingly prevalent. Indeed, there is evidence to support this prediction. In 1982, group gainsharing plans had been adopted by 7 percent of all U.S. corporations with 100 or more employees (compared with the 10 percent adoption rate for piece-rate pay plans). However, 34 percent of the group gainsharing plans were less than 2 years old, compared with only 2 percent of the piece-rate pay plans.[37] In light of these adoption rates, by 1986 group gainsharing plans will possibly be more widely used than individual output–based pay plans.

## INDIVIDUAL JUDGMENT–BASED MERIT REWARD SYSTEMS

The most common approach to rewarding performance among white-collar employees is the judgment-based merit reward system. Typically, some form of rating scale or ranking procedure is used to evaluate individual job performance, and this evaluation is used to determine various organizationally mediated rewards (or penalties), e.g., salary increase, promotion, and retention. Logically (and psychologically) such an approach makes good sense, for several reasons.

First, by tying job performance to various outcomes (favorable and unfavorable) employees should come to believe that a person's level of effort expenditure is a difference which makes a difference; consequently, average levels of work motivation should be high. Conversely, if job performance is *not* a path to various organizationally mediated rewards, many employees will conclude that effort expenditure does not pay off, average levels of work motivation (e.g., effort expenditure and creativity) will tend to be low, and attention will be directed at finding paths that do lead to rewards (e.g., "Who you know, not what you know"). Some individuals, those with a high need to achieve, will work hard despite the absence of reward and recognition. But it has been estimated that only a small minority of people, roughly 10 percent, have a high need to achieve.[38]

Second, to the extent that performance is the basis for rewards, rewards will be more highly valued. This will be so because performance-contingent rewards have psychological as well as inherent value. For example, the 7 percent merit salary increase in an organization where the average is 5 percent will likely be more highly valued, and more satisfying, than the across-the-board 7 percent increase. Conversely, the 5 percent merit salary increase obtained where the average is 7 percent probably will be less highly valued, and less satisfying, than the across-the-board 5 percent increase.[39] Certainly a person can take little credit for achieving another cost-of-living increase, or across-the-board raise; it merely signifies continued survival. But merit increases have psychological as well as financial value because they can convey meaningful information, namely, about job performance and competence, about how highly the person's contributions are regarded, and about future career prospects. In brief, merit reward systems *leverage* the value and satisfaction of rewards; this in turn should raise motivation.

Third, the extent to which performance is the basis for rewards will influence whether turnover is more prevalent among high-performing or low-performing employees. If all employees receive the same salary increase and other rewards, will they all be equally satisfied? Of course not.[40] The most productive employees will tend to be the least satisfied and the most likely to quit—many concluding that "there has to be a better way." In contrast, the least productive employees will tend to be the most satisfied and the least likely to quit. However, where performance is the basis for rewards, high performers will tend to be the most satisfied and the least likely to quit. Unfortunately, no matter what type of reward system an organization adopts, it is virtually impossible to satisfy all employees. But is it rational to invest in the satisfaction and retention of those who contribute the least?

So much for logic. What about evidence? Very little research has been conducted on the effectiveness of judgmental merit reward systems. Most of the research to date on reward systems has compared output-based and time-based pay plans; yet, ironically, most of today's workers do not produce standardized, countable outputs. Rather, there are numerous and important differences across types of legal cases, surgical procedures, and engineering problems; further, quality differences can be crucial in the performance of services—e.g.. all haircuts are not equal. Although objective measures are often available (e.g., dollars of billable legal work produced), such measures are usually only partial indicators of job performance. Hence, the use of judgment is inescapable in measuring the performance of many of today's workers. Accordingly, research on output-based reward systems cannot necessarily be extrapolated to judgment-based systems. It is important, therefore, to examine those (few) studies that have looked at the efficacy of judgmental merit reward systems.

Almost all organizations claim to employ judgmental merit reward systems. Yet, espoused policies are often different from actual practice. (Presumably this discrepancy results because the benefits and costs associated with saying something are often different from those associated with doing the same thing, that is, because talk is cheap.) Notwithstanding the claims, in practice organizations have not generally employed reward systems that are responsive to performance. On the basis of evidence from six systematic studies conducted during the 1960s, Lawler concluded:

Overall, therefore, the studies suggest that many business organizations do not do a very good job of tying pay to performance. This conclusion is rather surprising in light of many companies' very frequent claims that their pay systems are based on merit.[41]

While Lawler's evidence is somewhat dated, recent research suggests that the situation has not improved with the passage of time.[42] A 1983 survey conducted by the Public Agenda Foundation reported that only 22 percent of U.S. workers see a direct relationship between how hard they work and how much they are paid, and 73 percent said their job effort had declined as a result. The study concluded that to "a disconcerting degree," today's wage and reward systems "have uncoupled the traditional link between" job performance and "financial rewards and incentives on the job."[43]

Clearly, professing to have a merit reward system is one thing; having one is a different matter. But how can it be determined if a merit reward system is real or pretend? One way of assessing the robustness of a judgmental merit reward system is by computing the correlation between rated job performance and various organizationally mediated rewards (e.g., pay level, pay increase, job title). To date, only two studies have computed performance-reward correlations for different organizational units and compared these correlations with differences in average levels of work motivation or job performance.

In a study of three engineering organizations, all claiming to reward on the basis of merit, pronounced differences were found in performance-reward correlations. In one company nearly half of the variability in salaries could be attributed to performance differences; in another company less than 10 percent of the variability in salaries could be attributed to job performance—a fivefold difference in degree of association. Engineers' perceptions of reward system responsiveness (RSR) coincided with actual (as distinct from stated) reward system practices. More important, differences in RSR were strongly associated with intercompany differences in effort expenditure and job performance.[44]

In a study of ten branches of a large financial institution, performance-reward correlations were found to vary markedly. A negative association was observed in some branches (high performers receiving smaller pay increases than low performers); in other branches a strong positive relationship was found, with performance accounting for more than 40 percent of the variability in pay increases. As predicted, it was found that branches with a strong positive performance-reward correlation had higher average performance levels than branches with a weak performance-reward correlation. Moreover, the effects of performance-reward practices increased over time.[45]

A small number of other studies have also examined the effects of judgment-based merit reward systems. Using a sample of twenty-nine companies, relationships were examined between eight dimensions of perceived managerial practices and profit growth (the 5-year average annual growth rate). The single strongest correlate of profit growth was compensation, a dimension that was measured in terms of the extent to which compensation was based on performance, and competitive.[46]

A longitudinal field study reported on the turnover process in an organization (Exxon) where there was empirical evidence of a strong relationship between rated job performance and rewards (salary increases, time between salary increases, and job level). It was found over a 15-year period that the company consistently retained employees who were evaluated as superior performers; voluntary turnover centered among the low performers.[47]

As described in a recent field study, a university modified its reward policy, going from a system that rewarded evaluated job performance to one that issued equal percentage pay increases to all faculty. As predicted, those faculty members who felt equitably rewarded with the new (across-the-board) system were lower performers (based on self-assessments) than those who felt undercompensated. Also, those who felt undercompensated anticipated reduced future job performance, and increased effort toward finding alternative employment.[48]

Of course, as noted previously, logic dictates that in organizations where there is a weak (or negative) relationship between performance and rewards, the most competent and productive employees will tend to quit. With this in mind, consider the following descriptive account provided by a supervisor in a large municipal government (where pay increases and promotions are not based on job performance).

> Over the course of 15 years with the City . . . Agency, I have observed that policies, attitudes, and perverse techniques of administration and management have tended to drive out the most able employees in the work force. With good people leaving on a continuing basis, the agency finds itself saddled with an inordinate number of low performers, "crazies," and non-functioning people. . . . In my own unit I find it ever more difficult to retain the best worker, who tells me he wants to leave because he feels he is being dragged down by the low performers, dragged down to their level. Also he feels "burned out" because he has come to realize that his co-workers cannot perform well. Therefore he feels he has to put out more. In sum, I am doing my best to keep the worker because he is good for the job. Presently he is still on the job.[49]

Surely it would appear that this organization has found the "recipe" for organizational decline and degeneration. By decoupling job performance from virtually all organizationally mediated rewards (and penalties), it has apparently produced a low average level of motivation and has driven out many of the most competent, high-performing employees.

### Recent Trends in the Use of Judgment-Based Reward Systems

Three recent surveys of compensation practices all have reached the same conclusion: companies have substantially increased their efforts to tie pay more closely to performance.[50] As one commentator put it, many companies are "trying to use pay to reward employees for performing well, rather than for simply staying alive and on the payroll. Furthermore, they are trying to ensure that top performers get significantly larger raises than average performers."[51]

But efforts to relate pay more closely to performance are not exactly new. Nearly a decade ago, *Business Week* surveys reported that companies were expanding the range of pay raises they offered, and increasing the variability in the timing of these increases. Indicative of the big distinctions some companies were making in pay, the range of pay increases extended from 0 to 30 percent at Digital Equipment Corporation, and from 0 to 19 percent at Westinghouse Electric.[52]

Consistent with this emphasis, in recent years there has been growing use of special one-time payments to reward performance. The one-time payment has five advantages: (1) it can be given for a specific contribution, (2) it can be substantial (not being spread out over 52 weeks), (3) it can be awarded soon after the specific contribution, (4) it does not make the extra pay permanent (resembling an annuity), and (5) it increases flexibility in compensation administration (e.g., permitting total pay to exceed temporarily the salary range ceiling). As Robert Firth of Xerox noted, "If someone has demonstrated some absolutely unusual kind of performance and we want to reward him [or her], we can give [the person] a special merit award. At one time that was baked into their salary base forever. We're changing that and leaning more in the last two years toward the lump-sum, one-time payout. It's usually 10% of the individual's salary."[53] Similarly, many companies are turning to the use of performance bonuses in place of the customary annual salary increase. Increasingly, the emphasis is on current performance (i.e., "What have you done for me lately?"), rather than on the "faded press clippings" of achievements dating back many years or decades.

A promising example of a judgment-based merit reward system that incorporates a bonus component is the plan devised by James Brinks of the Wyatt Company. His plan combines a step-progression guideline, annual rate range adjustments, and a periodic bonus award based on performance. As Brinks has described it, ". . . all employees in a grade receive the same annual salary increase which includes range change and progression. After the going rate or midpoint is reached, annual increases are range changes only. Thus, all employees' base salaries in a grade end up at the midpoint. A bonus is then paid, preferably quarterly, though it could be semi-annually or annually, to distinguish performance. . . . *satisfactory* performers receive no bonus. *Good* performers can receive a bonus ranging from zero to the maximum of the good performance zone. . . . The *exceptional* performer should receive a minimum bonus of at least the top good performer and as much as the range maximum."[54] Although no effectiveness evidence has been published on the Brinks plan, several advantageous features might be noted. First, the plan separates pay increases into three components: rate range increases, which reflect changes in the cost of living or the market price of a job; progression increases, which are a reward for loyalty; and bonuses, which are awarded for good or exceptional current job performance. Second, because bonus awards may be given quarterly or semiannually, this should enhance work motivation (while adding somewhat to administrative costs). Third, given that base salaries rise no higher than the range midpoint, benefit costs will be reduced. Fourth, there is strong emphasis on evaluating and rewarding current performance.[55]

## Implementation Problems and Some Suggested Solutions

Two major problems have been identified in connection with judgment-based merit reward systems. Perhaps the paramount one is what industrial psychologists refer to as the "criterion problem." How can an organization be confident that managers will accurately and unbiasedly appraise the performance of subordinates, especially since for many of today's jobs there is no one comprehensive, objective performance indicator? Clearly there are no guarantees; some raters may make mistakes or be biased. But there are several steps that can be taken to deal with the performance measurement problem.

It is essential that a job analysis be conducted and that performance measures reflect all the important job responsibilities that should be accomplished. On the basis of this information, performance measures should be developed that are content-valid: they should not be deficient, ignoring important aspects of the job; nor should they be excessive, measuring things that are irrelevant. Yet the existence of relevant, content-valid measures does not ensure rater accuracy. Rater errors and rater biases remain important threats that must be minimized.

The use of multiple evaluations (i.e., judgments provided by two or more raters) can help reduce the effects of one rater's possibly idiosyncratic, or inaccurate views. In fact, simply knowing that ratings will be obtained from others will encourage raters to "get in line." At Intel Corporation, for example, three checks exist in the performance evaluation process: (1) it is required that the rater's boss review and approve each evaluation, (2) the personnel representative assigned to the employee's department must also approve the review (checking primarily for consistency), and (3) supervisors must meet to convert their separate ratings into a composite ranking. All three checks introduce additional—and frequently conflicting—points of view to the assessment process, increasing the chance of a fair evaluation.[56] Similarly, at another high-technology company, weighted evaluations are employed. The current immediate supervisor's rating is weighted 10, the evaluation of the supervisor's supervisor counts 8, and so forth.

Objectivity will also likely be enhanced by examining "hard" performance data, as well as information about overt (observable) job behaviors. Additionally, it has been demonstrated that rater training can significantly reduce a number of rater errors. Certainly raters should be encouraged to keep notes on subordinates' performance: reliance on memory and global impressions tends to perpetuate established opinions.

A second major problem is that all too often differences in merit pay increases are too small to motivate improved performance. Writing about the "folly of rewarding A while hoping for B," Steven Kerr cited the case of the large insurance company that awarded 5 percent raises to "outstanding" workers and 4 percent raises to virtually all other workers.[57] Of course, employees are rather adept at sizing up the trade-offs associated with performance alternatives, and they are quick to spot a "bad deal."[58] Evidence consistently indicates that employees seek to maximize their return on effort expenditure (ROE) in a fashion similar to the maximization of return on invested capital (ROI).[59] Apparently employees ask: What are the incremental benefits (and costs) associated with additional effort?[60]

One way to increase an individual's ROE is by using performance bonuses rather than annual salary increases. With bonuses, differences in payments can be substantial. In contrast, salary increases typically are but a small part of total compensation, especially as employees approach their job's pay range ceiling.

Another suggestion is the use of a mixed-consequence reward system. Research has shown that a very powerful motivational system is one that provides rewards for good performance, and that takes rewards away for poor performance.[61] However, if good performance merely leads to token increases in rewards while poor performance is ignored, many people will conclude that it pays to do as little as possible; performance will fall to the lowest acceptable level. A more effective approach, therefore, is to employ both rewards and penalties. *The consequences of performance should be leveraged across all levels of performance, not just the highest levels.* More specifically, people who are performing at low levels should be notified about performance deficiencies, and provided coaching or additional training if needed. Poor performers might also be denied pay increases until performance reaches a satisfactory level. If poor performance continues, counseling should be provided, and consideration should be given to job reassignment or termination. It is not unreasonable to make satisfactory job performance a condition of continued employment.

It would appear, though, that the biggest obstacle to creating substantial differences in outcomes (rewards and penalties) is not technical, but behavioral. It is not that reward systems prohibit the granting of sufficiently sizable pay increases (or decreases); rather it is that many managers are reluctant to make and defend such differences. Feelings of guilt, pity, and fear may inhibit managers from awarding markedly different pay increases (no less withholding an increase). Moreover, today employees who feel unfairly treated are relatively quick to grieve or go to court. This increases, further, the pressure many managers feel to treat employees the same. As Lawler has noted, in the past differential treatment might have entailed the "interpersonal discomfort in confronting an unhappy subordinate. Today, it may involve court appearances, financial losses for the organization, and considerable loss of face for the manager."[62] Moreover, a monograph on labor law adds:

> . . . very little can be done to completely insulate employers from lawsuits. Anyone with a grievance, a typewriter and a lawyer can file a lawsuit. None of these are in short supply in the United States.[63]

Certainly, it is not realistic to expect lower-level managers to uphold performance standards and to make sizable distinctions in merit rewards if higher-level managers do not lend their support to such efforts. Top management must make a vigorous and enduring commitment to the merit reward concept, and its imprimatur must be clearly communicated by actions—not just words—throughout all levels of the organization. In this vein, consider the comments of Andrew Grove, president of Intel Corporation:

> In spite of the criticisms [of performance appraisal and merit pay], I remain steadfast in my conviction that if we want performance in the workplace, somebody has to have the courage and confidence to determine whether we are getting it or not. We must also find ways to enhance what we are getting. . . . We are paid to manage our organizations. To manage means to elicit better performance from members of our organization. We managers need to stop rationalizing, and to stiffen our resolve and do what we are paid to do.[64]

A number of administrative problems have also been noted in connection with the use of judgment-based merit reward systems. Sometimes merit reward systems are so complicated that subordinates (and managers) do not understand how performance is evaluated and related to pay decisions. Other potential problems include the absence of timely feedback, or the lack of supervisory skill in providing performance feedback. While troublesome, these problems are not insurmountable. Merit reward systems need not be overly complex; managers can be trained in providing performance feedback; and timetables can be established to encourage the timely performance of required activities.

## REWARD SYSTEMS TO REDUCE ABSENTEEISM

During the average workweek more than 100 million hours are lost because of absenteeism. The annual cost of absenteeism in terms of lost productivity was estimated in 1978 to be as much as $26.4 billion.[65] More recently it has been suggested that this estimate may be too low.[66] In any case, it is indisputable that absenteeism is costly. To date, two major approaches have been used to reduce absenteeism: rewards for good attendance and penalties for excessive absences.

### Positive Reinforcement

Several studies have reported the successful use of rewards (positive reinforcement) to reduce absenteeism. However, a review of ten such studies found that most were of short duration (rarely longer than 4 months), and that most did not provide a cost-benefit analysis.[67] Examined on a cost-benefit basis, though, some of the "successes" actually yielded only modest or even negative results.[68] There have also been a few outright failures. In one case, a cash incentive increased the incidence of perfect attendance by 27 percent; but concomitant with this improvement, the company paid out $7500 in awards and experienced a 12.3 percent *increase* in overall absenteeism.[69]

There is an important problem in using rewards to reduce absenteeism. The employees who are rewarded are most often the same ones who had good attendance records before the incentive plan was introduced; but chronically absent employees typically are unaffected.[70] Apparently, workers willing to forgo a day's pay not to work are unlikely to choose to work in order to earn a day's pay plus a small incentive bonus (usually less than 1 percent of a day's pay).

A second (potential) obstacle to using rewards to improve attendance is the presence of a paid sick leave plan. Unfortunately, evidence indicates that paid sick leave plans nearly double the incidence of absenteeism.[71] It follows, therefore, that while most sick days are taken for legitimate reasons, almost as many would appear to be "imaginary illnesses." Thus, paid sick leave plans may nullify, or overwhelm, the effects of plans that would reinforce good attendance.

### Punishment

The second major approach to controlling absenteeism is by punishment, typically some form of progressive discipline. Although this policy is quite common, little research has been conducted on its efficacy. One study found that progressive discipline caused the type of absence to shift from short-term casual absences to longer-term "sickness" leaves. It was concluded that punitive sanctions to encourage attendance can have a negative effect, making the problem of absenteeism more intractable.[72]

A variant of the traditional progressive discipline policy that has received attention in recent years is the "no-fault" plan. With this plan, the organization makes no attempt to judge whether an absence is "excusable" or "nonexcusable," legitimate or not. Absences (or absence occurrences) are simply counted: if a predetermined number is exceeded, specified penalties occur. Because absences are not evaluated or categorized, this plan avoids the problem of inconsistent administration of attendance policies by supervisors (and the attendant complaints of favoritism and abuse). In one case study, an employee-management task force designed and implemented a no-fault attendance system. After 1 year, absenteeism declined from 6.7 to 1.1 percent, a reduction of 84 percent. Complaints of favoritism also decreased.[73]

Another punitive approach used to improve attendance is the withholding of rewards (extinction) in the face of high absenteeism. Such an approach was part of the labor agreement between the United Auto Workers and General Motors signed in 1979; it was also renewed in the 1982 agreement. The plan worked as follows. Workers absent more than 20 percent of their scheduled work time during the first 6 months of the year were given a warning and offered counseling. If these same workers exceeded the 20 percent rate during the second 6-month period, they faced temporary benefit cuts (e.g., in vacation pay, paid absence allowance, profit sharing). Absences due to major illnesses were not counted. After implementation of the plan, countable absences declined steadily, from 11.3 percent in 1981 to 10.3 percent in 1982, and to 8.8 percent in the first half of 1983—an overall decline of 22 percent.[74]

## Mixed-Consequence Systems

Conventionally, organizations have used one of the two major methods of controlling absenteeism: rewards for good attendance or punishment for excessive absences. An alternative to the traditional solution of using one method *or* the other (a single-consequence system) is the use of a mixed-consequence system, one that incorporates both rewards *and* penalties.

Several organizations have reported the use of a mixed-consequence system to control absenteeism: to date, results have been uniformly successful. Such a system was implemented in two industrial organizations. Nonmonetary rewards were provided for good attendance, and progressive discipline was initiated in the event of high absenteeism. Over the 1-year experimental period, absenteeism declined by 30 percent in one plant and by 32 percent in the other.[75]

Another successful mixed-consequence intervention was undertaken in a medical center. During the first year of the medical center's existence, 22 percent of available paid leave was taken; in the second year 37 percent was taken; and by the third year 65 percent was taken. Clearly there were signs of "Parkinson's law of sick leave abuse": The paid sick leave taken expands over time to equal the paid sick leave available.

The medical center implemented a mixed-consequence system that worked as follows. A small number of paid sick days (5 days), plus vacation days, and holidays were combined into a single paid leave account, over which the employee essentially had discretionary control. A minimum number of paid leave days had to be taken each year, and some days (5 to 10) could be converted to cash, if desired. The remaining sick days (7 days) were held in an extended illness account. Employees could draw on the extended illness account only after the paid leave account was fully exhausted. (A less onerous plan would have provided a deductible feature for major illnesses.) Employees were, therefore, rewarded for good attendance (receiving up to 5 extra days off and/or cash), and they were penalized for excessive absences (loss of vacation days or holidays). During the 30 months following introduction of this plan (1) the use of sick leave dropped by 65 percent (and even declined after adding the extra 5 days of discretionary leave), (2) overtime declined by 54 percent as planned absences replaced unplanned absences—after all, an employee cannot report that he or she will be out sick "a week from Monday," and (3) reactions to the plan were generally positive. When asked, employees said they liked the new plan because there was no need for deceit to take time off from work; a person could make plans for leisure-time activities with far less worry about having to work an extra shift; people had more self-respect and less resentment of coworkers; teamwork improved; and there were tangible rewards for good attendance (whereas before, there were none).[76]

As is the case with the no-fault plan, a mixed-consequence system removes the supervisor from the role of having to evaluate absences or punish subordinates. Consequently penalties are administered uniformly across infractions, employees, and supervisors. But unlike the no-fault concept, a mixed-consequence plan incorporates reinforcers as well as punishers. Although the mixed-consequence approach to absence control has been used primarily in health care organizations, the approach appears generalizable to other settings.[77]

## MISCELLANEOUS REWARD SYSTEMS

In addition to reward systems that are based on outputs, labor efficiency, evaluated job performance, and attendance behavior, many other types of reward systems have been implemented in organizations. Some reward creative ideas; others reward continued loyalty. There has also been considerable variety in the kinds of rewards provided: rewards have ranged from the mundane (merchandise gifts) to the inspirational (commendation letters). This section examines some of the different types of reward systems that have been used.

### Suggestion Systems

Suggestion boxes have been around for a long time, dating back to the mid-1800s, when Yale and Towne Manufacturing Company nailed up an idea box.[78] Possibly the first company to install a formal suggestion system was Eastman Kodak, which has had such a program in effect since 1898.[79] Currently there are approximately 3000 organizations with formal suggestion systems in the United States.[80]

The basic concept behind the suggestion system is simple: an organization shares the benefits resulting from employee suggestions. As one company has put it: "Good ideas pay off." But operating a suggestion system successfully is not as simple as it might appear. The National Association of Suggestion Systems recommends adoption of the following specific implementing practices.

1 Carefully define what constitutes a suggestion.
2 Draw up specific eligibility standards.
3 Explain the system clearly to all employees.
4 Evaluate each suggestion according to a formal procedure.
5 Ensure that a fair and reasonable award is made.
6 Explain in writing why a suggestion is rejected.
7 Establish an appeals procedure for employees who want their suggestions reconsidered.
8 Keep meticulous records, independent of the suggestion process, of ideas and proposals reviewed.[81]

Oftentimes a good deal of hoopla accompanies the issuance of awards. At H. R. Textron Company, winners get crisp $100 bills right on the factory floor, as cameras flash and coworkers applaud. The company also makes sure that local newspapers are promptly notified about people who are honored for their good ideas. In 1982, H. R. Textron paid out $31,449 in cash awards and spent

$20,000 administering its suggestion system; in return it obtained a first-year savings of $386,636.[82]

On a far bigger scale, IBM typically reviews 250,000 suggestions a year (compared to the 400 to 500 at H. R. Textron) and in 1982 paid out $12 million from the reported savings of $65 million. (The maximum possible award for a suggestion at IBM is $100,000, an amount that has been paid three times.) IBM has described its suggestion system as "extremely worthwhile."[83]

Yet there have also been times when coworkers have not applauded an individual's creativity. Mitchell Fein cites the case of a large, well known company which paid good wages, had excellent relations with its employees and union, and which promised no layoffs due to improvements resulting from suggestions.

> An employee developed improvements which eliminated three assemblers from each of six lines, and he received a cash award of $24,000. All eighteen displaced persons were given other jobs and their union seniority was fully protected. Management was proud of the innovative employee and he received wide publicity. Some employees were not that impressed: The award winner also received a truckload of wet concrete on his driveway and the windows of his house were smashed. Though no one lost his job, some employees apparently felt that eighteen jobs had been lost to the plant.[84]

Evidence regarding the average impact of suggestion systems is limited. As might be expected, participation rates (i.e., number of suggestions per employee) are directly related to the sharing formula. The participation rate is nearly 50 percent higher for suggestion systems paying 11 to 20 percent of total savings compared to those paying up to 10 percent.[85] All in all, it appears that suggestion systems have only a modest impact on productivity. Although the average *rate* of return is about 5 to 1 in terms of savings (which may be in time) to dollar outlays,[86] the average *amount* of return is small. One survey reported an average annual savings per employee of about $50, an amount comparable to an increase in productivity of roughly one-fifth of 1 percent.[87] The same survey reported that only about 15 percent of the companies with suggestion systems thought they were an effective program for improving productivity.[88]

## Nonfinancial Reward Systems

Whereas suggestion systems typically provide praise and recognition along with cash awards, many organizational reward systems offer only intangible reinforcers. In their survey of "excellent" companies, Thomas Peters and Robert Waterman found widespread use of social and psychological rewards.

> We found rich systems of monetary incentives; but we expected that. We also discovered an incredible array of nonmonetary incentives and an amazing variety of experimental or newly introduced programs. . . . Nothing is more powerful than positive reinforcement. Everybody uses it. But top performers, almost alone, use it

extensively. The volume of contrived opportunities for showering pins, buttons, badges, and medals on people is staggering at McDonald's, Tupperware, IBM, or many of the other top performers.[89]

What is striking is the readiness in some companies to commemorate good performance via public rituals (e.g., award ceremonies at dinners) or via the granting of special designations (e.g., salespeople who make the "One Hundred Percent Club," stores that make the weekly "honor roll"). Further, although these activities may seem "corny" and as "unabashed hoopla," Peters and Waterman report that people respond positively.[90]

Other forms of praise and recognition include letters of commendation, visits by top management, temporary use of a special parking spot, and of course, inclusion in the organization's newsletter of a photograph and write-up of the "employee of the month." Perhaps the most obvious form of recognition is a compliment provided by an employee's supervisor. Yet, although such compliments are cost-free, many managers find it difficult to offer praise and recognition. A recent survey found that cultural factors were the primary obstacle. One respondent was fearful "of appearing to be a 'soft' boss"; another admitted that "giving and receiving praise can be embarrassing, it's not macho." Relatedly, concern was expressed that praise may be seen as disingenuous: employees may "wonder what you have up your sleeve."[91]

A somewhat novel recognition program was implemented at Eastman Kodak's apparatus division. As part of the operator certification program, machine operators who consistently produced components that met rigid quality standards became certified. Once the operators became certified, only 25 percent of their work was inspected, instead of 100 percent. Further, the names of certified operators were posted on bulletin boards. However, if an operator's performance fell below a specified level, the operator was required to requalify for certification. Although hard data were not provided in the report describing this program, it was claimed that the program was helping to upgrade manufacturing quality.[92]

Another type of nonfinancial reward is release time. In some settings it is customary to allow workers to go home when their work is completed (e.g., mail carriers, refuse collectors). There is some (very limited) evidence that such a practice can be used to improve productivity. In one company, where performance had averaged 92 percent of the productivity standard, employees urged the use of release time. After such a plan was put into effect, the standard amount of output was achieved in 5 hours—an increase in productivity of approximately 74 percent. Yet management was not enthusiastic about the plan because it was getting only a relatively small increase in output (about 9 percent) for the same pay; yet there was considerable "wasted production potential."[93]

Very little systematic research has been conducted on the effects of nonfinancial rewards (e.g., recognition, special privileges) on employee performance. One survey found that in nonmanufacturing companies and in clerical tasks, output increased by 87 percent in response to nonfinancial rewards;

when applied in educational settings, the quality of performance improved by 21.9 percent.[94]

### Merchandise Gifts

Gold and silver watches have long been used as rewards for loyalty. More recently, watches and other gifts have increasingly been used to motivate improved work behavior or job performance. The case of Noble Drilling Corporation provides an illustration of a remarkably successful intervention.

In order to improve worker safety, Noble Drilling had previously (1) hired a full-time safety supervisor, (2) mandated weekly oil rig inspections, (3) instituted a program of required training, consisting of 52 topic units, and (4) initiated incentive programs that awarded savings bonds, watches, and cash to crews with good long-term safety records (e.g., no lost-time accidents for a year). Yet after nearly a decade of such activities, the disability accident rate at Noble Drilling in 1978 was 85.91 per 1000 hours worked, more than 70 percent above the industry average.

In 1979, Noble Drilling began awarding S&H Green Stamps to workers for meeting short-term safety goals. Workers received 25 Green Stamps for each hour worked whenever they completed a 2-week period without a lost-time accident. In addition to hourly stamps, workers could earn 5000 stamps if their crew went a month without an accident. James Connor, the safety director at Noble, stated:

> Initially the Green Stamps program was sort of a joke among the men. But the response in terms of injury reduction was phenomenal after about three months, when crew members started to realize how quickly the stamps could accumulate and how much they were worth in exchange for merchandise.[95]

After 1 year, and the expenditure of $70,000 for 30 million Green Stamps, plus $64,000 for watches and savings bonds, the injury rate declined to 18.07 per 1000 hours worked—64 percent below the industry average. Turnover decreased by nearly 25 percent, and Noble received a refund of $1 million from its insurer. Thus, there were considerable savings in both business and human terms.[96]

### Flexible Benefits

Fringe benefits amounted to 25 percent of the average employee's total compensation in 1960.[97] However, between 1965 and 1975 wages increased by 85 percent while benefits rose by 165 percent; consequently by 1981 benefits amounted to 37 percent of total compensation.[98] Notwithstanding the vast dollar expenditures on benefits, most benefit packages have seemingly been put together in a piecemeal fashion—benefits often being added simply because they are in vogue.

Yet today, employees are more heterogeneous as a group than ever before.

Accordingly, the utility of a particular benefit may vary markedly across individuals. Both spouses in a dual-career couple may not need family major medical insurance; a young employee may want extensive maternity benefits or child care assistance; an older employee may prefer increased pension contributions. Not surprisingly, therefore, when employees are allowed to "customize" their benefit package, upward of 80 percent make changes.[99] Further, there is reason to believe that employees tend to make benefit allocation decisions that are "responsible."[100] In any event, this potential problem can be addressed by requiring employees to have specified minimum levels of certain fringe benefits (e.g., medical insurance).

Obviously, the use of flexible benefits should increase the utility of the benefit package to the typical employee; this in turn should improve retention. Other possible advantages of a flexible benefit plan might be noted. First, such a program can help in communicating to employees information about the extent and cost of benefits provided. In one survey it was found that nearly two-thirds of the firms spent less than $10 per employee annually to communicate the benefit program. No wonder that in some organizations employees are able to recall less than 15 percent of the benefits to which they are entitled.[101]

Also, a flexible benefit plan can be a useful recruiting tool. At Educational Testing Service, an organization which has had a "flex" plan in place since 1974, it is believed that the plan helps in attracting competent professionals. In addition to a "core" set of benefits, employees at ETS can allocate between 3 and 6 percent of their base salary to a variety of benefits, such as a fully paid dental plan, extra vacation, or a matching retirement fund (the most popular choice).[102]

It has also been argued that implementation of a flexible benefit plan may improve an organization's climate. This might happen if the plan is seen as reflective of a high degree of management trust in employees, trust that they will make responsible choices.[103]

Despite the many potential advantages, flexible benefit plans have not been widely adopted. A survey of chief executives conducted in 1980 (by William M. Mercer) found that 65 percent considered flexible benefits a valuable tool; yet only 5 percent said their firms used such a practice.[104] Similarly, a 1981 survey of nearly 600 personnel managers reported an adoption rate of 5.3 percent.[105] Apparently the primary reason for the low rate of adoption is the cost of setting up and administering such a plan.[106] Yet evaluation evidence to date has been quite positive, albeit nonrigorous.

At American Can Company, 92 percent of covered employees thought they had substantially improved their benefit package by selecting among options.[107] At TRW, 96 percent of responding employees were "moderately satisfied" or "very satisfied" with the company's flexible benefit plan.[108] And a recent cost-benefit study asked 250 employees (1) how much they would personally pay for various benefits and (2) how they would allocate a fixed amount of money on benefits, given the actual costs of different benefits. Overall, it was found that implementation of a flexible benefit plan would increase the average utility of benefits to employees by $250 a year, at a cost to the organization of $420 *less* per employee.[109]

A few years ago Vincent Flowers and Charles Hughes wrote an article entitled "The Key to Motivation." Described in the journal's table of contents as "a succinct answer to the employee motivation problem," the article is presented here in its entirety:

> The results of a 20-year study are in. The answer to the question "What really motivates people?" is: Go ask your people.[110]

The use of flexible benefits does just that. It asks people what they want, recognizing that people differ and that people change.

### Job Security

During the past few years there has been considerable and growing interest in job security as an organizational reward. In part this interest may be attributed to the economic success achieved in Japan and the widely heralded practice there of granting guaranteed lifetime employment.[111] Another contributing factor has probably been the lagging productivity growth in the United States, coupled with a growing receptivity to new ideas. Yet it should be noted that there is a long history to the view that a lack of job security is an impediment to high productivity.

James F. Lincoln, former chairman of the highly successful Lincoln Electric Company, stated the case quite aptly in 1951.

> It is management's duty to make the worker secure in his job. Only so can the worker feel that he can develop the skill and apply the imagination that will do his job more efficiently, without fear of unemployment from the progress he makes.[112]

More recently, Mitchell Fein has argued that job security should be a *management* demand in labor relations.

> Since job security is such an important component of the work environment, managers must look upon job security as *an essential precondition to enhancing the will to work.* . . . In plants without job security workers stretch out the work if they do not see sufficient work ahead of them. They will not work themselves out of their jobs.[113]

Moreover, as the personnel manager of a company with a history of no layoffs has observed, job security cannot be conveyed (or created) merely by words. "The workers have to actually see over a period of years the results of the increased productivity before they become convinced that it is not a threat to their job security."[114]

Yet it would appear that job security, per se, does not assure high productivity: it may be a necessary condition, but it is not a sufficient one. There are many organizations in the United States (particularly in the public sector) where lifetime employment is virtually guaranteed, but which are lacking in vitality and productivity.[115] Indeed, in a study that correlated managerial practices with the 5-year average annual rate of growth in profits, it was found that profit growth was lowest when job security was either very high or very low. The researchers offered the following explanation: where job security is too high, performance problems tend to be ignored; where job security is too low, employees see little opportunity for personal growth and career development.[116]

It would appear, therefore, that it is useful to distinguish between two types of job security: job security that arises from adequate business or funding (economic job security), and job security that arises from a reluctance to fire (personal job security). While economic job security may be a precondition for motivation and productivity, personal job security may actually be detrimental to these goals.

Several steps have been identified that organizations can take to improve economic job security.[117] Briefly, these include:

**1** Issuing a policy statement to the effect that the organization will avoid layoffs if at all possible
**2** Using work-force buffers or "shock absorbers" such as overtime, temporary or part-time employees, and the subcontracting of work that employees could perform
**3** Work sharing, e.g., use of a 30-hour workweek if need be
**4** Wage sharing, i.e., cutting the pay of all workers in place of laying off some
**5** Redeploying workers to jobs or locations where needed (a practice that may entail cross-training employees to handle multiple jobs)
**6** Remaining "lean"—not overhiring during good times
**7** Arranging for the temporary assignment or "lending" of employees to other organizations
**8** Providing incentives for early retirement
**9** Permitting voluntary leaves of absence
**10** Deferring low-priority work until slack periods

A good deal of planning and effort is required to provide a high degree of economic job security. However, a number of benefits might also be anticipated. There should be relatively low expenditures for severance pay, unemployment insurance, health insurance (continued coverage), legal fees, and outplacement costs. The organization's reputation should also be enhanced.

Of course, the provision of economic job security is essentially a two-way street; it requires a good deal of employee cooperation—e.g., in sharing work, or accepting changes in job assignments. At IBM, for example, where there has not been a layoff in more than 40 years, more than 12,000 employees voluntarily accepted new positions (e.g., going from laboratories to sales and field engineering jobs) during one 5-year recessionary period. It is also expected at IBM that employees will work a reasonable amount of overtime to protect their job security.[118] At Honda's Marysville, Ohio, plant a job applicant is asked if he or she would be willing to be moved from job to job at management's discretion. That flexibility, Honda tells applicants, is necessary to minimize layoffs during business downturns. Applicants who refuse to go along are not hired.[119]

Whereas economic job security requires a high degree of employee cooperation, guaranteed lifetime employment presumes a far greater commitment by employees, a commitment to lifetime loyalty. There exists, clearly, a quid pro quo: higher levels of organizational assurance entail greater levels of employee cooperation, commitment, and loyalty. Yet there is reason to believe that there are limits on how far many U.S. workers are willing to go in exchanging predictability for opportunity. For example, at Kawasaki's manufacturing plants in Japan the company has a practice of guaranteed lifetime employment, but at its plant in Lincoln, Nebraska, the company offers a high degree of economic job security. As Robert C. Summers, the personnel manager at Kawasaki's Lincoln plant, has commented, "U.S. workers wouldn't want to trade independence to choose where to work in exchange for guaranteed employment."[120]

## SUMMARY

This chapter has examined evidence regarding the effectiveness of many different types of reward systems for improving work behavior, job performance, and organizational effectiveness. Summarizing results, it was found that individual output-based reward systems have reliably improved productivity, the median increase being approximately 30 percent. Group gainsharing plans have also consistently shown positive effects, the median performance improvement being 18 percent.

There is evidence that judgment-based reward systems can work, raising average levels of motivation and performance. However, the use of judgmental merit reward systems may raise a number of potential problems; these were discussed, along with possible remedies. But what are the alternatives to rewarding evaluated job performance? If rewards are instead based on longevity or personal favoritism, logic and evidence indicate that these approaches are recipes for organizational decline.

Reward systems have also been used to improve attendance behavior. Modestly successful results have been found for the two conventional approaches: rewarding attendance *or* punishing excessive absences. A highly promising alternative approach is a mixed-consequence system, one that incorporates both positive reinforcement (for good attendance) *and* punishment (for excessive absences).

Various miscellaneous reward systems were also reviewed. Evidence indicates the following: suggestion systems can be used cost-effectively to generate good ideas; nonfinancial rewards can be used to increase productivity (and are extensively used by highly effective organizations); merchandise gifts can be used to improve work behaviors; flexible benefit plans can raise the value to individuals of fringe benefits; and economic job security may be a precondition for high levels of work motivation and productivity.

Of course, more than one type of reward system can be employed at one time. Presumably, organizations will find it advantageous to reward people for appropriate work behaviors, as well as for their individual job performances and their collective effectiveness.

## NOTES

1  In this chapter the term "reward system" is conceptualized broadly. It includes attempts to influence work behavior and job performance by: providing rewards (positive reinforcement), permitting escape from or avoidance of unpleasant outcomes (negative reinforcement), withholding or discontinuing rewards (extinction), and providing unpleasant outcomes (punishment).

2  Claude S. George, Jr., *The History of Management Thought* (Englewood, Cliffs, N.J.: Prentice-Hall, 1968), pp. 10–11.

3  H. Jack Shapiro, "Pay Incentives and Work Motivations: Past and Present," *Psychological Reports,* 42 (1978), 124–126.

4  Allan N. Nash and Stephen J. Carroll, Jr., *The Management of Compensation* (Monterey, Calif.: Brooks/Cole, 1975), pp. 199–202. Some of the organizations surveyed apparently employed group output–based reward systems, a factor that may have reduced average effects.

5  Mitchell Fein, "Motivation to Work," in *Handbook of Work, Organization, and Society,* ed. Robert Dubin (Chicago: Rand McNally, 1976), p. 522.

6  E. A. Locke, D. B. Feren, V. M. McCaleb, K. N. Shaw, and A. T. Denny, "The Relative Effectiveness of Four Methods of Motivating Employee Performance," in *Changes in Working Life,* ed. K. D. Duncan, M. M. Gruneberg, and D. Wallis (Chichester, England: Wiley, Ltd., 1980), pp. 368–375.

7  Raymond A Katzell, Penney Bienstock, and Paul H. Faerstein, *A Guide to Worker Productivity Experiments in the United States 1971–75* (New York: New York Univ. Press, 1977), Abstracts 73, 103; Richard A Guzzo and Jeffrey S. Bondy, *A Guide to Worker Productivity Experiments in the United States 1976–81* (New York: Pergamon Press, 1983), Abstracts 13, 43, 48, 50, 55, and 63.

8  Gary P. Latham and Dennis L. Dossett, "Designing Incentive Plans for Unionized Employees: A Comparison of Continuous and Variable Ratio Reinforcement Schedules," *Personnel Psychology,* 31 (1978), 53–54.

9  Donald L. McManis and William G. Dick, "Monetary Incentives in Today's Industrial Setting," *Personnel Journal,* 52 (May 1973), 388–389.

10  Carl H. Driessnack, "Financial Impact of Effective Human Resources Management," *The Personnel Administrator,* Dec. 1979, p. 64. (This article first appeared in the Jan. 1976 issue of the same journal.)

11  Harold F. Rothe, "Output Rates among Welders: Productivity and Consistency Following Removal of a Financial Incentive System," *Journal of Applied Psychology,* 54 (1970), 549–551.

12  Charles N. Greene and Philip M. Podsakoff, "Effects of Removal of a Pay Incentive: A Field Experiment," *Proceedings of the 1978 National Meeting of the Academy of Management,* pp. 206–210. It is noteworthy that the difference in performance exceeded *ten* standard errors.

13  Edward E. Lawler III, "Reward Systems," in *Improving Life at Work,* ed. J. Richard Hackman and J. Lloyd Suttle (Santa Monica, Calif.: Goodyear, 1977), p. 223.

14  John Miner, in "Performance Appraisal: The Barrier to Pay for Performance," *Pro-

*ceedings, National Meeting of the American Compensation Association* (1978), p. 46.

15 Lawrence M. Miller, *Behavior Management* (New York: Wiley, 1978), p. 56. Note that this notion is called a "law," not a "theory" or a "hypothesis."

16 Edward E. Lawler III, *Pay and Organizational Effectiveness: A Psychological View* (New York: McGraw-Hill, 1971), pp. 37–60.

17 Mitchell Fein, "An Alternative to Traditional Managing," unpublished paper, (Hillsdale, N.J.), 1977, pp. 12–13.

18 E. A. Locke, D. B. Feren, V. M. McCaleb, K. N. Shaw, and A. T. Denny, "Relative Effectiveness," p. 379. Locke and his associates attribute this discrepancy to "ideological bias" (p. 379).

19 Office of Economic Research, New York Stock Exchange, *People and Productivity: A Challenge to Corporate America* (New York: New York Stock Exchange, 1982) p. 44. In total, the sample consisted of 1158 companies.

20 Edward E. Lawler III, *Pay and Organizational Effectiveness,* p. 7 (1935 estimate), p. 120 (1939 estimate); also Lyman W. Porter and Edward E. Lawler III, *Managerial Attitudes and Performance* (Homewood, Ill.: Irwin, 1968), p. 58 (1958 estimate); also *People and Productivity,* p. 44 (1982 estimate).

21 *People and Productivity,* p. 45.

22 Edward E. Lawler, "Whatever Happened to Incentive Pay?" *New Management,* 1 (1984), p. 38.

23 Harold G. Kaufman, *Obsolescence and Professional Career Development* (New York: Amacom, 1974), p. 4. Indeed, as noted in "The Basics in Trouble," *Newsweek,* 8 Sept. 1980, p. 56, only about 40 percent of U.S. workers produced goods (in 1980).

24 Edward E. Lawler III, "Merit Pay: An Obsolete Policy?" in *Perspectives on Behavior in Organizations,* ed. J. Richard Hackman, Edward E. Lawler III, and Lyman W. Porter, 2nd ed. (New York: McGraw-Hill, 1983), pp. 305–308.

25 Broadly defined, group gainsharing plans may be viewed as including profit sharing and even employee stock ownership plans. However, the effects of these plans on productivity are not known. While static (cross-sectional) data exist pertinent to the productivity and profitability of companies that have and do not have profit sharing and employee stock ownership plans, there is an absence of the before and after (longitudinal) data needed to assess effectiveness (see Mitchell Fein, "Motivation to Work," pp. 519–522). There is evidence, though, that as the size of the group sharing an incentive gets larger, the impact of the incentive plan diminishes [see R. Marriott, *Incentive Wage Systems* (London: Staples Press, 1968)]. Hence in large organizations, the motivational effects of profit sharing and stock ownership plans are likely to be small for most employees, such plans serving primarily as symbols of shared interests (see Edward E. Lawler, "Whatever Happened to Incentive Pay?" p. 41). (Of course, profit sharing and stock ownership plans can have an important impact on the motivation of top executives.)

26 See Arthur J. Ringham, "Designing a Gainsharing Program to Fit a Company's Operations," *National Productivity Review,* 3 (Spring 1984), 131–144; Linda S. Tyler and Bob Fisher, "The Scanlon Concept: A Philosophy as Much as a System," *Personnel Administrator,* 28 (July 1983), 33–37; and Andrew J. DuBrin, *Contemporary Applied Management* (Plano, Tex.: Business Publications, 1982), pp. 186–197. (Typically, also, savings resulting from new capital investments are reflected in a change in the "normal" ratio.)

**27** Mitchell Fein, "Motivation to Work," pp. 518–519.

**28** Edward E. Lawler III and Gerald E. Ledford, Jr., "Productivity and the Quality of Work Life," *National Productivity Review,* 1 (Winter 1981–82), 30.

**29** E. A. Locke, D. B. Feren, V. M. McCaleb, K. N. Shaw, and A. T. Denny, "Relative Effectiveness," pp. 376–377. However, because the performance improvement actually takes the form of a salary savings, it is not accurate to equate it with an increase in output (or productivity). Since salaries comprise about 57 percent of the dollar value of all goods and services produced (GNP), the 16 percent salary savings corresponds to an increase in outputs or productivity of 9.12 percent (57% × 16%). For evidence demonstrating the validity of this conversion, see Frank L. Schmidt and John E. Hunter, "Individual Differences in Productivity: An Empirical Test of Estimates Derived From Studies of Selection Procedure Utility," *Journal of Applied Psychology,* 68 (1983), 407–414.

**30** Mitchell Fein, "An Alternative to Traditional Managing," pp. 15–17, 37–41. (Typically, standards are changed with new capital investment.)

**31** *People and Productivity,* p. 33.

**32** Ibid., p. 48. Interestingly, the median productivity increase after only 6 weeks was 15 percent. Unlike some interventions, it does not take months or years to raise productivity. In this regard consider the comments of Mitchell Fein during his presentation, "Raising Productivity by Sharing Productivity Gains," at the 35th Annual Conference of the American Society for Personnel Administration (New York, 1 June 1983): "I asked the union representative how long it would take to increase productivity. His reply, 'Twenty minutes. Fifteen minutes to think about it, and five minutes to do it.'"

**33** U.S. General Accounting Office, *Productivity Sharing Programs: Can They Contribute to Productivity Improvement?* (Gaithersburg, Md.: U.S. General Accounting Office, 1981), p. 15. Moreover, it was found that among long-standing gainsharing plans, those in effect for more than 5 years, the average labor savings was 29 percent. Converted to outputs (see footnote 29), this corresponds to an increase in productivity of 16.5 percent. Further, it might be noted that roughly 60 percent of the gainsharing plans studied were implemented in facilities with unionized labor forces.

**34** E. A. Locke, D. B. Feren, V. M. McCaleb, K. N. Shaw, and A. T. Denny, "Relative Effectiveness," pp. 376–378.

**35** R. Marriott, *Incentive Wage Systems* (London: Staples Press, 1968).

**36** L. Miller and R. Hamblin, "Interdependence, Differential Rewarding and Productivity," *American Sociological Review,* 28 (1963), 768–778. In their review of 24 studies involving competitive and cooperative incentive plans, they found that the competitive (i.e., individual incentive) approach worked best when there was low task interdependence; however, when jobs were highly interdependent, the cooperative (i.e., group incentive) approach was superior.

**37** *People and Productivity,* pp. 44–45.

**38** Fred Luthans, *Organizational Behavior,* 3rd ed. (New York: McGraw-Hill, 1981), p. 160.

**39** Indeed, the person who receives a 7 percent merit increase where the average is 5 percent might even experience more satisfaction than the person who receives an 8 percent merit raise where the average is 10 percent. Consistent with this reasoning is the research evidence from 30 national surveys from 20 countries indicating that wealth is positively related to happiness *within* a culture. Clearly, therefore, evaluations of outcomes are relative. Would a person with an above-average income in a poor country (or community) be as happy given the same real income in a wealthy country (or community)? Perhaps there is something to be said for small ponds. See Richard A. Easterlin, "Does Money Buy Happiness?" *The Public Interest,* No. 30 (Winter 1973), 3–10.

40 Similarly, if all students in a course received the same grade, say a "C," would they all be equally pleased? Obviously, some would be disappointed, others highly delighted.

41 Edward E. Lawler III, *Pay and Organizational Effectiveness,* p. 158.

42 See *Industry Week,* 12 Jan. 1981, p. 11; see also *New York Times,* 5 Sept. 1983, p. 8.

43 *New York Times,* 5 Sept. 1983, p. 8.

44 Richard E. Kopelman, "Organizational Control System Responsiveness, Expectancy Theory Constructs, and Work Motivation: Some Interrelations and Causal Connections," *Personnel Psychology,* 29 (1976), 205–220; Richard E. Kopelman, "Merit Rewards, Motivation and Job Performance," *Research Management,* 20 (May 1977), 35–37. Along these lines, in a study of two hospitals, one that rewarded on the basis of seniority, the other on the basis of merit, employees more highly valued rewards in the latter hospital. See B. Schneider and L. K. Olson, "Effort as a Correlate of Organizational Reward System and Individual Values," *Personnel Psychology,* 23 (1970), 313–326.

45 Richard E. Kopelman and Leon Reinharth, "Research Results: The Effect of Merit-Pay Practices on White Collar Performance," *Compensation Review,* 14, No. 4 (1982), 30–40.

46 George G. Gordon and Bonnie E. Goldberg, "Is There a Climate for Success?" *Management Review,* 66 (May 1977), pp. 37–44.

47 George F. Dreher, "The Role of Performance in the Turnover Process," *Academy of Management Journal,* 25 (1982), 137–147.

48 Timothy J. Keaveny and Robert E. Allen, "The Implications of an Across-the-Board Salary Increase," unpublished research paper (No. 279), University of Wyoming, 1979, pp. 1–14.

49 Additional anecdotal evidence indicates that the situation described is not atypical. In several training sessions conducted for supervisors and professional staff employees in various agencies of the same municipal government, the following question was asked: "If you were to describe your agency as an animal, what animal comes to mind?" The most common response: "a turtle"; one person added, "rolled over on its back."

50 Robert B. McKersie and Janice A. Klein, "Productivity: The Industrial Relations Connection," *National Productivity Review,* 3 (Winter 1983–84), 26–35; Kenneth S. Teel, "Performance Appraisal: Current Trends, Persistent Progress," *Personnel Journal,* 59 (Apr. 1980), 298–300, 316; *New York Times,* 6 Oct. 1982, p. D23.

51 Kenneth S. Teel, "Performance Appraisal," p. 299.

52 See "The Tightening Squeeze on White-Collar Pay," *Business Week,* 12 Sept. 1977, pp. 82–94; also see "A Changing Pattern in Allocating Pay Hikes," *Business Week,* 23 June 1975, pp. 67, 70.

53 "The Tightening Squeeze on White-Collar Pay," *Business Week,* 12 Sept. 1977, p. 88.

54 James T. Brinks, "Is There Merit in Merit Increases?" *Personnel Administrator,* 25 (May 1980), 63–64. Coypright 1980, The American Society for Personnel Admin-

istration, 606 North Washington Street, Alexandria, Va. 22314. Reprinted by permission.

**55** Ibid., p. 64.

**56** Andrew S. Grove, "Keeping Favoritism and Prejudice Out of Evaluations," *Wall Street Journal,* 27 Feb. 1984, p. 26.

**57** Steven Kerr, "On the Folly of Rewarding A, While Hoping for B," *Academy of Management Journal,* 18 (1975), 778–779.

**58** Howard R. Smith, "Brother to the Ox," *Management Review,* 64 (Nov. 1975), 4–12. Along these lines, Edward E. Lawler III, in *Pay and Organizational Effectiveness,* has commented that "motivating people with financial rewards is not a piker's game" (p. 173).

**59** Richard E. Kopelman, "Across-Individual, Within-Individual and Return on Effort Versions of Expectancy Theory," *Decision Sciences,* 8 (1977), 651–662; Richard E. Kopelman, Andrew M. Liebman, and Gary A. Yukl, "Experimental Test of a Return on Effort Version of Expectancy Theory: Across-Person and Within-Person Analyses," *Journal of Management,* 4 (1978), 97–105; Charles W. Kennedy, John A. Fossum, and Bernard J. White, "An Empirical Comparison of within-Subjects and between-Subjects Expectancy Theory Models," *Organizational Behavior and Human Performance,* 32 (1983), 124–143.

**60** In other words, it is the *slope* (not the height) of the relationship between effort expenditure and outcomes that determines choices made among behaviors. As David Belcher commented in "Pay and Performance," *Compensation Review,* 12, No. 3 (1980), 17: "performance variance can best be accounted for by measuring the *difference* between the expected values of working hard and that of working at a more leisurely pace" (italics in original).

**61** Alan E. Kazdin, *The Token Economy* (New York: Plenum Press, 1977), pp. 69–73.

**62** Edward E. Lawler III, "Merit Pay: An Obsolete Policy?" p. 307.

**63** Lawrence Z. Lorber, J. Robert Kirk, Kenneth H. Kirschner, and Charlene R. Handorf, *Fear of Firing: A Legal and Personnel Analysis of Employment-at-Will* (Alexandria, Va: ASPA Foundation, 1984), p. 30.

**64** Andrew S. Grove, "Keeping Favoritism and Prejudice Out of Evaluations," *Wall Street Journal,* 27 Feb. 1984, p. 26. Reprinted by permission of the Wall Street Journal, © Dow Jones & Company, Inc. 1984. All rights reserved.

**65** Richard M. Steers and Susan R. Rhodes, "Major Influences on Employee Attendance: A Process Model," *Journal of Applied Psychology,* 63 (1978), 391.

**66** Michael K. Moch and Dale E. Fitzgibbon, "Absenteeism and Production Efficiency: An Empirical Assessment," paper presented at the 40th Annual National Meeting of the Academy of Management (Detroit, 1980).

**67** Loretta M. Schmitz and Herbert G. Heneman III, "Do Positive Reinforcement Programs Reduce Employee Absenteeism?" *Personnel Administrator,* 25 (Sept. 1980), 87–93.

**68** Richard E. Kopelman and George O. Schneller IV, "A Mixed-Consequence System for Reducing Overtime and Unscheduled Absences," *Journal of Organizational Behavior Management,* 3, No. 1 (1981), 17–28.

**69** George O. Schneller IV and Richard E. Kopelman, "Using Incentives to Increase Absenteeism: A Plan That Backfired," *Compensation Review,* 15, No. 2 (1983), 40–45.

**70** In the agricultural implement industry, for example, a paid time-off incentive plan was instituted, and awards were made to some 100,000 workers. However, according to Agis Salpukas, "The plan has had little effect on the workers who are chronically absent while those who come in normally have in effect gotten off a half-hour a week." See the *New York Times,* 6 Feb. 1976, pp. 1, 12.

71  D. Willings, "The Absentee Worker," *Personnel and Training Management,* 31, No. 12 (1968), 10–12.

72  Nigel Nicholson, "Management Sanctions and Absence Control," *Human Relations,* 29 (1976), 139–151.

73  Darrell Olson and Ruth Bangs, "No-Fault Attendance Control: A Real World Application," *Personnel Administrator,* 29 (June 1984), 53–56.

74  *Forbes,* 5 Dec. 1983, pp. 8, 10. General Motors reported that 75 percent of the employees who qualified for counseling in the first half of 1982 avoided the threatened benefit cuts during the second half of the year.

75  Robert W. Kempen and R. Vance Hall, "Reduction of Industrial Absenteeism: Results of a Behavioral Approach," *Journal of Organizational Behavior Management,* 1, No. 1 (1977), 1–21.

76  Richard E. Kopelman and George O. Schneller IV, "Mixed-Consequence System."

77  For a review of the specific features in seven such plans (and suggestions for an "ideal plan") see George O. Schneller IV, Richard E. Kopelman, and John J. Silver, Jr., "A Combined Leave Benefit System for the Control of Absenteeism in Health Care Organizations," *Hospital & Health Services Administration,* 27, No. 1 (1982), 63–74.

78  Gail Gregg, "The Power of Suggestion," *Across the Board,* 20 (Dec. 1983), 28.

79  William B. Werther, Jr., "Out of the Productivity Box," *Business Horizons,* 25 (Sept.–Oct. 1982), 58.

80  Gail Gregg, "The Power of Suggestion," p. 28.

81  Ibid., p. 31.

82  Ibid., p. 27.

83  Ibid., p. 31.

84  Mitchell Fein, "An Alternative to Traditional Managing," pp. 3–4.

85  Gail Gregg, "The Power of Suggestion," p. 29.

86  Ibid.

87  Robert B. McKersie and Janice A. Klein, "Productivity," p. 31.

88  Ibid.

89  Thomas J. Peters and Robert H. Waterman, Jr., *In Search of Excellence: Lessons from America's Best-Run Companies* (New York: Harper & Row, 1982), pp. 242, 269.

90  Ibid., pp. 239–240, 247, 269. Regarding the value and potency of token reinforcers, Peters and Waterman suggest to readers the following experiment: ". . . go back and look through closets and drawers as we recently did. We still have Boy Scout merit badges, trophies gathering dust, and a medal or two from some insignificant ski races held decades ago" (p. 268).

91  Judi Komaki, "Why We Don't Reinforce: The Issues," *Journal of Organizational Behavior Management,* 4 (Fall–Winter 1982), 97–100.

92  *Personnel Administrator,* 29 (Mar. 1984), 16.

93  Stanley M. Nealey, "Compensation Fungibility," *Proceedings of the 28th Annual Winter Meeting of the Industrial Relations Research Association,* pp. 154–155.

94  *Training/HRD,* 17 (July 1980), A6–7.

95  "Adding Incentives to Safety Training Cuts Injuries, Boosts Productivity," *Train-*

*ing/HRD,* 17 (July 1980), A3. Reprinted with permission from TRAINING, The Magazine of Human Resource Development. Copyright 1980, Lakewood Publications, Inc., Minneapolis, Minn. All rights reserved.

96  Ibid., pp. A2–3.

97  Philip Kienast, Douglas MacLachlan, Leigh McAlister, and David Sampson, "The Modern Way to Redesign Compensation Packages," *Personnel Administrator,* 28 (June 1983), 127.

98  Harold C. White, "Personnel Administration and Organizational Productivity: An Employee View," *Personnel Administrator,* 26 (Aug. 1981), 37. Also see *Time,* 27 June 1983, p. 54.

99  Robert B. Cockrum, "Has the Time Come for Employee Cafeteria Plans?" *Personnel Administrator,* 27 (July 1982), 67; also Stanley M. Nealey, "Compensation Fungibility," p. 156.

100  Stanley M. Nealey, "Compensation Fungibility," pp. 156–157.

101  Harold C. White, "Personnel Administration and Organizational Productivity," p. 38. On the basis of an extensive review of survey data, White concluded, *"Little attempt is made by most firms to maximize the potential of personnel administration practices for employee motivation and productivity"* (p. 38, italics in original).

102  *Wall Street Journal,* 24 Feb. 1981, p. 1.

103  *Time,* 27 June 1983, p. 54.

104  *Industry Week,* 12 Jan. 1981, p. 11.

105  Barry C. Campbell and Cynthia L. Barron, "How Extensively are HRM Practices Being Utilized by the Practitioners?" *Personnel Administrator,* 27 (May 1982), 69.

106  *Time,* 27 June 1983, p. 54.

107  Robert B. Cockrum, "Has the Time Come?" p. 67.

108  *Time,* 27 June 1983, p. 54.

109  Randall B. Dunham and Roger A. Formisano, "Designing and Evaluating Employee Benefit Systems," *Personnel Administrator,* 27 (Apr. 1982), 29–35.

110  Vincent S. Flowers and Charles L. Hughes, "The Key to Motivation," *Personnel Administrator,* 26 (Feb. 1981), 70. Copyright 1981, The American Society for Personnel Administration, 606 North Washington Street, Alexandria, Va. 22314. Reprinted by permission.

111  It should be noted, though, that in Japan this practice (granting guaranteed lifetime employment) generally only occurs in large companies, and is limited, typically, to male employees between the ages of 20 and 55 or 60 (depending on the mandatory retirement age). All told, only 25 percent of the labor force in Japan is covered by guaranteed lifetime employment. [See Nan Weiner, "The Japanese Wage System," *Compensation Review,* 14, No. 1 (1982), 47.] Furthermore, as William B. Werther, Jr., has put it, the application of Japanese employment practices in the U.S. "would be folly (and illegal)" ("Out of the Productivity Box," p. 55).

112  Mitchell Fein, "Motivation for Work," p. 512.

113  Mitchell Fein, "An Alternative to Traditional Managing," p. 40, italics in original.

114  John Savage, "Incentive Programs at Nucor Corporation Boost Productivity," *Personnel Administrator,* 26 (Aug. 1981), 33–36, 49. Copyright 1981, The American Society for Personnel Administration, 606 North Washington Street, Alexandria, Va. 22314. Reprinted by permission.

115  Marta Mooney, "A Time for Government Action," *National Productivity Review,* 3 (Winter 1983–84), 89. (This article summarized the results of the 1983 White House Conference on Productivity. At the conference there was debate, but no

agreement, on the advisability and feasibility of business moving toward greater employment security arrangements.)

116 George G. Gordon and Bonnie E. Goldberg, "Is There a Climate for Success?" pp. 42–43.

117 James F. Bolt, "Job Security: Its Time Has Come," *Harvard Business Review,* 61 (Nov.–Dec. 1983), 116–122; Marta Mooney, "Let's Use Job Security as a Productivity Builder," *Personnel Administrator,* 29 (Jan. 1984), 39–42, 44, 90; *People and Productivity,* pp. 18–20.

118 *The Career Development Bulletin,* 2, No. 4 (1981), 1–2.

119 Masayoshi Kanabayashi, "Honda's Accord: How a Japanese Firm is Faring on Its Dealings with Workers in U.S.," *Wall Street Journal,* 2 Oct. 1981, p. 25.

120 Robert C. Summers, "Applying Japanese Management Methods in America: Kawasaki at Lincoln, Nebraska," invited address at conference, Current Directions in Productivity—Evolving Japanese and American Practices, (New York, 22 Mar. 1982).

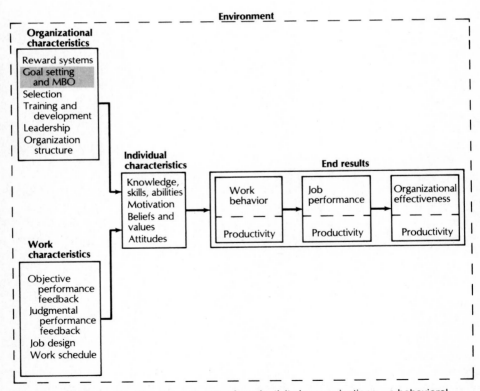

Conceptual framework of the determinants of productivity in organizations—a behavioral science approach.

# GOAL SETTING AND MANAGEMENT BY OBJECTIVES

Goal setting and management by objectives (MBO) are commonly treated as equivalent techniques in the academic and professional literatures. Reflective of this, four recent reviews have combined results for goal setting and MBO interventions.[1] Yet, there are numerous and seemingly important distinctions between the two interventions. The most obvious difference is in the target population: goal setting programs are typically conducted for hourly employees; MBO programs are generally undertaken for managerial and professional employees.

Although the setting of specific performance goals is an essential feature of MBO (note that MBO, unlike goal setting, usually entails setting multiple goals), MBO programs typically attempt to accomplish much more than simply setting goals and clarifying roles. MBO plans attempt to improve the planning process, to provide more effective performance appraisal reviews, to enhance managerial-subordinate communication, to ensure the timely correction of performance problems, and to further the personal development of the employee. In light of the differences between goal setting and MBO in terms of purpose and process, the two techniques are examined separately.

## GOAL SETTING

According to legend, Andrew Carnegie used to motivate his employees to increase steel production by writing in chalk on the factory floor the day shift's tonnage produced. The second shift would then be challenged to surpass this goal, and the day shift would then be challenged to meet the second shift's output, and so forth.

Although the utility of goals has long been suspected, formal research into the effects of goal setting is a relatively recent phenomenon. Controlled laboratory experiments were first conducted about 20 years ago, and numerous studies have been conducted since. Only a limited number of field investigations have been undertaken, however, most during the past 10 years. Interestingly, laboratory and field studies have generally agreed in results, yielding the following major findings:

**1** Specific goals (e.g., produce 42 units per hour) lead to higher levels of achievement than vague goals or admonitions (e.g., do your best, try your hardest). There is also evidence that specific goals lead to higher levels of task interest (and lower boredom) than do vague goals.

**2** Difficult (challenging) goals lead to higher levels of achievement than easy goals—provided the difficult goal is accepted. (This finding is in accord with Parkinson's law: Work expands to fill the time allotted for its completion. In terms of goal setting, work effort is adjusted to the perceived difficulty of the task goal.)[2]

**Empirical Results**

Eleven field studies provide data pertinent to the effects of goal setting on job performance; ten of these studies relate to quantity of output, and one to quality. These studies are briefly summarized here, in chronological order. (Studies dealing with the impact of goal setting on attitudes or job satisfaction are excluded from this reviw.)

**1** Latham and Kinne examined the productivity of logging crews (in terms of cords per hour worked). Half of the crews had been given production goals, half had not. Over a 3-month period productivity was 9 pecent higher in crews with production goals.[3]

**2** Latham and Baldes reported that when workers were told to do their best, logging trucks were loaded to about 60 percent of capacity. When workers were assigned the goal of loading trucks to 94 percent of maximum allowable weight, the average level of loading rose to around 90 percent and stayed at that level during the final 6 months of the 9-month study period.[4] The 50 percent improvement in work quality produced a savings of $250,000 over the study period; moreover, the 90 percent loading level continued for 7 years.[5] Interestingly, before the experiment began, many managers were extremely skeptical. Latham noted: "Some of the managers thought that [goal setting] was the funniest and most naive thing they'd ever heard of. They couldn't conceive how that would motivate anybody to do anything, because there wasn't any money involved, no recognition, and they, the truck drivers, would get nothing out of it."[6]

**3** Latham and Yukl examined the effects of assigned and participatory goal setting procedures among educated and uneducated woods workers. The average result during an 8-week experimental period was 17 percent higher productivity with goal setting.[7]

**4** Latham and Locke studied the effects of goal setting (in the form of time limits) on the productivity of wood-harvesting crews. Over a 3-month period, the crews with time limits were 1 percent more productive (in terms of cords per hour worked) than were the crews without time limits.[8]

**5** Latham and Yukl examined the effects of goal setting on the productivity of typists (in terms of lines typed per hour, corrected for errors). The average effect of goal setting over a 10-week period was an increase in productivity of 11 percent.[9]

**6** Kim and Hamner examined the effects of goal setting and feedback on a sample of blue-collar Bell System workers. The introduction of goal setting and feedback led to an average increase in productivity of 9 percent over 3 months.[10]

**7** Ivancevich reported that district sales managers used three different programs in managing salespeople. Five district sales managers used participative goal setting, six used assigned goal setting, and seven served as a comparison group (using "do your best"). Four objective measures served as performance criteria: the frequency of sales calls, the ratio of orders to sales calls, the direct selling cost, and a market penetration index. Combining the two goal setting groups together, the result was that after 6 months the goal setting groups outperformed the control group by 20 percent; however after 12 months the difference in performance was only 3 percent. The average difference in performance throughout the experiment was 15.5 percent.[11]

**8** Ivancevich examined the effects of a 2½-day goal setting training program and subsequent goal setting among skilled technicians. Over a period of 12 months, service complaints (an indicator of performance quality) decreased 21 percent more in the goal setting groups compared to the "do your best" group. Cost performance (an indicator of performance quantity) improved by 23 percent more in the goal setting groups. However, Ivancevich noted a "pronounced dissipation of performance and satisfaction improvement" approximately 9 months after the goal setting program had begun.[12]

**9** Dossett, Latham, and Mitchell examined the effects of goal setting and feedback on the job performance of female clerical employees. The performance criterion was a (relatively objective) behavioral observation scale. After the introduction of goal setting, performance scores increased by 9.5 percent over 8 months. There was some evidence of attenuating effects over time: performance scores improved by 10.6 percent over the first 4 months; however, the increase (over baseline) was only 8.5 percent during the second 4 months (reflecting a decline from the prior 4-month period).[13]

**10** Ivancevich and McMahon examined the effects of goal setting, feedback, and praise on the job performance of engineers over 9 months. The goal setting groups, in comparison with the control groups, showed 4 percent better cost performance, 7 percent better quality performance, and 2 percent poorer overtime hours performance. Thus, averaging results across the three criterion measures, performance in the goal setting groups was 3 percent better than in the control groups.[14]

**11** Kim studied the effects of goal setting and feedback on the sales performance of retail store salespersons. Standardized, adjusted sales were 31 percent higher in the goal setting groups compared with the control group over a 10-week period.[15]

### Summary and Conclusions

The effect of goal setting on productivity (or performance quantity) has ranged from an increase of 1 percent to an increase of 31 percent, the median improvement being an increase of 10.3 percent.[16] Clearly, the evidence indicates that goal setting raises productivity, and this effect is highly reliable.[17]

Why does goal setting work? In most general terms, it appears to be because goals and intentions influence behavior: a person who intends to do something does it. But why do people adopt goals? Apparently for a number of reasons related to psychological, social, and extrinsic job factors. The introduction of a difficult but attainable specific goal can add meaning to work and increase the satisfaction of performing well, especially on a repetitive job.[18] Also, goal setting can engender informal competition between (or among) individuals and groups adding to the social satisfaction, status, and respect of some workers. Further, the process of setting goals clarifies what management expects the worker to accomplish. As D. E. Law, a management consultant with Arthur Young & Company, has observed: "Basic to managing for productivity is the establishment of targets for optimal performance of specific functions. . . . If there are no such targets, productivity is a meaningless term, because the absence of specific objectives implies that management finds any level of performance acceptable."[19] Hence, goal setting may raise what is called "evaluation apprehension": employees may see possible benefits in "looking good" (e.g., job retention, pay increase) and possible costs in "looking bad." In this vein, recent research has directly examined why difficult goals raise motivation more than easy goals. It was found that difficult goals are generally more desirable (or highly "valent") than easy goals,[20] and it would appear that the greater desirability may result from psychological, social, or extrinsic considerations.

A number of additional, although less definitive, findings have also emerged from field studies performed to date. Although one might expect that participation in goal setting yields results superior to assigned goals, no clear productivity differences have emerged. When participation has yielded higher productivity it appears to have been because (1) participation resulted in individuals setting more difficult goals than when assigned, or (2) participation resulted in increased understanding of how to accomplish goals.[21]

A number of individual difference variables have been examined as possible moderators of the effects of goal setting on productivity. Unfortunately, as Locke, Saari, Shaw, and Latham noted in their comprehensive review article, "The only consistent thing about the studies of individual differences in goal setting is their inconsistency."[22] There is, however, some evidence that participation in goal setting, goal clarity, and feedback may be especially helpful to individuals with a high need for security concerning their job performance.[23]

Goal setting appears to have an enhanced positive effect when used in conjunction with incentives and objective performance feedback.[24] Also, longitudinal data indicate that the impact of goal setting on productivity diminishes somewhat with the passage of time. Further, examining results across studies, median productivity increases in studies lasting up to 3 months and in studies lasting longer than 3 months, were 11 percent and 9.5 percent, respectively.

It is important to recognize that there are other dimensions of goals to consider besides the three already mentioned (specificity, difficulty, and acceptance). According to Gary Yukl,[25] effective goals should be:

- Clear and concise
- Verifiable (capable of measurement or observation)
- Time bounded
- Cost effective (benefits justify costs)
- Mutually acceptable (to manager and subordinate)
- Consistent with policy
- Results oriented (not activity oriented)
- Relevant (to effective performance)
- Compatible with the goals of others
- Written (a copy being kept by both the manager and subordinate)

## MANAGEMENT BY OBJECTIVES

The discussion of management by objectives is divided into four sections. The first section describes what the process called MBO is about, the second provides frequently advanced reasons why the use of MBO should enhance productivity, the third section reviews the empirical results to date, and the fourth section summarizes these results and offers recommendations for action.

### A Description of the Process

The intervention called *management by objectives* is similar to goal setting, but far more comprehensive, involving many more activities than merely setting goals. And, as noted above, while goal setting programs have generally been used with hourly workers, MBO has typically been implemented with managerial and professional employees. Indeed, according to Edwin Locke, the key element in MBO is "the setting of specific performance goals by executives and managers."[26]

It is generally agreed that the first person to describe the MBO process was Peter Drucker in his 1954 book, *The Practice of Management.* Douglas McGregor later popularized MBO in his 1960 book, *The Human Side of Enterprise,* and George Odiorne contributed further impetus with his 1965 book, *Management by Objectives.*

Management by objectives has been referred to by a variety of names: management by results, work planning and review, performance-planning evaluation, the charter of accountability concept, and participative goal setting.[27]

These different labels and the normative (prescriptive) processes they describe usually reflect only minor variations in emphasis. Drucker and McGregor, for instance, emphasized the importance of participation and responsibility by the lower-level manager (hereafter called the manager) in setting objectives and planning how to accomplish them. In other words, they emphasized the motivational advantages arising from increased self-direction and self-control (autonomy). Odiorne, in contrast, emphasized the advantages of improved role clarification resulting from the manager and the higher-level executive (hereafter called the executive) having reached agreement on goals, targets, and priorities. Nearly all writers, however, have viewed MBO as emphasizing "proactive" management—planning for future accomplishments—rather than "reactive" management, putting out "fires" and finding out who's to blame.[28]

Although different writers have explicated somewhat different versions of the MBO process, the following list includes many of the suggested steps found in several versions of MBO.

1 Formulate organizational goals and strategic plans.
2 Identify key individual job responsibilities.
3 Assign priorities to these key responsibilities.
4 Set realistic and challenging objectives (performance targets) and milestones for participating individuals.
5 Obtain agreement on priorities, objectives, and milestones.
6 Formulate plans for achieving the agreed-upon objectives.
7 Implement plans and monitor interim results in terms of the milestones.
8 Take corrective action when required to attain objectives.
9 Review individual and organizational performance in terms of objectives.
10 Appraise overall performance, and strengthen motivation through effective management training and development, compensation, and career planning.

More succinctly stated, MBO is a three-step process which, according to Schuster and Kindall involves the "1) initiation periodically by the employee of a set of written performance goals or targets for himself; 2) discussion of the goals between the employee and his superior, followed by mutual agreement on a set of goals to which the employee is committed; and 3) periodic review (either formally or informally) by the employee and his superior to determine to what extent goals previously set have been met or exceeded."[29]

Although the process of MBO may not appear particularly revolutionary, some management experts consider it the best management idea to come along in decades.[30] The next section considers the rationales advanced to explain why the MBO process should enhance productivity.

### Reasons Why It Should Work

At least ten reasons have been put forward to explain why MBO should enhance productivity in comparison to the conventional (hierarchical or authoritarian) approach to management. These reasons are listed and briefly described next.

*Performance measurement.* MBO provides a relatively objective way of measuring job performance. Instead of relying on whether or not the executive is pleased with the manager's performance, MBO requires that good performance be defined in advance in terms of concrete events (e.g., reduce scrap loss by 5 percent). Performance evaluations should, therefore, be less subject to personal bias.

*Concrete feedback.* Because the criteria and target levels defining good performance have been identified and agreed upon, the manager need not worry, "I wonder how well I'm doing." Because the rules of the game and the methods of keeping score have been determined, the manager can ascertain how well he or she is doing simply by looking at interim results.

*Performance-reward tie.* Because performance is measured in a relatively objective fashion, it is possible to tie performance more closely to various organizationally provided rewards. Perhaps more important, to the extent that managers *perceive* that performance leads to (valued) rewards this should motivate them to improve performance.

*Proactive versus reactive.* MBO focuses on the future—it possesses a problem-solving orientation—rather than on the past (e.g., "Here's what you did wrong this time.")

*Specific goals.* Almost by definition, MBO creates specific goals to strive for rather than vague pleas such as "Do your best!" Evidence clearly indicates the superiority of specific goals in comparison with vague goals.

*Difficult goals.* Goals are set in MBO by mutual agreement between manager and executive. Hence, goals will tend to involve some degree of "stretch." After all, the executive will probably have to reach agreement with his (or her) boss on his (her) own objectives, and so on up the hierarchy.

*Organizational climate.* Because performance is judged by results, not personal opinion, the executive need no longer "play God." Thus, advocates of MBO argue that the manager can view the executive as coach or consultant or collaborator (someone whose role it is to help solve problems) rather than as judge or umpire (someone whose role it is to determine one's fate). This shift in roles should increase trust and improve the relationship between manager and executive.

*Growth and development.* Because the manager is responsible for defining responsibilities, setting priorities, selecting realistic targets and milestones, and planning the accomplishment of these targets, the manager will probably feel increased job responsibility and autonomy. These two conditions are likely to enhance managerial growth and development.

*Psychological ownership.* Managers will likely feel some sense of psychological ownership because areas of responsibility, priorities, and performance targets are set by mutual agreement. To the extent that there is real participation, objectives will be viewed as the manager's, not as somebody else's.

*Customized evaluations.* Because each manager's job situation will be different (presenting different opportunities and obstacles), each manager's objectives will be different. MBO allows for "tailor-made" objectives; each manager need not, therefore, be measured by the same yardstick.

A survey of more than 15,000 managers has revealed that there are four questions that managers want answers to: (1) What are my *real* job responsibilities? (as distinct from what may be written on an obsolete job description), (2) What standards of accomplishment apply to these areas of responsibility? (How good is good?), (3) What are the limits to my authority? (What am I allowed to do to accomplish these objectives?), and (4) At what level of proficiency am I now performing? (How'm I doing?)[31] Clearly, the process of MBO, at least in theory, provides specific answers to three of these questions.

### Empirical Results

Although there have been hundreds of articles praising the virtues of MBO,[32] Bruce Jamieson has observed that "it is still difficult to gain a clear perspective on the efficacy of MBO in terms of corporate and individual performance. There is a distressing lack of well-documented and well-controlled research using a before-and-after measurement design. Partial field experiments, case studies and survey reports of *reactions* to MBO have been published, but these together with the available case studies are not enough to provide sufficient evidence."[33]

Indeed, the first and second *Guide to Worker Productivity Experiments* (WPE1 and WPE2) listed only five studies that examined the effects of MBO on productivity (loosely defined). A recent comprehensive review by Jack Kondrasuk of MBO-*type* interventions, identified 95 "effectiveness studies." However, only 29 of the studies presented data on either productivity *or* job satisfaction, and in only 10 cases was Kondrasuk sure that MBO was actually used.[34] The following review examines the effects of MBO on productivity (or related criteria) in eight studies. The studies are reviewed in chronological order and, where possible, the impact of MBO on productivity is identified.

**1** Research at General Electric Company measured the impact of MBO in terms of rated managerial performance; productivity was not measured. It was found that specific goals helped improve managerial performance more than criticism and discussion of performance. Weak support was found for the superiority of participative versus assigned goals.[35]

**2** At Purex Corporation, MBO was implemented from the top down with considerable support from the chief executive officer. In this program goals were assigned rather than set via participation. Prior to the introduction of MBO, productivity was declining at an annual rate of 4.8 percent; 18 months after the introduction of MBO, productivity was increasing at an annual rate of 3.6 percent. Thus the change in productivity purportedly attributable to MBO was +8.4 percent.[36]

**3** In three plants of the Palos Company three different programs were employed. In one plant a 4-day MBO training session was conducted and MBO was introduced; in a second plant MBO training was conducted, MBO was implemented, and after 21 months there was an extensive follow-up program, consisting of letters, meetings, memos, and telephone conversations; in the third plant there was no intervention. Production quantity increased by 17 percent more in the two MBO plants than in the control plant after 6 months. However, after 24 months, productivity had improved by 28 percent in the plant that used MBO and had the follow-up, but it was virtually unchanged in the MBO-only plant and the control plant—changes in those plants were +0.6 percent and +0.5 percent, respectively. The average productivity increase, given MBO training and follow-up was 19.3 percent.[37]

**4** In seven Veterans' Administration hospitals MBO was installed to improve the performance of nurses. In the 60 wards where MBO was introduced, ratings of patient care increased significantly on one of five scales, and patient-interview responses were more positive, compared with responses in wards where MBO had not been introduced. Results were somewhat more positive after 6 than after 12 months.[38]

**5** In a company with a well-organized MBO program already in place it was found that perceived differences in MBO characteristics (e.g., participation, feedback, goal difficulty, goal specificity) were largely unrelated to rated managerial performance. However, when managers were divided into high and low need-for-achievement groups, two significant results emerged. Among low need-for-achievement managers, degree of participation was quite positively related to rated performance; among high need-for-achievement managers, amount of feedback was positively related to rated performance.[39]

**6** MBO was installed in twelve branches of a Maryland-based bank; twenty branches served as matched controls. Performance data were collected 6 and 12 months after the intervention. MBO did not significantly affect performance on any of ten pertinent performance criteria (e.g., number of checking accounts opened, dollar value of installment loans). In general, results were rather negative: the experimental (MBO) branches showed better results than the control branches in only 11 out of 29 specific comparisons.[40]

**7** MBO was introduced in one of two railroad repair shops. Productivity was on the average 5 percent higher in the control repair shop over the 8-month measurement period.[41]

**8** An MBO-type program was introduced in three district offices of the U.S. Equal Employment Opportunity Commission. Case closings per person increased by 68 percent. New charges were processed in approximately 65 days compared to nearly 2 years, prior to the intervention.[42]

Of the five empirical studies reporting objective performance data, the median increase in productivity attributable to MBO was 8.4 percent. Clearly, results to date present a mixed picture: sometimes MBO "works," and sometimes it does not; certainly the results are less than one might have expected given the numerous reasons why MBO should enhance productivity. Commenting on his two studies, Muczyk concluded: "Although MBO has been around since at least 1954 and has for the most part been accepted on faith, a number of companies, having tried it, are abandoning the approach. It appears that results of these studies do not constitute an isolated case."[43]

Similarly, William Reddin in his book, *Effective Management by Objectives,* has written: "While MBO is popular, it also has more clear failures than successes. Some consulting firms spend more time taking MBO out than putting it in."[44] The survey of the *Fortune* 500 companies conducted by Schuster and Kindall is consistent with Reddin's assertion. Schuster and Kindall found that roughly 35 percent of the *Fortune* 500 companies employed MBO-type programs. Among these companies, MBO was rated a success only 25 percent of the time and only 5 percent of these companies rated MBO as "highly successful." Hence, the overall success rate appears to be approximately 30 percent.[45]

### Summary and Conclusions

Where productivity changes could be measured (or approximated), the average effect of MBO was an increase of 8.4 percent. Although this is a meaningful improvement, the evidence also indicates that without an extensive follow-up effort, results may be short-lived. Accordingly, one management writer has suggested that "if the need is for an immediate burst of energy due to declining profits or shrinking markets, MBO can prove very valuable. For the long term it is less likely to maintain effort unless it is possible to reactivate goals frequently and perhaps shift the actual content of certain goals. . . ."[46] However, for reasons outlined below, this recommendation does not seem entirely sound.

Before implementing MBO it is very important to be clear why MBO is being introduced, what it is supposed to accomplish. Unfortunately, this understanding is rarely present in practice. According to Walter Wikstrom of the Conference Board, "very few companies have even specified what their MBO programs are for when they implement them. And that is what MBO itself is all about."[47] MBO appears far more useful as a long-term approach toward developing managerial talent than as a mechanism for measuring job performance and handling such administrative decisions as promotions and salary increases. To be sure, MBO is highly subjective and judgmental as a performance measurement tool. Across diverse individuals, different objectives of varying degrees of importance and difficulty will be accomplished with varying degrees of success. And judgments about success must be tempered by adjustments for uncontrollable factors. Thus, because so many judgments are involved in assessing performance, MBO is anything but objective as a means of evaluating performance across individuals.

Where MBO has worked it has required a considerable investment of time and managerial training to nurture it along during the early years. According to Schuster, "You've got to take the long-range view. You can't just plug MBO in. Union Carbide, for example, admits that it took 5 years to get its MBO program operating and 10 years to make it successful."[48] Clearly, MBO requires the development of several managerial skills (e.g., performance planning, delegation, performance feedback and interviewing)—skills which are often lacking. Further, successful application requires a lasting commitment from top management toward participation, risk-taking, and tolerance of failure (i.e., a climate of trust). Yet, in practice (according to Wikstrom) "to many managers MBO is just a joke. In one instance, a manager thought that the way to make MBO work was to set objectives so low that all his subordinates would get bonuses. [Subsequently that manager was] transferred out of that division which was known as the 'no-profit' section inside the company."[49]

Wikstrom has cited another instance of lack of understanding about what MBO is all about. "In one electronics firm it was very obvious that MBO wasn't working. They had 5,500 managers in their program and the man in charge was saying what a success it was because all of the managers had their MBO forms in on time. To me, this meant that MBO wasn't working at all. The fact that they all were in promptly suggested to me that the people were filling out the forms to get central management off their backs. These were, incidentally, the fanciest MBO forms I have ever seen. Their program has since ended."[50]

In short, although the introduction of MBO may provide an initial burst of energy, to use it for this purpose appears to be self-defeating. With a short-term perspective, an overall MBO program would probably miss the mark in so many cases that it would quickly lose legitimacy. Further, it would likely result in increased hostility and resentment among managers who felt trapped by their "own" objectives.[51] A short-term orientation might also focus attention exclusively on results ("the bottom line") without regard to how these results are achieved.[52] Lastly, it has been noted that producing effective goals requires a "long and continuing struggle."[53] (An excellent example of effective goal-setting is provided by Drucker in his user's guide to MBO: " 'Saving souls' as the mission of the church is totally intangible. At least, the bookkeeping is not of this world. However, the goal of bringing at least two-thirds of the young people of the congregation into the church and its activities is easily measured.")[54]

As has been emphasized, MBO requires a long-term perspective and an enduring commitment. If a short-term burst of energy is sought, perhaps a goal setting program (which is far more limited than MBO) should be implemented.

## NOTES

1 Gary P. Latham and Gary A. Yukl, "A Review of Research on the Application of Goal Setting in Organizations," *Academy of Management Journal,* 18 (1975), 824–845; Gary P. Latham and Edwin A. Locke, "Goal Setting—A Motivational Technique That Works," *Organizational Dynamics,* 8 (Autumn 1979), 68–80; E. A. Locke, D. B. Feren, V. M. McCaleb, K. N. Shaw, and A. T. Denny, "The Relative Effectiveness of Four Methods of Motivating Employee Performance," in *Changes in Working Life,* ed. K. D. Duncan, M. M. Gruneberg, and D. Wallis (Chichester,

England: Wiley, Ltd., 1980), pp. 363–388; and Edwin A. Locke, Lise M. Saari, Karyll N. Shaw, and Gary P. Latham, "Goal Setting and Task Performance: 1969–1980," *Psychological Bulletin,* 90 (1981), 125–152.

2 Judith F. Bryan and Edwin A. Locke, "Parkinson's Law as a Goal Setting Phenomenon," *Organizational Behavior and Human Performance,* 2 (1967), 258–275.

3 Gary P. Latham and Sydney B. Kinne III, "Improving Job Performance through Training in Goal Setting," *Journal of Applied Psychology,* 59 (1974), 187–191.

4 Gary P. Latham and J. James Baldes, "The Practical Significance of Locke's Theory of Goal Setting," *Journal of Applied Psychology,* 60 (1975), 122–124.

5 Gary P. Latham and Edwin A. Locke, "Goal Setting," p. 137.

6 John R. Hinrichs, *Practical Management for Productivity* (New York: Van Nostrand Reinhold, 1978), p. 45.

7 Gary P. Latham and Gary A. Yukl, "Assigned Versus Participative Goal Setting with Educated and Uneducated Woods Workers," *Journal of Applied Psychology,* 60 (1975), 299–302.

8 Gary P. Latham and Edwin A. Locke, "Increasing Productivity with Decreasing Time Limits: A Field Replication of Parkinson's Law," *Journal of Applied Psychology,* 60 (1975), 524–526.

9 Gary P. Latham and Gary A. Yukl, "Effects of Assigned and Participative Goal Setting on Performance and Job Satisfaction," *Journal of Applied Psychology,* 61 (1976), 166–171.

10 Jay S. Kim and W. Clay Hamner, "Effect of Performance Feedback and Goal Setting on Productivity and Satisfaction in an Organizational Setting," *Journal of Applied Psychology,* 61 (1976), 48–57.

11 John M. Ivancevich, "The Effects of Goal Setting on Performance and Job Satisfaction," *Journal of Applied Psychology,* 61 (1976), 605–612.

12 John M. Ivancevich, "Different Goal Setting Treatments and Their Effects on Performance and Job Satisfaction," *Academy of Management Journal,* 20 (1977), 406–419.

13 Dennis L. Dossett, Gary P. Latham, and Terence R. Mitchell, "Effects of Assigned Versus Participatively Set Goals, Knowledge of Results, and Individual Differences on Employee Behavior When Goal Difficulty is Held Constant," *Journal of Applied Psychology,* 64 (1979), 291—298.

14 John M. Ivancevich and J. Timothy McMahon, "The Effects of Goal Setting, External Feedback, and Self-Generated Feedback on Outcome Variables: A Field Experiment," *Academy of Management Journal,* 25 (1982), 359–372.

15 Jay S. Kim, "Effect of Behavior and Outcome Feedback and Goal Setting on Performance: A Field Experiment," unpublished paper, Ohio State University, 1982, pp. 1–15.

16 E. A. Locke, D. B. Feren, V. M. McCaleb, K. N. Shaw, and A. T. Denny, "Relative Effectiveness," pp. 370–371, 375, reported that the median effect of goal setting on productivity was an increase of 16 percent. Their higher estimate is attributable to four procedural differences between their review and the present one: (1) they included the results of two (very successful) objective feedback studies (yet dozens more might have been included if the two interventions are considered identical), (2) they included the results of four MBO interventions (but some, less positive, MBO interventions were excluded), (3) they included one study that did not take place in an organizational setting (they might also have examined the effects of

goals, say, on dieting), and (4) they measured magnitude of impact, by comparing the baseline score to the final level of performance—in contrast, the present review adopted the (more conservative) approach of comparing baseline to the average score during the entire experimental period.

**17** On the basis of their review of field and laboratory experiments ("Goal Setting and Task Performance"), Edwin A. Locke, Lise M. Saari, Karyll N. Shaw, and Gary P. Latham have noted that "99 out of 110 studies found that specific, hard goals produced better performance than medium, easy, do-your-best, or no goals. This represents a success rate of 90%" (p. 131).

**18** Gary P. Latham and Edwin A. Locke, "Goal Setting," pp. 135, 142–143; also see the vivid, first-hand description of how goal setting made a monotonous job more tolerable, in Donald F. Roy, " 'Banana Time'—Job Satisfaction and Informal Interaction," *Human Organization,* 18 (Winter 1959–1960), 158–168.

**19** Donald E. Law, "Managing for Productivity," *The Arthur Young Journal* (Summer–Autumn 1975), p. 8.

**20** Tamao Matsui, Akinori Okada, and Reiji Mizuguchi, "Expectancy Theory Prediction of the Goal Theory Postulate, 'The Harder the Goals, the Higher the Performance,'" *Journal of Applied Psychology,* 66 (1981), 54–58.

**21** Edwin A. Locke, Lise M. Saari, Karyll N. Shaw, and Gary P. Latham, "Goal Setting and Task Performance," pp. 137–139.

**22** Ibid., p. 142.

**23** Ibid., pp. 139–140.

**24** Ibid., pp. 136–137 (incentives), 133–136 (objective performance feedback).

**25** Gary Yukl, *Goal Setting* (Module E), Baruch Human Services Management Project, Management Development Curriculum (New York: Baruch College, 1979), p. E-III-2.

**26** Edwin A. Locke, "Toward a Theory of Task Motivation and Incentives," *Organizational Behavior and Human Performance,* 3 (1968), 186.

**27** Andrew D. Szilagyi and Marc J. Wallace, Jr., *Organizational Behavior and Performance* (Santa Monica, Calif.: Goodyear, 1980), p. 576.

**28** Anthony P. Raia, *Management by Objectives* (Glenview, Ill.: Scott, Foresman, 1974), p. 8.

**29** Fred E. Schuster and Alva F. Kindall, "Management by Objectives: Where We Stand—A Survey of the Fortune 500," *Human Resource Management,* Spring 1974, p. 9.

**30** Stephen Singular, "Has MBO Failed?" *MBA,* Oct. 1975, pp. 47, 48, 50.

**31** Virgil Rowland, *Evaluating and Improving Managerial Performance* (New York: McGraw-Hill, 1970).

**32** Stephen Singular, "Has MBO Failed?" *MBA,* Oct. 1975, p. 47.

**33** Bruce D. Jamieson, "Behavioral Problems with Management by Objectives," *Academy of Management Journal,* 16 (1973), p. 504.

**34** Jack N. Kondrasuk, "Studies in MBO Effectiveness," *Academy of Management Review,* 6 (1981), 421–424.

**35** John R. P. French, Emanual Kay, and Herbert H. Meyer, "Participation and the Appraisal System," *Human Relations,* 19 (1966), 3–19.

**36** Anthony P. Raia, *Management by Objectives.*

**37** John M. Ivancevich, "Changes in Performance in a Management by Objectives Program," *Administrative Science Quarterly,* 19 (1974), 563–574.

**38** E. D. Dyer, M. A. Monson, and M. J. Cope, "Increasing the Quality of Patient Care through Performance Counseling and Written Goal Setting," *Nursing Research,* 24 (1975), 138–144.

**39** Richard M. Steers, "Task-Goal Attributes, Achievement, and Supervisory Performance," *Organizational Behavior and Human Performance,* 13 (1975), 392–403.

**40** Jan P. Muczyk, "MBO in a Bank and a Railroad Company: Two Field Experiments Focusing on Performance Measures," *Proceedings of the 29th Annual Meeting of the Industrial Relations Research Association* (1976), pp. 13–17.

**41** Ibid., pp. 17–18.

**42** Lewis W. Taylor and L. S. Tao, "Management Initiatives and EEOC's Improved Productivity," Case Management Information on Series, Report No. 1, U.S. Office of Personnel Management (Jan. 1981), pp. 5–6.

**43** Jan P. Muczyk, "MBO in a Bank and a Railroad Company," p. 19.

**44** W. J. Reddin, *Effective Management by Objectives: the 3-D Method of MBO* (New York: McGraw-Hill, 1971), p. x.

**45** Fred E. Schuster and Alva F. Kindall, "Management by Objectives: Where We Stand," p. 9. It might also be noted that in the review by Jack Kondrasuk, "Studies in MBO Effectiveness," results were categorized as either "positive" or "not positive." It was found that the more rigorous the evaluation methodology employed, the less positive the results (p. 425).

**46** John B. Miner, *Theories of Organizational Behavior* (Hinsdale, Ill.: Dryden Press, 1980), p. 196.

**47** Stephen Singular, "Has MBO Failed?" p. 48.

**48** Ibid., p. 50.

**49** Ibid., p. 48.

**50** Ibid., p. 48.

**51** Harry Levinson, "Management by Whose Objectives?" *Harvard Business Review,* 48 (Jul.–Aug. 1970), 125–134.

**52** Harry Levinson, "Appraisal of What Performance?" *Harvard Business Review,* 54 (Jul.–Aug. 1976), 30–48; also see Lawrence M. Miller, *Behavior Management* (New York: Wiley, 1978), p. 89.

**53** Thomas P. Kleber, "Forty Common Goal-Setting Errors," *Human Resource Management,* 11 (Fall 1972), 10–13.

**54** Peter F. Drucker, "What Results Should You Expect?—A User's Guide to MBO," *Public Administration Review,* 36 (Jan.–Feb. 1976), p. 16. Unfortunately, a short-term perspective is likely to generate many of the mistakes on Thomas Kleber's list, "Forty Common Goal-Setting Errors," pp. 10–13.

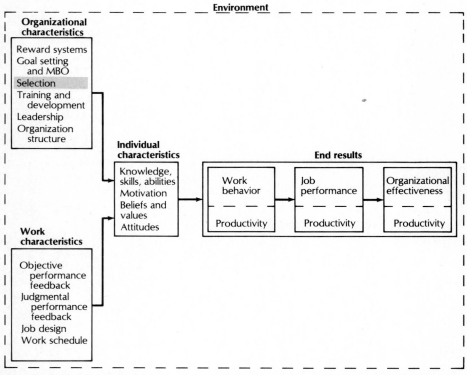

Conceptual framework of the determinants of productivity in organizations—a behavioral science approach.

# SELECTION

*Get me someone who is able and willing to do the job!* Surely this plea is ageless. Moreover, for centuries people have sought ways of determining *prior to employment* whether a person can and will do the job. Plato, it is said, advocated the use of military aptitude tests,[1] and some 300 years later (c. 50 B.C.) Varro suggested guidelines for the selection of farmhands: "Select for farm hands those who are fitted for heavy labor and have some aptitude for agriculture, which can be ascertained by trying them on several tasks and by inquiring as to what they did for their former master."[2] In addition to the examination of physical traits, job tryout, and the rating of prior training and experience, Varro advised using personal history data: "The foreman should have some education, a good disposition and economical habits, and it is better that he should be older than the hands, for they will be listened to with more respect than if they were boys."[3]

Some eighteen hundred years later, during the early days of industrialization, it was common for the foreman to look over the assembled applicants, choose those who appeared the most capable and send the rest away.[4] The application of scientific techniques to the process of selecting employees is, however, a relatively recent phenomenon.

In 1901, Frederick W. Taylor described the impact of physical strength on the productivity of pig-iron handlers. He stated, ". . . a man properly built for that work could load forty-five tons a day" (in contrast the average worker loaded 12 tons per day). Unfortunately, Taylor's study lacked adequate scientific controls.[5]

During the past 50 years an enormous literature concerning selection has emerged. Hundreds of articles and books have been written offering opinions about various selection techniques (e.g., how-to-do-it books on interviewing). This work, though, has been largely anecdotal and impressionistic. Additionally, many empirical studies have been conducted that focus on determining the validity coefficients of particular tests and criteria (i.e., how well tests explain or predict job success). Yet relatively few empirical studies have directly assessed the impact of selection devices on productivity (or output or costs). In part, this shortage of productivity-related effectiveness studies may reflect the search for competitive advantage: organizations have presumably seen little practical benefit in publicizing valuable proprietary information. But whatever the reasons for the scarcity of such studies, it is noteworthy that only during the past decade have selection studies reporting productivity effects been published. The present discussion reviews the evidence of effectiveness of four prominent selection devices (tests, interviews, personal history data, and reference checks), and a new approach (the realistic job preview). Subsequently, the focus turns to consideration of legal issues and strategies for selecting.

## IMPACT ON PRODUCTIVITY

The American Psychological Association, Division of Industrial and Organizational Psychology, has prepared and published a set of principles regarding the development and use of employee selection devices *(Principles for the Validation and Use of Personnel Selection Procedures)*. According to these guidelines, there are three axioms that underlie the process of employee selection:

1 Individuals differ in many ways.

2 Individual differences in personal characteristics and backgrounds are often reliably related to individual differences in behavior on the job.

3 It is in the best interest of organizations and employees that information about relevant differences between individuals be developed and used in selecting people for jobs.[6]

Accordingly, it follows that organizations should attempt to identify and measure relevant individual differences in "personal characteristics and backgrounds" so that valid inferences can be made about future job performance. Although more than a dozen methods have been used to accomplish this aim, the present discussion deals with the most widely used approaches.

### Tests

In recent years a number of reports have appeared that describe the effects of tests on productivity. These reports are described below (in chronological order), along with one study that examined the impact of tests on an index of "effective performance."

Stone and Ruch reported on the introduction of a testing program at the

Southern California Gas Company. The program, which accepted 50 percent of all applicants (who previously had passed an interview) reduced the turnover rate for typing clerks by 36 percent. When tests were used to select gas crew workers, turnover fell by 28 percent.[7]

These findings make it logical to ask about the financial impact of a reduction in turnover. Clearly, the impact depends on many factors, including the costs of recruiting, hiring, and training a replacement, and the lost productivity associated with the newcomer's social integration and acquisition of technical proficiency. As a general rule, the total cost of turnover increases with job responsibility. It has been estimated, for example, that the replacement cost of an insurance claim adjuster is roughly one-half a year's salary,[8] the replacement cost of a machine operator approximates one year's pay,[9] and the cost of replacing an engineer is roughly one and one-third times the annual salary.[10]

Returning to the Southern California Gas Company case, if we assume that the replacement cost of a clerk typist is roughly 25 percent of a year's salary and that the 36 percent reduction in turnover corresponds to a decrease of 18 percentage points, then the reduction translates into a salary savings of approximately 4.5 percent, and a productivity improvement of roughly 2.6 percent. (Because dollar outputs are, on average, roughly 175 percent of salaries, conversion of salary savings to outputs requires multiplication by 0.57. See Chapter 3, footnote 29.) Similarly, if the replacement cost of a gas crew worker is roughly one-half a year's pay, and the 28 percent reduction in turnover represents a 12 percentage point decrease, then the savings attributable to testing corresponds to an estimated 3.4 percent increase in productivity.

Booth, McNally, and Berry examined the use of two aptitude tests as potential predictors of effective performance among health care specialists in the U.S. Navy. Scores on the General Classification Test and the Arithmetic Reasoning Test were summed to predict the performance of hospital corpsmen and dental technicians. Effective performance was defined as completing training, remaining on the job for at least 2 years, and reaching a specified minimum pay level. Aptitude scores were trichotomized into three levels, and the proportions of effective hospital corpsmen with low, middle, and high aptitude scores were 45, 67, and 82 percent, respectively. The comparable results for dental technicians were 69, 77, and 91 percent.[11] Although tests had not actually been used to select health care specialists, the results indicate that large potential improvements in average performance would likely result from the use of tests, provided sufficient high-scoring applicants were available. Unfortunately, the published report provides no way to translate the expected average performance improvement into dollar or output terms.

Schmidt, Hunter, McKenzie, and Muldow presented data on the increased productivity which would likely result from the use of the Programmer Aptitude Test (PAT) to select programmers, compared with using no test (or a less valid test). In one plausible set of circumstances, the estimated increase in productivity resulting from one year's use of the PAT was roughly $65,000 per selected applicant; over the average job tenure of 10 years, the savings per selectee amounted to $6500 per year.[12] In output terms, this corresponds to an increase in productivity of roughly 20 percent.

Under these same circumstances, for all 618 programmers hired annually by the federal government, the total productivity increase would be $40 million. And if the entire population of computer programmers employed by the federal government had been hired using the PAT, the total increase in productivity would be $1.2 billion. Extending this to the economy as a whole, the productivity gain would be $10.8 billion.[13]

Further, Schmidt and his associates point out that substantial productivity gains can be achieved even if the predictive validity of a test is low, provided that the selection ratio (the proportion of applicants selected) is also low. For instance, a test with a rather low predictive validity (.25) will increase the proportion of successful new hires from 50 percent to 67 percent if the selection ratio is low (.10).[14] On the basis of their research on tests, the authors asserted that "it does make a difference—an important practical difference—how people are selected. . . . We conclude that the implications of valid selection procedures for work-force productivity are much greater than most of us have realized in the past."[15]

Kravetz has reported on the use of commercially available clerical tests (e.g., of filing ability and business vocabulary) in combination with patterned interviews to select clerical employees in four insurance companies and two manufacturing companies. Results indicated improvements in clerical productivity that ranged from 20 to 67 percent. Further, in one of the insurance companies clerical turnover declined from 37.1 percent in 1974 to 24.4 percent in 1979, a reduction of 34 percent. This reduction occurred while job employment opportunities were improving—which should have led to increased turnover. Noted Kravetz, "the developmental work involved in properly validating tests and establishing patterned interviews was negligible when one considers the benefits obtained."[16]

Schmidt and Hunter reported on the utility of a cognitive ability test that was used by the Philadelphia Police Department to select entry-level officers. It was estimated that if the department were to drop the use of the test, it would cost the city more than $170 million over a 10-year period. On a per employee basis, the loss due to discontinuance of the test would approximate $3500 per year, comparable to an annual reduction in productivity of 6.8 percent.[17]

Hunter and Hunter have reported on the expected increase in productivity that would result if the U.S. government were to hire new employees using the optimal combination of cognitive and psychomotor tests. (That is, cognitive and psychomotor test scores would be combined so that the former score is weighted more heavily in predicting performance on highly complex jobs, and less heavily in predicting performance on less complex jobs. The resulting average validity coefficient for government jobs would be .55.) Assuming that the top 10 percent of applicants were hired, the annual gain in productivity would be $15.61 billion. Since this gain would result from hiring 460,000 new employees each year with an average annual salary of $13,598 (in mid 1980), the anticipated annual increase in productivity would be 14 percent.[18]

The impact of using a strength test (the arm dynamometer, which measures pull pressure) was examined in connection with the selection of steelworkers at Armco, Inc. The performance criterion consisted of job-relevant samples of task performance (e.g., lifting and carrying a 60-pound jackhammer, using wire cutters, lifting 75-pound bags to and from a 4-foot-high table). The arm dynamometer test demonstrated an average validity coefficient of .84. Although it was observed that the top 10 percent of steelworkers accomplished eight to nine times as much work as the bottom 10 percent, it was "conservatively estimated" that the top 1 percent of steelworkers performed only twice as much work as the bottom 1 percent. Using this very conservative (inaccurate?) assumption, it was calculated that use of the arm dynamometer to select steelworkers would increase productivity by 19 percent; and if the test were used on a top-down basis to hire 80 percent men and 20 percent women, the test would still increase productivity by 13 percent compared with random selection. In view of the fact that Armco hired 1853 entry-level steelworkers in 1979, use of the strength test would have generated utility of $9.1 million annually (with merit selection) and $6.3 million annually (with hiring goals). Moreover, these estimates are low because they ignore (1) the costs associated with a higher risk of on-the-job injury to weaker workers and (2) the costs associated with a higher likelihood of job failure (and subsequent turnover).[19]

Cascio has described the doctoral dissertation research by Roche on the utility of the Test of Mechanical Comprehension for selecting radial drill operators. Compared with random selection, Roche found that use of the test would have increased productivity by 3.7 percent.[20] This relatively modest improvement is attributable to three somewhat unique features of the study. First, the estimated standard deviation of job performance (a measure of variability) in dollars was only 10 percent of the annual salary; typically the standard deviation in dollars is 40 percent of the annual wage.[21] Had the estimated standard deviation been 40 percent of the wage, the anticipated productivity improvement due to testing would have been approximately 15 percent. Second, the validity of the Test of Mechanical Comprehension was low (.31), compared with the average (private sector) test validity coefficient of .53.[22] Had the validity coefficient been .53, the expected improvement in productivity would have been approximately 6.3 percent. Third, the selection ratio was high (33 percent); had only 10 percent of applicants been hired, the expected improvement in productivity would have been 5.5 percent.

Fear and Ross have described the results of a new selection system that included the use of aptitude tests. Results were computed by comparing the new selection procedure with an earlier one which was evaluated and found cost effective and "quite good." They found that (1) absenteeism declined 42 percent, (2) turnover declined 28 percent, (3) social insurance program claims declined 51 percent, (4) reported accidents declined 25 percent, (5) the number of compensation cases declined 33 percent, (6) the frequency of lateness declined 33 percent, (7) grievances declined 82 percent, and (8) disciplinary actions declined 28 percent. The estimated dollar savings associated with just the first three indicators was $1 million, or roughly $3000 per employee hired.

Hence, the overall improvement in productivity approximated 5.7 percent.[23]

To sum up, the use of ability and aptitude tests in selecting employees has been consistently effective in increasing productivity. Improvements have ranged from 2.6 percent to 43.5 percent, the median result being an increase in productivity of 10.4 percent.[24] Although studies have primarily entailed the *introduction* of tests, there have been a couple of (sketchy) reports of the results of discontinuing tests. For example, Schmidt and Hunter reported that

> Some years ago, U.S. Steel selected applicants into their skilled trades apprentice programs *from the top down* based on total score on a valid battery of cognitive apti-tude tests. They then lowered their testing standards dramatically, requiring only minimum scores on the tests equal to about the seventh-grade level and relying heav-ily on seniority. Because their apprentice training center kept excellent records, they were able to show that (a) scores on mastery tests given during training declined markedly, (b) the flunk-out and drop-out rates increased dramatically, (c) average training time and training cost for those who *did* make it through the program increased substantially, and (d) average ratings of later performance on the job declined.[25]

While the discussion of testing has repeatedly referred to the utility of tests, it should be kept in mind that utility is in part a function of test validity. Recently, research on test validity has produced two remarkable findings. First, it has been demonstrated that four measurement problems have been primar-ily responsible for the inconsistent results reported in many prior studies. When these problems are controlled for, particularly the impact of sample error arising from small sample size, predictive validities rise substantially.[26] In other words, pooling results across studies (and making other adjustments) shows tests to be far more valid than when using small samples. (For example, in a small sample, one extremely deviant score can significantly lower apparent validity.) Clearly, users need be concerned about the actual, not the apparent, validity of a test. Second, and perhaps of even greater significance, it has been found based on examining 698 separate studies involving 368,000 individuals, that it is possible to generalize validity results not just across companies for a given job, but also across families of related jobs. In this regard, Kenneth Pearl-man concluded: "these findings in essence lay the groundwork for a science, rather than a technology, of personnel selection, since they imply a basic ratio-nality, relative simplicity, and consequent generalizability of the human attrib-ute factors underlying the structure of work, rather than the apparent chaos, complexity, and situational specificity of job analysis and test validation results that have long characterized the field."[27] In more pragmatic terms, one might ask, "How can these results be used by personnel managers faced with the practical problems of selection?" Pearlman, Schmidt, and Hunter provide an answer: "Thus, to apply any of the validity generalization results ... one would only need to collect sufficient job analysis information on the *occupa-tion* in question to appropriately classify it ... under the DOT [*Dictionary of Occupational Titles*] definition. ... following such classification, the potential usefulness of various test results could then be assessed in light of our validity generalization results."[28] Indeed, Hunter has recently concluded that "the research base now exists to justify selection using cognitive and psychometric ability [tests] for all [12,000] jobs in the DOT, i.e., virtually all jobs in our economy."[29]

There are many types of tests that organizations can employ: e.g., achievement, knowledge, work sample, aptitude, leaderless group discussions, in-basket, business simulations and—combining several tests—assessment centers. Discussing the validity evidence for each type of test is clearly beyond the scope of this book. Although there is clear and impressive evidence that achievement tests can materially improve the effectiveness of hiring decisions, the use of such tests is not without problems. Some of these problems are discussed at the end of the chapter.

### Interviews

In 1963, Marvin Dunnette and Bernard Bass offered the following assessment of the interview as a selection device: "The personnel interview continues to be the most widely used method for selecting employees, despite the fact that it is a costly, inefficient, and usually invalid procedure."[30] Roughly 10 years later, it was observed that, "In spite of the impressive evidence demonstrating its limited reliability and questionable predictive value, the traditional selection interview continues to be used by almost all organizations as an important step in personnel decisions."[31]

More recently, in 1981, Mary Tenopyr commented as follows:

> The history of validity for the interview is, to say the least, dismal. The interview, despite various innovations over the years, has never been consistently shown to improve selection. At best it introduces randomness to the selection process; at worst, it colors selection decisions with conscious or unconscious biases. As such, the interview represents a poor alternative to testing, although it may be viewed favorably by groups who stand to profit from its potential biases.[32]

Underscoring these views, a recent meta-analysis (a study of studies) of interview validity research found a mean validity coefficient of .14 (based on 10 correlational results drawn from samples with 2694 people). In contrast, it will be recalled that the mean validity coefficient for the optimal combination of ability tests is .53 (based on 425 correlational results from samples with some 32,000 people). Comparing the two selection methods in terms of their ability to account for (or "explain") variations in rated job performance, interviews account for 1.96 percent ($.14^2$), and tests 28.09 percent ($.53^2$) of performance variability—nearly a fifteen-fold difference in explanatory power.[33] In terms of practical utility—i.e., impact on productivity—tests are nearly four times as useful as interviews (.53 divided by .14).

On a more positive note, a number of steps might be taken to improve the psychometric adequacy (reliability and validity) of selection interviews. First, a structured interview should be developed that is based on a job analysis which indicates important job-related behaviors and skills. Second, interviewers should be trained in the conduct of the structured interview, in order to minimize numerous sources of bias and error. Third, multiple interviews should be conducted whenever possible, with the resulting composite assessment used in the decision process. (In general terms, the psychometric adequacy of interviews will be improved to the extent that (1) they are made more objective and standardized, (2) they are comprehensive, and (3) they are based on more data—that is, the psychometric adequacy of interviews will be improved to the extent that they are made more like tests.)

The first two suggestions (the use of structured interviews and interviewer training) were recently adopted by McDonald's Corporation in connection with the hiring of store managers. McDonald's implemented a new interviewing program in the two regions (out of their twenty-five regions) with the highest turnover rate. The two regions combined had been hiring some 2500 management trainees each year because annual turnover averaged 52 percent. A job analysis identified ten characteristics of effective job performers (including ability to make logical decisions quickly, concern for achievement and willingness to delegate and check for results, and initiative and originality). Specific questions were then developed to tap each of these dimensions. For example, with respect to initiative and originality, applicants were asked: "In your previous position, what did you do differently from your predecessor? What did you do with your time, and what resulted? Give me some examples of projects you started on your own. What did you do to make your job more rewarding, more satisfying, or easier?" After the new interviewing procedure was introduced, the turnover rate declined from 52 percent to 34 percent over a 2½-year period. Also, the time required to interview an applicant was reduced by half. Although no profitability data were presented in connection with the intervention, a prior study at McDonald's revealed that stores with the lowest turnover were the most profitable. Finally, the new interviewing procedure purportedly resulted in hiring better-qualified applicants, but evidence to substantiate this claim was not presented. At the minimum, though, the two empirically demonstrated savings were comparable to an increase in productivity of roughly 5 percent.[34]

### Personal History Data

Weighted application blanks (WABs) and biographic information blanks (BIBs) are two selection methods which rely on self-reported personal history data. Brief descriptions of three studies that illustrate the potential utility of personal history data as a selection device follow.

Cascio has reported on the development of a ten-item weighted application blank that was used to predict turnover among clerical employees. Although the turnover rate for all clerical employees averaged 48 percent, use of the WAB would have reduced first-year turnover to 28 percent. In other words, use of the WAB would have increased the probability of hiring long-tenure applicants from 52 percent to 72 percent.[35] Assuming a replacement cost of 25 percent of annual salary, the expected reduction in turnover would be comparable to an increase in productivity of roughly 3 percent.

In 1982 Love reported on the utility of the Aptitude Inventory Battery (AIB), a weighted biographical inventory used to select life insurance salespersons. The criterion of interest was the proportion of new life insurance agents who became "good" agents—defined as (1) surviving in the business for at least 12 months after being hired and (2) producing sales in the top half of all surviving agents. It was found that without the AIB, a company had to hire 588 agents in order to have 100 "good" agents. Using the AIB, however, the number of hires needed to yield 100 "good" agents depended on the AIB cutoff score: with a cutoff score of 307, 472 hires were needed; with a score of 312, 341 hires were needed; and with a score of 317, only 258 hires were needed. Obviously, more applicants would have to be screened (and available) at higher AIB cutoff levels. Accordingly, a cost-benefit analysis was performed, indicating that the optimal cutoff score was 312. At this score, hiring 100 "good" agents costs $2,400,000. In contrast, without the AIB, the same result costs $3,450,000. Hence, use of the AIB reduces the cost of hiring "good" agents by about one-third.[36] Furthermore, there is evidence that optimal use of the AIB produces additional profit per agent (not just for "good" agents) of $10,007 over and above the average profit of $9,387.[37] Thus, over the expected job tenure of a life insurance agent, optimal use of the AIB can be expected to increase profits by 18.8 percent per annum.[38]

Use of a WAB to hire circulation route managers was studied in connection with a major metropolitan newspaper. In the focal organization, turnover among circulation route managers was very high—51 percent quit within 3 months of hire—and this had a negative effect on the performance and job tenure of newspaper carriers, as well as on subscriber service, collections, and circulation expansion. The WAB model yielded 83 percent correct predictions of job tenure; however, the variables that were predictive of job tenure changed over time. Interestingly, many of the traditional assumptions of personnel interviewers were found to be erroneous. Although the conventional wisdom was that "people with too much education don't last on that job," and that "hiring an unemployed applicant is less desirable than an employed applicant," these views proved incorrect. Indeed, of the twelve specific factors that the newspaper's interviewers actually used to reach a hiring decision, three showed a small positive correlation with tenure, four were unrelated, and five were negatively related. In short, intuitive assumptions require empirical validation to serve as useful hiring criteria. Given the estimated direct cost of turnover of approximately $7500 per circulation route manager, use of the model would have increased productivity by at least 6 percent.[39]

A good summary of the research on personal history data as a basis for employee selection has been provided by Wayne Cascio in *Applied Psychology in Personnel Management*.

Properly cross-validated WABs and BIBs have been developed for many occupations including life insurance agents, service station managers, salesclerks, . . . engineers, architects, research scientists. . . . In sum, even after satisfying the legal requirements for using personal history data, . . . [criterion measures] can be predicted with an appreciable degree of accuracy. Ease of development, . . . low cost, potentially high predictive validity, and an easily accessible data base make such a procedure especially attractive.[40]

Hunter and Hunter's recent meta-analytic research provides a more quantitative assessment of the validity of personal history data as a predictor of job success. They reported a mean validity coefficient of .37 for personal history data as a predictor of job performance (based on twelve correlational results with a total sample of 4429 people). Of the eleven selection devices Hunter and Hunter examined, personal history data had the third highest validity coefficient (the two highest validity coefficients were for tests, with .53, and for job tryout, with .44).[41]

The reader should note that the most effective personal history data selection models are tailor-made to fit a specific job or firm. Stone and Ruch, therefore, warn potential users to "be wary" of biographic data techniques that are promoted as "useful in many organizations for a variety of jobs or occupations."[42]

**Reference Checks**

One common form of reference check is the letter of recommendation. Recent research, however, has cast serious doubt on the validity and utility of recommendation letters. In an ingenious study, researchers examined two letters of recommendation for each of forty applicants, each of forty recommenders having provided letters for two applicants. On the basis of the sample of eighty recommendation letters the researchers concluded that:

**1** Recommenders tend to use the same distinctions (dimensions, criteria), and even the exact same terms, in evaluating different individuals.

**2** There is little agreement between raters regarding distinctions, and the lack of consensus is not attributable to length of acquaintance.[43]

In brief, recommendation letters appear to tell more about the perceptual set of the perceiver than about characteristics of the perceived. Recommenders tend to write the same (or a similar) reference letter for many if not most individuals for whom references are requested.

A more useful type of reference check is the structured request for factual information. For entry-level jobs, Fear and Ross recommend a form letter which asks for information about dates of employment, positions held, reasons for termination, and number of days absent during the last 12 months of employment.[44]

The meta-analysis by Hunter and Hunter found a mean validity coefficient of .26 for reference checks in predicting job performance (based on ten correlational results from a total sample of 5389 people).[45] Somewhat surprisingly, of the eleven selection devices examined, reference checks yielded the fourth highest level of predictive validity. The seven selection devices with lower predictive validities were amount of experience, .18; interview, .14; rating of training and/or experience, .13; academic achievement (class rank or grade point average), .11; rating of education, .10; measures of interests, .10; age, $-.01$.[46]

### Realistic Job Previews

In recent years realistic job previews (RJPs) have received a good deal of attention as a selection device. The major premise behind the use of RJPs is that providing accurate and complete information to job applicants should lessen subsequent disillusionment; consequently, this should increase job satisfaction, lower turnover, and possibly increase job performance. Somewhat akin to a medical vaccination, the RJP exposes the person to a small dose of organizational reality, thereby "inoculating" the individual against a larger, more extensive exposure.[47] Further, it has been argued that RJPs may be useful because they help newcomers cope better with unpleasant job characteristics— that is, newcomers have advance warning that allows them time to discover methods of dealing with difficult aspects of the job.[48] It has also been suggested that the RJP may enhance attitudes toward the employing organization because it fosters perceptions of high credibility, honesty, and openness.[49]

What does the evidence indicate? In general, job applicants or recruits who receive RJPs are less likely to leave an organization than those who do not. A recent review of eleven empirical studies found that turnover rates averaged 19.8 percent in RJP groups versus 25.5 percent in control groups.[50] Assuming a replacement cost of 75 percent of one year's salary, the 6.7 percentage point reduction in turnover translates into a productivity gain of approximately 3 percent. It is noteworthy that while the average reduction in turnover was 6.7 percentage points, the reduction was considerably higher on complex compared to entry-level jobs (9.4 vs. 1.9 percentage points, respectively).[51]

Offsetting the general reduction in turnover is the tendency for the job offer acceptance rate to decline in the face of unfavorable information.[52] For example in a study more recent than the review cited above, RJPs were used to hire some basic-care technicians in a residential facility for retarded persons. Turnover rates in the RJP and control groups were 46 percent and 51 percent, respectively. However, the hiring rate (the proportion of individuals who accepted job offers and actually appeared for assignment) was only 37 percent with the RJP groups versus 46 percent in the control groups.[53]

With respect to the impact of RJPs on job performance, generally no significant effects have been found.[54] In light of the evidence indicating modest performance effects, Todd Jick and Leonard Greenhalgh have suggested that RJPs may be too limited in scope. In their view, job applicants need more than task-related information to get a realistic job preview; applicants should also receive information about the organizational climate, what life is like inside the organization. Jick and Greenhalgh argue, therefore, for the use of realistic organizational previews (ROPs), although they present no evidence to support the utility of ROPs.[55]

## LEGAL ISSUES

According to Robert Guion, "employment practice is by nature discriminatory, and it must be so. An employer cannot be expected to take all applicants regardless of their qualifications; he is expected to be able to distinguish between those who are qualified and those who are not . . . in talking about discrimination, then, a clear distinction must be made between discrimination which is necessary and right and discrimination which is unfair. Unfair discrimination exists when persons with equal probabilities of success on the job have unequal probabilities of being hired for the job."[56]

The statistical procedures used in making selection decisions typically assume that the object is to maximize a criterion (e.g., expected performance). However, in recent years the maximization assumption has been challenged by those who argue for making selection decisions based on social grounds. One social purpose is to increase the representation of minorities and disadvantaged persons in the work force. Neither assumption is inherently incorrect, nor are the two purposes entirely incompatible; further, there are legitimate reasons to base selection decisions on both goals.[57]

It should be noted, though, that with respect to whether unfair discrimination exists, the burden of proof falls on the employer. The employer must show that a given selection device actually predicts job performance for all categories of applicants. This requirement necessitates the conduct of careful job analyses, the development of reliable and relevant criterion measures, and the completion of appropriate validity analyses.[58]

The Uniform Guidelines on Employee Selection Procedures (published in 1978), and the subsequent Interpretive Questions and Answers (published in 1979) represent only a small portion of relevant legal opinion. The issue of legal requirements is a vast and complex one. Nevertheless, it is important to note a couple of concepts which are central to compliance. *Adverse impact* is defined as "a substantially different rate of selection in hiring, promotion, or other employment decision which works to the disadvantage of members of a race, sex, or ethnic group."[59] In the absence of demonstrated validity and job relatedness, adverse impact is prima facie evidence of unfair discrimination. In practice, the rule of thumb is that adverse impact exists if the selection rate for any race, sex, or ethnic group is less than 80 percent of the rate of the largest group of applicants. Another important concept is the notion of the "bottom line." Owing to administrative and prosecutorial discretion, the federal government usually has not required validation evidence for every component of the selection process if there is no adverse impact. However, Greenlaw and Kohl point out that "the guidelines are very clear in indicating that the 'bottom line' concept in no way prohibits either governmental intervention or the rights of individuals to pursue court action."[60] Indeed, in a recent court decision (Connecticut *v.* Teal) the U.S. Supreme Court ruled that the absence of adverse impact at the "bottom line" does not permit an employer to select or promote people on the basis of a test that has an adverse impact.[61]

In response to the complex legal and measurement issues associated with employee selection, the American Psychological Association, Division of Industrial and Organizational Psychology, has published the set of selection principles mentioned at the beginning of this chapter. This document, consisting of more than eighty recommendations concerning procedures, documentation, generalization, and implementation, concluded: "Hundreds of lower court decisions have been rendered based on EEOC guidelines and on interpretations of the U.S. Supreme Court decisions. These guidelines and the court decisions sometimes conflict with precepts set forth in these *Principles*. . . . the researcher or practitioner may need to perform additional analyses in order to satisfy these guidelines or case law. . . . it would be folly for the researcher or practitioner to ignore relevant legislation, subsequent rule-making, and case law in developing strategies for the validation and use of personnel selection procedures."[62]

Predictably, employers have been generally reluctant to use tests and other selection devices. A 1976 Bureau of National Affairs survey of nearly 200 companies found that only 42 percent of the companies used tests to select employees; in contrast, a similar survey conducted in 1963 found that tests were used by 90 percent of the responding companies.[63] Mary Tenopyr, in her article, "The Realities of Employment Testing," noted that the "legal requirements for testing are probably the primary cause of the decline in test use. Nothing in the literature indicates that tests are less valuable selection tools than they were, but many articles . . . inform employers of the regulations and government advisories in test use."[64] In this vein, Felix M. Lopez has observed that "employers don't believe that you can have fair employment procedures and maintain high selection standards." Yet if "unscientific and unsound selection procedures" continue to be used, "eventually there will be a day of reckoning: the company will not be able to get the work done."[65]

## SELECTION STRATEGIES

As Guion so eloquently put it, "Few would argue with a policy statement to the effect that it is nice to have employees who are productive, are likely to stay, will show up regularly for work, and will not steal."[66] Yet how are these goals to be accomplished within the requirements of the law? Three major options are available to the organization. The first option is to use random selection (and most of the time there will be no adverse impact). Apparently, the uncertainties associated with testing have led many employers to conclude that the advantages are not worth the risk. Moreover, this reasoning has increasingly been extended to other selection devices (e.g., application blanks, interviews). The result, according to John Miner, is that "some organizations are moving precipitously close to random hiring, with all the implications for subsequent performance failure that such an approach involves."[67] More recently, Fear and Ross commented, "many companies have become so intimidated by EEO regulations that they have completely abandoned any kind of genuine selection program for entry-level people. . . . The *indiscriminate* hiring that has replaced the previous selection program in such companies not only is unnecessary but also can [lead to] high turnover and loss of productivity . . . [and] bankruptcy."[68]

Of course, testing is legal—provided that the test is valid—and Miner argues that there are two important reasons why testing should not be abandoned despite increased government surveillance of all aspects of selection:

> If some employing organizations, such as AT&T, continue to use valid tests these organizations are in a position to skim the top of a local labor force—male and female, black and white. Those who abandon testing will tend to abandon other selection procedures also as pressure for validation increases there too; inevitably they will move eventually to random hiring. But random hiring where everyone is employing randomly is one thing; random hiring in a labor market where a number of employers are actively selecting on a scientific basis is quite different. Under the latter conditions there may well be so little of the type of talent needed remaining in a local labor force that performance and productivity are seriously hampered. The situation is not unlike that occurring with the use of advertising, where if some companies invest, others in the industry are under strong pressure to follow suit, merely to remain in competition.
>
> Another consideration in any decision regarding abandoning testing relates to the basic position taken by EEOC and other government enforcement agencies—"if an employer doesn't have a proper distribution of minorities in its workforce, he is guilty unless he can prove the imbalance is job related." . . . The way to show that an imbalance is job related is to demonstrate that qualities needed for effective job performance are lacking in a segment of the labor force with which fair employment laws are concerned. . . . Thus, discontinuing testing rather than providing protection against charges may well serve to eliminate the possibility of an effective and entirely justified defense; a charge of discrimination may accordingly be upheld for lack of test data.[69]

A second strategy is to develop and use valid selection procedures even if an adverse impact should result. As noted previously, this requires a thorough program of documented research demonstrating all relevant bases for making valid inferences about future job performance. Pertinent to this strategy are the 515 validity studies conducted over a 45-year period by the U.S. Employment Service. On the basis of this research and other evidence, Schmidt and Hunter have concluded that, "Professionally developed cognitive ability tests are valid predictors of performance on the job and in training for all jobs. Cognitive ability tests are equally valid for minority and majority applicants and fair to minority applicants in that they do not underestimate the expected job performance of minority groups."[70]

Ironically, the method of selection that has been found to be the most valid for predicting job performance, testing, has also been by far the most controversial. Compared to the next best predictor, job tryout, testing explains an additional 40 percent of the variance in job performance. With respect to predicting performance on jobs for which applicants are already trained, ability tests are the second most valid predictor (.53), slightly less valid than work samples (.54).[71] Yet social critics have focused on written tests in connection with unfair discrimination in employee selection.[72] This attention has had the unfortunate effect of causing many organizations to rely more heavily on less valid selection devices (e.g., the employment interview). However, increased reliance on the interview can create even more serious compliance problems, given the difficulty of interview validation. Indeed, it has been suggested that interview validation is likely to become an important "battle area" in the 1980s.[73]

A third approach involves the use of selection devices which have been validated, coupled with a policy of avoiding adverse impact—notwithstanding the demonstrated validity of the selection devices employed. Two mechanisms can be employed to avoid adverse impact: (1) minimum competency selection and (2) top-down hiring with employment goals (quotas).

The minimum competency approach involves setting a low cutoff score, typically one standard deviation below average (i.e., at the 15th percentile), and then randomly selecting individuals who are above the cutoff point.[74] The top-down selection approach with employment goals works as follows. If, for example, an organization plans to hire 10 percent of all applicants, the top 10 percent of each group is hired.

In comparing the effectiveness of these two mechanisms it is evident that the minimum cutoff approach has two major disadvantages: it leads to selecting majority as well as minority applicants with lower ability; and it usually does not fully satisfy affirmative action goals. Schmidt and Hunter have noted that minimum competency systems "result in productivity losses 80% to 90% as great as complete abandonment of valid selection procedures."[75] Consequently, the low cutoff score approach wipes out virtually all of the benefits associated with the predictive power of tests. This happens because "employee productivity is on a *continuum* from very high to very low, and the relation between ability test scores and employee job performance and output is almost invariably linear. Thus a reduction in minimum acceptable test scores at any point in the test score range results in a reduction in the productivity of employees selected."[76]

With respect to the second problem, Hunter and Hunter have concluded that the minimum competency approach is "vastly inferior" to top-down hiring with quotas. "Quotas guarantee that the hiring rate [e.g., 10 percent] is the same in each group. But low cutoff scores do NOT equalize hiring rates." The low cutoff method "achieves only a poor approximation of racial balance."[77]

Although top-down hiring with quotas is far more effective than minimum competency selection, both in terms of productivity and the achievement of social goals, the former approach raises a host of legal, social, and moral questions (e.g., reverse discrimination). While not ignoring these questions, it is important to recognize that all methods of accomplishing important societal objectives are neither equally effective nor equally efficient.

## SUMMARY

This chapter has examined five techniques that organizations can use in selecting people who are able and willing to do the job: tests, interviews, personal history data, reference checks, and realistic job previews. In terms of impact on productivity, evidence indicates that tests have the largest positive effect, on the average raising productivity by 10.4 percent; at the other extreme, realistic job previews generally have not materially improved productivity, the average increase being roughly 3 percent.

Ironically, there seems to be an inverse relationship between the predictive validity of a selection device—how good a job it does in predicting performance—and its acceptability. Although tests have shown the highest predictive validity, their use is most controversial. In contrast, the selection interview, notwithstanding its dismal record in predicting job performance, is the most widely accepted and frequently used selection device. However, to the extent that interviews are standardized, structured, comprehensive, and objective—i.e., they resemble oral tests—predictive validity (and utility) is thereby improved.

Personal history data and reference checks can also be useful in raising productivity, the former technique being generally more effective than the latter. Indeed, evidence indicates that the use of personal history data in selection is superior to all major techniques with the exception of tests and work samples.

Because all selection techniques, with the possible exception of random hiring, are inherently discriminatory, attention must be paid to ethical and legal considerations. While increased productivity is clearly a desirable end, another important social goal is increased work-force participation by minorities and disadvantaged persons. Two major strategies exist for accomplishing both sets of purposes; however neither strategy is maximally successful in all respects; each has certain drawbacks.

## NOTES

**1** Robert M. Guion, "Recruiting, Selection, and Job Placement," in *Handbook of Industrial and Organizational Psychology,* ed. Marvin D. Dunnette (Chicago: Rand McNally, 1976), p. 781.

**2** Claude S. George, Jr., *The History of Management Thought* (Englewood Cliffs, N.J.: Prentice-Hall, 1968), p. 24.

**3** Ibid.

**4** Robert M. Guion, "Recruiting, Selection, and Job Placement," p. 777.

**5** Charles D. Wrege and Amedo G. Perroni, "Taylor's Pig-Tale: A Historical Analysis of Frederick W. Taylor's Pig-Iron Experiments," *Academy of Management Journal,* 17 (1974), 8–9.

**6** American Psychological Association, Division of Industrial-Organizational Psychology, *Principles for the Validation and Use of Personnel Selection Procedures,* 2d ed. (1980), p. 4.

**7** C. Harold Stone and Floyd L. Ruch, "Selection, Interviewing, and Testing," in *ASPA Handbook of Personnel and Industrial Relations: Staffing Policies and Strategies,* ed. Dale Yoder and Herbert G. Heneman (Washington, D.C.: The Bureau of National Affairs, 1974) I, 4:137–138.

**8** Wayne F. Cascio, *Costing Human Resources: The Financial Impact of Behavior in Organizations* (Boston: Kent, 1982), p. 19.;

**9** Gary P. Latham and Kenneth N. Wexley, *Increasing Productivity through Performance Appraisal* (Reading, Mass.: Addison-Wesley, 1981), pp. 3–4.;

**10** Gopi R. Jindal and Carl H. Sandberg, "What it Costs to Hire a Professional," *Research Management,* 21 (July 1978), 26–28.

**11** Richard F. Booth, Michael S. McNally, and Newell H. Berry, "Predicting Performance Effectiveness in Paramedical Occupations," *Personnel Psychology,* 31 (1978), 581–588.

**12** Frank L. Schmidt, John E. Hunter, Robert C. McKenzie, and Tressie W. Muldrow, "Impact of Valid Selection Procedures on Work-Force Productivity," *Journal of Applied Psychology,* 64 (1979), 622–623.

**13** Ibid., p. 624.

**14** Ibid., p. 610.

**15** Ibid., p. 624.

**16** Dennis J. Kravetz, "Selection Systems for Clerical Positions," *Personnel Administrator,* 26 (Feb. 1981), 39–42.

**17** Frank L. Schmidt and John E. Hunter, "Employment Testing: Old Theories and New Research Findings," *American Psychologist,* 36 (1981), 1128; also see John E. Hunter and Ronda F. Hunter, "Validity and Utility of Alternative Predictors of Job Performance," *Psychological Bulletin,* 96 (1984), 72. An unusual aspect of this study is that savings are computed based on the number of employees rather than the number of selectees. The loss due to test discontinuance would be higher if computed on the (more conventional) per selectee basis.

**18** John E. Hunter and Ronda F. Hunter, "Validity and Utility," p. 93. Although the average validity coefficient for ability tests in predicting job performance is .53, the average validity coefficient is .55 for government jobs. It is slightly higher because there are relatively fewer low-complexity jobs in government than in industry.

**19** John D. Arnold, John M. Rauschenberger, Wendy G. Soubel, and Robert M. Guion, "Validation and Utility of a Strength Test for Selecting Steelworkers," *Journal of Applied Psychology,* 67 (1982), 588–604. Productivity estimates are after converting salary savings to outputs.

**20** Wayne F. Cascio, *Costing Human Resources,* pp. 148, 177–180.

**21** The explanation for this marked discrepancy is that Roche actually computed the standard deviation of the individual's contribution to *profits,* not job performance.

Hence, Roche's measure substantially underestimated the variability in job performance. See John E. Hunter and Frank L. Schmidt, "Fitting People to Jobs: The Impact of Personnel Selection on National Productivity," in *Human Performance and Productivity: Human Capability Assessment,* ed. Marvin D. Dunnette and Edwin A. Fleishman (Hillsdale, N.J.: Lawrence Erlbaum Associates, 1982), I, 248, 254–255.

22 John E. Hunter and Ronda F. Hunter, "Validity and Utility," pp. 90, 93.

23 Richard A. Fear and James F. Ross, *Jobs, Dollars, and EEO: How to Hire More Productive Entry-Level Workers* (New York: McGraw-Hill, 1983), pp. 11–14.

24 The median result excludes the Roche study, which was flawed (see footnote 21).

25 Frank L. Schmidt and John E. Hunter, "Employment Testing," p. 1130.

26 Kenneth Pearlman, Frank L. Schmidt, and John E. Hunter, "Validity Generalization Results for Tests Used to Predict Training Success and Job Proficiency in Clerical Occupations," *Journal of Applied Psychology,* 65 (1980), 373–406. See also Frank L. Schmidt, John E. Hunter, and Kenneth Pearlman, "Progress in Validity Generalization: Comments on Callender and Osburn and Further Developments," *Journal of Applied Psychology,* 67 (1982), 835, 843–844. In connection with the crucial importance of sampling error, the authors state: "We have found that, except when study sample sizes are very large, most of the variance in observed correlations that is due to artifacts is due only to one artifact—simple sampling error. . . . validity generalization is a very robust phenomenon; it can be demonstrated using only corrections for simple sampling error" (p. 844).

27 Kenneth Pearlman, "Job Families: A Review and Discussion of Their Implications for Personnel Selection," *Psychological Bulletin,* 87 (1980), 24.

28 Kenneth Pearlman, Frank L. Schmidt, and John E. Hunter, "Validity Generalization Results," p. 398, italics added.

29 John E. Hunter, "Test Validation for 12,000 Jobs," paper presented at the January 13, 1983 meeting of the Metropolitan New York Association for Applied Psychology (New York City), p. 1. Also see *Test Validation for 12,000 Jobs: An Application of Job Classification and Validity Generalization Analysis to the General Aptitude Test Battery,* U.S. Employment Service Research Report No. 45 (Washington, D.C.: U.S. Department of Labor, 1983), pp. 1–50.

30 Marvin D. Dunnette and Bernard M. Bass, "Behavioral Scientists and Personnel Management," *Industrial Relations,* 2 (1963), 117.

31 C. Harold Stone and Floyd L. Ruch, "Selection, Interviewing, and Testing," p. 4:148.

32 Mary Tenopyr, "The Realities of Employment Testing," *American Psychologist,* 36 (1981), 1123. Tenopyr noted that during the 3 years from 1978 to 1980 only one published validation study for the interview was found; however, during the same period approximately 50 published studies reported how vulnerable interviews and resumé reviews are to biases or irrelevancies of various sorts.

33 John E. Hunter and Ronda F. Hunter, "Validity and Utility," p. 90. Moreover, if interview and test scores are both used to predict performance and weighted equally, the resulting composite would have a lower validity than tests alone.

34 Robert L. Desatnick, "How HRD Took the Bite Out of McDonald's High Turnover," *Training/HRD,* 19 (Sept. 1982), 42–45.

35 Wayne F. Cascio, "Turnover, Biographical Data, and Fair Employment Practice," *Journal of Applied Psychology,* 61 (1976), 576–580. Note that it is important to test

the validity of WABs and BIBs in samples independent from those used to develop the prediction model—i.e., to perform a cross-validation. This is necessary because the procedure used to select and/or weight items picks up not only those items that genuinely predict the criterion, but also those that by chance are predictive in the particular sample studied. Cross-validation eliminates the capitalization on chance association phenomenon. Returning to the Cascio study, the predictive validity of the WAB in cross-validation samples was .58 for minority applicants and .56 for nonminority applicants.

**36** William D. Love, "Putting a Dollar Value on Productivity Enhancement through Personnel Selection," data presented at the conference, "Current Directions in Productivity—Evolving Japanese and American Practices," (New York City) March 1982. The presentation was based on the Life Insurance Marketing and Research Association (LIMRA) report, "Cost-Effective Selection: The AIB in Combination Operations," Research Report 1981-9.

**37** Steven H. Brown, "Validity Generalization and Situational Moderation in the Life Insurance Industry," *Journal of Applied Psychology,* 66 (1981), 668. Also see the LIMRA report, "Profits and the AIB: In United States Ordinary Companies," Research Report 1978-6.

**38** Information on the job tenure of life insurance agents was obtained from the LIMRA report, "The Manpower and Production Survey: United States Ordinary Agent Experience," pp. 1–2.

**39** Daniel G. Lawrence, Barbara L. Salsburg, John G. Dawson, and Zachary D. Fasman, "Design and Use of Weighted Application Blanks," *Personnel Administrator,* 27 (Mar. 1982), 47–53.

**40** Wayne F. Cascio, *Applied Psychology in Personnel Management* (Reston, Va.: Reston Publishing, 1978), pp. 202–203. Reprinted by permission of Reston Publishing Company, a Prentice-Hall Company, 11480 Sunset Hills Road, Reston, Va. 22090.

**41** John E. Hunter and Ronda F. Hunter, "Validity and Utility," pp. 87–90.

**42** C. Harold Stone and Floyd L. Ruch, "Selection, Interviewing, and Testing," p. 4:132.

**43** James C. Baxter, Barbara Brock, Peter C. Hill, and Richard M. Rozelle, "Letters of Recommendation: A Question of Value," *Journal of Applied Psychology,* 66 (1981), 296–301.

**44** Richard A. Fear and James F. Ross, *Jobs, Dollars, and EEO,* pp. 95–97.

**45** John E. Hunter and Ronda F. Hunter, "Validity and Utility," p. 90.

**46** Ibid.

**47** Paula Popovich and John P. Wanous, "The Realistic Job Preview as a Persuasive Communication," *Academy of Management Review,* 7 (1982), 571: also see Bernard L. Dugoni and Daniel R. Ilgen, "Realistic Job Previews and the Adjustment of New Employees," *Academy of Management Journal,* 24 (1981), 580.

**48** Bernard L. Dugoni and Daniel R. Ilgen, "Realistic Job Previews and the Adjustment of New Employees," p. 580.

**49** Ibid.

**50** Richard R. Reilly, Barbara Brown, Milton R. Blood, and Carol Z. Malatesta, "The Effects of Realistic Previews: A Study and Discussion of the Literature," *Personnel Psychology,* 34 (1981), 830–833.

**51** Ibid.

**52** Todd D. Jick and Leonard Greenhalgh, "Realistic Job Previews: A Reconceptualization," paper presented at the 40th Annual Meeting of Academy of Management (Detroit), 1980, p. 1.

**53** E. S. Zaharia and A. A. Baumeister, "Job Preview Effects During the Critical Initial Employment Period," *Journal of Applied Psychology,* 66 (1981), 19–22.

**54** Todd D. Jick and Leonard Greenhalgh, "Realistic Job Previews," p. 1.

**55** Ibid., passim.

**56** Robert M. Guion, "Employment Testing and Discriminatory Hiring," *Industrial Relations,* 5 (1966), 26.

**57** Sheldon Zedeck and Milton R. Blood, *Foundations of Behavioral Science Research in Organizations* (Monterey, Calif.: Brooks/Cole, 1974), pp. 108–109.

**58** Ibid., pp. 134–135.

**59** Paul S. Greenlaw and John P. Kohl, "Selection Interviewing and the New Uniform Federal Guidelines," *Personnel Administrator,* 25 (Aug. 1980), 76.

**60** Ibid.

**61** "Is Quota Hiring on the Horizon? Adverse Impact Defense Invalid," *Resource,* Aug. 1982, pp. 1, 6.

**62** American Psychological Association, Division of Industrial-Organizational Psychology, *Principles,* pp. 21–22.

**63** Donald L. Grant, "Issues in Personnel Selection," *Professional Psychology,* 11 (1980), 380.

**64** Mary Tenopyr, "Realities," p. 1121. Tenopyr added, "The general reaction appears to be to flee from objective selection procedures rather than to attempt to comply with the guidelines."

**65** Michael Reiner, "It's Not Easy Getting 'Equal'," *Great Neck Record,* 18 Sept. 1980, p. 1A.

**66** Robert M. Guion, "Recruiting, Selection, and Job Placement," p. 778.

**67** John B. Miner, "Psychological Testing and Fair Employment Practices: A Testing Program That Does Not Discriminate," *Personnel Psychology,* 27 (1974), 49.

**68** Richard A. Fear and James F. Ross, *Jobs, Dollars, and EEO,* p. 27.

**69** John B. Miner, "Psychological Testing," p. 61.

**70** Frank L. Schmidt and John E. Hunter, "Employment Testing," p. 1128.

**71** John E. Hunter and Ronda F. Hunter, "Validity and Utility," p. 91. (It should be noted that the Uniform Guidelines stipulate that at the time of validation, the employer should examine alternative predictors—including other types of tests— that might be equally valid but have less adverse impact).

**72** Wayne F. Cascio, *Applied Psychology in Personnel Management,* p. 114.

**73** Paul S. Greenlaw and John P. Kohl, "Selection Interviewing," p. 79.

**74** Frank L. Schmidt and John E. Hunter, "Employment Testing," p. 1130.

**75** Ibid. Additionally, the authors noted that if an organization the size of the federal government were to move from selection based on rankings on valid tests to a minimum competency selection system with the cutoff at the 20th percentile, yearly productivity gains would be reduced from $15.6 billion to $2.5 billion. In short, it would cost an extra $13.1 billion annually to obtain the same level of output.

**76** Ibid. Schmidt and Hunter continued: "A decline from superior to average performance may not be as visible as a decline from average to poor performance, but it can be just as costly in terms of lost productivity."

**77** Ibid. Returning to the example of the federal government, the use of top-down hiring with quotas (TDHQ) would yield an annual productivity gain of $14.8 billion, whereas the minimum competency method (MCM) would yield an annual productivity gain of $2.5 billion (versus $15.6 billion using top-down hiring). Thus the opportunity cost of achieving employment goals would be 800 million dollars with TDHQ (15.6 − 14.8), compared to $13.1 billion with MCM (15.6 − 2.5), the latter cost being 16.5 times greater than the former. Moreover, MCM would still not achieve employment goals as well as TDHQ.

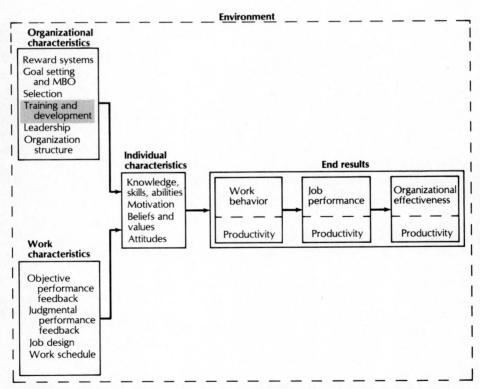

Conceptual framework of the determinants of productivity in organizations—a behavioral science approach.

# CHAPTER 6

# TRAINING AND DEVELOPMENT

In the world of work, the terms *training* and *development* refer to planned efforts by an organization to facilitate the learning of job-related behaviors by employees. Although it is commonplace to talk about training nonmanagers and developing managers, the two terms are used interchangeably in this discussion. It is useful, however, to distinguish between training and education. Typically, training implies a process whereby learned outcomes can be specified in terms of particular behavioral responses; in contrast, if particular behaviors cannot be specified, or if the learning is expected to transfer knowledge to a variety of situations, the process can be classified as education. It has been suggested that whereas training narrows the range of responses among trainees, education broadens the range.[1]

## TRAINING: A SYSTEMS PERSPECTIVE

Three purposes are generally associated with the conduct of training: developing skills, imparting knowledge (information, rules, concepts), and influencing attitudes. Whatever the primary purpose, it is important to adopt a comprehensive view of the training process. Ideally, training should be seen as an ongoing system, a process consisting of three phases: diagnosis, delivery, and evaluation.[2]

### Diagnosis

First, a diagnosis or needs assessment should be performed at three levels of analysis: the organization (*where* is training needed and *when?*), the job activity (*what* kinds of training are needed?), and the individual (*who* needs training?). In other words, prior to conducting training it should be determined (1) whether the organization (or one or more subunits) is failing to meet goals and objectives and if it is, whether this is the result of deficiencies in knowledge, attitude, or skill; (2) what kinds of tasks need to be performed, and what instructional content is necessary to generate the required behaviors; (3) whether there are current or anticipated future shortages in particular skills; and if so, (4) which particular individuals need what specific kinds of training. Notwithstanding the logic of needs assessment, it is common to see a given type of training employed throughout an entire organization—across all levels, departments, locations, and people. No wonder employees are often heard to comment "I have no idea why I've been told to go to that training center" or "I knew just about everything they told to go to that training center" or "I knew just about everything they taught in this program."[3]

As Irwin Goldstein has noted, machinists examine the type of job to be done (of course) before choosing their tools. However, training specialists still need to be warned about matching the solution to the problem.[4] A vivid illustration of this situation has been provided by Anthony Putman.[5]

*Super Trainer:* "So, what did you find out from your interviews at the finishing plant?"

*Novice Trainer:* "Man, have they got problems over there! Morale is lousy, turnover is way too high, and they've got a whole new crop of supervisors running around trying everything imaginable to cope."

*Super Trainer:* "Hmmm . . . sounds like they need some supervisory skills training."

*Novice Trainer:* "That's exactly what the plant manager said! (Pause) So, what exactly is supervisory-skills training?"

*Super Trainer:* (Smiling indulgently) "No problem, kid. We can give them some stuff on positive discipline, maybe some Maslow, be sure to hit them with a little Theory X–Theory Y, right? And I just saw this great new package on listening for productivity, we could. . . ."

A caricature? Perhaps, but the picture may not be too far removed from common practice. Notes Goldstein, the field of training is dominated by a "fads approach" which places heavy emphasis on developing and adopting new techniques. Just as children have gone "from yo-yos to hoola hoops to skate boards [to video games] . . . training directors [have gone] from sensitivity training to organizational development to behavioral role modeling."[6] *Clearly, an accurate diagnostic needs assessment should be performed prior to the design and delivery of training.* Trainers should be mindful of the legendary recipe for rabbit stew, which begins: "First, catch a rabbit."[7]

### Delivery

The second phase of the training process should entail the provision of training. There are, of course, numerous training methods, both on- and off-the-job:

lecture, case study, role play, simulation, programmed instruction, apprenticeship, vestibule training, job rotation, and others. Broadly speaking, each of the three purposes of training implies a different training methodology: (1) skill building implies an emphasis on practice; (2) imparting knowledge suggests a presentation mode; and (3) changing attitudes implies a high degree of participation.[8]

### Evaluation

The third phase of the training process should entail the evaluation of training in terms of criteria (i.e., learning objectives) derived from the first (need assessment) phase. Training should not be evaluated solely in terms of changes in knowledge, skills, and attitudes; it is also important to measure success in terms of on-the-job performance. Finally, the results of the evaluation phase should be used to modify subsequent needs assessments and training interventions.[9]

Evaluations of training effectiveness can take four forms: participant reactions, measures of learning, behavioral criteria, and end-result measures. Unfortunately, in practice the situation with respect to the evaluation of training is "absolutely deplorable."[10] Only a small proportion of training programs are ever evaluated, and where evaluations are performed, the most common approach is to examine trainee reactions.[11] To understand why this approach is inadequate, consider the following account of training evaluation, as conducted by a medium-sized bank.

[The bank] develops its managers by giving them a monthly series of lectures by prestigious outside speakers . . . The effectiveness of these training sessions [is] ritualistically evaluated by the loudness of the audience's clapping and cheerfulness at the end of the session. Used also is a short, two-item comment sheet that can be voluntarily filled out by any of the participants and mailed to the training department. The questionnaires received by the training department are largely favorable, thereby demonstrating that the fees paid to the [speakers are] worth it, and that the training staff is succeeding in its mission.[12]

Although participant reactions are the most commonly examined indicator of training effectiveness, they are also the least unbiased. The opinions expressed by all those who are involved—the trainees, the trainers, the managers who selected trainees, and the personnel manager who contracted for the training—may all be self-serving. In brief, the problem is that those who rate the programs may see greater benefits in *positive* evaluations than in *accurate* evaluations.

Tests of knowledge or skill are often used to evaluate training programs, comparing scores before and after training, or between trained and untrained groups. While improvements in knowledge or skill (or attitudes) may be necessary conditions for improved job performance, they are not sufficient conditions. Immediately after training, trainees may be able to respond successfully to substantive questions, or be able to demonstrate specific skills. But the crucial question is whether this evidence of "learning" is manifested in terms of modified on-the-job behavior.

All too often it has been demonstrated that the knowledge of concepts and the possession of "insights" has little bearing on work behavior and job performance.[13] Consequently, it is important to measure what people actually *do* on the job. Several types of behavioral observation scales can be used toward this end.[14] However, even a training program that modifies behavior raises the question of worth: is it justifiable in cost-benefit terms? Increasingly, there has been a call for a "bottom-line" demonstration of the utility of training.

While there are few who would argue with the notion of accountability, or with the pragmatic demonstration of the utility of training, it should be noted that it is very difficult to gauge the effects of training in *dollar* terms. Ron Zemke cites the following story, told by Ian McLaughlin.

> When I was training director for Del Monte Corp., I once ran before-and-after tests to prove the value of a specific training program. We did an outstanding needs analysis, put on a terrific program and the results were top-notch. The following three months saw this district move to the top third in sales of the item we wanted to see improvement in. I turned in a report showing dollar increases and everything else I could think of.
>
> Then the deluge! The product manager claimed credit for his support of the effort. The local sales managers said they had concentrated their efforts on the item after our workshop and claimed credit. The regional sales manager pointed out that if headquarters wanted a sales workshop on one item, it obviously must be important, so he had exerted pressure on the item.
>
> All in all, I learned several lessons from the episode. . . . profitability is never a one-department or one-action result. . . . training is part of the total action plan, not a poor relative and not a panacea.[15]

To be sure, this example does not deny the importance of evaluating training; but it does point out the difficulty of isolating the economic effects attributable to one contributory function or program. Certainly it is less problematic to identify the effects of training in terms of observable behaviors, or even in terms of the quantity of output produced.

Thus far, some definitions have been presented, and a widely accepted systems approach to training has been described. The discussion next focuses on the extent of training activity, and the empirical literature pertinent to the impact of training on productivity. A number of general guidelines are inductively developed on the basis of this review. The chapter concludes with an examination of two new training technologies (behavior modeling, and programmed and computer-assisted instruction), and one traditional approach (on-the-job training).

## THE EXTENT OF TRAINING ACTIVITY

Training is a big business. In 1980, public and private organizations spent more than $30 billion for employee training—roughly half the amount spent on all higher education—*excluding* the salaries of trainees.[16] Calculated on this basis, AT&T alone spent $1.7 billion in 1980. Evidently, it was expensive to conduct an average of 12,000 courses daily at 1300 different training sites.[17] Moreover, when salaries are *included* in estimates of the training enterprise, the annual cost rises to nearly $100 billion.[18] And there are reasons to believe that training expenditures will grow over time—even though at present more than 90 percent of all private organizations have some type of systematic training program.[19] As technological advances continue, the demand for training will likely increase; and competitive pressures may have an impact. According to Edward Denison and William Ouchi, "Japanese companies typically provide each worker with twenty full days of training each year, while comparable firms in the United States provide about one day of training each year."[20] Additionally, as organizations hire and promote more women, minorities, older individuals, and handicapped persons, many coming to the job less well prepared than the traditional work force, training will become even more critical to organizational efficiency and effectiveness.[21]

## THE EMPIRICAL LITERATURE

Ironically, despite the vast resources devoted to training, the empirical literature is rather skimpy: the "studies" that exist are largely anecdotal, impressionistic, and opinion-based. Irwin Goldstein noted in 1980 that since the previous major review of the training literature (in 1971), more than 3000 additional publications had appeared. Regarding these new additions, Goldstein commented: "nontheoretical and nonempirical articles which toast a new technique or discuss the general need for training constitute the largest segment of the training literature . . . the vast majority of writing in this area is not empirical, theoretical, or thoughtful. . . . There is a desperate need for high quality empirical investigations that examine the usefulness of training technologies."[22] Moreover, because sound empirical studies are "few and far between . . . there are few generalizations concerning the relevance of particular technologies for particular behaviors."[23]

While there has been a shortage of high-quality training studies, there has been no shortage of studies. The first and second *Guide to Worker Productivity Experiments* (*WPE1* and *WPE2*) both reported that training was the most frequently reported approach to productivity improvement. Specifically, although fourteen different technologies were employed in the 207 different field studies reviewed in *WPE1* and *WPE2,* training was employed in 59 of the studies. One reason for the wide use of training is that many approaches to productivity improvement require implementation by supervisory personnel who in turn need training—e.g., MBO, job redesign, positive reinforcement, participative leadership. After classifying studies in terms of the principal intervention employed, 41 of the studies *primarily* involved training. A review of these studies, as well as others not included in *WPE1* and *WPE2,* provides the basis for the following six generalizations.

**1** Job-specific training programs are generally more effective than general educational programs. One highly successful training intervention, for example, involved step-by-step instruction and practice in handling specific problems connected with the work of tax auditors for the Indiana Department of Revenue. Trainees showed a 39 percent drop in required supplemental audits per auditor.[24] In contrast, consider the following example of diffusive, non-job-specific training. The case involved an attempt to build participatory management in an engineering organization. As one of the training consultants put it: "We gave supervisors eight to twelve hours of training, but it really wasn't too worthwhile. We discussed motivation theory *à la* Maslow, discussion techniques *à la* Maier, and so forth. But the supervisors were so handicapped in trying to apply all this stuff. They got so bogged down that nothing happened."[25] Although trainees may be truly intrigued with theories, will they function more effectively Monday morning? Compounding the problem, some trainers reason that if one theory is good, ten theories must be ten times better.[26] Consequently, the result is a "training" program that provides "a taste of what all management theories have to offer."[27] Instead, it would seem more fruitful to provide job-specific training, instruction in the work behaviors required for successful job performance.

**2** Lengthy training programs are generally more successful than short training programs. One successful program cited in *WPEI* entailed 220 hours of training (to prepare psychiatric workers for promotion); another successful program involved 104 hours of training (to prepare supervisors to implement job enrichment). In contrast, two rather unsuccessful programs were described as providing "brief instruction" and "short-term training." Unfortunately, these examples involve numerous differences besides the duration of training. This problem is largely avoided by examining training programs of differing durations that focus on the same set of skills. In connection with training managers to avoid rating errors in performance evaluations, one experiment used workshops and group discussions which lasted 6 to 8 hours. Compared with a control group, the trained employees showed significantly fewer rating errors and significantly greater accuracy. However, two other rater training programs, lasting from 5 minutes to 1 hour, brought about no lasting behavioral changes.[28] Similarly, in another study it was found that simply lecturing individuals to recognize and avoid rating errors was not successful.[29] It would seem, therefore, that Joan Harley and Lois Koff are correct in suggesting that short-term training programs should be renamed "over the rainbow training." They write:

> Zap! You are exposed to a two-hour shot of delegation and you become so effective at giving orders that you never have to take the course again in your career.
> Zap! One-half day of motivation and all workers reporting to you will be more cooperative and productive evermore.
> Zap! . . . Wrong.[30]

Promises of instant solutions and miracle cures are suggestive of the early "snake oil" vendors. Unfortunately, changing human behavior takes time.

**3** Programs that entail practice and active participation tend to be more effective than those involving only passive learning (e.g., lectures, films). Successful programs often use such techniques as role-playing exercises, experiential simulations, on-the-job coaching, and the imitation of effective models. Moreover, it might be not entirely fortuitous that lengthy training programs are superior to short ones; the superiority may in large part result from the greater opportunity for individuals to *practice* new behaviors. Similarly, evidence indicates that one of the best predictors of academic achievement is the actual time spent on academic tasks. Notes G. Christian Jernstedt, *only* time spent directly on academic tasks correlates with academic achievement; time spent in the learning environment but not directly on academic tasks is largely unrelated to academic achievement.[31]

**4** Programs that provide feedback along with training tend to be more successful than those that provide training without feedback. For example, in an intervention focusing on the sanitation practices of kitchen workers—specifically, hand-washing behavior—training alone improved work behavior by 21.7 percent. Training combined with feedback increased required hand washing by 203.1 percent.[32] Paul Mali has put it quite cogently: "The adage 'practice makes perfect' is wrong. But practice with feedback, review, analysis, and change does make perfect."[33]

**5** Programs providing visual examples of effective job performance (positive models) tend to be more successful than those that do not. Two explanations have been advanced to support this conclusion: (1) seeing an effective model raises the trainee's belief in his or her self-efficacy (via identification with the model), and (2) a visual presentation provides the clearest possible description of the required work behaviors.[34] Evidentiary support for this conclusion is provided by the almost uniformly positive results of behavior modeling training (described below).

**6** Management support for training is particularly important if a training program is to succeed. Indeed, it is important that all levels of management support training; otherwise training programs can fall apart.[35] Illustrative of this problem is the case of the training program conducted for 96 counselors in 17 field offices. Because managers in the field offices felt no stake in the training, they gave the counselors little time off to attend training. Not surprisingly, the counselors in turn showed little interest in training.[36] Clearly, without management commitment people will be sent off to training with messages such as: "We have to send somebody and it might as well be you," or "Go this time and get it over with." With this send-off the "trainer" will be confronted with a roomful of disinterested and possibly sullen, resentful attendees.[37] One way that top management can signal its support is by making a substantial commitment to training. Perhaps this is yet another reason why long-term training efforts tend to be more successful than short-term efforts.

As mentioned above, *WPE1* and *WPE2* reviewed 41 studies that were primarily concerned with training. Of these, 34 pertained to job performance and 7 dealt with the retention of disadvantaged, hard-core unemployed workers.

The results of these interventions can be summarized as follows: (1) training improved job performance in roughly 85 percent of the studies, and (2) training proved effective in 3 of the 7 studies concerned with the retention of disadvantaged persons. Only 6 of the performance-related studies reported productivity data; the median result was an increase in productivity of 13.8 percent. Fourteen studies evaluated training effectiveness in terms of rated performance. However, because raters were generally aware of the purpose of the training and knew who was trained and who was not, the interpretation of these results is problematic.

## THREE PROMINENT TRAINING METHODS

### Behavior Modeling

In the 1980 *Annual Review of Psychology,* Goldstein commented that the training "method that has generated the most excitement is clearly behavioral role modeling or applied learning."[38] Behavior modeling basically consists of a four-step procedure: (1) presentation of key concepts (learning points, principles), (2) observation of a model that utilizes the principles (often shown on a videotape), (3) rehearsal of appropriate behaviors by role playing, and (4) provision of social reinforcement and feedback from the trainer and other members of the group.[39] Hence, this technique combines the presentation mode (the trainer identifies key points and the model demonstrates their application), the active practice mode (imitative rehearsals), and the participative mode (group discussion and critique of the videotape and role plays). Although it may not appear to be a "big deal," the combination of conceptualizing, observing, and practicing specific behaviors, coupled with social reinforcement and feedback is a powerful technique.

A number of recent studies provide evidence demonstrating the effectiveness of behavior modeling. Latham and Saari used behavior role modeling to train first-level line supervisors in improving interpersonal skills. Although the impact on productivity was not measured, the training had a significant positive effect on four indicators: training reactions, learning measures, behavioral criteria, and rated performance. Notwithstanding the inherent limitations of reactions as an indicator of training effectiveness, Latham and Saari's findings in this regard are so vivid that they merit attention. In their words:

> Participation in the training program was mandatory. Attendance records were monitored regularly by the vice president with the prior knowledge of the trainees. In situations where an absence was unavoidable, a make-up session was held. Thus, it may not be surprising that many foremen were initially unreceptive to the program. The lack of receptiveness was evident at the initial training classes when supervisors stared at the floor with observable frowns.
>
> In the practice sessions, the trainees who were asked to take the role of an hourly worker frequently behaved in an extremely uncooperative manner. This was done to show the trainers "the way things really are" and why this program was a waste of their time. By the third session, however, this behavior had changed. Supervisors

playing the role of an employee announced publicly to the group that "This program really works; there is no way I can outmaneuver him when he sticks to those damn learning points." Concerns initially expressed to the effect that the company was trying to get everyone to act exactly the same way gave way to such comments as, "Did you notice that none of us are doing the same thing and yet we are all following these key points?" Other representative comments included, "most training isn't worth ———; it works in the classroom but not on the job. With this program, it is just the opposite. It is much easier to do on the job what we learned here than it is to do it in front of all of you."[40]

Further, the trainees performed significantly better than did their counterparts in the control group (1) on a learning test administered 6 months after training, (2) on behavioral simulations collected 3 months after training (and scored by evaluators who did not know which supervisors had received training), and (3) in terms of performance ratings obtained 1 year after training.

Jerry Porras and Brad Anderson reported another successful behavior modeling intervention. A training program designed to teach supervisory skills was conducted at a Champion International plywood plant in Oregon. Four indicators suggested positive results. First, supervisory behaviors (as perceived by subordinates) improved markedly in the trained group in comparison to the control group. Second, productivity increased by an average of about 5 percent during the 6-month postintervention period. It is noteworthy that although productivity declined initially after training, it was 17 percent higher at the end of the postintervention period. Third, a monthly savings of approximately $45,000 was achieved from reduced waste of raw materials. Fourth, grievances, absenteeism, and turnover decreased in the trained group. The researchers concluded: "These findings indicate that the modeling-based change program substantially affected the behavior of first-line supervisors in the experimental plant. Subsequent change in plant performance and labor relations indices imply that the new problem-solving orientation of supervisors also led to other, more profound improvements in plant efficiency and effectiveness."[41]

Nine studies involving behavior modeling were reviewed in *WPE1* and *WPE2*. In eight cases results were positive; in one case results were mixed. Although some of these studies have been criticized because of weaknesses in experimental design,[42] the concatenation of evidence would seem to discount some of the concerns regarding methodological rigor. Consider the following additional, albeit sketchy, evaluative reports:

• Executives at the Lukens Steel Company concluded that behavior modeling saved the company $1 million a year through increased productivity. Evidence consistent with this claim was provided by examination of the performance ratings of trained and untrained managers. After behavior modeling training, 65 percent of the trained managers were rated at least "above average," compared to 28 percent of the untrained managers.[43]

• At AT&T, an independent panel rated first-level supervisors on their performance during a posttraining assessment. Among the supervisors who had previously undergone behavior modeling training, 29 percent were evaluated as having "exceptionally" good supervisory skills, compared with 9 percent of untrained supervisors. Also, 55 percent of trained supervisors were judged "above average," compared with 23 percent in the control group.[44]

• A company that trained 345 supervisors using behavior modeling asked for anonymous comments in response to the statement: I feel better equipped to supervise people as a result of the program. Of 342 supervisors who replied, 43 percent responded "strongly agree," 54 percent responded "agree," and 3 percent responded "undecided." No one responded "disagree" or "strongly disagree."[45]

• Edited videotapes were used to permit individuals to serve as their own models. Self-modeling improved the productivity of handicapped workers by 15 percent during the 2-week intervention period. In comparison, productivity declined by 3 percent in the control group.[46]

In light of these positive results it is not surprising that many organizations have implemented behavior modeling training in recent years. In 1980, more than 500,000 people received behavior modeling training.[47] Further, by 1982 three management consulting firms (alone) had conducted behavior modeling training for some 750 companies.[48]

What makes behavior modeling so effective in comparison with other training techniques? Certainly an important factor is that behavior modeling trains employees to develop specific skills; it does not teach abstract theories or attempt to change attitudes. Rather, behavior modeling focuses on specific, commonly encountered problems, and the training proceeds one problem at a time. For example, in supervisory skills training, typical issues include dealing with a rule infraction, motivating a poor performer, and handling a discrimination complaint.

### Programmed and Computer-Assisted Instruction

Programmed instruction (PI) is a training method characterized by (1) specific learning objectives, (2) self-paced learning, (3) logically sequenced component steps (frames), (4) active responding (which allows the assessment of comprehension), and (5) feedback of results. Variants of PI (e.g., teaching machines, programmed texts) have been used to train people to perform a wide variety of functions, including sales, machine operation, and supervision. For example, a retail gift shop chain uses PI to train the temporary salespeople hired during the Christmas season. The training program deals with such topics as check cashing, customer relations, handling refunds, operating the cash register, merchandise display, and sales slips. The chain reportedly has 98 percent of all trainees on the floor and selling within 6 hours.[49]

What can be concluded about the effectiveness of PI? The results of more than 100 studies using PI indicate that the major advantage is that it nearly always decreases the amount of time required for training. Trainees can typically be taught the same information as by other methods in about one-third the time.[50]

In many respects, computer-assisted instruction (CAI) is similar to PI. However, CAI offers a number of unique advantages: after diagnosing the trainee's needs, it is possible to teach, drill, test, and grade in an individualized manner. Further, CAI allows more rapid interaction than PI, and it can update, flashback, review, and explain in various modes—including animation. And the mode of presentation can be individualized too.

An example of the successful application of CAI is provided by Control Data's PLATO system, which took 19 years to develop. Using this system, new computer programmer analysts were trained in 19 days instead of the 44 days of classroom instruction previously required. The company reported an "improvement in the training content as well as a cost savings of $5,000 per student." Similarly, in connection with the maintenance of computer equipment, two new courses reduced the cost of customer engineer training by "approximately $700,000 per year."[51] The cost of operating Control Data's system was $7 per hour in 1975, but had decreased to under $2 per hour by 1980. In comparison, conventional types of training cost from $18 to $75 per hour, depending in large measure on the amount of lost work time and the travel time required.[52] The use of CAI, though, permits training to be conducted *where* and *when* it is convenient. Also, CAI can often be provided on short notice: if, for example, a sales meeting is canceled, salespeople can profitably spend time taking a brief refresher course.

Another successful application of CAI has been reported in connection with the training of bank tellers. Ironically, bank tellers are responsible for large amounts of cash, they importantly influence customer goodwill, and their performance directly bears on the efficiency of operations—yet bank tellers are low paid and routinely quit. Traditional bank teller training programs consist of 3 weeks of classroom instruction and a few weeks of on-the-job training. Typically, after a 90-day probation period, 25 to 100 percent of the tellers quit, in part because the trainees have not mastered the more than 200 different transactions they may be called on to handle. The use of CAI has been shown to (1) improve knowledge acquisition (from 82.5 to 97 percent), (2) halve the training time required, and (3) lower the turnover rate.[53]

In a study comparing the efficiency of CAI and PI, CAI produced a substantial and significant reduction in the time required to train electronic technicians. Specifically, IBM reported a 10 percent reduction in training time using CAI compared with using programmed texts.[54]

### On-the-Job Training

The most widely used training method involves assigning trainees to experienced workers or supervisors for on-the-job training (OJT). Often the experienced worker is directed, "Teach Charlie your job." Charlie is then expected to learn by the observation and imitation of effective job performance. Although OJT is relatively economical, there are potential problems. The trainers may resent the extra responsibilities; and they may not do their best if they are concerned about job security (e.g., some trainees may have more *organizational* tenure than some trainers). Additionally, trainers may not be motivated to train all trainees equally well. James Hayes provides the following illustration of poor quality control in OJT.

> The personnel manager brings a new, green employee over to a supervisor and says, "Show him how to use one of your machines, and put him to work." So the supervisor tells the new worker: "You put this piece of metal on the machine like this. You step on the foot lever and press the hand lever. Try it. No, that's a reject. Try it again. Take your time. Try it once more. No, you don't seem to get the hang of it."
>
> So the supervisor goes to the foreman and says: "The new guy can't understand that complex machine. We'd better give him a job pushing boxes around and get someone else for the machine job. I have a brother I think could do the work." The foreman agrees.
>
> So the supervisor brings in his brother and says: "Let me explain how to use this machine. You put the piece of metal on the machine like this, slap it with the side of your hand so it's flush with the bar, press down on the foot lever, and on this particular machine if you bounce the lever about an inch off the floor as you quickly yank the handle, it'll come out nicely. Try it. Great!"[55]

## SUMMARY

This chapter has argued for a systems approach to training: a diagnosis of training needs should precede the design and development of training; and subsequent to delivery, an evaluation of training effectiveness should be performed to determine if learning objectives were accomplished. In brief, training should entail a recurring cycle of planning, action, and controlling.

Today, training is an important undertaking in the United States: cash outlays (alone) approximate one-half the entire cost of higher education. Moreover, trends suggest that training will play an ever more prominent role in influencing organizational productivity.

Although much has been written about the need for training, and about the "virtues" of specific training techniques, empirical studies have been scarce, and high quality studies scarcer still. Notwithstanding the unevenness of the literature, several general guidelines can be offered with confidence. A training program should focus on specific job-related behaviors, include a demonstration of the successful performance of those behaviors, allow adequate time for active practice, provide feedback and, where appropriate, positive reinforcement, and be actively supported by all levels of management.

The most prevalent method of training is on-the-job training. Yet this approach has several disadvantages, including a possible lack of uniformity in training content and quality. Two more systematic methods that have shown considerable promise are behavior modeling and computer-assisted instruction.

## NOTES

1 William McGehee, "Training and Development Theory, Policies, and Practices," chapter in *ASPA Handbook of Personnel and Industrial Relations: Training and Development,* ed. Dale Yoder and Herbert G. Heneman (Washington, D.C.: Bureau of National Affairs, 1977), V, 5:5.
2 Irwin L. Goldstein, *Training: Program Development and Evaluation* (Monterey, Calif.: Brooks/Cole, 1974), pp. 17–25; see also Kenneth N. Wexley and Gary P. Latham, *Developing and Training Human Resources in Organizations* (Glenview, Ill.: Scott, Foresman, 1981), pp. 28–100; see also Sheldon Zedeck and Milton R. Blood, *Foundations of Behavioral Science Research in Organizations* (Monterey, Calif.: Brooks/Cole, 1974), pp. 138–157.
3 Kenneth N. Wexley and Gary P. Latham, *Developing and Training Human Resources,* p. 53.
4 Irwin L. Goldstein, "Training and Organizational Psychology," *Professional Psychology,* 11 (1980), 422.
5 Anthony O. Putman, "Designing from the Logic of People," *Training and Development Journal,* 35 (May 1981), 125.
6 Irwin L. Goldstein, "Training and Organizational Psychology," p. 422. (Goldstein credits this analogy to John P. Campbell.)
7 Anthony O. Putman, "Designing from the Logic of People," p. 128.
8 Max H. Forster, "Training and Development Programs, Methods, and Facilities," in *ASPA Handbook of Personnel and Industrial Relations: Training and Development,* ed. Dale Yoder and Herbert G. Heneman (Washinton, D.C.: Bureau of National Affairs, 1977), V, 5:36.
9 Irwin L. Goldstein, *Training,* pp. 17–25.
10 Irwin L. Goldstein, "Training and Organizational Psychology," p. '423. Also see Max H. Forster, "Training and Development Programs," p. 5:55. Goldstein noted that in the 1950s, only about one company in forty scientifically evaluated its supervisory training programs; similarly, in a 1971 U.S, Civil Service catalog of educational training programs, only six out of fifty-five programs indicated the existence of validity evidence of any kind.
11 Irwin L. Goldstein, "Training and Organizational Psychology," p. 424. In a 1968 survey of 154 companies that conducted training evaluations, 77 percent emphasized the use of reaction measures. Frequently trainee reactions were assessed by rather informal "eyeball" methods.
12 Kenneth N. Wexley and Gary P. Latham, *Developing and Training Human Resources,* p. 99.
13 A case study that vividly illustrates this point is provided by Kenneth N. Wexley and Gary P. Latham, *Developing and Training Human Resources,* p. 86.
14 See Gary P. Latham and Kenneth N. Wexley, *Increasing Productivity through Performance Appraisal* (Reading, Mass.: Addison-Wesley, 1981), pp. 37–77.
15 Ron Zemke, "Ten Ways to Undermine Your HRD Effort," *Training/HRD,* 19 (Dec. 1982), 26. Copyright 1982, Lakewood Publications, Inc., Minneapolis, Minn. All rights reserved. Reprinted with permission.

**16** Marianna Ohe, "Business Educates Employees," *American Business,* Sept. 1981, p. 2.

**17** Ibid.

**18** Kenneth N. Wexley and Gary P. Latham, *Developing and Training Human Resources,* p. 15.

**19** Irwin L. Goldstein, "Training and Organizational Psychology," p. 421.

**20** Edward F. Denison and William G. Ouchi, "The Breakdown-Slowdown Lowdown: Defining the Productivity Decline," *Management,* 1 (Fall 1981), 13.

**21** Kenneth N. Wexley and Gary P. Latham, *Developing and Training Human Resources,* p. 6.

**22** Irwin L. Goldstein, "Training in Work Organizations," *Annual Review of Psychology,* 31 (1980), 231, 262–263; © 1980 by Annual Reviews Inc. Reproduced with permission.

**23** Irwin L. Goldstein, "Training and Organizational Psychology," p. 424.

**24** John L. Mikesell, John A. Wilson, and Wendell Lawther, "Training Program and Evaluation Model," *Public Personnel Management,* 4 (1975), 405–411.

**25** John R. Hinrichs, *Practical Management for Productivity* (New York: Van Nostrand Reinhold, 1978), p. 71.

**26** Joan Harley and Lois Ann Koff, "Training Traps: Reasons, Results and Remedies," *Personnel Administrator,* 25 (Aug. 1980), 35.

**27** Ibid.

**28** Gary P. Latham and Kenneth N. Wexley, *Increasing Productivity,* pp. 105–107; also Kenneth N. Wexley and Gary P. Latham, *Developing and Training Human Resources,* pp. 216–218.

**29** Kenneth N. Wexley, and Gary P. Latham, *Developing and Training Human Resources,* p. 217.

**30** Joan Harley and Lois Ann Koff, "Training Traps," pp. 34–35. Reprinted from the August 1980 issue of *Personnel Administrator,* copyright 1980, The American Society for Personnel Administration, 606 North Washington Street, Alexandria Virginia 22314.

**31** *Training,* 20 (Aug. 1983), 70.

**32** E. Scott Geller, Serena L. Eason, Jean A. Phillips, and Merle D. Pierson, "Interventions to Improve Sanitation During Food Preparation," *Journal of Organizational Behavior Management,* 2 (1980), 229–240.

**33** Paul Mali, *Improving Total Productivity* (New York: Wiley, 1978), p. xi.

**34** Peter W. Dowrick and Marie Hood, "Comparison of Self-Modeling and Small Cash Incentives in a Sheltered Workshop," *Journal of Applied Psychology,* 66 (1981), 394–397; also Charles C. Manz and Henry P. Sims, Jr., "Vicarious Learning: The Influence of Modeling on Organizational Behavior," *Academy of Management Review,* 6 (1981), 105–113. To enhance the process of ego-identification, some consultants strongly encourage the use of actual employees as models. Apparently there is greater identification with real employees who are filmed on the organization's premises and who speak using the organization's terminology than with actors who are used as models.

**35** Bernard L. Rosenbaum, "Behavior Modeling Based Training Programs," address presented at the 1980 Conference of the American Society for Training and Development (Anaheim, Calif.), pp. 2–4.

**36** Raymond A. Katzell, Penney Bienstock, and Paul H. Faerstein, *A Guide to Worker*

*Productivity Experiments in the United States 1971–75* (New York: New York Univ. Press, 1977), p. 125.

37 Joan Harley and Lois Ann Koff, "Training Traps," p. 34. Further, Irwin L. Goldstein, "Training and Organizational Psychology," notes additional managerial obstacles to effective training: (1) production standards which do not permit supervisors to send employees for training on a regular basis, (2) supervisors who reject practices taught in training, and (3) unresolved conflicts in goals and objectives among different organizational subunits (pp. 425–426).

38 Irwin L. Goldstein, "Training in Work Organizations," p. 260.

39 Bernard L. Rosenbaum, *How to Motivate Today's Workers* (New York: McGraw-Hill, 1982), pp. 107–110. Rosenbaum adds two additional steps: transferring training to the job, and management reinforcement.

40 Gary P. Latham and Lise M. Saari, "Application of Social Learning Theory to Training Supervisors through Behavioral Modeling," *Journal of Applied Psychology,* 64 (1979), p. 242.

41 Jerry I. Porras and Brad Anderson, "Improving Managerial Effectiveness through Modeling-Based Training," *Organizational Dynamics,* 9 (Spring 1981), 74; also, the newsletter, *MOHR Developments,* 1 (Spring 1981), 1, 3–4.

42 William McGehee and William L. Tullar, "A Note on Evaluating Behavior Modification and Behavior Modeling as Industrial Training Techniques," *Personnel Psychology,* 31 (1978), 477–484.

43 "Imitating Models: A New Management Tool," *Business Week,* 8 May 1978, pp. 119–120.

44 "How One Company Trains Supervisors to Motivate Safe Worker Practices," *Alert* (published by the Research Institute of America), 4 July 1979 p. 4.

45 Bernard L. Rosenbaum, "New Uses for Behavior Modeling," *The Personnel Administrator,* 23 (July 1978), 27–28.

46 Peter W. Dowrick and Marie Hood, "Self-Modeling and Small Cash Incentives," pp. 394–397.

47 James C. Robinson and Dana L. Gaines, "Questions to Ask Before Using Behavior Modeling," *Training/HRD,* 17 (Dec. 1980), 71.

48 "Training Bosses," *Time,* 7 June 1982, p. 61.

49 Kenneth N. Wexley and Gary P. Latham, *Developing and Training Human Resources,* p. 135.

50 Ibid., p. 137. Wexley and Latham note that contrary to the claims of proponents, PI does not seem to improve either the amount of knowledge acquired or its retention over time when it is compared with conventional lecture methods.

51 William C. Norris, *Technology for Company-Employee Partnership to Improve Productivity,* Monograph No. 17 (Minneapolis, Minn.: Control Data Corporation, June 1981) pp. 2, 16.

52 Ibid., p. 16.

53 "Teller Training Can Put Money in the Bank," *Training/HRD,* 20 (Mar. 1983), 8.

54 Kenneth N. Wexley and Gary P. Latham, *Developing and Training Human Resources,* p. 138.

55 "Want to Be a Better Boss? Advice from an Expert," *U.S. News & World Report,* 21 Mar. 1977, p. 68. (James Hayes was president of the American Management Associations.)

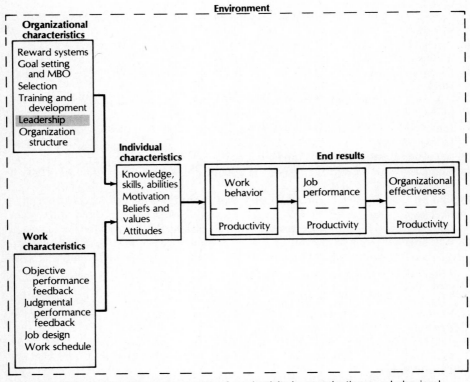

Conceptual framework of the determinants of productivity in organizations—a behavioral science approach.

# LEADERSHIP

Among the many questions about leadership that have been researched by behavioral scientists, three have received the most attention: Who should be the leader?; What kinds of leader behaviors are most promotive of group effectiveness?; and How much control (power, participation, influence) should work group members be given? Unfortunately, although hundreds of *correlational* leadership studies have been conducted (relating scores on one variable to scores on another), very few studies have examined, experimentally, the impact of *changes* in leadership practices on productivity. Nevertheless, this chapter examines the leadership literature as it relates to improving the productivity of people at work. Two relatively recent leadership practices are also considered: (1) quality circles and (2) the amalgam of techniques frequently called the Japanese approach to leadership.

## WHO SHOULD BE THE LEADER?

*The question "Who ought to be boss" is like asking "Who ought to be the tenor in the quartet?" Obviously, the man who can sing tenor.*

Henry Ford[1]

People have long enjoyed reading biographies of the great men and women of history—the powerful figures who are often described as "natural leaders." Not surprisingly, behavioral scientists have also been fascinated by this issue: Are there particular traits (personal characteristics and abilities) that predispose people to leadership success? Certainly, if such traits exist, it would be possible to determine *beforehand* who ought to be the leader—and who should sing tenor.

As of 1970, Ralph Stogdill had examined 287 studies dealing with leader traits.[2] Although some traits were moderately predictive of leadership effectiveness (e.g., vigor, self-confidence, dependability, originality), results were generally neither very strong nor consistent.[3] In part, the inconsistent findings reflected differences in other factors. Leadership effectiveness is influenced by many variables besides leader traits (e.g., the characteristics and expectations of group members, the prevailing organizational climate, the task to be performed), and these factors have differed across studies. Also, small sample sizes in some studies (i.e., sampling error) may have contributed to result variability. Further, many of the trait measures used may have lacked psychometric adequacy (reliability, validity): to be sure, calling a scale a measure of "integrity" does not necessarily make it so.

### Three Promising Trait Approaches

**Contingency Theory of Leadership**   One trait approach that has achieved a high level of predictive validity, under certain circumstances, is Fred Fiedler's contingency theory of leadership. According to Fiedler, there are two types of leaders, those who are task-oriented, primarily motivated to accomplish goals, and those who are relationship-oriented, primarily motivated to achieve good relationships among group members. Fiedler believes that leadership orientation is an enduring personality characteristic; hence he argues that the "fit" between the leader's orientation and the situation determines leadership effectiveness. This explains why inexperienced individuals assigned the role of leader often perform as well in terms of group effectiveness as experienced leaders who may have had years of "training":

> When we talk about leadership behavior we are talking about fairly deeply ingrained personality factors and habits of interacting with others. These cannot be changed easily. . . . In fact, as we have seen, not even four years of military academy and 5 to 17 years of subsequent experience enable a leader to perform significantly better on different tasks than someone who has had neither training nor experience.[4]

According to Fiedler's theory, task-oriented leaders perform best in situations which are highly favorable or highly unfavorable; in contrast, relationship-oriented leaders perform best in moderately favorable situations. The theory predicts, therefore, that if the same type of training and experience are given to both task- and relationship-oriented leaders, the training will be dysfunctional for some of the leaders. Training that improves the performance of one type of leader will likely prove detrimental to the performance of the other type.[5]

Strube and Garcia have conducted a comprehensive review of 145 tests of Fiedler's theory—all known tests performed after the original 33 on which the theory was based. Combining the data from 145 tests produced a remarkable significance level: the likelihood of obtaining these results by chance alone was less than .01 $\times$ 1 trillion $\times$ 1 trillion.[6] Strube and Garcia concluded, "The model as a whole was overwhelmingly supported. . . . Given that it took 13 years to generate the present validation evidence consisting of 145 hypothesis tests, it is unlikely that the model will be disconfirmed in the near future."[7]

On the basis of his theory, Fiedler has developed an approach to leadership training, Leader Match, that attempts to change the leadership situation to fit the leader, rather than vice versa. Leader Match has been tested in 12 studies, 5 in civilian organizations and 7 in the military. In all 12 studies results were statistically significant and supported Leader Match training.[8] Further, Leader Match training is highly cost-effective: training consists of a self-administered programmed workbook that requires only 5 to 12 hours to complete.

Yet, it should be noted that under certain conditions, Leader Match requires that leaders deliberately impair goal clarity or damage leader-group relations.[9] It is also not clear from the research evidence whether Leader Match has worked because of a better leader-situation fit, or whether improvement resulted from other factors (e.g., leaders being more self-confident). Consequently some management writers remain skeptical about the use of Leader Match as a means of improving leader effectiveness.[10]

**Need for Power**    A second trait approach to leadership that has reported good predictive validities is the research on the need for power. In an early study, McClelland and Burnham found that 80 percent of high-performing sales managers in a large company had a stronger need for power than for affiliation; among low-performing sales managers only 10 percent had a stronger need for power than for affiliation. Similar results were found for managers in research, product development, and operations: for these managers 73 percent of the high-performing and 22 percent of the low-performing managers had a stronger need for power than for affiliation. McClelland and Burnham emphasize, though, that the effective managers showed a high need for *socialized* power (influence used in building organizations), rather than for personal power (used for one's own aggrandizement).[11]

More recently, McClelland and Boyatzis have examined the success of 237 managers at AT&T over periods of 8 and 16 years. It was predicted that managers having the leadership motive pattern would outperform those who did not. The *leadership motive pattern* (LMP) was defined as a high need for power, a low need for affiliation, and a high degree of self-control (socializing the need for power). Results were supportive for nontechnical managers: after 8 years, 66 percent of managers with the LMP were promoted, compared with 36 percent without the LMP; after 16 years the promotion rates were 79 percent and 57 percent, respectively. The presence or absence of the LMP was not, however, predictive of career success among technical managers. Apparently, technical managers were promoted more on technical and verbal skills than on leadership qualities.[12]

Why is a strong need for socialized power, coupled with a relatively weak need for affiliation, an effective leadership motive pattern? McClelland and Burnham provide a good explanation in their article, "Good Guys Make Bum

Bosses." When the need to be liked predominates, leaders tend to make "wishy-washy decisions." Wanting to stay on good terms with their subordinates, such leaders care more about the happiness of individuals than about the effectiveness of the work unit; hence, they make exceptions to rules and violate the fundamental principle of fairness. Bending the rules alienates workers, undermines faith in the organizational reward system, and causes the less favored to feel their behavior has little influence over events.[13]

In this vein, Van Fleet relates the sad story of George S., an experienced worker promoted to first-level supervisor in a furniture manufacturing plant. George wanted to succeed in his new position, but he also very much wanted to be liked. George allowed his former peers to prolong coffee breaks and lunch breaks; he said nothing when people came in late for work; he accepted all sorts of excuses for absenteeism; and he approved poor quality work. The result?

> In less than two months after George had taken over the department, it was in complete shambles. Production had fallen off . . . quality had slipped badly . . . accidents had increased . . . several hundred yards of expensive fabric had been ruined . . . housekeeping had become sloppy and slipshod . . . the men were careless about everything . . . [and eventually] . . . management gave up and fired George.[14]

George's problem, according to Van Fleet, was trying to be liked rather than respected. The problem might also be viewed characterologically: George had a far stronger need for affiliation than for socialized power.

**Motivation to Manage**   A relatively new construct, the motivation to manage, is conceptually similar to the need for power. The motivation to manage consists of the following six components:[15]

1 A favorable attitude toward authority
2 A desire to compete
3 A desire to be assertive
4 A desire to direct others and exercise power
5 A desire to stand out and be the center of attention
6 A desire to carry out routine administrative tasks

Two decades of research on the motivation to manage have led John Miner to conclude that (1) people with a high motivation to manage are more likely to become managers and that (2) managers with a high motivation to manage are more likely to function successfully in that role (compared to those with a low motivation to manage).

Miner found, however, that between 1960 and 1973 the average motivation to manage scores of college business students declined steadily and substantially; and average scores remained at a low level between 1973 and 1980.[16] Miner commented:

> Although the future appears to offer the prospect of an abundance of *intellectual* managerial talent, in the sense of requisite knowledge and intelligence to meet the challenges of the managerial role, a sizable body of research now exists to indicate that *managerial* motivation will be in short supply.[17]

More recently, Miner and Smith have noted that as older managers (with relatively high levels of motivation to manage) leave the work force, they are being replaced by men and women who lack the motivational drive to meet the managerial role requirements successfully. Consequently, "we face right now something like a 15-year deficit in managerial talent."[18]

Longitudinal research on managerial careers at AT&T during the past 20 years provides evidence supporting this conclusion. Comparing first-level managers in the 1970s with their counterparts in the 1950s, no differences were found in a number of respects (e.g., the need to achieve, dogmatism). However, marked declines were noted in the desire to lead others, in the desire for upward mobility, and in expectations of career advancement. The 1970 cohort strongly desired a nurturing role (to be generous, to treat others with kindness and empathy—in short, to love others, not to lead them). The principal researchers concluded, "With due respect to the virtues of human warmth and kindness, who is going to run our corporations in the future?"[19]

## WHAT LEADER BEHAVIORS PROMOTE GROUP EFFECTIVENESS?

### Consideration and Initiating Structure

A second major area of leadership research has centered around the different types of work behaviors leaders can exhibit. Much of the research has focused on the distinction between two broad categories of leader behaviors: *Initiating Structure,* which refers to task-oriented behaviors such as role clarification, goal setting, criticism and discipline, and *Consideration,* which encompasses such person-oriented behaviors as expressing concern, support, and warmth, sharing information, and representing subordinates' interests.

Numerous studies have been conducted regarding leader behaviors, but results have been far from consistent. It would appear that only one finding warrants much confidence: the more considerate the leader, the higher the average level of job and supervision satisfaction among work group members. Consideration has not been found to be a reliable predictor of job performance, and Initiating Structure has not been reliably predictive of either satisfaction or performance.[20] In light of the long history of inconsistent research results, leadership has been described as one of the "most researched and least understood" of all management concepts.[21]

### Path-Goal Leadership Theory

One attempt at "making some sense" out of decades of seemingly inconsistent findings has taken the form of the path-goal theory of leadership. *Path-goal theory,* in essence, identifies boundary conditions (moderator variables) that purportedly influence the relationship between leader behaviors and two outcome variables, satisfaction and performance. One such moderator identified by path-goal theory is task complexity. Evidence suggests that this, indeed, may be a relevant factor. For example, it has been found that Consideration is especially predictive of satisfaction where task complexity is low (a condition typically accompanied by low intrinsic motivation and by low pay)—i.e., where the quality of supervision is practically "the only game in town."[22] There is also some evidence that Initiating Structure impairs satisfaction on noncomplex tasks (possibly because structuring is felt as redundant and is resented) and that Initiating Structure enhances performance and satisfaction on complex tasks (where structuring may provide useful technical information).[23] Yet the reader should be aware that tests of hypotheses derived from path-goal theory have not been consistently supportive. Also, since tests have been correlational, average effects in terms of productivity improvement are unknown. Given these limitations, John Miner has offered the following overall assessment: "Applications have not been developed and guidelines for managerial action have not been sufficiently spelled out. . . . it appears premature to draw inferences about the use of the [path-goal] theory in management practice."[24]

One reason why past research on leader behaviors has not been very useful is that the two major categories (Consideration and Initiating Structure) are far too broad. Widely-used measures of Initiating Structure encompass eight different types of leader behaviors: role clarification, goal setting, performance emphasis, criticism and discipline, problem solving, planning, coordinating, and delegation. Prominent measures of Consideration cover five different types of leader behaviors: warmth and support, decision participation, structuring rewards, praise and recognition, and representation. As Gary Yukl has noted, the broader the categorization of leader behaviors, "the less useful it is for determining what makes a leader effective in a particular situation."[25]

### Leader Behavior with Marginal Performers

Relatively few studies have examined leadership effectiveness as it relates to more "fine-tuned" leader behaviors. One study reporting positive results was conducted by O'Reilly and Weitz. Focusing on criticism and discipline, O'Reilly and Weitz studied the behaviors of first-level supervisors in a retail store chain. Some supervisors, classified as having an "employee orientation," gave relatively few oral or written warnings to employees who performed poorly; these supervisors typically allowed much time to pass before dealing with performance problems; they were also reluctant to terminate poorly performing employees. In contrast, supervisors with a "confrontative orientation" gave more frequent oral and written warnings, allowed less time to pass between warnings and dismissal, and were more likely to terminate poorly performing employees. Performance rating data, based primarily on annual unit sales and costs, were obtained for 113 supervisors. Supervisors with an "employee orientation" had significantly lower performance ratings than those with a "confrontative orientation."[26] Although the former were more patient, it would appear that fervently hoping that "things will work out" is not a successful pattern of leader behavior.

## Management by Walking Around

Another leader behavior that has received increasing attention of late relates to performance emphasis. A number of writers have argued the advantages of *management by walking around* (MBWA), i.e., active, hands-on involvement rather than distant order-giving.[27] Saul Gellerman has provided a rich account of how some supervisors enact MBWA, based on the observation of twelve production supervisors employed by a major food processing company. The behavior of supervisor C, a highly rated supervisor whose shift's productivity was among the highest, was described as follows:

> For the most part, C was no conversationalist. His contacts were brief. . . . But they were also easy, with a touch of banter. . . . C seemed to know his people well, and his manner made his inspection of their work, which after all is a control function, easier to tolerate. . . . C was constantly on the move. . . . The operators saw a lot of him, but never had to endure a concentrated dose of scrutiny. . . . C tried to turn his visits into welcome, if brief, respites from monotony. He even encouraged gentle ribbing and harmless jokes at his expense.[28]

John Doyle, a Hewlett-Packard executive, offered the following rationale for MBWA: "That's how you find out whether you're on track. . . . If you don't constantly monitor how people are operating, not only will they begin to wander off track but also they will begin to believe you weren't serious about the plan in the first place. So, management by wandering around is the business of staying in touch with the territory all the time."[29]

Thomas Peters and Robert Waterman, in their book *In Search of Excellence,* provide anecdotal evidence regarding the utility of MBWA. They quote a manager at General Motors who contrasted the performance of two giant auto plants:

> I know this sounds like caricature, but I guess that is how life is. At the poorly performing plant, the plant manager probably ventured out on the floor once a week, always in a suit. His comments were distant and perfunctory. At South Gate, the better plant, the plant manager was on the floor all the time. He wore a baseball cap and a UAW jacket. By the way, whose plant do you think was spotless? Whose looked like a junk yard?[30]

Finally, in connection with leader behaviors, behavioral *consistency* has been found to be related to leadership effectiveness, especially where task demands vary. Apparently, when workers must deal with an uncertain task situation, consistent leader behavior enhances worker motivation and satisfaction.[31]

## HOW MUCH CONTROL SHOULD WORKERS BE GIVEN?

A considerable body of literature has accumulated on the effects of participative decision making on group effectiveness. One of the earliest social psychological experiments contrasted the effects of democratic, laissez-faire, and autocratic styles of leadership.[32] Yet, as Locke and Schweiger have observed

No issue in the field of organizational behavior and industrial relations is more loaded with ideological and moral connotations than that of worker participation in decision making. . . . Systems of management which do not stress [participation] have been accused of being "exploitative," "dictatorial," "ahuman," and even "neo-Nazi" . . . [reflecting an] "authoritarian-materialistic" culture.[33]

Although some academics have adopted the position, "I don't care what the evidence shows about participation, it's a moral issue," another view is "whatever works is what counts" (within limits, of course). Because the debate centers on values (people's satisfaction vs. economic pragmatism), it is not readily resolvable.

Three studies, however, provide a balanced perspective on the effects of participative leadership. One experiment, conducted by Powell and Schlacter, involved six groups of employees at the Ohio Bureau of Traffic. Two groups were allowed only indirect participation (the leaders could confer with higher management), two groups were allowed limited direct participation (the members could confer with higher management on some issues), and two groups were allowed broad decision-making responsibility (the groups themselves made all decisions on some issues). The researchers hypothesized that increased participation would result in increased productivity. The results failed to support this prediction. In Powell and Schlacter's words:

> The research suggests that while participative management techniques may produce involved, happy workers, it does not necessarily achieve productive results for the organization.[34]

A second, and more positive, intervention was reported by John Hinrichs in *Practical Management for Productivity*. At one plant of the AHM Corporation (a pseudonym for a large automobile manufacturer), some management planners decided to ask workers on the assembly line for their ideas about plant layout for a new model. As Hinrichs relates the process, "rap sessions" were held in various departments. Many employees presented their ideas and were glad to contribute. Others said, "Don't bother me. Do what you gotta do, pal, just let me do my job." The overall result was the smoothest start-up in the history of the plant. Further, in the body shop, where the weld discrepancy had been roughly 35 percent, management approached the workers, saying, "We need your help to try to find out why we're having these problems." Within months the average weld discrepancy was reduced to 1.5 percent, an improvement of 95 percent. A member of AHM's training department explained the company's objectives:

> We're not trying to make people happy. What we're trying to do is involve them, utilize their talents. We started to believe that people have some smarts and that they want some control over their own jobs. . . . If people just tell you about their problems, you get nowhere. But when you start involving people, meaningfully, in tasks which affect their jobs, they start to derive some satisfaction from that . . . [and] we know we'll get productivity too.[35]

A third application of participative leadership was undertaken among white- and blue-collar employees in a large aerospace-defense firm. Over a 4-year period, productivity improvements were reported in 27 out of 40 work groups where participative leadership was employed. On the average, productivity increased by roughly 15 percent, approximately 4 percent per annum. It is notable, though, that the intervention combined at least seven different behavioral science techniques: training, goal setting, feedback, job and work flow redesign, organization restructuring, and participative decision making. Unfortunately, participative leadership was discontinued, reportedly because of a cutback in aerospace-defense contracts.[36]

There have been numerous other attempts at improving productivity via participative leadership. Six such experiments were listed in the first and second *Guide to Worker Productivity Experiments in the United States* (*WPE1* and *WPE2*). In the most comprehensive review to date, Edwin Locke and his associates reviewed 16 studies on participative leadership. They found that the average increase in productivity associated with participation was 0.5 percent.[37] Combining results from all (three) surveys, the average impact of participation was an increase in productivity of 3.5 percent.

### Boundary Conditions for Participation

Although the median effect of participation on productivity has been found to be virtually nil, the range of results in the Locke survey was from $-24$ percent to $+47$ percent, with half the studies reporting positive results. It appears, therefore, that participative leadership is effective in some situations. Clearly, a key task is identifying the boundary conditions that reliably influence the effectiveness of participation.

One boundary condition is motivation to participate: if group members do not want to participate in decision making, a participative leadership style is unlikely to prove successful. John Ivancevich tested this hypothesis using a sample of project engineers. Engineers were classified into three groups: those who had participated in fewer decisions than they desired (a condition called "decision deprivation"), those who had participated in more decisions than desired ("decision saturation"), and those who had participated in as many decisions as desired ("decision equilibrium"). As predicted, engineers in the decision equilibrium group had significantly higher performance ratings and cost-effectiveness results than engineers in the decision deprivation or saturation conditions.[38]

Although it is widely assumed that subordinates want to participate as fully as possible in the decision-making process, evidence (besides Ivancevich's) indicates considerable diversity in this regard.[39] When Honda attempted to implement participative leadership in its Marysville, Ohio, plant many managers declined the invitation, responding, "We'll do whatever you decide."[40]

A second boundary condition is ability to contribute. If work group members possess little relevant information or knowledge, participation may waste time and effort at best, and possibly harm decision quality. Consider the case of Nonlinear Systems, a manufacturer of electrical measuring instruments with a history of rapid growth in sales and profits. After consulting several eminent advocates of participatory leadership, and after years of planning, Nonlinear Systems introduced major changes aimed at making the company thoroughly democratic. Five years later the program was abandoned because of increasingly severe problems in sales, costs, and losses (which replaced profits). One commentator offered the following explanation of what went wrong.

> The seven vice presidents formerly had been vigorously active in the midst of daily problems and were more or less expert in their individual specialties. Under participative management these men were practically immobilized as "sideline consultants."[41]

The key problem at Nonlinear Systems, according to Locke and Schweiger, was the separation of responsibility from knowledge. The attempt to give everyone equal say "led to the most competent employees being prevented from acting on their judgment. . . . A profit-making organization survives by the discovery and application of knowledge relevant to its product and market. . . . From the point of view of an organization, employee satisfaction must be considered a means to an end (i.e., a necessary condition for long-term profitability), not an end in itself. . . . employee feelings have no market price."[42] An executive at General Motors put it quite succinctly: it is possible that workers "on the carton-folding operation really have nothing to contribute to almost anything important about running a container company."[43]

A number of other factors have been identified as possible boundary conditions pertinent to the effectiveness of participative leadership. These include the questions of (1) whether the leader desires to share power and influence (some will be threatened by the prospect); (2) whether the leader possesses the requisite skills to use participation effectively; and (3) whether time pressures are too great (since participative decision making typically takes longer than more directive methods).[44]

Two additional limiting factors should be noted regarding participation. First, organizations adopting participatory leadership cannot expect immediate results. At Westinghouse, increased participation was viewed as part of a "cultural revolution" and management expected "to wait two years before seeing any results, and ten years before the benefits took full effect."[45] Second, participative leadership may be incompatible with bold leadership. As one corporate president commented, "I'm quite willing to present my ideas, indeed I am insistent about it. . . . You cannot please everyone, but as a leader you had better say firmly, 'This is a northbound train—those wishing to go south had better get off at the next station.'"[46]

Pertinent to the issue of strong leadership, it is notable that in the 1970s several major U.S. corporations experimented with team management at the top of the organization (the "office of the chief executive"). At Aetna, team management was initially described as "a process by which all of us can bring our own backgrounds, intelligence, and judgment to company problems."[47] After a 4-year trial period, Aetna abandoned team management because it "tended to lead to delays or impede the decision-making process on occasion."[48] So far, there is no evidence that team management at the top of an organization enhances organizational effectiveness or productivity compared to individual leadership.

## QUALITY CIRCLES

A recent and popular participative leadership program is the quality circle. A *quality circle* (QC) is a small group of employees, usually from the same work unit, who voluntarily meet on a regular basis to identify, analyze, and solve work-related problems they have encountered.

This idea, first applied in Japan in the early 1960s—primarily to improve product quality—impressed a visiting management team from Lockheed in 1973. Reportedly the Lockheed group was astonished to find that shop-floor workers sometimes solved problems that had baffled engineers.[49] In 1974 Lockheed's Missile and Space division became the first U.S. organization to adopt the practice. Growth in the United States was virtually exponential: by 1977 approximately 50 U.S. organizations had implemented QCs; by 1982 it was estimated that QCs were functioning in some 2000 organizations.[50] In 1982 at least 5 U.S. corporations had 500 or more ongoing QCs: Hewlett-Packard, Honeywell, Westinghouse, Hughes Aircraft, and Texas Instruments.[51] While the preponderance of applications has been in manufacturing companies, QCs have also been implemented in service organizations (e.g., J.C. Penney, American Express, Lincoln National Life Insurance).

The QC concept is quite simple, but in some ways very different from conventional participatory leadership approaches. In QCs (1) the choice of projects is left up to the group, (2) the group as a whole (not a subcommittee) analyzes and solves problems, (3) training is provided for all group members, and (4) recognition is granted to the entire group (although the supervisor may be the one who gets promoted). In light of these distinctive characteristics, it has been suggested that the QC concept represents a "radical shift" from conventional practices, and that the implied requisite changes are "earthshaking," tantamount in many cases to a "cultural revolution."[52] Certainly it is clear that effective implementation requires more than bringing workers together, forming groups, and turning them loose.

### Steps for Implementation

Five activities appear necessary to get QCs functioning effectively. First, it is necessary to obtain top management's active support. Permission is insufficient: top management's involvement and commitment are essential.[53] Support should be manifested in several ways, including:

- providing required resources (time, information, funding)
- responding to suggestions promptly, offering full explanations when ideas are rejected
- accepting reasonable suggestions, and being especially tolerant early on
- removing impediments to problem solving and implementation
- establishing a steering committee, comprised of top-level executives, that has overall responsibility for the QC effort (and that may also serve to review QC suggestions)

Second, it is important that middle managers be involved in the QC effort. Middle managers should not simply be directed to cooperate. At the minimum they should be briefed about the program's objectives, organization, and their roles in the process. Middle managers who feel threatened by QCs can and will subvert them: QC meetings will be canceled due to work pressures; requests for information will be ignored. Employees will then conclude that the QC effort is a sham.

Third, union leaders should be involved in the planning and implementation of a QC effort. Although several national union leaders have been outspoken advocates of the QC concept, local units may be resistant. Local union leaders may fear the loss of jobs if efficiency improves, and may see the program as exploitative and manipulative, solving management's problems without providing any material benefits to workers. To the extent that QCs improve cooperation between workers and management, they may be viewed as undermining the need for a strong union.[54] As William Roehl, assistant director of organizing for the AFL-CIO, has said, "A number of well-meaning people believe that quality circles can lead to improvements in the work place. But what they don't know is that they can also be part of a company's union-busting strategy . . . [giving] workers the impression that all their problems will be solved by quality circles, which implies that there's no need for unions."[55]

A fourth essential activity is training the QC members and leader. (The QC leader should be the first-level supervisor; this preserves the supervisor's status and authority.) Evidence shows that training is crucial in determining the quality of QC activity.[56] Leaders should be trained in group process techniques and problem-solving skills. Under an autocratic leader, a QC is unlikely to succeed; rather the leader should act as a "discussion moderator," not as the "boss." Members, too, should be trained in group process techniques (such as brainstorming) and problem-solving skills (such as Pareto analysis and statistical sampling).

A fifth important step is the creation of the role of facilitator or involvement coordinator. A facilitator typically assists QC efforts by helping to organize QCs; training leaders and members; coordinating the work of various QCs; acting as a liaison between QCs and other departments (e.g., gathering data); guiding QCs during their initial meetings; and aiding in keeping QCs "on track."

Clearly, QCs require a good deal of planning, preparation, and follow-through. As Fred Riley of Hewlett-Packard put it, an organization cannot simply "start a program, walk away, and assume it is going to run by itself. You just can't do that. It is going to take a lot of work for a long time."[57] A QC effort should proceed at a slow, deliberate pace: if it is not successful the first time, employees will not be likely to go along with such an effort again.[58] Yet many managers reason that if 10 QCs are good, 100 would be great—apparently ignoring the considerable burden involved in getting just 10 QCs to function successfully.[59]

## Boundary Conditions for QC Success

A number of factors bear on QC effectiveness besides implementation activities. In general, if the organizational "climate" or "culture" is not right, there is a considerable risk of failure.[60] Three factors appear important in this regard. First, there should be a high degree of mutual labor-management trust. Management must trust workers enough to share sensitive information, and workers must trust management not to translate increased efficiency into fewer jobs.[61] This may explain why few Japanese-owned companies in the United States have implemented QCs. As one Japanese manager commented, "*First, we need good two-way communication and mutual understanding. Mutual credit is needed; otherwise it's almost impossible for us to introduce such things.*"[62] Second, there should be a history of prior worker participation. It has been argued that QCs are difficult to implement in a highly centralized, hierarchical structure.[63] Third, (this factor has been suggested by Kenichi Ohmae of McKinsey & Company) the work force must be intelligent and reasonably well educated. Ohmae pointed out that it is no coincidence that the Japanese companies most successful with QCs (e.g., Hitachi) are also well known for fine recruiting and training programs.[64] Similarly, it may not be pure happenstance that the five U.S. companies with more than 500 QCs (Hewlett-Packard, Honeywell, Westinghouse, Hughes Aircraft, and Texas Instruments) are all in high-technology industries.

## Effectiveness Evidence

Widespread adoption of QCs in the United States, has occurred despite a lack of reliable evidence that QCs work here, or for that matter that they work in Japan. The authors of a recent review noted that to date there has not been a single published study reporting the effects of QCs in the United States where data were collected before and after the QC intervention and compared with a control group.[65]

Although the literature on QCs is extensive, it consists of case studies, anecdotal accounts, and opinions. Illustrative of some of the "success stories" are the case studies from Martin Marietta and Honeywell. At its New Orleans plant, 445 Martin Marietta employees participated in QCs. Compared with the company as a whole, those in QCs had a 44 percent lower absenteeism rate, a

65 percent lower accident rate, and a 76 percent lower rate of attrition.[66] At Honeywell, 12 QC teams documented a savings of $86,430 coupled with a 36 percent reduction in assembly costs.[67]

There have also been failures. A manufacturer of molded rubber products established QCs to deal with the problem of declining product quality. With the approval of the union, employees were asked to volunteer and a number of QCs were started, but the result was little change in quality.[68] A similar outcome was reported in connection with the 101-store Ralph's Grocery chain. While QCs were found to be worthwhile in their warehouses, results were disappointing in retail stores. The chief executive officer commented: "To be honest, we're a little disappointed. Some of the quality circles have turned into nothing but social groups. That's not to say we haven't had some minor successes; we have, but we're still looking for a major success."[69]

Case studies of successful QC applications often report a ratio of benefits to costs ranging from 2 to 1 to 8 to 1. However, two recent surveys of 70 companies with QCs found that in about 70 percent of the companies the ratio was less than 1 to 1.[70] It also appears that cost-benefit estimates often overstate the actual effectiveness of QCs in three ways. First, there is a clear bias toward reporting successes, not failures. Second, often only out-of-pocket costs are examined, excluding costs associated with the time spent in training, meetings, and general administration, as well as overhead expenses. Third, savings are often in the form of a reduction in the time required to perform a task. Typically it is assumed (but not demonstrated) that the time saved was spent productively, rather than, say, in resting or socializing.[71]

In light of the lack of solid evidence of effectiveness, it is not surprising that summary assessments vary markedly. Perhaps the most enthusiastic endorsement is provided by Dewar and Beardsley, two former Lockheed managers who became QC consultants. In their book *Quality Circles* they wrote:

> Quality Circles can be the most effective tool with which to effect genuine productivity and work quality improvement in any industry, business, institution, or government agency in any culture or country.[72]

Advocates often claim such additional benefits as lessened conflict and improved communication between employees and managers; heightened worker morale, motivation, and creativity; enhanced problem-solving and leadership skills among employees and managers; lowered costs, reduced turnover, grievances, and absenteeism; and greater identification with the organization.[73]

On the other hand, there are critics of the QC concept. For example, Leighton Smith, of Arthur Andersen's Tokyo office, has commented:

> There is only one objective an organization should have if it installs quality control circles—and it is *not* to improve productivity; nor is it to cut costs. It is simply to improve morale, no more, no less. . . . In fact, the Japanese don't expect a quality circle to cut costs. Introduction of one actually reduces productivity by 2½ percent,

which is typically the amount of extra time workers spend conducting the business of a circle.[74]

Along these lines, Robert Cole has pointed out that QCs do not work very well in many Japanese companies. Even in the best programs, as few as one-third of the circles work well, another third are borderline, and one-third simply make no contribution at all.[75]

Another commentator, Yoshi Tsurumi, argues that roughly 80 percent of a company's productivity and product quality problems can only be solved by top management. In his view QCs are a superficial fad and have little to do with organizational effectiveness.[76]

A final criticism is that the value of QCs is short-lived. Often QCs first address problems that group members find personally annoying but which do not contribute to productivity (the "pebble-in-the-shoe" phase). Then, members may attend to organizationally significant problems. However, employees may use up their ideas and "run out of gas" within a few months.[77]

Given the absence of rigorous research, it appears that the "jury is still out." Certainly, QCs are a promising intervention; but the extent to which they can raise productivity and have sustained value remains to be seen.

## JAPANESE LEADERSHIP PRACTICES

Recently a great deal of attention has been paid to the leadership and management practices used in Japan. Among the many best sellers on this topic have been *Theory Z,* by William Ouchi, and *The Art of Japanese Management,* by Pascale and Athos.[78] Although some of the practices described are uncommon in the U.S. (and likely to remain so—e.g., lifetime employment, deliberately slow promotions, early morning exercises), others appear transferable in varying degrees.

Japanese companies often express a great deal of concern for the well-being of their employees. Hatvany and Pucik note that "in most Japanese companies, *human assets are considered to be the firm's most important and profitable assets in the long run.* Although the phrase itself sounds familiar, even hollow, to many American managers.... [in Japan] this management orientation is backed up by a well-integrated system of strategies and techniques that translate this abstract concept into reality."[79] More specifically, Hatvany and Pucik note that

> It is established practice for managers to spend a lot of time talking to employees about everyday matters ... managers do consciously attempt to get to know their employees, and they place a premium on providing time to talk. The quality of relationships developed with subordinates is also an important factor on which a manager is evaluated. Various company-sponsored cultural, athletic, and other recreational activities further deepen involvement in employees' lives.[80]

A second Japanese leadership practice, also reflective of Consideration, is the minimization of status differences. At Honda's Marysville, Ohio, plant all employees, from top executives to newly hired workers, wear the same white uniform bearing the company's insignia and the wearer's first name. All employees are referred to as "associates," and there are no special privileges such as private offices, separate dining facilities and washrooms, reserved parking spaces, and private secretaries.[81]

Japanese organizations typically share a lot of information with employees at all levels. At Sony's U.S. plants, for example, management keeps workers informed about the company's plans and goals via monthly plantwide meetings.[82] As Samadi (Chris) Wada of Sony Corporation of America put it, "Workers should be a part of the family. We want them to know everything about Sony."[83]

A fourth Japanese leadership practice relates to participation in decision making. The widely heralded approach called *ringi* involves obtaining the unanimous consent (not necessarily approval) of managers and work groups. Ouchi has contrasted the Japanese approach with the method used in many U.S. corporations.

> In the typical American organization, the department head, division manager, and president typically each feel that "the buck stops here"—that they alone should take the responsibility for making decisions. . . . When an important decision needs to be made in a Japanese organization, everyone who will feel its impact is involved in making it . . . that will often mean sixty to eighty people directly involved in making the decision. A team of three will be assigned the duty of talking to all sixty to eighty people and, each time a significant modification arises, contacting all the people involved again. The team will repeat this process until a true consensus has been achieved. Making a decision this way takes a very long time, but once a decision is reached, everyone affected by it will be likely to support it.[84]

Another format for participation is, of course, the quality circle. It has been estimated that roughly 15 percent of all Japanese workers participate in QCs. However, in many companies in Japan participation is virtually mandatory.[85] Still another approach to worker participation is the roundtable meeting. In some Japanese companies top executives meet with a small number of workers, answer questions, and listen to, if not resolve, employee complaints.[86]

Japanese managers also tend to be expert at MBWA. Supervisors are often deliberately deprived of offices so that they can be with subordinates on the shop floor all day, instructing and helping whenever necessary.

Thus, in large measure Japanese leadership practices consist of being considerate, providing structure, and promoting participation. What is unique is the high quality way in which Japanese managers carry out the leadership function. Johnson and Ouchi have commented:

> The Japanese simply outmanage us when it comes to people. We've done very well coping with the inanimate elements of management. But a shocking number of American managers are really inept at dealing with people.[87]

Similarly, John Ebby of Ford of Japan has commented: "By and large we can give the Japanese good marks for being more people-conscious than the West.

We [Americans] tend to think of people as assets that can be moved around."[88]

One aspect of Japanese leadership practice that deserves special emphasis is the concern for creating a corporate identity. Japanese firms frequently articulate a corporate philosophy, a logically consistent set of organizational beliefs and values. Leaders attempt to translate the philosophy into action by explicit policies and by the creation of symbols, myths, and legends. At Sony Corporation of America, for example, management continually articulates (and acts on) such values as "taking pride in product quality," and "being part of the Sony family." These values are embodied in policies on layoffs and pay cuts: "No father can lay off his children or say, 'You have to skip your lunch but I'll have my lunch.'"[89]

Legends and stories play an important part in the shaping of corporate culture, and in creating a common purpose. The chairman of Sony Corporation flew from Japan to Alabama to attend a party celebrating a plant achievement. Although thanked by local management for his attendance, the chairman declined the offer to go to bed; instead he attended parties for the other two shifts at the plant.[90] So what? Narrowly viewed, the chairman's behavior underscored the corporate philosophy that "the dedication of workers cannot be bought; it must be earned." More broadly, the chairman's behavior illustrates the idea that a value embodied in a specific story is more believable and better-remembered than when stated abstractly. Stories, whether based entirely or partly on real events, form an important part of organizational culture.[91]

Probably the single most important idea in the recent best-seller, *In Search of Excellence,* is that leadership consists primarily of infusing new and enduring values, creating a transcendent purpose through symbols, ideologies, rituals, and myths.[92] The "excellent" companies were found to have rich cultures that supported a common sense of purpose. Although cynics may deride the idea that culture is important, Peters and Waterman argue that man is "quite strikingly irrational," seeking both to achieve as an individual and to find meaning in a social endeavor.[93]

## SUMMARY

An enormous body of literature has developed in connection with leadership. An early approach, focusing on enduring characteristics of people, sought to identify traits that would reliably predict leadership effectiveness. While initial results were disappointing, recent studies have shown some promise. Today there is a more balanced view of traits: it is recognized that certain traits do increase the likelihood of leader effectiveness, but of course they do not guarantee it.[94]

Research on leader behaviors has produced few reliable findings. Moreover, it is not at all clear whether leader behaviors are more the cause of subordinate performance or the result of it. It is clear, though, that the two major categories of leader behavior (Consideration and Initiating Structure) are too broad and all-encompassing to provide useful guidelines.

Although participative decision making was originally assumed to enhance leader effectiveness, research to date has not supported this view. (In fact, the average increase in productivity associated with participative leadership has been less than 4 percent.) Hence, over time more and more qualifications have been placed on the premise that participation increases productivity.[95] At present it appears that participation seems to work when small groups of workers voluntarily focus on solving specific, work-related problems that they are motivated to solve (i.e., Quality Circles). However, a need for rigorous research remains regarding the magnitude and persistence of effect of QCs on productivity.

Japanese leadership practices have received a great deal of attention recently, but of those practices that are transferable to the United States, little appears unique. Rather, Japanese managers simply do a better job of leading people. They also appear to be more aware of the importance of shaping organizational culture to create a transcending sense of shared purpose.

## NOTES

1 Center for Creative Leadership newsletter, 1979.

2 Gary A. Yukl, *Leadership in Organizations* (Englewood Cliffs, N.J.: Prentice-Hall, 1981), pp. 68–70.

3 Ibid., pp. 67–70.

4 Fred E. Fiedler, "How Do You Make Leaders More Effective? New Answers to an Old Puzzle," *Organizational Dynamics,* 1 (Autumn 1972), 15. Further, a longitudinal (20-year) study of managerial careers at AT&T has found that, on average, managerial ability does not improve with experience. See Michael M. Lombardo, "How Do Leaders Get to Lead?" *Issues & Observations* (report by the Center for Creative Leadership), 2 (Feb. 1982), 1. That it is hard to change leader behaviors has also been reported by Chris Argyris in "Leadership, Learning and Changing the Status Quo," *Organizational Dynamics,* 4 (Winter 1976), 42.

5 Fred E. Fiedler, "The Effects of Leadership Training and Experience: A Contingency Model Interpretation," *Administrative Science Quarterly,* 17 (1972), 453–469.

6 Michael J. Strube and Joseph E. Garcia, "A Meta-Analytic Investigation of Fiedler's Contingency Model of Leadership Effectiveness," *Psychological Bulletin,* 90 (1981), 315.

7 Ibid., p. 316.

8 Kenneth N. Wexley and Gary P. Latham, *Developing and Training Human Resources in Organizations* (Glenview, Ill.: Scott, Foresman, 1981), p. 156.

9 Chester A. Schriesheim and Steven Kerr, "Theories and Measures of Leadership: A Critical Appraisal of Current and Future Directions," in *Leadership: The Cutting Edge,* ed. James G. Hunt and Lars L. Larson (Carbondale, Ill.: Southern Illinois University Press, 1977), p. 54.

10 Ibid., pp. 51–56; also see John B. Miner, *Theories of Organizational Behavior* (Hinsdale, Ill.: Dryden Press, 1980), pp. 316–324.

11 David C. McClelland and David H. Burnham, "Power is the Great Motivator," *Harvard Business Review,* 54 (Mar.–Apr. 1976), 102–104.

12 David C. McClelland and Richard E. Boyatzis, "Leadership Motive Pattern and

Long-Term Success in Management," *Journal of Applied Psychology,* 67 (1982), 738–742.

**13** David C. McClelland and David H. Burnham, "Good Guys Make Bum Bosses," *Psychology Today,* 9 (Dec. 1975), 41–42.

**14** James K. Van Fleet, *The 22 Biggest Mistakes Managers Make and How to Correct Them* (West Nyack, N.Y.: Parker Publishing, 1973), p. 127; © 1973 by Parker Publishing Company, Inc., West Nyack, New York. Reprinted by permission of the publisher.

**15** John B. Miner, *Motivation to Manage* (Atlanta, Ga.: Organizational Measurement Systems Press, 1977), p. 29; also see John B. Miner and Norman R. Smith, "Decline and Stabilization of Managerial Motivation over a 20-Year Period," *Journal of Applied Psychology,* 67 (1982), 298.

**16** John B. Miner, "The Real Crunch in Managerial Manpower," *Harvard Business Review,* 51 (Nov.–Dec. 1973), 146–158 (for the 1960–1973 period); John B. Miner and Norman R. Smith, "Decline and Stabilization," pp. 297–305 (for the 1973–1980 period).

**17** John B. Miner, "The Real Crunch in Managerial Manpower," *Harvard Business Review,* 51 (Nov.–Dec. 1973), 158. Copyright © 1973 by the President and Fellows of Harvard College; all rights reserved.

**18** John B. Miner and Norman R. Smith, "Decline and Stabilization," p. 302.

**19** Ann Howard and Douglas W. Bray, "Today's Young Managers: They Can Do It, but Will They?" *The Wharton Magazine,* 5 (Summer 1981), 26.

**20** Gary A. Yukl, *Leadership in Organizations,* pp. 108–113; also see Abraham K. Korman, *Organizational Behavior* (Englewood Cliffs, N.J.: Prentice-Hall, 1977), pp. 165–166.

**21** Alan C. Filley, Robert J. House, and Steven Kerr, *Managerial Process and Organizational Behavior,* 2d ed. (Glenview, Ill.: Scott, Foresman, 1976) p. 211.

**22** John B. Miner, *Theories of Organizational Behavior* (Hinsdale, Ill.: Dryden Press, 1980), p. 346.

**23** Ibid., pp. 340–346.

**24** Ibid., p. 348.

**25** Gary A. Yukl, *Leadership in Organizations,* p. 120.

**26** Charles A. O'Reilly and Barton A. Weitz, "Managing Marginal Employees: The Use of Warnings and Dismissals," *Administrative Science Quarterly,* 25 (1980) 467–484.

**27** William G. Ouchi, *Theory Z: How American Business Can Meet the Japanese Challenge* (New York: Avon Books, 1982), pp. 176–177. MBWA is also mentioned repeatedly by Thomas J. Peters and Robert H. Waterman, Jr., in their book, *In Search of Excellence: Lessons from America's Best-Run Companies* (New York: Harper & Row, 1982), pp. 122, 262, 289.

**28** Saul W. Gellerman, "Supervision: Substance and Style," *Harvard Business Review,* 54 (Mar.–Apr. 1976), 90–91. Copyright © 1976 by the President and Fellows of Harvard College; all rights reserved.

**29** *The HP Way* (Palo Alto, Calif.: Hewlett-Packard, 1980), p. 10. Courtesy of Hewlett-Packard Company.

**30** Thomas J. Peters and Robert H. Waterman, Jr., *In Search of Excellence,* p. 262.

**31** Ramon J. Aldag and Arthur P. Brief, "Relationships between Leader Behavior Variability Indices and Subordinate Responses," *Personnel Psychology,* 30 (1977), 419–426; also see Saul W. Gellerman, *Motivation and Productivity* (New York: American Management Associations, 1963), p. 43.

**32** K. Lewin, R. Lippitt, and R. White, "Leader Behavior and Member Reaction in Three 'Social Climates,'" in *Group Dynamics: Research and Theory,* ed. Dorwin Cartwright and Alvin Zander, 2d ed. (Evanston, Ill.: Row, Peterson & Company, 1960).

**33** Edwin A. Locke and David M. Schweiger, "Participation in Decision-Making: One More Look," in *Research in Organizational Behavior,* ed. Barry M. Staw (Greenwich, Ct.: JAI Press, 1979), I, 266–267.

**34** Reed M. Powell and John L. Schlacter, "Participative Management—A Panacea?" *Academy of Management Journal,* 14 (1971), 172.

**35** John M. Hinrichs, *Practical Management for Productivity* (New York: Van Nostrand Reinhold, 1978), pp. 90–93.

**36** Ibid., pp. 67–76.

**37** E. A. Locke, D. B. Feren, V. M. McCaleb, K. N. Shaw, and A. T. Denny, "The Relative Effectiveness of Four Methods of Motivating Employee Performance," in *Changes in Working Life,* ed. K. D. Duncan, M. M. Gruneberg, and D. Wallis (Chichester, England: Wiley Ltd., 1980), pp. 363–388. It should be noted, though, that 5 of the 16 studies reviewed by Locke et al. pertained to participation in goal setting. When these 5 studies are omitted from the analysis (they are included in the present review in connection with goal setting), the median effect of participation on productivity becomes 0.0 percent. In discussing their results, Locke et al. commented as follows: "Our findings may surprise or even shock many social scientists. For the last several decades ideological bias . . . has led many of them to deny the efficacy of money and to emphasize the potency of participation. The results of research to date indicate that the opposite would have been more accurate" (p. 379); copyright 1980 by John Wiley & Sons, Ltd. Reprinted by permission of the publisher. Along these lines, John Miner has reviewed research on participation in connection with Douglas McGregor's Theory Y. Miner concluded that, "Such positive findings as have been obtained involve job satisfaction, not performance or productivity" (John B. Miner, *Theories of Organizational Behavior,* p. 286). In a related vein, a recent U.S. Government report, *The Elusive Bottom Line: Productivity in the Federal Workforce,* offered the following overall assessment: "*Poor supervisory skills have an adverse effect on productivity, but good supervisory skills have only a marginally positive effect.* Although this statement has a dry sound in black and white, in fact it represents a rather startling variance from the conventional wisdom upon which much of the Federal Government's personnel policy has been based in recent years, namely that improving supervisor's [sic] skills will have a direct and substantial effect on employee productivity. The present data indicates that this can be expected only when the quality of supervision is poor and is brought up to acceptable levels" (Washington, D.C.: U.S. Merit Systems Protection Board, May 1982), p. 18, italics in original.

**38** John M. Ivancevich, "An Analysis of Participation in Decision Making Among Project Engineers," *Academy of Management Journal,* 22 (1979), 253–269.

**39** John B. Miner, *Theories of Organizational Behavior,* p. 282.

**40** Masayoshi Kanabayashi, "Honda's Accord: How a Japanese Firm Is Faring on Its Dealings With Workers in U.S.," *Wall Street Journal,* 2 Oct. 1981, p. 25.

**41** Edwin A. Locke and David M. Schweiger, "Participation in Decision-Making," pp. 325–326.

**42** Ibid., pp. 326–328.

**43** Thomas H. Fitzgerald, "Why Motivation Theory Doesn't Work," *Harvard Business Review,* 49 (July–Aug. 1971), 43.

**44** Edwin A. Locke and David M. Schweiger, "Participation in Decision-Making," pp. 321–322; also J. B. Ritchie, "Supervision," in *Organizational Behavior: Research and Issues,* ed. George Strauss, Raymond E. Miles, Charles C. Snow, and Arnold S. Tannenbaum (Madison, Wis.: Industrial Relations Research Association, 1974), pp. 65–71.

**45** Jeremy Main, "Westinghouse's Cultural Revolution," *Fortune,* 15 June 1981, p. 76. Along these lines, Rensis Likert commented that changes in management practices toward increased participation (System 4) *"apparently require an appreciable period of time before the impact is fully manifest in corresponding improvement in the end-result variables"* [*The Human Organization: Its Management and Value* (New York: McGraw-Hill, 1967), p. 81; italics in original].

**46** *Report from the Center for Creative Leadership,* 5 (Feb. 1978), 2.

**47** "Aetna: Where Group Management Didn't Work," *Business Week,* 16 Feb. 1976, p. 77.

**48** Ibid.

**49** Joseph L. Krieger and Joe W. Lee, "Productivity Improvement through Use of Quality Control Circles: Concepts and Practices in Historical and Cultural Perspectives," *Proceedings, Eastern Academy of Management* (1982), p. 56.

**50** Sud R. Ingle, "There Is No Limit to What We Can Do Together," *BNAC Communicator,* 2 (Spring 1982), 4; also see Dan Shannon, "Productivity: Quality Circles for Supermarkets," *New York Times,* 18 April 1982, p. F19.

**51** Roy G. Foltz, "QWL's Effect on Productivity," *Personnel Administrator,* 27 (May 1982), 20; Mary T. Kohler and Everett R. Wells, "Quality Circles at Hughes Aircraft," *National Productivity Review,* 1 (Summer 1982), 312; Thomas J. Peters and Robert H. Waterman, Jr., *In Search of Excellence,* pp. 60, 277. It might be noted that QCs are given different names in different organizations: e.g., "employee participation groups" (GM), "involvement teams" (Motorola, Control Data), "people involvement programs" (Texas Instruments).

**52** Thomas J. Peters and Robert H. Waterman, Jr., *In Search of Excellence,* pp. 241–242; also "Test Your Company's Climate before Installing Quality Circles," *Training/HRD,* 19 (Nov. 1982), 13; see also William B. Werther, Jr., "Quality Circles: Key Executive Issues," *Journal of Contemporary Business,* 11, No. 2 (1982), 20.

**53** William B. Werther, Jr., "Quality Circles," pp. 18–21.

**54** Gerald D. Klein, "Implementing Quality Circles: A Hard Look at Some of the Realities," *Personnel,* 58 (Nov.–Dec. 1981), 14–16; also see Robert Wood, Frank Hull, and Koya Azumi, "Evaluating Quality Circles: The American Application," *California Management Review,* 26 (Fall 1983), 49.

**55** "Quality Circles Grow, Stirring Union Worries," *Wall Street Journal,* 22 Sept. 1981, p. 29.

**56** Roland A Dumas, "QCs' Critical Ingredient," *Training,* 20 (June 1983), 15.

**57** Charles G. Burck, "What Happens When Workers Manage Themselves," *Fortune,* 27 June 1981, p. 65. Similarly, William B. Werther, Jr., "Quality Circles," has noted that successful implementation requires more than the decision by top management to "get some circles started" (p. 18).

**58** Nina G. Hatvany, comment during her presentation, "Japanese Management Practices and Productivity," at the BNA conference, "Current Directions in Productivity—Evolving Japanese and American Practices," 22 Mar. 1982 (New York City).

**59** William B. Werther, Jr., "Quality Circles," p. 22. Furthermore, given that facilitators can typically handle about 10 QCs, adding 100 QCs would require an additional 10 facilitators. Because facilitators should be well known to organizational participants, finding 10 such people may not be an easy task. See also William B. Werther, Jr., "Quality Circles and Corporate Culture," *National Productivity Review,* 1 (Summer 1982), 304.

60  "Test Your Company's Climate before Installing Quality Circles," p. 13; also William B. Werther, Jr., "Quality Circles,," pp. 25–26.

61  Nina Hatvany and Vladimir Pucik, "Japanese Management in America: What Does and Doesn't Work," *National Productivity Review,* 1 (Winter 1981–1982), 71; also see Yoshi Tsurumi, "Japanese Productivity," *The Dial,* 2 (Sept. 1981), 48–49. Tsurumi notes: "Most Japanese managers recognize that establishing QCs is not the first but the last step in building a company's commitment to product quality and productivity."

62  Nina Hatvany and Vladimir Pucik, "Japanese Management in America," p. 71.

63  Mignon Mazique, "The Quality Circle Transplant," *Issues & Observations,* 1 (May 1981), 2–4; also William B. Werther, Jr., "Quality Circles," p. 20.

64  Kenichi Ohmae, "Quality Control Circles: They Work and Don't Work," *Wall Street Journal,* 29 Mar. 1982, p. 18.

65  Robert Wood, Frank Hull, and Koya Azumi, "Evaluating Quality Circles," p. 49.

66  "How Quality Circles Work in the U.S.," *Resource,* Nov. 1982, p. 9.

67  "Honeywell Quality Circles: Part of a Growing American Trend," *Journal of Organizational Behavior Management,* 3, No. 4 (1981–1982), 99.

68  Ronald N. Ashkenas and Todd D. Jick, "Productivity and QWL Success without Ideal Conditions," *National Productivity Review,* 1 (Autumn 1982), 383.

69  Dan Shannon, "Productivity," p. F19.

70  Robert Wood, Frank Hull, and Koya Azumi, "Evaluating Quality Circles," p. 43.

71  Kenneth D. Ramsing and John D. Blair, "An Expression of Concern about Quality Circles," *Proceedings, 42nd Annual National Meeting of the Academy of Management* (1982), p. 326. Further, as Wood et al. have noted, success stories should be viewed somewhat skeptically because "those telling the story are often either the managers responsible for the program or consultants who are selling QCs. The story tellers have something to gain" ("Evaluating Quality Circles," p. 13).

72  Robert Wood, Frank Hull, and Koya Azumi, "Evaluating Quality Circles," p. 43.

73  Ibid., pp. 44–46.

74  Leighton F. Smith, comments during presentation, "Japan's Industrial Environment," at the Arthur Andersen & Co. conference, "Productivity: The Japanese Formula," 13 Oct. 1981 (New York City); Smith was also quoted in Roy G. Foltz, "QWL's Effect on Productivity," p. 20.

75  Kenneth D. Ramsing and John D. Blair, "Concern about Quality Circles," p. 327. Robert Cole is the director at the Center for Japanese Studies at the University of Michigan. In his survey of 176 companies that had adopted QCs as of 1981, 60 percent were lukewarm or unhappy with the results. See Jeremy Main, "The Trouble with Managing Japanese-Style," 2 Apr. 1984, p. 50.

76  Yoshi Tsurumi, "Japanese Productivity," p. 49.

77  R. Wood, F. Hull, and K. Azumi, "Evaluating Quality Circles," p. 24; also see Gerald D. Klein, "Implementing Quality Circles," pp. 17–20.

78  Other books include Satoshi Kamata's *Japan in the Passing Lane: An Insider's Account of Life in a Japanese Auto Factory,* (New York: Pantheon Books, 1983) and Ezra F. Vogel's *Japan as Number One: Lessons for America.* (Cambridge, Mass.: Harvard University Press, 1979).

79  Nina Hatvany and Vladimir Pucik, "Japanese Management: Practices and Produc-

tivity," *Organizational Dynamics,* 9 (Spring 1981), 7, italics in original; © 1981 AMACOM, a division of American Management Associations, New York. All rights reserved. Reprinted by permission of the publisher.

**80** Ibid., pp. 16–17; © 1981 AMACOM, a division of American Management Associations, New York. All rights reserved. Reprinted by permission of the publisher. Also see Yoshimatsu Aonuma, "A Japanese Explains Japan's Business Style," *Across The Board,* 18 (Feb. 1981), 49; also see Wilfrid C. Rodgers, "How to Raise Productivity," *Boston Globe,* 16 May 1981, p. 16.

**81** Arnold Abrams, "Japanese Cars Find Ohio Roots," *Newsday,* 5 Dec. 1982, pp. 7, 98; also John Holusha, "Honda Plant Brings Touch of Japan to Ohio," *New York Times,* 26 Apr. 1983, pp. 1, D23.

**82** Chris Wada, comments during presentation, "Sony Company Productivity Concepts and Practices," at the BNA conference, "Current Directions in Productivity—Evolving Japanese and American Practices," Mar. 22, 1982 (New York City); also see Wilfrid C. Rodgers, "How to Raise Productivity," p. 16.

**83** Chris Wada, "Sony Company Productivity Concepts and Practices."

**84** William G. Ouchi, *Theory Z,* pp. 36–37; also see Yoshimatsu Aonuma, "A Japanese Explains," p. 48. As Hatvany and Pucik, "Japanese Management," noted, the process of *ringi* does not require unanimous approval; rather what is sought is the unanimous consent to implement a decision—i.e., opposing parties may lend consent knowing that their views may be adopted at a later time (pp. 15–16).

**85** Kae H. Chung and Margaret Ann Gray, in "Can We Adopt the Japanese Methods of Human Resources Management?" *Personnel Administrator,* 27 (May 1982), 43, estimate that 12.5 percent of Japanese workers participate in QCs. However, Hirotaka Takeuchi, in his article "Productivity: Learning from the Japanese" [*California Management Review,* 23 (Summer 1981), 9], estimates a participation rate of up to 20 percent.

**86** Chris Wada, "Sony Company Productivity Concepts and Practices."

**87** *Newsweek,* 8 July 1974, p. 60.

**88** John Holusha, "Japan's Productive Car Unions," *New York Times,* 30 Mar. 1983, p. D19.

**89** Chris Wada, "Sony Company Productivity Concepts and Procedures."

**90** Ibid.

**91** William G. Ouchi, *Theory Z,* pp. 35–36.

**92** In this regard, Thomas J. Peters and Robert H. Waterman, Jr. (*In Search of Excellence*) quote extensively from the writings of academics. For example, they cite Selznick's comment that leadership involves "the reworking of human and technological materials to fashion an organization that embodies new and enduring values" (p. 85). Andrew Pettigrew's conception of the leadership role is also noted: the leader "is the creator of symbols, ideologies, language, beliefs, rituals, and myths" (p. 104). Moreover, Joanne Martin is noted for observing that organizations are "systems composed of ideas, the meaning of which must be managed" (p. 104).

**93** Thomas J. Peters and Robert H. Waterman, Jr., *In Search of Excellence,* p. 86.

**94** Gary A. Yukl, *Leadership in Organizations,* pp. 70, 90–91.

**95** J. B. Ritchie, "Supervision," p. 62.

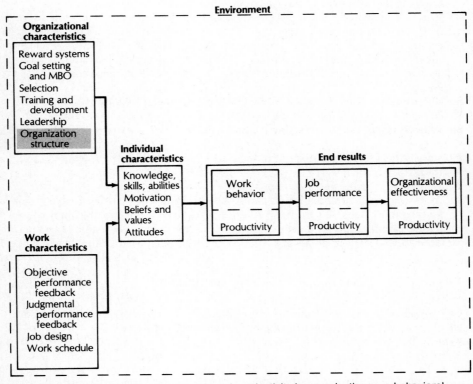

Conceptual framework of the determinants of productivity in organizations—a behavioral science approach.

# CHAPTER 8

# ORGANIZATION STRUCTURE

Metaphorically speaking, organization structure is the skeleton of the organizational entity; it provides the frame for the managerial processes, systems, and behaviors which emerge and develop. Of course, conceptual clarity requires greater precision in the definition of terms; accordingly, this is the first issue addressed in this chapter. Next, some limitations in the research literature are noted, along with general reactions to organization structure interventions. Subsequently, the empirical research evidence pertinent to the most widely examined dimensions of organization structure is reviewed. Although the empirical literature is extensive, almost all studies have been correlational; very few experiments have been reported. The empirical data are therefore supplemented somewhat liberally with opinions and brief descriptive accounts of structural interventions.

## DEFINITIONS AND LIMITATIONS

The term *organization structure* refers to the formal arrangements that exist in an organization, that is, (1) how jobs are defined and combined (specialization, formalization, departmentalization), (2) the distribution of authority, responsibility, and control (centralization, coordination), and (3) the size and shape of the organization (the number of organization members, the number of levels, span of control, administrative intensity). The discussion in this chapter examines seven dimensions of organization structure.

Frequently, a distinction is made between the intended, designed, idealized (or preferred) set of *formal* organizational arrangements (which are often documented on paper in organization charts and position descriptions) and the actual, "living," emergent set of *informal* arrangements that exist. This distinction is important conceptually and empirically. Researchers have used diverse methods of measuring organization structure: some have relied on written documents (the so-called "institutional measures" which emphasize intended formal arrangements) and others have used questionnaire surveys ("perceptual measures" which highlight existing informal arrangements). Not surprisingly, institutional and perceptual measures have shown low convergence, empirically.[1]

Many studies have been conducted regarding organization structure. Indeed, two recent reviews examined nearly 200 relevant works.[2] Yet most of the empirical literature has dealt with (1) interrelationships between structural dimensions (e.g., the relationship between centralization and formalization) and (2) relationships between structural dimensions and various nonperformance variables (e.g., employee attitudes, climate, and job satisfaction). In one review article, Dan Dalton and his associates observed that "the association between structural variables and performance . . . has largely been ignored."[3]

Unfortunately, the studies pertinent to organizational effectiveness that do exist have yielded few consistent findings. Dalton and associates concluded that "The literature on structure-performance relationships is among the most vexing and ambiguous in the field of management and organizational behavior. Evaluations and generalizations concerning the nature and directions of these relationships are tenuous."[4] Why has this been so? Several explanations might be advanced. First, there has been great diversity in conceptualizations of organization structure. Some theorists have identified 3 dimensions, others, 7 or 8 dimensions; and one writer has identified 16 different dimensions.[5] Further, operational measures have varied as well: there are at least 10 different operational measures of the construct, centralization. Second, to the extent that interrelationships exist among structural dimensions, results have likely been affected by the combination of variables examined (and how the interdependencies are handled). Third, studies have focused on different units of analysis, some on entire organizations, others on subunits (departments, work groups), and still others on different jobs. Fourth, results have also varied because of differences in many important nonstructural variables. Comparing data across organizations, for example, assumes constancy in such key factors as strategy, operating systems, managerial styles, employee skills, financial resources, and technology. As Peters and Waterman have noted, organization structure is "only a small part of the total issue of management effectiveness. The very word 'organizing,' for instance, begs the question, 'Organize for what?'"[6]

## SOME GENERAL VIEWS

Often, structural solutions are viewed as cures for all organizational ills. Peter Drucker has commented that many "businesses, especially large and complex ones, suffer from the disease of 'organizitis.' . . . Reorganization is going on all

the time. . . . And no organizational solution ever lasts long, indeed few organizational arrangements are even given enough time to be tested and worked
out in practice."[7] Apparently this phenomenon is not new. Consider the observations of Petronius (ca. 66 A.D.):

> We trained hard . . . but every time we were beginning to form into teams, we would
> be reorganized. I was to learn later in life that we tend to meet any new situation by
> reorganizing—and what a wonderful method it can be for creating the illusion of
> progress while producing inefficiency and demoralization.[8]

Although most managers and consultants know *intellectually* that the formal organization structure—the boxes, charts, dotted lines, position descriptions and the like—is not the organization, but only a schematization of it, too
often managers and consultants act as if structural changes necessarily produce
changes in work behavior and organizational functioning.[9] A few years ago a
task force assembled by McKinsey & Company contacted consultants and
executives who were known for their skill and experience in organization
design. The task force found that "All were disillusioned about the usual structural solutions. . . . Not suprisingly, then, a single blunt instrument—like structure—is unlikely to prove the master tool that can change organizations with
best effect."[10]

Apart from the general opinions about structural interventions, a good deal
of research and writing has been conducted. The findings are reviewed in the
next section. The reader should be cautioned, though, that since most studies
were correlational, assessment of the impact of structural variations in terms
of productivity is difficult.

## RESEARCH ON STRUCTURAL DIMENSIONS
### Size

Anecdotal evidence supports the idea that organization size is negatively
related to effectiveness, in other words, it supports the idea that smaller is better. At Motorola, for example, president John Mitchell has observed that
"something just seems to go wrong when you get more [than 1000] people
under one roof. . . . somehow, like magic, things start to go wrong."[11] Similarly,
Gordon Engdahl of 3M has stated that "We are keenly aware of the disadvantages of large size. We make a conscious effort to keep our units as small as
possible because we think it helps keep them flexible and vital. When one gets
too large, we break it apart. We like to say that our success in recent years
amounts to multiplication by division."[12] Indeed, of 3M's 91 manufacturing
plants in the United States, only 5 employ more than 1000 people. While the
mean number of employees per unit is 270, the median is but 115.[13] One more
illustration: Johnson & Johnson, a $5-billion company, consists of 150 inde-
pendent divisions each with average sales of just over $30 million. Chief exec-
utive James Burke asserts, "We have periodically studied the economics of
consolidation . . . [however] we believe that a lot of the efficiencies you are sup-

posed to get from economies of scale are not real at all. They are elusive. Once you get your big monster going, you are going to create inefficiencies that you don't know are there."[14]

In their survey of "excellent" companies, Peters and Waterman reported finding many examples of small 10-person project groups "that were regularly more innovative than fully equipped R&D and engineering groups with casts of hundreds."[15] In a wide variety of settings and *"in almost every case,"* Peters and Waterman found that the small unit was more efficient because its staff was better motivated than those in large facilities.[16] A second explanation was, also advanced: small size leads to rapid action which accelerates learning; in contrast, large size entails high costs of communication and decision making which often overwhelm technologically determined economies of scale. In light of these findings (which certainly could be better documented), Peters and Waterman concluded:

> Regardless of industry, it seems that more than 500 or so people under one roof causes substantial and unanticipated problems. More significant, even for the cost-oriented companies, small is not only more innovative but also more productive.[17]

Survey data, relating size to various indicators of organizational effectiveness, are not nearly so clear-cut. With respect to *total* organizational size, seventeen systematic surveys have been conducted. No reliable relationship has emerged between total size and three effectiveness measures: financial success, labor relations, and turnover. There is some limited evidence, though, that larger organizations experience greater absenteeism;[18] but this may merely reflect the existence of a paid sick leave program.

As Peters and Waterman would have predicted, evidence indicates that *subunit* size is negatively related to organizational performance and positively related to absenteeism and turnover. The larger the size of the subunit, the lower the level of performance (in 5 out of 6 cases), the higher the rate of absenteeism (in 9 out of 11 studies), and the higher the rate of turnover (in 3 out of 4 cases).[19] Perhaps the existence of relationships at the subunit level but not at the total organizational level reflects the reduced impact of other variables (e.g., technology) *within* organizations as compared to *across* organizations.

In two studies (one involving subunits, the other entire organizations), size was positively related to performance on structured, routine tasks, but negatively related to performance on unstructured, ambiguous tasks.[20] Yet the positive relationship between size and performance on structured tasks may be only transitory. Hull, Hage, and Azumi found that the most cost-effective (and generally large) factories in the early 1970s were more likely to be out of business in the 1980s than their less cost-effective (and smaller) counterparts.[21] Apparently, large facilities tend to be less adaptive, which threatens their long-term survival. The following case study provides a dramatic illustration.

> Ten years ago Ford Motor Co. built a plant to produce 500,000 tons of iron engine blocks a year. Erected on the principle that mass production means lower costs, it was four stories high and large enough to enclose 72 football fields. But the plant,

designed to produce V-8 engines, turned out to be too big and too specialized. When new designs for lighter engines followed the oil crunch, Ford discovered that retooling the huge plant was prohibitively expensive. It shut down the factory, moving operations to a 30-year-old, smaller plant.[22]

## Shape

A widely discussed dimension of organization structure is *shape,* the number of levels in the hierarchy (also referred to as vertical differentiation). Organizations with many levels are usually described as tall, those with few levels, as flat. Conceptually, organization shape is one aspect of organizational complexity; other components include the number of departments (horizontal differentiation) and the number of job titles (specialization). A fourth, and infrequently examined, aspect of complexity is the spatial dispersion of subunits.

There is a diverse, but far from rigorous, body of evidence pertinent to the effects of organization shape on effectiveness. It would appear, from anecdotal accounts, that flat organizations fare better than tall ones. It may not be entirely due to chance, for instance, that highly successful Japanese companies generally have flatter shapes than comparable U.S. firms. Whereas there are five levels between the chairman and the first-line supervisor at Toyota, at Ford there are more than fifteen. Not surprisingly, Ford recently cut more than one-quarter of its middle management staff.[23] One steel company in the U.S. which formerly had thirty-two levels between the president and hourly workers now operates with eighteen.[24] At Brunswick Corporation, president Jack F. Reichert has mandated that no more than six layers of management separate him from any employee. Crown Zellerbach recently eliminated three layers of management.[25]

Summarizing the results of their survey of "excellent" companies, Peters and Waterman concluded:

> We found . . . *less layering* at most of the excellent companies. . . . Excessive layering may be the biggest problem of the slow-moving, rigid bureaucracy . . . a kind of Parkinson's law of management structure sets in: extra levels of management mainly create distracting work for others to justify their own existence. Everyone appears busy; but in reality it is simple management featherbedding.[26]

Echoing this point, management consultant Frederick Hornbruch argues that too many organizational levels "is almost a guarantee that the organization will be afflicted with corporate artereosclerosis." Yet, "In these times of accelerating kaleidoscopic change, an organization must be dynamic."[27]

Certainly the case of Nucor Corporation, a steel company, is consistent with these opinions. It is indisputable that Nucor has performed well in the steel business. Between 1971 and 1980 sales rose from $65 million to $480 million while profits rose from under $3 million to more than $45 million. Yet in 1981 there were only five levels in the entire organization: the chief executive officer, vice presidents and general managers, department managers, supervisors and professionals, and nonexempt employees. There were no executive vice presidents or group vice presidents, no assistant vice presidents or group managers, no assistant managers or deputy assistants.[28]

Four surveys have examined the relationship between number of hierarchical levels and measures of organizational effectiveness. In three of these cases a negative relationship was found.[29] One study, a survey of forty-four Japanese industrial organizations, found a significant negative association between number of levels and innovativeness (defined in terms of patents per employee). In the fourth study, a curvilinear relationship emerged; effectiveness was highest with three or fewer, or six or more levels.[30]

### Administrative Intensity

*Administrative intensity* is the ratio of administrative (supervisory, staff, clerical) employees to production employees. Clearly, there is an overlap between administrative intensity and organizational shape: tall organizations tend to have more administrative personnel. As might be expected, the weight of opinion is that administrative intensity is negatively related (detrimental) to organizational performance.

John Cicco, a management consultant, has noted that as companies grow they tend to devote proportionately less and less time and effort to producing goods and services. Hence, Cicco states, "a firm's productivity is inversely related to the time spent managing it."[31]

In light of the trend toward increased administrative intensity, J. W. Forrester of MIT has argued that increased productivity is *not* an efficient solution to problems of low organizational (or national) productivity growth. He reasons that administrative (overhead) personnel have grown to represent as much as 90 percent of the working population in government and some service industries; and even in manufacturing an indirect labor force of 75 percent of total employees is quite common. Thus, higher productivity among the small fraction of employees who directly produce goods and services will have little impact—and possibly no impact if a corresponding increase occurs in overhead (e.g., people who expedite, monitor, study, manage, arbitrate, and regulate). Forrester suggests, therefore, that instead of attempting to improve productivity directly, the focus should be on reversing the trend out of production. Put simply, increasing the proportion of the work force in direct production from 10 to 20 percent would virtually double productive efficiency.[32]

Many corporations are now adopting this perspective. In the words of Jack F. Reichert of Brunswick Corporation, "We've been rewarding bookkeepers as if they created wealth. U.S. business has to make more beans rather than count them several times."[33] Acting on this view, Brunswick recently eliminated the positions of chief operating officer and group vice president, cut the headquarters staff by 40 percent, and required divisions to report directly to the chief executive.[34] Along these lines, recent reductions in managerial staffs have approximated 20 percent at Firestone, 40 percent at Chrysler, 20 percent at Crown Zellerbach, and 15 percent at Alcoa. General Electric cut its strategic planning department by 60 percent and expanded the authority of general managers.[35]

At Chrysler it is now a cardinal rule that new ideas can pass through no more than five executives.[36] Presumably, the intent is to avoid confirming Mollison's bureaucracy hypothesis: "If an idea can survive a bureaucratic review and be implemented, it wasn't worth doing."[37]

A common corollary of a high degree of administrative intensity is an elaborate system of checks and balances. Typically, checks and balances result in forms and documents that must be prepared, circulated, computerized, accounted for, and filed. As a consequence, decision making tends to get bogged down. A former manager at a large corporation commented:

> What should have taken two weeks to a month took two years. The checks and balances were such that they precluded you from making a colossal mistake, but they also precluded you from [developing] something that was unique and novel and revolutionary.[38]

Unfortunately, only a limited amount of systematic survey evidence is available on the effects of administrative intensity. Two out of the three studies conducted during the past two decades found a negative relationship between administrative intensity and measures of organizational performance.[39] These results are generally consistent with the opinions and anecdotes cited above. Another study, a survey of Japanese industrial companies, found that administrative intensity was negatively related to economic performance (sales per employee) but positively related to innovativeness (patents per employee).[40] This latter finding is not surprising given the criterion of patents per employee: production workers are far less likely to be awarded patents than are administrative personnel (such as technical professionals).

### Horizontal Differentiation and Specialization

As previously noted, two dimensions of organizational complexity are *horizontal differentiation* (the number of different departments in an organization, or sections per department), and *specialization* (the number of different job titles). Logically, a high level of horizontal differentiation or specialization should complicate internal communication and slow decision-making processes, thereby impairing organizational effectiveness. Empirically, however, no clear-cut relationships have emerged between horizontal differentiation and specialization, on the one hand, and various measures of organizational performance, on the other.[41] The weight of evidence suggests a tendency toward a negative association, though, when the criterion is productive efficiency.[42] Results have been mixed with respect to the criterion of innovativeness. Horizontal differentiation and specialization were negatively related to innovativeness in two surveys of profit-seeking organizations, and positively related to innovativeness in two surveys of nonprofit organizations.[43] It might be noted that while the former studies used relatively objective measures of innovativeness (patents and awards), the latter studies used subjective judgments of innovativeness.

## Span of Control

As conventionally defined, *span of control* refers to the number of subordinates a manager supervises. Although the optimal span of control was widely discussed many years ago, little empirical research has been conducted on this issue. Because a wide span of control is consistent with general, rather than close, supervision and with delegation of decision-making authority, it has been argued that a wide span promotes high employee motivation, productivity, and innovation. Unfortunately, it appears that only two empirical studies have been conducted during the past two decades. George Farris found a positive relationship between span of control and performance in a longitudinal study of engineers.[44] More recently, Barry Armandi and Edgar Mills, in a survey of savings and loan associations, reported a positive relationship between the number of people reporting to the president and profitability.[45] The limited evidence available is therefore consistent with the premise that a wide span of control enhances productivity. Three caveats should be noted, though. First, it is likely that too wide a span has deleterious effects; hence, a curvilinear relationship probably exists. Second, it is not clear whether span of control functions more as a cause or as an effect of organizational performance. Third, because a wide span of control is usually accompanied by decentralized decision making and general supervision, it may be these latter factors that predominantly influence performance.

## Centralization

In centralized organizations authority (or decision-making power) is of course concentrated at the upper levels of the hierarchy; in decentralized organizations relatively more authority is delegated to lower levels (the "lowerarchy"). Concomitant with the trend toward smaller organization size, many companies are pushing authority far down the hierarchy. For example, each of Dana Corporation's approximately ninety operating units is headed by a manager with full authority for virtually all functions. These individuals (called "store managers") are responsible for developing unit financial control systems, and for making all decisions regarding purchasing and personnel—functions commonly centralized in large companies.[46] At 3M, an organization that has been described as "radically decentralized," each of the forty divisions shares a common goal: 25 percent of current sales must come from products that did not exist 5 years before.[47]

A growing number of large companies, many with a history of centralized decision making, have been headed toward greater decentralization. Crown Zellerbach, a forest products company, has "sawn off" three layers of management from its container group, leaving plant managers accountable for plant success or failure. Each of the container group's sixteen plant managers is now responsible for credit, labor, marketing, and sales decisions.[48] Similarly, at Xerox, general managers of the company's twenty-four strategic business units now pick the products they want to develop and the technologies they will use, decisions that were formerly made by corporate headquarters staffs. In fact, most of the corporate staffs at Xerox no longer exist, or they have had their size and power drastically cut. A *Business Week* article asserted that the "redistribution of power resulted in a substantial decline in the time it takes Xerox to develop new products along with big reductions in manufacturing costs."[49]

Peters and Waterman found that "virtually all of the [excellent] companies we talked to placed high value on pushing authority far down the line, and on preserving and maximizing practical autonomy for large numbers of people."[50] Regarding future management practice, Peters offers the following prediction: "Look at the way truly decentralized companies outperform centralized companies ... it's a trend that [will] force itself on even the most reluctant CEOs."[51]

One obstacle to decentralizing is that delegation of decision-making authority implies an organizational climate that supports risk taking. Not many managers will exercise initiative and stick their necks out if top management is intolerant of mistakes. John Savage of Nucor Corporation, describes his company's climate as follows:

> I remember when I first started to work for Nucor and I was sitting down with Ken Iverson, president of Nucor. Ken told me, "John, you are going to make at least three mistakes with this company in the first few years that you are with us. Each one of these mistakes is probably going to cost us $50,000. I want you to be aggressive and I want you to make decisions and I just want to provide one word of caution. We don't mind you making the mistakes but please just don't make them all in one year."[52]

Survey data regarding the effects of decentralization are not so clear cut, however, at least not at first glance. Fourteen studies have examined the relationship between degree of centralization and judgmental ("soft") measures of organizational effectiveness such as rated performance and alienation. In six cases centralization was negatively related to effectiveness criteria (as might be predicted), and in eight cases no association was found.[53] Turning to studies employing relatively objective ("hard") effectiveness measures, three found centralization to be negatively related to performance, one reported no relationship, and five found centralization to be positively related to performance.[54] For example, in two studies of human service organizations, a high degree of centralization was associated with (1) less employee concern about larger, organizational issues and (2) increased time available for direct service delivery. Perhaps, therefore, the effects of centralization on organizational effectiveness are influenced by task complexity: where tasks are simple, well understood, and repetitive, centralization may be more efficient; where tasks are complex and nonrepetitive, decentralization may be more efficient. Certainly, there is a substantial body of evidence supporting such a contingency approach to organization design.[55]

With respect to the criterion of innovativeness, two studies (one of Japanese, the other of American industrial organizations) reported a negative relationship between centralization and innovation (patents per employee).[56] Keeping in mind Peters and Waterman's definition of excellence (continuously innovative large companies), a certain degree of lawfulness emerges from the research to date. When organizational effectiveness is defined in terms of innovativeness, or when technology is complex, requiring innovative solutions, centralization is generally negatively related to organizational success.

The limited number of field experiments to date that have focused on structural changes have primarily dealt with decentralization. Studies reporting objective performance data have employed such changes as the creation of cross-functional problem-solving teams, decentralization of the management of subunit operations, and the establishment of a task force to design changes in operations. In these experiments, structural changes have produced a median increase in productivity of 12.4 percent.[57] Ironically, although many management writers have expressed pessimism about structural solutions, the effects in the limited number of studies reported to date have been consistently positive and quite robust.

### Formalization

Although definitions vary, conceptualizations of *formalization* generally focus on the extent to which organizational rules, procedures, role definitions, and internal communications are written and explicit rather than oral and implicit. In effect, to the extent that formalization exists, role clarity should be improved and the behavior of role incumbents should be standardized and predictable.

On the basis of 41 years of experience at IBM, Clair Vough has observed that it is relatively easy to increase organizational formalization; however, elimination of written rules and procedures requires many approvals and carries considerable risk for the proposer. Indicative of this phenomenon, Vough points out that the purchasing manual at IBM "fills two volumes, even though its essential substance could be boiled down to two pages."[58] Admiringly, Vough notes that Dana Corporation has reduced a full volume of procedures to a folded, pocket-size card.[59]

Fifteen surveys have examined the relationship between degree of formalization and indices of organizational performance. In eight studies positive relationships were found; four studies reported no association; two found a negative relationship; and one found a positive association when the environment was stable, but a negative association when the environment was turbulent.[60] All told, the weight of evidence suggests that formalization generally enhances organizational performance, especially when task complexity is low. Apparently, the advantages of role clarity outweigh the possible disadvantages associated with increased standardization (i.e., the individual is less able to "do his own thing").

Yet formalization may be detrimental to innovativeness, to creativity, and, therefore, to the long-term survival of the organization. Comments Fletcher Byrom of Koppers, "Of all the things that I have observed in corporations, the most disturbing has been a tendency toward over-organization, producing a rigidity that is intolerable in an era of rapidly accelerating change."[61] Two surveys have examined the relationship between formalization and innovation. In both cases, a negative association was found.[62] Thus, a dilemma exists: organizations may have to choose between (1) standardization, conformity, and short-term efficiency and (2) creativity, adaptability, and long-term viability.

## SUMMARY

A review of the systematic survey evidence indicates that it is a risky business to offer universal prescriptions regarding organizational structuring: the research findings are not all that consistent. Yet the weight of evidence does suggest greater organizational productivity if (1) subunits are small, (2) there are relatively few hierarchical levels, (3) administrative intensity is controlled (e.g., not too many deputy assistants or staff specialists), (4) the structure is not too complex horizontally (e.g., it has a limited number of departments), and (5) managers have relatively wide spans of control. Where technology is relatively noncomplex and the environment relatively stable, evidence suggests that centralization of decision-making and a high degree of formalization promote efficiency. However, where technology is complex and the environment turbulent, organizations must be innovative: hence, decentralization, reduced formalization, and increased administrative intensity of technical professionals are functional.

In the short run, it appears that there is a trade-off between productive efficiency and innovativeness. Both aspects of organizational effectiveness are important, yet difficult to achieve simultaneously.[63] One approach to dealing with this dilemma is to subordinate one objective. Another approach is to adopt hybrid organization structures in which organizational arrangements vary across subunits. This approach is apparently widely practiced among Peters and Waterman's "excellent" companies; it is, reportedly, common for units to be "spun off" with an explicit mandate to be innovative.

While tension exists between concern for the short run and for the long run, the issue of organization structure is far from confused. Systematic evidence exists as to which approaches tend to work best and under what conditions.

## NOTES

1  Eric J. Walton, "The Comparison of Measures of Organization Structure," *Academy of Management Review,* 6 (1981), 155–160.
2  Dan R. Dalton, William D. Todor, Michael J. Spendolini, Gordon J. Fielding, and Lyman W. Porter, "Organization Structure and Performance: A Critical Review," *Academy of Management Review,* 5 (1980), 49–64; Louis W. Fry, "Technology-Structure Research: Three Critical Issues," *Academy of Management Journal,* 25 (1982), 532–552.

3 Dan R. Dalton et al., "Organization Structure and Performance," p. 49.

4 Ibid., p. 60.

5 Richard S. Blackburn, "Dimensions of Structure: A Review and Reappraisal," *Academy of Management Review,* 7 (1982), 59–66.

6 Thomas J. Peters and Robert H. Waterman, Jr., *In Search of Excellence: Lessons from America's Best-Run Companies* (New York: Harper & Row, 1982), p. 8.

7 Peter F. Drucker, *Management: Tasks, Responsibilities, Practices* (New York: Harper & Row, 1973), p. 549.

8 In Laurence J. Peter, *Peter's Quotations* (New York: William Morrow, 1977), p. 83. However, one Latin scholar, J. P. Sullivan, doubts the authenticity of this attribution to Petronius. See *Petronian Society Newsletter,* 11, Nos. 1/2, and 12, No. 1 (May 1981), p. 5.

9 Robert H. Waterman, Jr., Thomas J. Peters, and Julien R. Phillips, "Structure Is Not Organization," *Business Horizons,* 23 (June 1980), 14 (italics added).

10 Ibid., pp. 14, 16.

11 Thomas J. Peters and Robert H. Waterman, Jr., *In Search of Excellence,* pp. 32, 274.

12 *Wall Street Journal,* 5 Feb. 1982, p. 1.

13 Ibid. Parenthetically, an important facet of Japanese manufacturing methods is the so-called "focused factory." According to Leighton Smith, a consultant with Arthur Andersen & Co. (Tokyo), Japanese manufacturers typically employ no more than 300 persons at a given location. Smith made this observation in his talk, "Japan's Industrial Environment," at the conference, "Productivity: The Japanese Formula," Oct. 13, 1982 (New York City).

14 "The 88 Ventures of Johnson & Johnson," *Forbes,* 1 June 1972, p. 24. Also see Thomas J. Peters and Robert H. Waterman, Jr., *In Search of Excellence,* pp. 309–310.

15 Ibid., pp. 112–113.

16 Ibid., p. 321, italics in original.

17 Ibid., p. 275. See also Norman Macrae's article, "Intrapreneurial Now: Big Goes Bust," in *The Economist,* 17 Apr. 1982, pp. 67–72. Macrae notes that "Since the mid-1960s the thousand biggest firms in the United States have as a group been sensibly reducing their labour forces, and more than the whole of the 15m [million] private-sector jobs created since then have come in smaller firms—the majority of the new extra jobs at any one time being in firms less than five years old. . ." (p. 67).

18 See Dan R. Dalton et al., "Organization Structure and Performance," pp. 51–54; also see Judith R. Blau, and William McKinley, "Ideas, Complexity, and Innovation," *Administrative Science Quarterly,* 24 (1979), pp. 200–219; also see Charles A. Glisson and Patricia Yancey Martin, "Productivity and Efficiency in Human Service Organizations as Related to Structure, Size, and Age," *Academy of Management Journal,* 23 (1980), pp. 21–37; also see Koya Azumi and Frank Hull, "Predictors of Productivity and Innovation in Japanese Factories," *Proceedings, 19th Annual Meeting of the Eastern Academy of Management* (1982), pp. 59–64. It should be noted that the 17 surveys did not each examine all three criterion variables.

19 Dan R. Dalton et al., "Organization Structure and Performance," pp. 51–54.

20 Robert C. Cummins and Donald C. King, "The Interaction of Group Size and Task Structure in an Industrial Organization," *Personnel Psychology,* 26 (1973), 87–94; also Frank Hull and Jerald Hage, "A Systems Approach to Productivity and Inno-

vation in Industrial Organizations," unpublished Working Paper A-1 (Dec. 1981), Rutgers University, pp. 1–43. These two studies were not included with the surveys previously mentioned.

21 Frank Hull, Jerald Hage, and Koya Azumi, "Innovation and Organization Design: America vs. Japan," a preliminary report to the National Science Foundation, Feb. 1983.

22 Thomas J. Peters and Robert H. Waterman, Jr., *In Search of Excellence,* p. 112.

23 Ibid., p. 313.

24 Comment by Carla S. O'Dell, during her talk at the Conference Board conference, "Compensation Planning and the Recession," Nov. 3, 1983 (New York City).

25 "The Shrinking of Middle Management," special report in *Business Week,* 25 Apr. 1983, pp. 54, 56.

26 Thomas J. Peters and Robert H. Waterman, Jr., *In Search of Excellence,* p. 270, italics in original; also see the comments of D. L. "Dutch" Landen in the *National Productivity Review,* 1 (1982), 349.

27 Frederick W. Hornbruch, Jr., *Raising Productivity: Ten Case Histories and Their Lessons* (New York: McGraw-Hill, 1977), p. 197.

28 John Savage, "Incentive Programs at Nucor Corporation Boost Productivity," *Personnel Administrator,* 26 (Aug. 1981), 33–34.

29 See Koya Azumi and Frank Hull, "Predictors of Productivity," pp. 62–63; also Edwin M. Bridges, Wayne F. Doyle, and David J. Mahan, "Effects of Hierarchical Differentiation on Group Productivity, Efficiency, and Risk Taking," *Administrative Science Quarterly,* 13 (1968), pp. 305–319; also John M. Ivancevich and James H. Donnelly, Jr., "Relation of Organizational Structure to Job Satisfaction, Anxiety-Stress, and Performance," *Administrative Science Quarterly,* 20 (1975), pp. 272–280; also Barry R. Armandi and Edgar W. Mills, Jr., "Organizational Structure and Efficiency: A Causal Analysis," paper presented at the 41st Annual Meeting of the Academy of Management, 1981, pp. 1–20.

30 Leo Meltzer and James Salter, "Organizational Structure and the Performance and Job Satisfaction of Physiologists," *American Sociological Review,* 27 (1962), pp. 351–362.

31 John A. Cicco, Jr., "Wanna Fix Your Firm?" *New York Times,* 5 Jan. 1982, p. A15.

32 Jay W. Forrester, "More Productivity Will Not Solve Our Problems," *Business and Society Review,* No. 35 (Fall 1980), p. 15. Also see John E. Ullmann, "Whitecollar Productivity and the Growth of Administrative Overhead," *National Productivity Review,* 1 (1982), 290–300.

33 "A New Era for Management," special report in *Business Week,* 25 Apr. 1983, p. 52.

34 "The Shrinking of Middle Management," p. 54.

35 Ibid., p. 56; "A New Era for Management," p. 52.

36 "The Shrinking of Middle Management," p. 56.

37 Mollison's Bureaucracy Hypothesis appeared in *The Industrial Psychologist,* 18 (May 1981), 7.

38 "The Shrinking of Middle Management," p. 55.

39 See Dan R. Dalton et al., "Organization Structure and Performance," pp. 53–57.

40 Koya Azumi and Frank Hull, "Predictors of Productivity," pp. 61–63.

41 See Dan R. Dalton et al., "Organization Structure and Performance," pp. 56–58.

42 Barry R. Armandi and Edgar W. Mills, Jr., "Organizational Structure and Efficiency"; Jerald Hage, "Theory Construction before Research: An Example with an

Axiomatic Theory of Organizations," unpublished paper, 1975 (cited by Armandi and Mills); and Koya Azumi and Frank Hull, "Predictors of Productivity," pp. 61–63.

**43** Koya Azumi and Frank Hull, "Predictors of Productivity"; Judith R. Blau and William McKinley, "Ideas, Complexity, and Innovation" (negative relationships); J. Victor Baldridge and Robert A. Burnham, "Organizational Innovation: Individual, Organizational, and Environmental Impacts," *Administrative Science Quarterly*, 20 (1975), 165–175; Jerald Hage and Robert Dewar, "Elite Values Versus Organizational Structure in Predicting Innovation," *Administrative Science Quarterly*, 18 (1973), 279–290 (positive relationships).

**44** George H. Farris, "Organization Factors and Individual Performance: A Longitudinal Study," *Journal of Applied Psychology*, 53 (1969), 87–92.

**45** Barry R. Armandi and Edgar W. Mills, Jr., "Organizational Structure and Efficiency."

**46** Thomas J. Peters and Robert H. Waterman, Jr., *In Search of Excellence*, p. 112.

**47** Ibid., pp. 232–233.

**48** "The Shrinking of Middle Management," pp. 54, 56.

**49** Ibid., p. 54.

**50** Thomas J. Peters and Robert H. Waterman, Jr., *In Search of Excellence*, p. 310.

**51** "The Shrinking of Middle Management," p. 54.

**52** John Savage, "Incentive Programs at Nucor Corporation Boost Productivity," *Personnel Administrator* 26 (Aug. 1981), p. 35. Copyright 1981, The American Society for Personnel Administration, 606 North Washington Street, Alexandria, Va. 22314. Reprinted by permission.

**53** See Dan R. Dalton et al., "Organization Structure and Performance," pp. 57–59.

**54** Negative relationships between centralization and performance were reported by Robert A. Luke, Jr., Peter Block, Jack M. Davey, and Vernon R. Averch, "A Structural Approach to Organization Change," *Journal of Applied Behavioral Science*, 9 (1973), 611–635; also Johannes M. Pennings, "Dimensions of Organizational Influence and Their Effectiveness Correlates," *Administrative Science Quarterly*, 21 (1976), pp. 688–699; also George G. Gordon and Bonnie E. Goldberg, "Is There a Climate for Success?" *Management Review*, 66 (May 1977), 37–44. No relationship was found by David G. Bowers, "Organization Control in an Insurance Company," *Sociometry*, 27 (1964), 230–244. Positive relationships were reported by Charles A. Glisson and Patricia Yancey Martin, "Productivity and Efficiency"; David A. Whetten, "Coping with Incompatible Expectations: An Integrated View of Role Conflict," *Administrative Science Quarterly*, 23 (1978), 254–271; Koya Azumi and Frank Hull, "Predictors of Productivity"; Jerald Hage, "Theory Construction before Research"; and Steven K. Paulson, "Causal Analysis of Interorganizational Relations: An Axiomatic Theory Revised," *Administrative Science Quarterly*, 19 (1974), pp. 319–337.

**55** An exhaustive review of the technology-structure literature is provided by Louis W. Fry in "Technology-Structure Research: Three Critical Issues," *Academy of Management Journal*, 25 (1982), pp. 532–552. Fry reports strong support for a technology-structure relationship. Moreover, there is evidence that the "fit" between technology and structure influences organizational success: e.g., Tom Burns and G. M. Stalker, *The Management of Innovation* (London: Tavistock, 1961); Joan Woodward, *Industrial Organization: Theory and Practice* (London: Oxford University Press, 1965); and Paul R. Lawrence and Jay W. Lorsch, *Organization and Environment* (Boston: Harvard Graduate School of Business Administration, 1967).

**56** Koya Azumi and Frank Hull, "Predictors of Productivity"; Frank Hull and Jerald Hage, "A Systems Approach."

**57** Pertinent studies and effects are as follows: Rossall J. Johnson, "Problem Resolution and Imposition of Change through a Participative Group Effort," *The Journal of Management Studies,* 11 (1974), 129–142 (12 percent reduction in delays); Rensis Likert, "Improving Cost Performance with Cross-Functional Teams," *Conference Board Record,* 12 No. 9 (1975), 51–59 (mean increase in productivity/production of 22 percent); Robert A. Luke, Jr., Peter Block, Jack M. Davey, and Vernon R. Averch, "A Structural Approach" (a 4.5 percent increase in sales); Stephen Schwartz, "Decentralizing a Community Mental Health Center's Service Delivery System," *Hospital & Community Psychiatry,* 25 (1974), 740–742 (12.4 percent more cases handled); Stephen A. Stumpf, "Using Integrators to Manage Conflict in a Research Organization," *Journal of Applied Behavioral Science,* 13 (1977), 507–517 (98 percent more reports).

**58** Clair F. Vough, *Productivity: A Practical Program for Improving Efficiency* (New York: Amacom, 1979), p. 145.

**59** Ibid.

**60** See Dan R. Dalton et al., "Organization Structure and Performance," for descriptions of seven field studies. Additional pertinent studies include those by Charles A. Glisson and Patricia Yancey Martin ("Productivity and Efficiency"), D. A. Whetten ("Coping with Incompatible Expectations"), Steven K. Paulson ("Causal Analysis of Interorganizational Relations"), Jerald Hage ("Theory Construction before Research"), Koya Azumi and Frank Hull ("Predictors of Productivity"), Barry R. Armandi and Edgar W. Mills, Jr. ("Organizational Structure and Efficiency"), Paul E. Mott [*The Characteristics of Effective Organizations* (New York: Harper and Row, 1972)], and J. J. Molnar and D. L. Rogers ["Organizational Effectiveness: An Empirical Comparison of the Goal and System Resource Approaches," *The Sociological Quarterly,* 17 (1976), 401–413].

**61** Speech delivered to Carnegie-Mellon Graduate School of Industrial Administration, 1976 (cited in Thomas J. Peters and Robert H. Waterman, Jr., *In Search of Excellence,* p. 50).

**62** Koya Azumi and Frank Hull, "Predictors of Productivity," pp. 61–63; Jerald Hage and Michael Aiken, "Program Change and Organizational Properties," *American Journal of Sociology,* 72 (1967), 503–519.

**63** In this regard Peter F. Drucker, *Management,* has commented that the innovative organization realizes that "maintenance of the present business is far too big a task for the people in it to have much time for creating the new, the different business of tomorrow. [Yet, innovative organizations] also realize that taking care of tomorrow is far too big and difficult a task to be diluted with concern for today. Both tasks have to be done. But they are different" (p. 799).

PART **THREE**

# IMPROVING PRODUCTIVITY: MODIFYING WORK CHARACTERISTICS

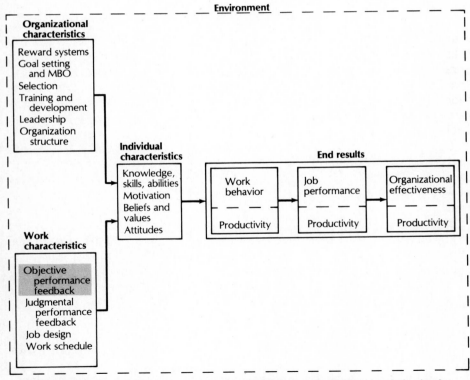

Conceptual framework of the determinants of productivity in organizations—a behavioral science approach.

# PERFORMANCE FEEDBACK: OBJECTIVE INDICATORS

During his first term as mayor of New York City, Ed Koch was often seen asking people in the street, "How'm I doing?" Responses, of course, varied: some constituents replied, "You're doing good"; others were less enthused. Evaluations tended to be both global and highly subjective. Few people provided specific, factual information, such as the percentage change in subway crime, or in unemployment. This chapter deals with the latter type of feedback—its effects and why and when it works.

*Objective feedback* is information about work behavior or job performance that is relatively factual and incontrovertible. Examples include days absent, miles per gallon, units produced. In contrast, many commonplace indicators of work behavior and job performance are relatively *subjective:* e.g., ratings of initiative, leadership skill, and sense of responsibility. Although it is tempting to consider the distinction between objective and subjective indicators as one of kind, it is really one of degree; all human measurement entails some degree of judgment. Measured output implies judgment about quality; and even attendance implies that the individual is both at work and working. Yet the distinction seems important: it is widely agreed that relatively objective indicators are preferable to relatively subjective ones. At the very minimum, they should provide more accurate information.

The results of 42 field studies that entailed the provision of objective feedback are reviewed next. It might be noted that research on objective feedback is a relatively recent phenomenon: 8 of the 42 studies were published in the 8 years from 1969 through 1976; the remaining 34 studies were published in the eight years from 1977 through 1984. In 14 of the interventions, the feedback pertained to work behaviors, i.e., to input processes related to *how* people attempt to accomplish goals. In 28 interventions feedback was provided concerning a variety of performance indicators, and in 13 of these studies feedback pertained to outputs. Consistent with the conceptual framework presented earlier (in Chapter 2), it is presumed that work behaviors are an antecedent of job performance, which in turn should be a determinant of outputs (goods produced, services performed).

### OBJECTIVE FEEDBACK: IMPACT ON WORK BEHAVIOR AND JOB PERFORMANCE

Table 9-1 summarizes the results of fourteen studies that examined the effects of objective feedback on behavioral criteria. The sample populations were highly diverse, including blue-collar workers, such as bus drivers, vehicle maintenance employees, kitchen workers, and white-collar workers, such as cashiers, telephone reservation clerks, and clinical therapists. Three methods of providing feedback were primarily employed: private individual feedback, public individual feedback, and public group feedback. Typically, feedback was used in conjunction with other interventions such as praise, public recognition, goal setting, and training. Results were obtained over treatment periods that ranged in duration from 1 week to 14 months, the median time period being 10.25 weeks. Increases in desired behaviors (or decreases in undesired behaviors) ranged from 4 to 429 percent, the median improvement being 47.5 percent. In all cases the results were positive. There was some evidence, though, that the effects of objective feedback tended to diminish with the passage of time. Comparing short- and long-duration interventions, median improvements in behavioral criteria were 49.5 percent and 41.4 percent, respectively.

Table 9-2 summarizes the results of twenty-eight studies that examined the effects of objective feedback on various indicators of job performance. Notwithstanding the diversity of sample populations, the many types and combinations of feedback provided, and the variety of accompanying interventions employed, the impact of objective feedback was uniformly positive. The effects of objective performance feedback were examined over treatment periods ranging from 1 week to 4 years, the median time period being 29.5 weeks. In all twenty-eight studies performance improved, with increases ranging from 5 to 482 percent, the median being 34.3 percent. Somewhat surprisingly, results appeared to strengthen with the passage of time: long-duration interventions showed more positive effects than short-duration interventions (46.4 percent vs. 32.8 percent).

Although the median performance improvement was an increase of 34.3 percent, this does not mean that productivity on the average improved to this extent. Some objective performance indicators were not too comprehensive, focusing only on component aspects of performance (e.g., truck turnaround time, the timeliness of reports). Thirteen studies did report comprehensive measures of performance, and in these studies objective feedback yielded a

**TABLE 9-1**
EFFECTS OF OBJECTIVE FEEDBACK ON WORK BEHAVIOR

| Study number and year | Sample | Type of feedback | Other interventions | Impact on work behavior | Comments |
|---|---|---|---|---|---|
| 1 1976[a] | 30 telephone reservation clerks for Aer Lingus | Pvt. I. Pub. G. | GS | 66.5% reduction in undesired verbal behaviors; 84.4% increase in desired verbal behaviors; over-all effect was a 77.9% improvement—after 3 months | Clerks had a positive reaction to the program |
| 2 1978[b] | 80 employees in a mental health organization | Pub. I. (posting of replies to suggestions offered) | | 222.7% increase in the number of suggestions offered over 32 weeks | 98% of employees said the program should be continued |
| 3 1978[c] | 6 therapists at a health service center | Pvt. I. Pub. G | T, P, R, GS | 429% increase in the percentage of graphs (of client behavior) completed; over 8.5 weeks | Pvt. I. was superior in impact to Pub. G.; Pvt. I. + Pub. G. was superior to Pvt. I. |
| 4 1978[d] | Supervisors and staff at 30 university laboratories | Pvt. G. (sent to supervisor) | P | 45.4% reduction in observed frequency of hazards over 7 to 14 months | Feedback was adopted as a permanent part of a new safety system |
| 5 1978[e] | 28 employees in 2 departments of a food manufacturing plant | Pub. G. | T, GS, R | 32.5% increase in the proportion of observed work incidents performed safely; over 11 weeks | Lost time accidents in the plant declined by 80% after 1 year |
| 6 1979[f] | All salespersons in 5 departments of a department store | Pub. G. | T, R | 95% increase in the percentage of customers approached by salespeople; service behavior score rose by 4%; over 5 to 11 weeks | |

**TABLE 9-1**
EFFECTS OF OBJECTIVE FEEDBACK ON WORK BEHAVIOR (*Continued*)

| Study number and year | Sample | Type of feedback | Other interventions | Impact on work behavior | Comments |
|---|---|---|---|---|---|
| 7 1979[g] | All workers in a fast-food snack bar | Pub. G. | | 94% reduction in employee theft over a 1 to 4 week period | |
| 8 1980[h] | 55 employees in a city's vehicle maintenance department | Pub. G. | T, GS | 41.4% improvement in behavioral safety scores over 34 to 36 weeks | 83% decrease in the number of lost-time accidents; employees had a favorable reaction to the program |
| 9 1980[i] | 11 front-line employees in a fast-food restaurant | Pvt. I. | T, P, R | 58% increase in friendliness behavior (smiling) over a 1.5 to 10 week period | |
| 10 1980[j] | 9 kitchen workers in a large cafeteria at a university | Pvt. I. | T | 203.7% increase in the frequency of handwashing over 3 weeks | In comparison, training alone increased the frequency of handwashing by only 21.7% |
| 11 1981[k] | 20 clerical employees in the home office of a large insurance company | Pub. I. Pub. G. | P | 9% reduction in absenteeism over 3 months (previously feedback alone without P resulted in a 50% decrease in absenteeism over 6 weeks) | The department manager failed to praise as required; apparently the use of P was quite alien |
| 12 1981–1982[l] | 21 clinical therapists at a psychological services center | Pub. I | T | 21.0% average reduction in 4 types of charting errors over 29 weeks | Feedback affected only the *specific* behaviors targeted |
| 13 1982[m] | 100 transit operators (bus drivers) at a regional transportation authority (325 operators in control group) | Pub. I. Pub. G. | TR, team competition | 24.9% reduction in accident rate (compared to control group) over 18 weeks; over last 10 weeks the improvement was 35.2% | Annualized savings of $9400; if extended to all drivers it would have been $30,500 |

| 14 | 1983[n] | 15 part-time cashiers in a retail drugstore | Pub. G. Pub. I. | TR + GS | 21.7% improvement in punctuality; 20.7% increase in the percentage of required checkout behaviors performed; 24% reduction in cashiered money discrepancies—over 38 days | Both Pub. I. and Pub. I + TR (and GS) were far more effective than Pub. G. |

*Note:* Pvt. I. = private individual, Pub. I. = public individual, Pvt. G. = private group, Pub. G. = private group, Pub. G. = public group, GS = goal setting, T = training, P = praise, R = public recognition, TR = token reinforcers.

[a] Stephen A. Allen, "Aer Lingus—Irish (B)," Case #9-477-640 (Boston: Intercollegiate Case Clearing House, 1976), pp. 1–20.

[b] H. Robert Quilitch, "Using a Simple Feedback Procedure to Reinforce the Submission of Written Suggestions by Mental Health Employees," *Journal of Organizational Behavior Management*, 1 (1978), 155–163.

[c] Gerald L. Shook, C. Merle Johnson, and William F. Uhlman, "The Effect of Response Effort Reduction, Instructions, Group and Individual Feedback, and Reinforcement on Staff Performance," *Journal of Organizational Behavior Management*, 1 (1978), 206–215.

[d] Beth Sulzer-Azaroff, "Behavioral Ecology and Accident Prevention," *Journal of Organizational Behavior Management*, 2 (1978), 11–44.

[e] Judi Komaki, Kenneth D. Barwick, and Lawrence R. Scott, "A Behavioral Approach to Occupational Safety: Pinpointing and Reinforcing Safe Performance in a Food Manufacturing Plant," *Journal of Applied Psychology*, 63 (1978), 434–445.

[f] Robert L. Collins, Judi Komaki, and Stephen Temlock, "Behavioral Definition and Improvement of Customer Service in Retail Merchandising," paper presented at the 87th Annual Meeting of the American Psychological Association (New York), 1979, pp. 1–12.

[g] Patrick McNees, Sharon W. Gilliam, John F. Schnelle, and Todd Risley, "Controlling Employee Theft through Time and Product Identification," *Journal of Organizational Behavior Management*, 2 (1979), 113–119.

[h] Judi Komaki, Arlene T. Heinzmann, and Loralie Lawson, "Effect of Training and Feedback: Component Analysis of a Behavioral Safety Program," *Journal of Applied Psychology*, 65 (1980), 261–270.

[i] Judi Komaki, Milton R. Blood, and Donna Holder, "Fostering Friendliness in a Fast Food Franchise," *Journal of Organizational Behavior Management*, 2 (1980), 151–164.

[j] E. Scott Geller, Serena L. Eason, Jean A. Phillips, and Merle D. Pierson, "Interventions to Improve Sanitation During Food Preparation," *Journal of Organizational Behavior Management*, 2 (1980), 229–240.

[k] Dale B. Silva, Phillip K. Duncan, and Donald Doudna, "The Effects of Attendance-Contingent Feedback and Praise on Attendance and Work Efficiency," *Journal of Organizational Behavior Management*, 3, No. 2 (1981), 59–69.

[l] Lee W. Frederiksen, William T. Richter, Jr., Richard P. Johnson, and Laura J. Solomon, "Specificity of Performance Feedback in a Professional Service Delivery Setting," *Journal of Organizational Behavior Management*, 3, No. 4 (1981–1982), 41–53.

[m] Robert S. Haynes, Randall C. Pine, and H. Gordon Fitch, "Reducing Accident Rates with Organizational Behavior Modification," *Academy of Management Journal*, 25 (1982), 407–416.

[n] T. J. Newby and P. W. Robinson, "Effects of Grouped and Individual Feedback and Reinforcement on Retail Employee Performances," *Journal of Organizational Behavior Management*, 5, No. 2 (1983), 51–68.

**TABLE 9-2**
EFFECTS OF OBJECTIVE FEEDBACK ON JOB PERFORMANCE

| Study number and year | Sample | Type of feedback | Other interventions | Impact on outputs and/or other objective performance criteria | Comments |
|---|---|---|---|---|---|
| 1 1969[a] | 18 metal workers in India | Pub. I. | | 11.8% increase in output over 1 week (explicit KR vs. no KR) | 3.3% increase in output in group with vague feedback |
| 2 1970[b] | 25 staff employees in 3 units of a residential child-treatment facility | Pub. I. Pub. G. | | 76% increase in the proportion of possible training sessions actually conducted; over 21 to 24 weeks | Performance improved in the absence of direct, daily supervision |
| 3 1973[c] | Sales and shipping employees at Emery Air Freight | Pvt. I. Pub. G. | GS, P, R | 150% increase in frequency of time meeting customer service standard; 110% increase in frequency of full use of containers—over 4 years | Annualized savings of roughly $1 million |
| 4 1974[d] | 9 staff employees in a residential child-treatment facility | Pvt. I. | T, public notice of ind. job assignments | 105% increase in the percentage of new jobs and procedures performed within 1 week of assignment; over 3 months | The combination of KR and T was more effective than either component alone |
| 5 1975[e] | 43 die casting operators | Pvt. I. Pub. G. | P, E | 6.1% increase in production over 36 weeks | Annualized savings of $77,000 |
| 6 1975[f] | 17 mental health technicians in 4 residential child-treatment units | Pub. I. | T, GS, an instructional memo (in 2 units) | 357% increase in the proportion of patients participating in planned activities; over 2 to 8 weeks | Prior training and an instructional memo had no effect |
| 7 1976[g] | 4 groups of 113 blue-collar, unionized service workers | Pvt. I. | GS, P | 7.9% improvement in cost performance; 11.6% increase in service—over 3 months (also 13.6% improvement in safety) | Best results were obtained in the group which used all interventions |

| No. | Subjects | Sector | Code | Results | Results |
|---|---|---|---|---|---|
| 8 1977[h] | 8 mental health technicians | Pub. I. | | 120% increase in group therapy sessions; 150% increase in one-on-one therapy sessions; 70% increase in daily routine duties; over 4 to 8 weeks | Decrease in staff conflict and in patient complaints |
| 9 1977[i] | Production employees in 3 plants | Pub. G. | GS | 18.8% average increase in productivity over 2 years (excluding effects in one plant due to other factors) | 75% decline in grievance rate; increase in employee suggestions for improving performance |
| 10 1978[j] | 58 plant managers; 92 truck drivers | Pvt. I. (to both plant managers and truck drivers) | TR | 12% increase in total shipping productivity over 29 weeks (also a 43.9% decrease in truck turnaround time) | |
| 11 1978[k] | 32 nonunionized industrial workers at PPG Industries | Pvt. I. Pub. G. | P, E | 8.7% increase in productivity over 4 months | Productivity was higher with both forms of feedback than with Pub. G. alone |
| 12 1978[l] | Doffers in a textile yarn mill | Pvt. I. Pub. G. | GS, P | 74.6% reduction in the incidence of high bobbins (which cause tangles in thread) over 8 weeks | When feedback was discontinued the incidence of high bobbins increased by 64% |
| 13 1978[m] | 1 draftsman in an engineering firm | Pvt. I. | | 72.2% increase in time spent working over 4 weeks (and sustained during follow-up after 11 weeks) | Marked improvement in punctuality |
| 14 1978[n] | 4 textile machine operators at PPG Industries | Pvt. I. | GS, P | 7.8% increase in output over an average study period of 32 weeks | Annualized savings of $3500: improved relationships between operators and the foreman |

**TABLE 9-2**
EFFECTS OF OBJECTIVE FEEDBACK ON JOB PERFORMANCE (*Continued*)

| Study number and year | Sample | Type of feedback | Other interventions | Impact on outputs and/or other objective performance criteria | Comments |
|---|---|---|---|---|---|
| 15 1978[o] | 195 truck drivers for textile company | Pvt. I Pub. G. | R, TR | 5.1% increase in miles per gallon; 56.7% increase in use of company-owned fuel terminals—over 2 years | Dollar savings from increased fuel efficiency described as "very substantial" |
| 16 1978[p] | 23 inspectors at Eastman Kodak | Pvt. I. Pub. G. | GS, P | 30% increase in productivity over 40 weeks | Annualized savings of $105,000; increased contact between workers and supervisor; job seen as more interesting |
| 17 1978[q] | 6 repair shop workers | Pub. G. | GS | 20% increase in productivity over 22 weeks | Annualized savings of $57,200 |
| 18 1979[r] | Approx. 150 sewing machine operators in a garment factory | Pub. G. | GS | 62% reduction in defective garments ("seconds") over 12 months | Pay satisfaction declined |
| 19 1979[s] | Approx. 12 workers in a personnel department of a federal agency | Pvt. I. | GS, P, PWA, TO, CL | 69.7% average improvement in 11 output measures over 7 months | 9 of 11 performance indicators improved, 1 was unchanged, and 1 showed a decline |
| 20 1979[t] | Clerical employees in the payroll office of a large city personnel department | Pvt. I. Pub. G. | | 37.6% decrease in average backlog of work over 8 weeks | Backlogs decreased in 17 out of 18 categories; 1 was unchanged |
| 21 1980[u] | 3 sales correspondents in an industrial products company | Pvt. I. | More complete sales information from salesmen | 67% reduction in price quotation turnaround time over roughly 3 years | Contributed to a 45% increase in sales and a 78% increase in profits |

| # | Year | Setting | Type | Intervention | Results | Notes |
|---|---|---|---|---|---|---|
| 22 | 1980[v] | Back-office employees in the trust department of the Marine Midland Bank | Pvt. I. Pub. G. | P, R, and group problem solving | 71.9% reduction in outstanding daily accounts receivable (increasing cash flow); over 1 year | Annualized savings of $440,350 (assuming a 15% cost of money) |
| 23 | 1980[w] | All employees in 16 departments of a large state hospital | Pvt. G. Pub. G. | | 83% increase in staff treatment programs, staff treatment hours, and client participation hours with private group feedback over 15–23 weeks; 178% increase in the same three criteria with public group feedback over 38 weeks | Work-related conversations increased among employees at all levels |
| 24 | 1980[x] | Tellers and financial consultants in 10 branches of a Midwestern bank (and 10 comparison branches—CBs) | Pvt. G. | Group problem solving (in some units) | 15.2% increase in work efficiency; 46.5% increase in work quality (compared to CBs)—over 1 year | Feedback included objective and subjective components; also the intervention was not implemented in some branches—and marginally adopted in others |
| 25 | 1981[y] | 6 employees on a machine-paced manufacturing operation at Cramer Products, Inc. | Pub. G. | P | 26% increase in productivity over 1 week (due to a reduction in preparation time) | 2100% return on investment |
| 26 | 1981[z] | Independent appraisal firm that reported to the branch claim department of a casualty insurance co. | Pvt. I. Pub. G. | GS | 482% increase in the proportion of timely automobile accident reports filed over 18 months (from 17% to 99.3%) | Job performance improved of employees working for another co. |
| 27 | 1982[aa] | 209 engineers in 5 locations | Pvt. I. (from 3 sources: supervisor, coworkers, and self) | GS, R | 5.4% increase in 3 objective indicators in the feedback only groups; 5.5% increase in the feedback + GS groups—over 9 months | Self-generated feedback was superior to externally generated feedback |

**TABLE 9-2**
EFFECTS OF OBJECTIVE FEEDBACK ON JOB PERFORMANCE (*Continued*)

| Study number and year | Sample | Type of feedback | Other interventions | Impact on outputs and/or other objective performance criteria | Comments |
|---|---|---|---|---|---|
| 28 1984[bb] | 93 salespeople in 4 branches of a large retail organization | Pvt. I. Pvt. G. | GS | 12.2% increase in mean sales performance in the 3 experimental groups over 10 weeks; 0% change in the control group | Behavioral + outcome feedback was superior to either component alone |

*Note:* Pvt. I. = private individual, Pub. I. = public individual, Pvt. G. = private group, Pub. G. = public group, GS = goal setting, P = praise, R = public recognition, TR = token reinforcers, PWA = preferred work assignments, T = training, TO = training opportunities, CL = commendation letters, KR = knowledge of results, E = encouragement.

[a]P. S. Hundal, "Knowledge of Performance as an Incentive in Repetitive Industrial Work," *Journal of Applied Psychology,* 53 (1969), 224–226.

[b]Marion Panyan, Howard Boozer, and Nancy Morris, "Feedback to Attendants as a Reinforcer for Applying Operant Techniques," *Journal of Applied Behavior Analysis,* 3 (1970), 1–4.

[c,]"At Emery Air Freight: Positive Reinforcement Boosts Performance," in *Organizational Behavior and Management: A Contingency Approach,* ed. Henry L. Tosi and W. Clay Hamner (Chicago: St. Clair Press, 1974), pp. 113–122. This article first appeared in the Winter 1973 issue of *Organizational Dynamics.*

[d]Dale A. Pommer and Darlene Streedback, "Motivating Staff Performance in an Operant Learning Program for Children," *Journal of Applied Behavior Analysis,* 7 (1974), 217–221.

[e]Everett E. Adam, Jr., "Behavior Modification in Quality Control," *Academy of Management Journal,* 18 (1975), 662–679.

[f]H. Robert Quilitch, "A Comparison of Three Staff-Management Procedures," *Journal of Applied Behavior Analysis,* 8 (1975), 59–66.

[g]Jay S. Kim and W. Clay Hamner, "Effect of Performance Feedback and Goal Setting on Productivity and Satisfaction in an Organizational Setting," *Journal of Applied Psychology,* 61 (1976), 48–57.

[h]Robert Kreitner, William E. Reif, and Marvin Morris, "Measuring the Impact of Feedback on the Performance of Mental Health Technicians," *Journal of Organizational Behavior Management,* 1 (1977), 105–109.

[i]Peter G. Kirby, "Productivity Increases through Feedback Systems," *Personnel Journal,* 56 (Oct. 1977), 512–515.

[j]Alex Runnion, Twila Johnson, and John McWhorter, "The Effects of Feedback and Reinforcement on Truck Turnaround Time in Materials Transportation," *Journal of Organizational Behavior Management,* 1 (1978), 110–117.

[k]Gerald D. Emmert, "Measuring the Impact of Group Performance Feedback versus Individual Performance Feedback in an Industrial Setting," *Journal of Organizational Behavior Management,* 1 (1978), 134–141.

[l]Michael McCarthy, "Decreasing the Incidence of 'High Bobbins' in a Textile Spinning Department through a Group Feedback Procedure," *Journal of Organizational Behavior Management,* 1 (1978), 150–154.

[m]P. A. Lamal and A. Benfield, "The Effect of Self-Monitoring on Job Tardiness and Percentage of Time Spent Working," *Journal of Organizational Behavior Management,* 1 (1978), 142–149.

172

[m]H. Wayne Dick, "Increasing the Productivity of the Day Relief Textile Machine Operator," *Journal of Organizational Behavior Management*, 2 (1978), 45–57.

[n]Alex Runnion, Jesse O. Watson, and John McWhorter, "Energy Savings in Interstate Transportation through Feedback and Reinforcement," *Journal of Organizational Behavior Management*, 1 (1978), 180–191.

[p]L. Eldridge, S. Lemasters, and B. Szypot, "A Performance Feedback Intervention to Reduce Waste: Performance Data and Participant Responses," *Journal of Organizational Behavior Management*, 1 (1978), 258–266.

[q]Albert Stoerzinger, James M. Johnston, Kim Pisor, and Craig Monroe, "Implementation and Evaluation of a Feedback System for Employees in a Salvage Operation," *Journal of Organizational Behavior Management*, 1 (1978), 268–280.

[r]James L. Koch, "Effects of Goal Specificity and Performance Feedback to Work Groups on Peer Leadership, Performance, and Attitudes," *Human Relations*, 32 (1979), 819–840.

[s]Craig E. Schneier and Robert Pernick, "Increasing Public Sector Productivity through Organizational Behavior Modification: A Successful Application," paper presented at the 39th National Meeting of the Academy of Management (Atlanta), 1979, pp. 1–15.

[t]Richard E. Kopelman, unpublished data, 1979.

[u]Lucien Rhodes, "It Pays to Be on Time," *Inc.*, June 1980, pp. 59–64.

[v]John K. Milne and Stephen X. Doyle, "Rx for Ailing Bank Trust Departments," *The Bankers Magazine*, 163 (Jan.–Feb. 1980), 54–57.

[w]Donald M. Prue, Jon E. Krapfl, James C. Noah, Sherry Cannon, and Roger F. Maley, "Managing Treatment Activities of State Hospital Staff," *Journal of Organizational Behavior Management*, 2 (1980); 165–181.

[x]David A. Nadler, Cortlandt Cammann, and Philip H. Mirvis, "Developing a Feedback System for Work Units: A Field Experiment in Structural Change," *The Journal of Applied Behavioral Science*, 16 (1980), 41–59.

[y]J. Michael Frost, B. L. Hopkins, and Rodney J. Conrad, "An Analysis of the Effects of Feedback and Reinforcement on Machine-Paced Production," *Journal of Organizational Behavior Management*, 3, No. 2 (1981), 5–17.

[z]Barbara J. Rowe, "Use of Feedback and Reinforcement to Increase the Telephone Reporting of Independent Automobile Appraisers," *Journal of Organizational Behavior Management*, 3, No. 2 (1981), 35–40.

[aa]John M. Ivancevich and J. Timothy McMahon, "The Effects of Goal Setting, External Feedback, and Self-Generated Feedback on Outcome Variables: A Field Experiment," *Academy of Management Journal*, 25 (1982), 359–372.

[bb]Jay S. Kim, "Effect of Behavior Plus Outcome Goal Setting and Feedback on Employee Satisfaction and Performance," *Academy of Management Journal*, 27 (1984), 139–149.

173

median increase (in productivity) of 15.2 percent. This finding closely corresponds to the observation of Milne and Doyle that objective feedback interventions alone produce an increase in productivity of 14 percent.[1] With respect to the durability of the impact of objective feedback on outputs, median results for long- and short-duration interventions were 17.0 percent and 16.1 percent, respectively.

Seven of the forty-two studies reported data on the dollar savings resulting from the feedback intervention. Annualized savings ranged from $3500 to $1 million, with a median of $77,000. In large part, though, the amounts saved were a function of the number of employees involved in the intervention. The Emery Air Freight program yielded a savings of $1 million and involved roughly 2000 employees; in contrast, the $3500 savings was achieved with 4 textile machine operators. Therefore, a more meaningful measure of the financial impact of objective feedback is the annualized savings per employee. On this basis, annualized savings ranged from $500 per employee (at Emery Air Freight) to $9533 (6 repair shop operators), the median being $1791.

## ADVANTAGES OF OBJECTIVE FEEDBACK

There are six advantages to objective feedback as a technique for improving productivity. First, it can be based on data that are already being generated; little change may be required in existing procedures.

Second, the provision of objective feedback is a relatively simple matter, requiring little investment of time or money. The initial cost of development is often less than $1000; yet, as noted previously, the median financial savings has been $77,000 per year.

Third, the use of objective feedback has good "face validity."[2] Feedback is a natural (although not always welcome) means of control. It does not require contrived events, such as a lottery; rather, it usually requires only minor changes in day-to-day routines.

Fourth, the results of objective feedback are evident rapidly; often improvements occur within a day. In contrast, it has been found that job enrichment and participation programs typically take 1½ to 3 years to yield results;[3] and major changes in managerial practices can take 3 to 7 years to demonstrate positive effects.[4]

Fifth, objective feedback systems can often be implemented in settings where few other interventions are feasible. In public agencies and not-for-profit organizations it may be very difficult to institute an incentive plan or to redesign jobs; however, there should be few impediments to providing objective feedback.[5]

Sixth, the use of objective feedback generally enhances the effects of other productivity improvement techniques. Training combined with feedback, for example, usually yields performance improvements far in excess of those that result from training alone. In one study, training alone increased sanitation practices—specifically, hand-washing behavior—among kitchen workers by

21.7 percent. Training combined with objective feedback led to an increase of 203.1 percent in (required) handwashing. The researchers concluded: "the present investigation indicates only minimal behavioral effects of the popular education approach to improving sanitation practices, but showed promising behavioral consequences of a feedback intervention."[6]

It might also be noted that feedback has been found to raise satisfaction and internal work motivation, particularly for nonstimulating jobs.[7] There is also evidence that individual feedback has a greater impact than group feedback;[8] and it appears that public feedback has a greater effect than private feedback.[9] However, no research study has directly compared the twofold effects of group vs. individual and public vs. private feedback.[10]

## WHY OBJECTIVE FEEDBACK WORKS

There are two primary reasons why feedback works: (1) it enhances the desire to perform well, i.e., it functions as a motivator, and (2) it cues learned responses or serves to develop new responses, i.e., it functions in an instructional capacity.

### Objective Feedback as a Motivator

Several explanations have been advanced as to why objective feedback motivates increased productivity. Although these explanations are interrelated, each is discussed separately.

**Feedback Corrects Misconceptions** People often have distorted perceptions of their work behavior and job performance. Objective feedback calls attention to these misperceptions and may motivate corrective action. A dramatic example of this is provided by the Emery Air Freight study.

> Executives at Emery were convinced that containers were being used about 90 percent of the times they could be used. Measurement of the actual usage—a measurement made by the same managers whose guesses had averaged 90 percent—showed that the actual usage was 45 percent, or half the estimate.[11]

Subsequently, Emery Air Freight initiated a motivational program consisting of performance measurement and feedback, goal setting, and positive reinforcement (praise, recognition). The program increased container usage from 45 percent to 95 percent. Similarly, the motivational program raised customer service so that the standard was met 90 percent of the time, compared with the prior level of 30 to 40 percent. The person responsible for designing and implementing the motivational program at Emery noted that objective feedback was the critical variable in explaining the success of the program.[12] In his words, "most managers genuinely think that operations in their bailiwick are doing well; a performance audit that proves they're not comes as a real and unpleasant surprise."[13]

Another illustration of the disconfirmation role of objective feedback is provided by the case of the telephone reservation clerks at Aer Lingus. The clerks were provided with profiles of their verbal behaviors obtained from unobtrusive work samples of twenty telephone calls per employee. The feedback caused one telephone clerk to comment as follows:

> When asked previously whether I used the customer's name I would have said—and believed—"Of course, we were trained to do that." I was really surprised when I saw objective evidence on how little I was actually doing it.[14]

As a result of the monitoring and feedback program, use of the customer's name by the thirty clerks rose by 87.5 percent. The frequency of interrupting by the telephone clerks dropped by 100 percent.[15]

These examples underscore Chris Argyris's contention that there is often a big difference between what people say they do (espoused theories) and what they really do (theories-in-use). In his words, "few people are aware that the theories they espouse are not the theories they use. Why should people espouse theories that are not their theories-in-use? One reason is because they are blind to the fact that they do not behave according to their espoused theories."[16] While it is notable that people often do not do what they say or think they do, what is perhaps even more remarkable is that people are *unaware* of this incongruence.

To the extent that feedback is objective, valid, and hence, incontrovertible, it offers the possibility of informing an individual about his or her false self-perceptions. Clearly, the use of such feedback has been found to motivate improved work behavior and job performance; presumably, this has been due in part to the correction of inaccurate self-perceptions.

**Feedback Creates Internal Consequences**  In the absence of performance feedback, it is unlikely that people will have either positive or negative feelings about themselves as a result of their job performance. The provision of feedback, however, allows one to experience positive or negative feelings about one's self as a result of performance, i.e., a greater degree of internal work motivation. Several examples of the impact of objective feedback on internal work motivation can be found in the literature.

After the introduction of objective performance feedback among cash management clerks at Marine Midland Bank, the average level of cash balances was reduced by 72 percent. A supervisor commented, "People are now trying to solve problems before they occur. People are looking to help out other individuals rather than just saying 'that's not my job.' I can say as a supervisor that it has a big impact on my own feelings toward the people who work for me. I feel a sense of accomplishment. . . . Give your employees a chance to 'make their day,' and they will make yours too."[17]

An objective performance feedback system was installed in the emergency room of a large hospital in Manhattan. The primary purpose of the intervention was to improve the completeness of reports filled out by emergency room clerks. One week after the introduction of the system, the proportion of complete reports submitted rose from 67 percent to 95 percent. The clerks reportedly experienced increased job satisfaction. One clerk said, "I used to go home evenings wondering what I had done . . . now I look at my feedback report and can see what I have accomplished."[18]

In short, objective performance feedback allows the individual to "keep score"; improvements or decrements in the individual's score may be a source of satisfaction or dissatisfaction. (Imagine how much commercial success a bowling alley would have if it placed a curtain in front of the pins, thereby preventing bowlers from knowing their scores.) Yet, it should be noted that knowledge of results is probably only a necessary, not a sufficient, condition for internal work motivation—by itself it may not be sufficient to "turn people on." Other relevant factors include the incumbent's perceptions of the meaningfulness of work and responsibility for results, as well as the individual's desire to grow and achieve.

**Feedback May Entail Social Consequences**   In situations where objective performance feedback is provided by an employee's supervisor or by public posting of data, the individual (or work group) will typically experience social consequences. Empirically, social consequences have been shown to improve job performance in a wide variety of work settings. For example, in a case involving 195 experienced truck drivers, private recognition was provided by letters of commendation and public recognition was provided by posting at each terminal the names of drivers who achieved 6 miles per gallon. These two forms of recognition, coupled with social and token extrinsic reinforcers, served to reduce energy consumption substantially for 2 years. According to company personnel, the "drivers enjoy their work more because of the amount and quality of feedback and recognition they receive for performance."[19]

In a mental health setting, all staff suggestions and comments were publicly posted, and responses were posted as well. However, anonymity was assured if desired; participants did not have to sign their names. The net result was that 1.8 suggestions were generated per employee per year, considerably above the national average rate of 0.08 in federal government agencies, and 0.4 in private industry, where sizable contingent cash awards are frequently offered. According to the researcher, many rapid improvements resulted, and 98 percent of the staff recommended that the program be continued.[20]

The use of recognition in improving performance does not require that performance feedback be uniformly positive. An interesting illustration of this point comes from the world of professional sports. Dave Anderson of *The New York Times* provides the following anecdote concerning Frank Robinson's first year as manager of the Cleveland Indians.

> Buddy Bell, now with the Texas Rangers, was the Indians' third baseman then. Buddy Bell was even-tempered, quiet, a hard worker, the organizer of the team's Fellowship of Christian Athletes Services. But midway through Frank Robinson's first season, Buddy Bell confronted him. "I can't play for you," Buddy Bell told him, "You ignore me. You don't pat me on the back when I'm going good. You don't chew me out when I'm going bad." [Apparently, Frank Robinson responded to this criticism.] By the end of that season, however, Buddy Bell confronted Frank Rob-

inson again. "I just want you to know," he said, "that I enjoyed playing for you." . . . The last day of that 1975 season, Frank Robinson was in the Indians' dugout in Fenway Park when the phone rang. Darrell Johnson, then the Boston Red Sox manager was calling from the other dugout. "For the last third of the season," Darrell Johnson told him, "you were the best manager in the league."[21]

Across such diverse groups as truck drivers, hospital employees, professional baseball players (and others), it is evident that recognition through performance feedback is an important motivator of improved work performance. While cynics may deride the utility of social reinforcers, viewing them as patronizing and demeaning, it can be argued that recognition is a largely underutilized incentive in American industry. Perhaps out of necessity, nonprofit and voluntary organizations have often relied heavily on recognition as a reward for various kinds of contributions; and there are reports of the extensive use of social reinforcers (e.g., insignias, titles) in Socialist countries. Yet, not only can social reinforcers be used in concert with extrinsic rewards, it is likely that feedback and recognition enhance the effects of tangible reinforcers.[22]

**Feedback Creates External Consequences**  The process of measuring and feeding back objective behavioral or performance data tends to generate a heightened sense of evaluation apprehension. Individuals want to "look good" to gain whatever rewards might result from managerial approval, and conversely, individuals want to avoid "looking bad" and the accompanying adverse consequences resulting from managerial disapproval.[23] In his book *Feedback and Organization Development* Nadler has written, "One way in which data collection generates energy is through implied sanctions or rewards. The fact that an activity is measured through data collection sends a message that some potentially powerful individual or group feels that the activity being measured is an important one."[24] Thus, the process of measurement and feedback represents a two-edged sword: there is the threat of punishers or relative deprivation on the one hand, and the possibility of rewards on the other. Indeed, objective measurement and feedback alerts people to the many possible forms of comparison: against their own prior levels of accomplishment, against the accomplishments of others, against some standard level of achievement (or goal), and against some combination of these bases for comparison.

There is some evidence that the implied threat or promise of external consequences is an important reason for the motivational effect of objective feedback. Two studies are particularly illuminating on this point.

In the case of the draftsman who was asked to monitor the time he spent working, objective measurement and feedback led to a 72 percent increase in the percentage of time actually spent working. The authors wrote, "The fact that the subject's behavior changed so dramatically with the onset of self-monitoring lends plausibility to the interpretation that the behavior changes were the result of perceived aversive consequences for failure to meet acceptable levels of performance."[25]

In a study of eight hospital technicians, individual performance scores were publicly posted. Improvements occurred for all technicians on all focal tasks: group therapy sessions increased by 120 percent, one-on-one therapy sessions increased 150 percent, and daily routine activities increased by 70 percent. One plausible reason for the increased rate of working is that public feedback increased competition among individuals for peer and/or supervisory approval.[26]

Whereas the absence of performance measurement and feedback implies that management finds any level of performance to be acceptable, institution of measurement and feedback signals that management is interested in how proficient each individual (or work group) is.[27] What is important, the message conveyed by objective measurement and feedback—not merely by words—is that inefficient workers may be treated less favorably than others, possibly penalized, or even terminated; in contrast, meritorious contributors may in fact be recognized and rewarded.

### Objective Feedback as an Instructional Device

The second primary reason why objective feedback increases productivity is because it instructs. Objective feedback can direct attention to the specific kinds of behaviors that should be performed and the levels of activity or proficiency that should be achieved.

In connection with the instructional role of feedback, Lawrence Miller, in *Behavior Management,* noted that "a typical reaction to substandard performance is to assume that there is a problem in the employee's motivation. . . . [Often,] a more fruitful approach is to assume there is a problem in clarity of performance expectations and timely, objective feedback of results to the employee."[28]

It is unfortunate, perhaps, that the term "feedback" is used to describe such a wide variety of informational activities. When managers hear about objective feedback for the first time, a common reaction is "we already use feedback." But the similarity in terminology should not be confused with actual techniques. The feedback many managers give and receive consists of global evaluations and general impressions (e.g., "your overall performance is not bad; the quantity of work is good, but the quality could be improved"). In contrast, a crucial feature of objective feedback is that it *targets* or *pinpoints specific tasks or activities.*[29] Objective feedback tends to be frequent, focused, and factual.

A good illustration of the instructional capability of objective feedback is provided by an intervention in a mental hospital. Over a decade, management had attempted to make the transition from a custodial to a treatment orientation. Unfortunately, what resulted was a high degree of role ambiguity and poor job performance. However, upon institution of public objective feedback, staff treatment hours increased by 178 percent. The researchers concluded that objective feedback "provided instruction to hospital staff in defining their job responsibilities."[30] Moreover, the intervention increased the amount of treatment-related information exchanged by hospital staff employees at all levels, in both professional and social encounters.[31]

Also pertinent to the instructional and correctional capability of feedback is research by Tharp and Gallimore. They studied the verbal behavior of John Wooden at fifteen practice sessions with his team. (John Wooden coached the UCLA basketball team to 10 national championships in 12 years.) Tharp and Gallimore found that at least 75 percent of Wooden's comments contained informational content. Most of his comments were specific statements of what to do and how to do it, rather than motivational communications. Indeed, Wooden was more than five times as likely to instruct than he was to praise or reprimand only.[32]

Not only can feedback inform people about the activities they should be performing, it can also provide information about standards of proficiency. Notes management consultant Jewell Westerman, "people who are measured know what's expected of them." While working on productivity measurement at Travelers Insurance Company, Westerman found that white-collar workers often had "piles of work in front of them, but they [did not] know if they were supposed to get it all out [the same day]. They need[ed] feedback" and information about work standards.[33] Insurance companies, such as Travelers, have pioneered in the area of work measurement for white-collar employees. The discussion next turns to an examination of some descriptive (and largely non-empirical) accounts of the application of work measurement and feedback.

## DESCRIPTIVE REPORTS OF OBJECTIVE PERFORMANCE MEASUREMENT AND FEEDBACK PROGRAMS

Unquestionably, the most common application of objective performance measurement and feedback has been on repetitive blue- and white-collar jobs. In such settings it is not uncommon to see work standards developed and used in budgeting, work scheduling, worker assignment, and procedural improvement efforts. Such information is also useful in evaluating and rewarding performance, for use with MBO and goal setting programs, for assessing the effects of training programs, and most generally, for raising productivity consciousness.[34] In view of the numerous benefits that may result from objective performance measurement and feedback, it is not surprising that organizations have increasingly been implementing measurement systems.

At the Metropolitan Life Insurance Company, the practice of work measurement has been ongoing since 1947. Productivity information is collected first at the individual level of analysis, and such data are converted into individual production reports (see Figures 9-1 and 9-2). It might be noted that in recent years, individual production reports have increasingly been produced electronically and automatically, on a real time basis.

Because the white-collar work force has grown roughly three times as rapidly as the blue-collar work force during the past 15 years, organizations have become more attentive to measuring white-collar work performance. Further, in light of the particularly rapid growth in the numbers of professional, technical, and managerial employees, efforts have greatly expanded to measure work outputs on high-level white-collar jobs. Some examples follow.

Beginning in 1972, a companywide monitoring effort was launched at Detroit Edison under the aegis of its president. By 1974, 80 percent of all employees were covered by work-measurement procedures. It was intended that these procedures would identify underperformance or overstaffing, and also provide a basis for corrective action.[35] By 1979, measurement at Detroit Edison was extended to include engineers, lawyers, and accountants. According to Arnold Benes, general auditor for Detroit Edison, the process was "slow coming, but we've made some real advances." Further, Benes has noted that "for years everybody has been concentrating on the guy with the wrench, but [now] they're looking in the mirror and saying, 'It's me, the white-collar guy, who needs measuring and improving.'"[36]

Of course, this is a lot easier said than done. As one banking executive has observed, "It's easy to measure the output on the assembly lines. . . . But what's the output of a lawyer or auditor? You just can't count how many audits or cases he handles because they are of all different types and of all different quality."[37] Consequently, in measuring the work of high-level professionals,

**FIGURE 9-1**
Count sheet. (*Reprinted by permission of the Metropolitan Life Insurance Company.*)

**Name:** Ann Jones

**Position:** Claim Approver

**Week of:** 1/21/77

| Transaction | Monday | Tuesday | Wednesday | Thursday | Friday | Total |
|---|---|---|---|---|---|---|
| Completed basic claims | ⦀⦀ ⦀⦀ ⦀⦀ (15) | ⦀⦀ ⦀⦀ (10) | ⦀⦀ // (7) | ⦀⦀ ⦀⦀ / (11) | ⦀⦀ // (7) | 50 |
| Completed EME claims | ⦀⦀ ⦀⦀ ⦀⦀ /// (18) | ⦀⦀ /// (8) | ⦀⦀ (5) | ⦀⦀ ⦀⦀ ⦀⦀ (15) | ⦀⦀ / (6) | 52 |
| Completed basic and EME claim | //// (4) | ⦀⦀ //// (9) | ⦀⦀ ⦀⦀ //// (14) | ⦀⦀ / (6) | ⦀⦀ ⦀⦀ (10) | 43 |
| Completed comprehensive claims | /// (3) | ⦀⦀ /// (8) | ⦀⦀ / (6) | //// (4) | ⦀⦀ // (7) | 28 |

**Instructions**
Enter a tick mark for each completed claim in the appropriate box above. A completed claim means that a decision has been made to either pay the claim or decline it, or that the charges do not reach the deductible amount. Each claim is to be counted only once.

**Name:** Ann Jones                                   **Week Ending:** 1/14/77

ACTIVITY

| Transaction | Mon. | Tues. | Wed. | Thurs. | Fri. | Week total | Std. | Mins. reqd. |
|---|---|---|---|---|---|---|---|---|
| Basic claim | 16 | 12 | 20 | 15 | 22 | 85 | 5.2 | 442 |
| EME claim | 10 | 11 | 6 | 25 | 18 | 70 | 6.4 | 448 |
| Basic and EME claim | 28 | 8 | 25 | 24 | 8 | 93 | 7.3 | 679 |
| Comprehensive claim | 2 | — | 4 | 2 | 7 | 15 | 9.0 | 135 |

|  | **Total minutes required for measured work** | **1704** |
|---|---|---|

MINUTES AVAILABLE

| | Mon. | Tues. | Wed. | Thurs. | Fri. | |
|---|---|---|---|---|---|---|
| Normal | 450 | 450 | 450 | 450 | 450 | 2250 |
| Overtime | | | | 60 | | + 60 |
| Absence/vacation | | 225 | | | | − 225 |
| Special work | | | | | | − |
| Other | | | | | | − |
| Company-sponsored act. | | | | 80 | | − 80 |
| Loan | | | | | | − |
| | | | | **Total minutes available = 2005** | | |
| Waiting for work | | | | | | − |
| | | | | **Net minutes available = 2005** | | |

| **Total minutes required ÷ Net minutes available = Individual performance** | | | |
|---|---|---|---|
| 1704 | ÷ 2005 | = | 85 % |

**FIGURE 9-2**
Claim approver's individual production report. (*Reprinted by permission of the Metropolitan Life Insurance Company.*)

attempts have focused on identifying relevant performance indicators, coupled with the assigning of weights to reflect varying levels of task difficulty and complexity. (Note that for a lawyer, the number of cases tried may not be a relevant indicator of job performance; the better the lawyer's advice, the fewer the number of cases that need to be tried.)[38] At the Bank of North America, for instance, analysts studied the job of lending officer and identified seven different major activities. Subsequently the bank started measuring such things as the number of loans that became problems, and the number of new accounts generated for other parts of the bank.[39]

Along these lines, a law firm in Chicago looked at the dozen different types of cases it handled and then ranked them according to difficulty. The firm used output measures, adjusted for weighted levels of difficulty to assess the productivity of its lawyers. This procedure was reportedly helpful in controlling the growth in staff size.[40] However, a far more sophisticated approach to work measurement for lawyers was employed by Marvin Mundel at the U.S. Department of the Interior, Office of the Solicitor. On the basis of extensive discussions with the legal staff, Mundel identified nine major categories of legal services performed (e.g., contracts, torts, leases, and patents and copyrights). Within these categories various types of legal activities were identified, and standard times were assigned to these specific activities on the basis (initially) of informed judgments. The resulting reporting and measurement system was used to monitor the productivity of the entire legal staff. A sample workload reporting form is shown in Figure 9-3. During its first 6 years of existence the program reportedly increased productivity by more than 25 percent, and yielded an annual salary savings of $1.5 million. One way in which the system improved productivity was that by measuring work backlogs it was possible to shift lawyers temporarily from low- to high-backlog locations.[41]

Mundel has also reported the application of productivity measurement to other professional occupations, including veterinarians, analytical chemists, news reporters, grant reviewers, and hospital administrators. Interestingly, in connection with the work of researchers, Mundel notes that it is not possible to measure *productivity* because each output is unique—representing an advance in the state of the art. However, Mundel has shown that it is possible to apply *work* measurement (not productivity measurement) to the research role, by comparing actual and estimated standard times for completing component steps in a given project.

Similarly, Robert Ranftl at Hughes Aircraft has concluded that the productivity of engineers and scientists cannot "possibly" be measured "with a number." Yet he has asserted, cryptically, that this "shouldn't be a hangup, and isn't any excuse for not improving productivity." But how can an improvement in productivity be obtained and known if it cannot be measured with a number? The answer, according to Ranftl, is to develop (as technical managers did at Hughes Aircraft) dozens of measurements to evaluate the performance (not productivity) of engineers and scientists, including the number of errors in work performed, the backlog of problems, and the "degree of professional-

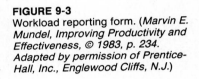

| (1) | (2) | (3) | (4) | (5) | (6) | (7) | (8) | (9) |
|---|---|---|---|---|---|---|---|---|
| MATTER CODE (4 Digits) | NUMBER PENDING START OF PERIOD | NUMBER RECEIVED DURING PERIOD | TOTAL PENDING AND RECEIVED | NUMBER PROCESSED DURING PERIOD | WEIGHT VALUE OF MATTER (Nos) | VALUE OF MATTERS PROCESSED (Nos) (Col. 5×6) | NUMBER OF MATTERS PENDING END OF PERIOD (Col. 5−3) | VALUE OF PENDING MATTERS (Nos) (Col. 8×6) |

United States Department of the Interior, Office of the Solicitor — Workload Analysis Report. 4 Week period ___ thru ___. Reporting Organization ___

Total Count / Total Matter Weight / Non-matter Factor / Gross Weighted Value / Remarks

**FIGURE 9-3**
Workload reporting form. (*Marvin E. Mundel, Improving Productivity and Effectiveness, © 1983, p. 234. Adapted by permission of Prentice-Hall, Inc., Englewood Cliffs, N.J.*)

ism in getting work done." These indices, says Ranftl, provide a "rough feel" for whether "things are going up or down."[42]

Another approach to measuring the performance of engineers and scientists was employed by Latham and Mitchell at Weyerhaeuser Company. Rather than relying on partial performance indicators or on subjective ratings of overall performance, they focused on whether engineers and scientists engaged in appropriate, and avoided inappropriate, work *behaviors*. In other words, instead of making highly judgmental assessments of an end-result variable, job performance, they turned to an antecedent of performance, work behavior.[43] Although their approach—the use of behavioral observation scales—has many advantages, it does not preclude examining various objective, partial performance indicators. To the contrary, it would seem that a preferable measurement strategy would be to use a combination of partial performance indicators (which are highly objective), behavioral observations (moderately objective), and supervisory and peer judgments of overall performance (relatively subjective).

In the public sector too, the potential utility of work measurement has increasingly been recognized by managers. On the basis of their study of human resource management practices in eight of the most progressive cities, one team of researchers concluded as follows:

The greatest change in personnel management in the cities that our research indicates [should be instituted] is the building-in of productivity or performance measurement and evaluation as the critical ingredients in all the processes and decisions. . . . To achieve greater productivity in the government through better personnel management clearly requires the use of performance measurement as the basis for personnel-related decisions.[44]

.   In a similar vein, Fred Lane has issued a related plea with respect to improving productivity in higher education: "you can measure, or at least measure approximately, many of the outcomes of higher education. It is better to approximate how you are doing than to have no feedback whatsoever on academic effectiveness."[45]

## SUMMARY

People in various settings are increasingly recognizing the benefits associated with objective performance measurement and feedback. The present review of 42 field interventions found that objective feedback is a productivity improvement technique that does not *usually* work, it virtually *always* works. In all cases results were positive. On the average, work behaviors improved by 47 percent, job performance indicators improved by 34 percent, and overall outputs (productivity) increased by 15 percent. Further, objective feedback was found to be highly cost-effective, results typically were evident rather rapidly, and there was little evidence that the effects attenuated with time.

Why does objective feedback work? For two reasons: it energizes behavior (it motivates), and it directs or cues behavior (it instructs). Where might objective performance measurement and feedback be profitably applied? In virtually all settings where managers are responsible for accomplishing goals or objectives. Wherever people are accountable for results, a good early step (after a job analysis has been performed) is to start counting. Even a crude measurement effort can help raise productivity, and analysis and interpretation of the resulting data can help compensate for limitations in the figures that emerge.

## NOTES

1  John K. Milne and Stephen X. Doyle, "Rx for Ailing Bank Trust Departments," *The Bankers Magazine,* 163 (Jan.–Feb. 1980) 57.
2  Albert Stoerzinger, James M. Johnston, Kim Pisor, and Craig Monroe, "Implementation and Evaluation of a Feedback System for Employees in a Salvage Operation," *Journal of Organizational Behavior Management,* 1 (1978), 269.
3  Mitchell Fein, "Improved Productivity through Worker Involvement," Paper presented at the 42nd National Meeting of the Academy of Management, (New York, 1982), p. 11.
4  Rensis Likert, *New Patterns of Management* (New York: McGraw-Hill, 1961).
5  Donald M. Prue and John A. Fairbank, "Performance Feedback in Organizational Behavior Management: A Review," *Journal of Organizational Behavior Management,* 3, No. 1 (1981), 2.
6  E. Scott Geller, Serena L. Eason, Jean A. Phillips, and Merle D. Pierson, "Interventions to Improve Sanitation During Food Preparation," *Journal of Organizational Behavior Management,* 2 (1980), 239.

7 Jay S. Kim and Randall S. Schuler, "The Nature of the Task as a Moderator of the Relationship between Extrinsic Feedback and Employee Responses," *Academy of Management Journal,* 22 (1979), 157–162.

8 Gerald L. Shook, C. Merle Johnson, and William F. Uhlman, "The Effect of Response Effort Reduction, Instructions, Group and Individual Feedback, and Reinforcement on Staff Performance," *Journal of Organizational Behavior Management,* 1 (1978), 206–215; Gerald D. Emmert, "Measuring the Impact of Group Performance Feedback versus Individual Performance Feedback in an Industrial Setting," *Journal of Organizational Behavior Management,* 1 (1978), 134–141.

9 See H. Robert Quilitch, "A Comparison of Three Staff-Management Procedures," *Journal of Applied Behavior Analysis,* 8 (1975), 59–66, and also Robert Kreitner, William E. Reif, and Marvin Morris, "Measuring the Impact of Feedback on the Performance of Mental Health Technicians," *Journal of Organizational Behavior Management,* 1 (1977), 105–109, for evidence of the powerful effects of public individual feedback—and average increase of 235 percent. In contrast, studies reporting the effects on performance of private individual feedback reported a median increase of 68.5 percent (see Table 9-2, studies 4, 7, 10, 13, 14, 19, 21, and 26).

10 Moreover, it might be hypothesized that an interaction will be found, the greatest effects occurring with public individual feedback, and the weakest effects with private group feedback.

11 "At Emery Air Freight: Positive Reinforcement Boosts Performance," in *Organizational Behavior and Management: A Contingency Approach,* ed. Henry L. Tosi and W. Clay Hamner (Chicago: St. Clair Press, 1974), p. 113. (This article first appeared in the Winter 1983 issue of *Organizational Dynamics.*)

12 "At Emery Air Freight," p. 117.

13 Ibid., p. 114.

14 Stephen A. Allen, "Aer Lingus—Irish (B)," case #9-477-640 (Boston: Intercollegiate Case Clearing House, 1976), p. 7.

15 Ibid., p. 20.

16 Chris Argyris, "Theories of Action That Inhibit Individual Learning," *American Psychologist,* 31 (1976), 639, 642.

17 John K. Milne and Stephen X. Doyle, "Rx for Ailing Bank Trust Departments," p. 57.

18 Lynda D. Baydin and Alan P. Sheldon, "Stephen Doyle (D)," case #9-474-026 (Boston: Intercollegiate Case Clearing House, 1973), p. 1.

19 Alex Runnion, Jesse O. Watson, and John McWhorter, "Energy Savings in Interstate Transportation through Feedback and Reinforcement," *Journal of Organizational Behavior Management,* 1 (1978), 189.

20 H. Robert Quilitch, "Using a Simple Feedback Procedure to Reinforce the Submission of Written Suggestions by Mental Health Employees," *Journal of Organizational Behavior Management,* 1 (1978), 155–163.

21 Dave Anderson, "Frank Robinson's Return," *New York Times,* 15 Jan. 1981, p. D21. Copyright © 1981 by The New York Times Company. Reprinted by permission.

22 Alex Runnion et al., "Energy Savings in Interstate Transportation"; also related, albeit tangentially, to the issue of the additivity of feedback and external incentives is the study by Gary P. Latham, Terence R. Mitchell, and Dennis L. Dossett, "Importance of Participative Goal Setting and Anticipated Rewards on Goal Difficulty and Job Performance," *Journal of Applied Psychology,* 63 (1978), 163–171. The positive effect of feedback on internal motivation has been noted by Edward L.

Deci in "Paying People Doesn't Always Work the Way You Expect It To," *Human Resource Management,* Summer 1973, pp. 28–32.

23 For an extensive discussion of evaluation apprehension see Howard L. Fromkin and Siegfried Streufert, "Laboratory Experimentation," in *Handbook of Industrial and Organizational Psychology,* ed. Marvin D. Dunnette (Chicago: Rand McNally, 1976), pp. 437–439.

24 David A. Nadler, *Feedback and Organization Development: Using Data-Based Methods* (Reading, Mass.: Addison-Wesley, 1977), p. 60.

25 P. A. Lamal and A. Benfield, "The Effect of Self-Monitoring on Job Tardiness and Percentage of Time Spent Working," *Journal of Organizational Behavior Management,* 1 (1978), 147.

26 Robert Kreitner, William E. Reif, and Marvin Morris, "Measuring the Impact of Feedback," pp. 105–109.

27 Donald E. Law, "Managing for Productivity," *The Arthur Young Journal,* Summer–Autumn 1975, p. 8.

28 Lawrence M. Miller, *Behavior Management* (New York: Wiley, 1978), p. 210.

29 Anne W. Riley and Lee W. Frederiksen, "Organizational Behavior Management in Human Service Settings: Problems and Prospects," *Journal of Organizational Behavior Management,* 5, Nos. 3–4 (1983), p. 11; also see Lawrence M. Miller, *Behavior Management,* pp. 77–79, 242–245.

30 Donald M. Prue, Jon E. Krapfl, James G. Noah, Sherry Cannon, and Roger F. Maley, "Managing Treatment Activities of State Hospital Staff," *Journal of Organizational Behavior Management,* 2 (1980), 180.

31 Ibid., pp. 178–180.

32 Roland G. Tharp and Ronald Gallimore, "What a Coach Can Teach a Teacher," *Psychology Today,* 10 (Jan. 1976), 74–78.

33 Lawrence Rout, "White-Collar Workers Start to Get Attention in Productivity Studies," *Wall Street Journal,* 7 Aug. 1979, p. 19.

34 See Irving H. Siegel, *Company Productivity: Measurement for Improvement* (Kalamazoo, Mich.: Upjohn Institute, 1980); also Marvin E. Mundel, *Measuring and Enhancing the Productivity of Service and Government Organizations* (Tokyo: Asian Productivity Organization, 1975).

35 Irving H. Siegel, *Company Productivity,* pp. 58–59.

36 Lawrence Rout, "White-Collar Workers," p. 1.

37 Ibid.

38 Marvin E. Mundel, *Productivity of Service and Government Organizations,* see chapter 9.

39 Lawrence Rout, "White-Collar Workers," p. 1.

40 Ibid., p. 19.

41 Marvin E. Mundel, *Productivity of Service and Government Organizations,* chapter 9.

42 Lawrence Rout, "White-Collar Workers," p. 19.

43 Gary P. Latham and Terence R. Mitchell, "Behavioral Criteria and Potential Reinforcers for the Engineer/Scientist in an Industrial Setting," *JSAS Catalogue of Selected Documents in Psychology,* 6, No. 3 (1976), Ms. 1316, p. 83.

44 Selma J. Mushkin and Frank H. Sandifer, *Personnel Management and Productivity in City Government* (Lexington, Mass.: Lexington Books, 1979), p. 97.

45 Frederick S. Lane, "A Practical Approach to Improving Productivity in Higher Education: 'This is Serious,'" paper presented at the 1980 Meeting of the American Council on Education (San Francisco), p. 6.

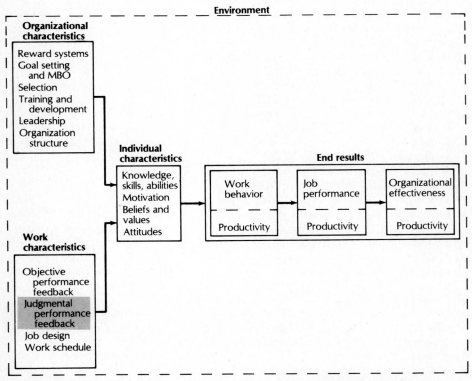

Conceptual framework of the determinants of productivity in organizations—a behavioral science approach.

# CHAPTER 10

# PERFORMANCE FEEDBACK: JUDGMENTAL INDICATORS

Judgmental measures of job performance are typically used because other, more objective (i.e., countable) indicators are unavailable.[1] In many jobs, and particularly in managerial jobs, it is often difficult to identify a comprehensive objective criterion against which subjective appraisals can be compared. Consequently, it is very hard to ascertain the validity of subjective performance appraisals.[2] Of 217 companies in a Conference Board study that reported having a performance appraisal system for managers, only 1 company had initiated an appraisal validation study—and that study was never completed.[3] Similarly, there has been a paucity of academic research examining (1) the validity of judgmental performance appraisal measures in terms of objective criteria and (2) the impact of judgmental performance feedback on objective criteria.[4]

A body of research has been produced, however, on improving the measurement properties (e.g., reliability, validity) of various judgmental performance indicators. This and related research has addressed four major issues: the design (format) of the measurement instrument, the performance evaluation process, characteristics of the rater, and the performance appraisal interview. Although most of this literature does not demonstrably relate to productivity, it is nevertheless relevant: measurement considerations place an upper bound on the validity and utility of subjective measures of performance. Accordingly, this chapter: (1) reviews research on the aforementioned four major issues related to subjective performance appraisals, (2) offers some specific suggestions toward enhancing the validity and legality of subjective performance appraisals, and (3) presents guidelines for implementing a performance measurement program.

## MAJOR ISSUES IN JUDGMENTAL PERFORMANCE APPRAISAL

### Design of the Performance Measurement Instrument

Although there are several types of judgmental evaluation instruments, the most widely used method is the rating scale.[5] A recent survey of 216 companies found that in 57 percent of all cases the primary performance evaluation technique was the rating scale, often accompanied by narrative comments.[6] Similarly, a survey of published research studies found that in 72 percent of all cases the primary criterion was a performance rating.[7] The present discussion, therefore, focuses primarily on the design of performance rating instruments.

For many years performance ratings were largely used to measure personality traits and broad performance characteristics. Typical dimensions were dependability, stability, initiative, maturity, loyalty, and aptitude. However, making judgments about such broad and often ill-defined dimensions raised many questions about the validity, reliability, and imperviousness to bias of such measures.

Raters may have very different ideas about the meaning of a trait such as "initiative." Some raters may define initiative in terms of self-reliance, others in terms of aggressiveness, and still others in terms of creativity, and so on. Of course, this kind of ambiguity does little to minimize the potential for various rater errors. Some raters tend to be rather lenient, others rather stringent; and some raters will be inclined to rate an individual high or low on all dimensions because of an overall impression—the halo error. Unfortunately, the halo error is not just a problem confronting a few unskillful raters; there is evidence that it reflects common cognitive processes underlying all evaluations. In making judgments, raters assign each ratee to a category, and the initial assignment colors subsequent judgments in two ways: by the selective screening of information and by various attributional tendencies.[8]

Partly in response to the problems associated with trait ratings, there has been an accelerating trend toward the measurement of observable work behaviors. Certainly there is less ambiguity associated with such specific, overt work behaviors as "prepares and distributes an agenda prior to the meeting," or "begins and ends the meeting on time," than there is with the trait "quality of leadership." There has been, consequently, a great deal of research examining the merits of various types of behavioral rating formats, such as, behaviorally anchored rating scales (BARS), behavioral expectation scales (BES), and behavioral observation scales (BOS).[9]

Taken as a whole, there are a number of advantages to using behavioral measures rather than making judgments about traits, broad performance dimensions, or overall job performance. First, behavioral measures, correctly developed, are comprehensive, encompassing all important aspects of the job. In contrast, some supervisors have rather idiosyncratic ideas about what constitutes good performance—e.g., "the good worker has a clean desk." Behavioral indicators attempt to substitute a more complex and content-valid categorization scheme for those which raters will use if left to their own devices.[10]

Second, behavioral indicators are relatively more objective than judgments about the person per se, since the former focus attention on overt, observable phenomena. Third, there is evidence that behavioral measures have slightly superior measurement characteristics when compared with more conventional assessments using graphic rating scales.[11] Fourth, and perhaps of greatest importance, behavioral indicators provide more useful (and psychologically more acceptable) information for individual improvement purposes.[12] Individuals who are told to improve their "leadership and communication skills" or their "sense of responsibility" are unlikely to know exactly what to do differently, assuming they are motivated to improve and are not so affronted by the assessment that they reject it entirely. In contrast, behavioral indicators define role requirements in terms of specific job behaviors. Fifth, behavioral measures provide performance feedback without the delays associated with end-result measures. While it may, for example, take years for the operational or financial results of an engineer's performance to be evident, behavioral indicators provide more timely information. (Indeed, today's financial results may actually reflect job performance that occurred a decade ago.) Thus, given the advantages of behavioral over nonbehavioral measures, it is not surprising that the former have been described as offering "immediate improvements in evaluation systems."[13]

Although many studies have compared behavioral and nonbehavioral measures in terms of various measurement (psychometric) properties, only a few studies have examined the impact of use of behavioral measures on objective performance indicators. One such study compared the effects of two judgmental evaluation methods, behavioral expectation scales (BES) and trait ratings, in terms of attitudes and job performance. The research involved two groups of engineers, (each rated by a different method) who responded to questionnaires after 6 and 18 months and for whom performance data were available. At the outset of the study, attitudes and three performance indices were essentially the same in both groups. After 18 months the BES group showed significantly better attitudes, especially in connection with the perceived equity of the ratings, the meaningfulness and clarity of performance feedback, and (lower) job-related tension. Further, scheduling performance improved dramatically in the BES group but only marginally in the other group. Adding to the impressiveness of the results were the following two considerations: raters had received no training in the use of BES scales, and the new performance evaluation system was in place for only the 18 months of the study.[14]

A second study examining both behavioral indicators and objective performance data found strong correlations between behavioral observation scale (BOS) scores and measures of productivity ($r = .47$), and attendance ($r = .66$). The researchers suggested that "the advantage of behavioral criteria is that it allows the manager to determine 'how' and 'why' performance on cost-related variables can be maintained or improved."[15]

Another recent study reported on the development and validation of a performance appraisal instrument for managerial employees. On the basis of an extensive job analysis to determine the knowledge, skills, and abilities (KSA) required for successful job performance, twelve performance dimensions were identified (see Figure 10-1). A modified behavioral expectation scale (BES) procedure was employed to develop anchors, and content validity was established by having 158 managers review the dimensions with respect to job importance. More than 75 percent of the managers rated each of the twelve dimensions as important or extremely important in terms of successful job performance. Evidence of convergent validity was obtained by correlating each of the twelve performance factor ratings with an accomplishment-based MBO evaluation.

**FIGURE 10-1**
DIMENSIONS OF MANAGERIAL JOBS: 12 PERFORMANCE FACTORS

| | |
|---|---|
| 1 Administration | Smoothly carrying out the activities required by organization's rules, policies, and procedures in getting the job done |
| 2 Job knowledge | The expertise or area of specialized knowledge that the individual brings to bear in the job |
| 3 Forecasting and planning | Anticipating trends or probable occurrences and setting the requirements for the actions and resources needed to deal with them |
| 4 Innovation | The degree to which individuals search for, create, and apply new ideas, methods, techniques, or processes to improve the manner in which work is performed |
| 5 Communication skills | The degree and skill with which individuals communicate all matters of importance—problems, obstacles, successes, instructions, orders, directives, etc.—to their superiors, peers, and subordinates |
| 6 Initiative | Taking action beyond what is necessarily called for. Originating action rather than just responding to events |
| 7 Being responsible | The degree to which individuals carry out work responsibilities and obligations in a reliable, punctual manner without the need for close supervision |
| 8 Work relationships | Promoting harmonious and cooperative relationships with work associates leading to a reduction of personal pressure and stress and increased productivity |
| 9 Salesmanship | Convincing others, by word or by example, to accept or to act in harmony with their wishes. (This does not include directives and orders from a base of power.) |
| 10 Decision making | Selecting from alternatives a particular course of action and committing to it |
| 11 Leadership | Motivating and getting results through others |
| 12 Selection and development of personnel | Selecting competent individuals and effectively training and appraising them to develop their best capabilities for the organization |

*Source:* Donald H. Brush and Lyle F. Schoenfeldt, "Management Performance Appraisal: Validation and Application," unpublished paper, Rensselaer Polytechnic Institute, 1981, pp. 9–11.

The mean correlation was rather robust ($r = .53$), and the multiple correlation (using all twelve rating scores as predictors) was quite impressive ($R = .75$). Thus, the researchers provided evidence of both content and convergent validity for their rating instrument.[16]

As noted above, there have been numerous studies pertinent to the design of rating scales; however, a review of the research on questionnaire development is beyond the scope of this chapter. A few specific findings are illustrative of the results of this research. Evidence indicates that scales should have at least three rating points, but no more than nine.[17] Scales should contain items reflective of unfavorable, as well as favorable outcomes.[18] And the provision of dimension clarifying statements, in addition to behavioral descriptors for specific items, usually improves the psychometric properties of a behaviorally based rating scale.[19]

### The Evaluation Process

Performance appraisals can serve a number of purposes, including (1) providing information pertinent to administrative decisions (e.g., compensation, promotion, work-force planning, layoffs), (2) providing feedback useful for individual development (e.g., identifying areas for improvement, action planning for career development), (3) providing information useful for research purposes (e.g., validation of selection devices and training programs), and (4) providing justification and documentation for personnel decisions—a purpose that is rarely acknowledged.

There is wide agreement that the more objectives an organization tries to accomplish via its performance appraisal system, the less successful the system is likely to be. Certainly, the early research on performance appraisal at General Electric is consistent with this conclusion. When the performance appraisal system was used for both administrative and developmental purposes, there was a nonfulfillment of the developmental functions.[20] More recent research by Brinkerhoff and Kanter confirms the general conclusion that more can be less.[21]

Consider the problem which often arises when managers are required to use performance appraisal ratings both for administrative and developmental purposes. A recent study found that, "when required to give feedback to subordinates, supervisors significantly distorted their feedback to make it more positive for low performers and . . . this effect was most pronounced for those [subordinates] for whom they [supervisors] believed poor performance was due to lack of ability."[22] To the extent that subordinates need accurate feedback in order to improve, this finding is rather disquieting. Compounding the problem, distorted ratings—resulting from having to share evaluations with subordinates—may threaten the achievement of administrative objectives.

More concretely, Brinkerhoff and Kanter have noted that, "in one large company, employee relations staff sometimes laughed at the appraisals they saw because they would often have independent information that an employee rated 'outstanding' was constantly complained about by his manager."[23] Along these lines, the situation frequently arises where a manager may want to terminate an employee for poor performance, but is unable to do so because the manager has consistently given the employee satisfactory or better evaluations.[24] Of course, not only do distortions occur on rating forms, they also occur with evaluative essays. To facilitate comprehension, a guide to the accurate interpretation of terms used in evaluative essays is provided in Figure 10-2.

A second issue related to the appraisal process is the type of information obtained. There is evidence that the accuracy of performance ratings is enhanced when objective performance criteria are established.[25] Yet for many

**FIGURE 10-2**
TERMS USEFUL IN PERFORMANCE EVALUATION AND THEIR MEANINGS

| Term | Meaning |
| --- | --- |
| Average employee | Not too bright |
| Exceptionally well qualified | Has committed no major blunders to date |
| Active socially | Drinks heavily |
| Wife is active socially | She drinks too |
| Character and integrity above reproach | Still one step ahead of the law |
| Zealous attitude | Opinionated |
| Quick thinking | Offers plausible excuses for errors |
| Takes pride in his work | Conceited |
| Takes advantage of every opportunity to progress . | Buys drinks for the boss |
| Forceful and aggressive | Argumentative |
| Outstanding | Frequently in the rain |
| Indifferent to instruction | Knows more than his seniors |
| Stern disciplinarian | A bastard |
| Tactful in dealing with superiors | Knows when to keep mouth shut |
| Approaches difficult problems with logic | Finds someone else to do the job |
| A keen analyst | Thoroughly confused |
| Definitely not the "desk" type | Did not go to college |
| Expresses himself well | Speaks English fluently |
| Often spends extra hours on the job | Miserable home life |
| Conscientous and careful | Scared |
| Meticulous in attention to detail | A nit picker |
| Demonstrates qualities of leadership | Has a loud voice |
| Shows exceptionally good judgment | Lucky |
| Maintains professional attitude | A snob |
| Keen sense of humor | Has vast repertoire of dirty jokes |
| Strong adherence to principles | Stubborn |
| Career minded | Back-stabber |
| Gets along extremely well with superiors and subordinates alike | A coward |
| Slightly below average | Stupid |
| A very fine employee of great value to the organization | Gets to work on time |

*Source: The Industrial Psychologist, 18 (Nov. 1980), 6.*

of today's (white-collar) jobs, it is difficult or impossible to identify *compre-hensive* objective indicators: those that exist tend to be deficient, measuring only a portion of the total domain of job responsibilities. Performance evalu-ations based solely on such limited indicators can have dysfunctional conse-quences: employees may attend only to what is being measured, i.e., to "play-ing the game."[26] Trying to "look good," managers may focus solely on short-term, "bottom-line" results, ignoring how results are obtained, i.e., the price in terms of employee development or customer relations.[27] It is, therefore, advis-able that performance appraisals be based on multiple indicators, combining both objective data and subjective evaluations. The use of trait ratings, how-ever, should be discouraged, given their susceptibility to rating errors and rater bias. Further, with respect to employee development, all rating approaches are not equal. Not only do trait ratings yield vague injunctions, such as, improve your "sense of responsibility," they also often point to characteristics over which people have little control, such as their self-confidence or cheerfulness.

A third process-related issue concerns who does the rating. Where possible it is desirable to obtain multiple evaluations.[28] In one engineering organization, for example, technical professionals are evaluated by all knowledgeable super-visors, present and past. A weighting system is employed whereby the present supervisor's rating counts 10, the prior supervisor's rating 8, and so forth. Sim-ilarly, the rating by the supervisor's supervisor counts 8, and the rating by that person's supervisor counts 6.

The use of multiple ratings minimizes the possible biases resulting from a single rater's idiosyncratic categorization system.[29] Such a method also mini-mizes the dynamics of power and the resulting uncertainties that figure so prominently in organizational reality.[30] Research suggests that the individual who is evaluated by a low-power manager may be at a distinct disadvantage.[31]

Alan Patz has underscored the threat that political considerations represent to valid performance appraisals. In his words, "The most obvious barrier to effective performance appraisal is . . . [employee] suspicion (if not certainty) that data falsification for selfish purposes actively persists. Most [employees] believe that superiors attempt to work the appraisal system to their own advan-tage by consciously or unconsciously reporting false evaluations of their sub-ordinates."[32] Clearly, the use of multiple evaluations minimizes both the impact of inaccurate, biased evaluations and the motivation to produce such evaluations.

A fourth important aspect of the performance appraisal process is the extent to which performance evaluations count in terms of organizationally mediated outcomes (e.g., salary, job title, and so forth). If performance evaluations do not importantly influence various indicators of career success, they will likely come to be regarded as "academic."[33]

Fifth, raters should conduct frequent evaluations and they should provide ratees with continuing feedback regarding performance—certainly more fre-quent than an annual interview. Advantages associated with frequent feedback include (1) the provision of more timely information for developmental purposes, (2) a potential reduction in rater errors (e.g., halo, leniency), (3) a reduction in the level of apprehension or anxiety experienced by both raters and ratees, because each evaluation is only one of many, and (4) a possible reduction in ratee defensiveness and motivation to argue over a given rating, again because it is only one of many.[34] Of course, too-frequent evaluations may be more costly than worthwhile, and may even be seen as indicative of excessively close supervision.[35] Nevertheless, it is often the case that frequent feedback is necessary for the evaluator to be "heard," and for the message to "sink in."[36]

Sixth, raters should be competent. This issue is discussed in the next section.

Seventh, and finally, an effective performance appraisal system requires managerial support, particularly from top management. In this regard, consider the fairly common problem faced by a major bank. The personnel function developed a good, workable (MBO type) performance appraisal system which got nowhere with the organization's line managers. Top management provided neither sanctions nor rewards for using the program "and it fell by the wayside as just another 'personnel program.'"[37]

## Characteristics of the Rater

Much research has been conducted on the effects of various rater characteristics on rater accuracy and effectiveness. These studies can be grouped into two categories, those examining relatively enduring personal characteristics of the rater, and those examining characteristics more amenable to change. Illustrative of the first set of studies are those focusing on the effects of rater sex, race, age, job performance, cognitive complexity, and intelligence. With respect to these variables the following results have been found: (1) no reliable effects occur on account of differences in age, sex, or cognitive complexity;[38] (2) slightly higher ratings are given, on the average, to subordinates of the same race;[39] (3) high-performing raters are less prone to committing the leniency error, and make greater distinctions in the ratings they assign—i.e., they are more likely to "spread out" their ratings;[40] and (4) more intelligent raters typically provide more valid performance ratings.[41]

Of greater practical utility, it would appear, are studies that have focused on variables organizations can more readily influence. In this category are studies relating to improving rater competence through training. Evidence indicates clearly that rater training programs are sorely needed; apparently there are very few "naturally gifted" raters. Unfortunately, simply warning people about possible errors (i.e., lecturing them about rater errors) does not reduce the frequency of their occurrence.[42] (Presumably, the recipients of the lecture think the information is being provided for the benefit of the other attendees.) What is required is a workshop conducted according to the principles of learning, namely, active participation, knowledge of results, and practice. Effective rater training apparently requires 6 to 8 hours of workshop training.[43]

Although most of the training programs to date have focused on the use of rating forms, training is perhaps even more urgently needed in the observation and recording of day-to-day work behaviors. Unfortunately, human recollections are generally not very accurate. People tend to forget some facts and "refabricate" others to fill in the gaps; further, they tend to adjust their recollections to fit their values and expectations. In short, because people are not very careful observers, distortions occur in what they remember.[44]

Memory-related errors can be reduced, however, through the routine use of behavior sampling and the recording of particularly noteworthy behaviors for consideration when evaluation decisions are to be made.[45] Evidence is strong that the typical rater is cognitively unprepared to summarize adequately a great many observations if no record has been kept throughout the appraisal period.[46] Yet in practice the systematic observation and recording of work behaviors does not occur. Instead, raters tend to rely upon broad stereotypic impressions of the ratee, i.e., the cognitive categorization process.[47]

For appraising performance on high-level white-collar jobs, it is particularly important that work sampling, careful observation, and the recording of critical incidents take place. On these jobs, comprehensive, objective indicators are rarely present; hence it is especially difficult to evaluate performance. Further complicating matters, high-level white-collar jobs often entail complex tasks, lack clear-cut goals, involve outcomes that are unpredictable, and are highly dependent on the work of other people.[48] Given these obstacles to accurate performance appraisal, the presence of skilled evaluators is all the more difficult to accomplish, yet important to achieve. Certainly, the more demanding the performance appraisal situation, the truer the ancient Chinese proverb: the palest ink is clearer than the best memory.

### The Performance Appraisal Interview

There is considerable evidence that managers in general are reluctant to conduct performance appraisal interviews (sometimes called performance reviews). This reluctance is manifested in several ways: managers may avoid holding an interview altogether, or if this is not possible, postpone the performance review until the last possible minute when, on the way to catch a plane, they hurriedly hold a perfunctory meeting to take care of the "personnel department's new forms."[49] Hall and Lawler have documented the occurrence of such practices, labeling the phenomenon the "vanishing performance appraisal." When Hall and Lawler questioned managers about the frequency of performance appraisal interviews they were told, "Sure, we do it every six months." However, on speaking to subordinates, they discovered that not only did appraisal interviews not take place, many employees did not know there existed a formal performance appraisal system.[50] Apparently, many managers held discussions that were so cursory, subordinates did not realize they had participated in performance appraisal interviews.[51]

Additional evidence of the pervasive reluctance to hold performance appraisal interviews is provided by the Center for Creative Leadership's survey of 1450 managers. The good news was that 88 percent of the managers reported receiving performance appraisal feedback via a formal interview. The bad news was that 14 percent of the managers reported that the entire interview lasted less than 30 minutes and 60 percent reported that the review took between 30 and 60 minutes. Only 14 percent reported having an appraisal interview that lasted an hour or more.[52]

Why are managers so reluctant to provide complete, accurate, and timely information to subordinates in a face to face meeting? One explanation is provided by Felix Lopez, author of the book *Personnel Interviewing*. Lopez has shown the following transcript to hundreds of practicing managers.[53]

*Jim:* You wanted to see me, Mr. Manager?
*Mr. Manager:* Yes, Jim. I would like to talk with you about your work this past year.
*Jim:* Oh, fine. (Pause) Has it been ok?

When asked to describe what ensued, the vast majority of the managers stated that Mr. Manager was largely critical of Jim's performance; Jim had a negative emotional reaction (he was angry, sullen, defensive, or depressed); and that Jim's job performance subsequently declined. In brief, the experience of most managers is that performance appraisal interviews not only "don't work," they are counterproductive.

A second reason why managers are reluctant to conduct performance appraisal interviews is that the process is emotionally costly. Managers believe (probably correctly) that employees who are given unfavorable evaluative feedback will have reduced liking for the manager who provided the feedback. Calling criticism "the atomic bomb of human relations," Mortimer Feinberg notes that managers not only have to criticize and judge (playing "umpire"), they must also live with the people they judge (being part of the "home team").[54] Consequently some managers, when conducting performance appraisal interviews, "fudge or misrepresent their evaluations to avoid the embarrassment and conflict inherent in criticizing a subordinate's performance."[55] Further, managers may be fearful of the anger, hostility, and possible threats of low-performing subordinates; they may also feel guilty (unconsciously) about damaging a subordinate by giving low evaluations;[56] and they may feel an uncomfortable sense of pity for such an individual. No wonder many managers and subordinates approach the performance appraisal interview with great feelings of apprehension, as if it were "time for their punishment."[57]

In a more constructive vein, a growing research literature has accumulated concerning the conduct of the performance appraisal interview. The following factors have been found to contribute to an effective interview.[58]

**1** *Participation.* The subordinate has an opportunity to express his or her thoughts and feelings, i.e., the subordinate's self-assessment. To increase participation the manager might ask about the subordinate's greatest recent job successes, and the manager might inquire about the job-related problems encountered.

**2** *Supportive behavior.* The manager evinces a friendly, helpful, constructive attitude, is respectful, and recognizes good job performance. Supportiveness is also indicated by scheduling a follow-up meeting and by ending the interview on a positive note.

**3** *Mutual goal setting.* The manager and the subordinate agree on specific future goals.

**4** *Solving performance problems.* The manager helps find solutions to job-related problems, removing obstacles to performance.

**5** *Limited amount of criticism.* Only a few performance problems or deficiencies are discussed, because generally speaking, more is less effective.

**6** *Amount of threat experienced.* The more threatening the interview, the less effective it is.

**7** *Self-development planning.* The subordinate perceives a high degree of influence in planning for his or her self-development.

**8** *Proportion of air time.* The manager spends roughly an equal amount of time talking and listening.

**9** *Job performance vs. personality.* The manager discusses specific job-related behaviors (critical incidents) and performances (results), rather than general personality traits.

**10** *Adequate time allowed.* The manager allots enough time to cover thoroughly the issues at hand. The manager should ensure that outside events (e.g., telephone calls) do not interrupt the discussion.

**11** *Subordinate preparation.* Subordinates should be encouraged, if not required, to analyze prior to the interview their job responsibilities, the problems encountered, and their level of job performance. (This increases participation, creates a more equal distribution of air time, and makes it more likely that specific performance-related problems will be identified and resolved.)

Although all eleven factors have been found to influence the subordinate's satisfaction with the performance appraisal interview, or the subordinate's satisfaction with the supervisor, only four of these factors have been found to influence work motivation and job performance. In probable (descending) order of impact these latter factors are (1) setting future performance targets (goal setting), (2) clearing up job-related obstacles and problems, (3) involving the subordinate in self-development planning, and (4) supportive supervisory behavior.

Unfortunately, in practice performance appraisal interviews generally fail to produce positive improvements in subordinate performance because managers lack the required interviewing skills.[59] Moreover, managers often have very inaccurate ideas of how they actually conduct the performance appraisal interview. Research has repeatedly found that managers (self-servingly) overestimate the extent to which they invite participation, are supportive, and so forth.[60] And merely telling the manager to "be more supportive" is unlikely to change the manager's behavior. With behavior-based training, however, managers can be taught many of the critical skills involved in conducting an effective performance appraisal interview.[61]

## TOWARD A VALID AND DEFENSIBLE APPRAISAL SYSTEM

As noted previously (Chapter 4), managers eagerly seek answers to the following four questions: "What am I really supposed to accomplish?"; "What are the limits to my authority?"; "How good is good?"; and "How'm I doing?". Clearly, a valid and defensible performance appraisal system will provide comprehensive, accurate, and timely answers to all four questions. Yet, in practice managers (and nonmanagers) often have to rely on indirect, obscure sources of information for answers. In connection with the last question ("How'm I doing?"), employees may make inferences based on how friendly the boss is or they may seek clues by talking with secretaries or by noting whether they are invited to particular meetings.[62] From the world of professional baseball, Jim Bouton has provided a vivid account of how he obtained performance feedback.

> . . . you could always tell how you were doing by the way the [pitching coach] said good morning. If he said, "Well now, good morning Jimsie boy," that meant you'd won your last two or three games and were in the starting rotation. If he nodded his head to you and said, "Jimbo, how are you doin', how are you doin'?" you were still in the starting rotation, but your record probably wasn't much over .500. If he just said, "Mornin'," that meant you were on your way down, that you'd probably lost four out of five and it was doubtful if you would be getting any more starts. If he simply looked at you and gave a solemn nod, that meant you might get some mop-up relief work, or you might not, but you definitely weren't starting anymore and would never get into a close game again. And if he looked past you, over your shoulder as if you didn't exist, it was all over and you might as well pack your bag because you could be traded or sent down at any moment.[63]

Of course, unlike pitching, many jobs lack clear performance feedback that is provided by the work itself (e.g., games won, earned run average). Indeed, the president of a major company wrote that the performance standard for his job consisted of the following criterion: "The Chairman thinks I am doing a good job."

It would seem that there must be "a better way" of defining job responsibilities, delimiting authority, setting standards, and measuring job performance than is often the case in practice. Certainly, the courts are more demanding in what they view as a valid performance appraisal system. Latham and Wexley have noted that "the courts have developed a deep skepticism of appraisal techniques involving supervisory judgments that depend almost entirely on subjective evaluation. . . . The courts have specifically condemned procedures based on trait scales . . . [that employ] vague terms such as commitment, initiative, and aggressiveness, that are not defined in terms of overt observable behavior."[64]

The cornerstone of a valid performance appraisal is the job analysis.[65] This is made explicit by the federal government's *Uniform Guidelines:*

> There shall be a job analysis which includes an analysis of the important work behaviors required for successful performance. . . . Any job analysis should focus on work behavior(s) and the tasks associated with them. (Sec. 14.C.2)

It is noteworthy that behaviorally based performance appraisal measures, unlike conventional rating scales, require for their development the conduct of a job analysis.

Unfortunately, the legal situation is not as clear-cut as might ideally be the case. On a positive note, the courts have begun to recognize that for many jobs, comprehensive objective indicators of performance neither exist nor are to be found. For example, in the case of Rogers *v.* International Paper Company, the Eighth Circuit Court of Appeals observed that subjective criteria "are not to be condemned as unlawful per se, for in all fairness to the applicants and employers alike, decisions about hiring and promotion in supervisory and managerial jobs cannot realistically be made using objective standards alone."[66] However, on a less positive note, court decisions and the *Uniform Guidelines* themselves are not always consistent with existing laws.[67] Yet despite the tenuousness of the present situation, personnel decisions still must be made on the basis of performance appraisals. Indeed, "the personnel professional, continuously faced with the possibility of charges of illegal discrimination, must find ways of ensuring [that] personnel decisions are made in a way which will satisfy the scrutiny of law enforcement agencies and the courts."[68] Certainly, the task of assessing performance is not an easy one under the best of conditions.

> The typical manager has many duties, only some of which involve the direct supervision of subordinates. . . . Direct information about subordinates' job behavior is often fragmentary; direct personal contact with subordinates may be minimal and restricted to a particular set of situations, depending on the nature of the job. Jobs themselves are incompletely understood, and specific duties may be inadequately described or entirely unspecified, especially at higher managerial levels . . . and it should be realized that . . . most people charged with evaluating others have many other activities that also must be performed and thus a limited amount of time that can be spent on observation and evaluation.[69]

One possible response to this situation is to give up in despair. Alternatively, notwithstanding the problems, organizations can resolve to act constructively toward the development of an acceptable and defensible performance appraisal system. In this quest, the development of a valid performance measurement system becomes the first order of business.[70] Having established the relevance and validity of a given performance measurement method, the next major task is to ensure that the system is legally defensible. Based on their review of some twenty recent court cases, Klasson and his associates have identified what they believe are the basic *minimum* requirements of a defensible system. They suggest that organizations adhere to the following specific recommendations.[71]

**1** The process should be formalized, completely documented, standardized, and to the extent possible, objective in nature. Further, there should be statements regarding the purposes of appraisals; use by management should be mandatory; there should be complete disclosure of the bases of evaluation; and due process procedures should exist.

**2** Standards of performance should exist for all positions, based on a thorough, formal job analysis.

**3** Performance standards (behaviors, traits, or results) should be job-related and relevant to successful job performance.

**4** Weights for the component dimensions of performance evaluations should be fixed in advance, and supervisory evaluations should be only one component of the overall performance appraisal process.

**5** Appraisers should be adequately trained in the use of appraisal techniques.

**6** Appraisers should have substantial opportunities to observe a representative sample of an employee's job-related performance.

**7** Multiple appraisers should be used if it enhances the overall quality of assessment.

**8** The administration and scoring of performance appraisals should be standardized and controlled.

**9** Opportunities for promotion and transfer should be posted and this information should be made available to potentially interested individuals.

**10** An employee-initiated promotion and transfer procedure should exist which does not require the immediate supervisor's recommendation.

### IMPLEMENTATION OF A PERFORMANCE MEASUREMENT AND FEEDBACK SYSTEM

The remainder of this chapter is concerned with the concrete steps organizations can take toward the successful implementation of a performance measurement and feedback system. The suggestions that follow are pertinent to implementing both objective and judgmental performance feedback systems.[72]

**1** *Visible top management support.* Development of a successful performance measurement system requires effort and commitment from top management. Only top management can provide the "imprimatur of authority."[73]

**2** *Mechanisms for insuring middle management and supervisory commitment.* Middle managers can easily sabotage a performance evaluation program. For such a program to succeed, managers must see conducting appraisals as critical to their own role success.[74] One mechanism for increasing support is early training and exposure to the program. There is evidence that when supervisors are trained to use a new system before lower-level personnel, program implementation is superior compared to when supervisors are trained after lower-level personnel.[75]

The case of Aer Lingus provides a dramatic illustration of the power of middle managers. At the Dublin office, the new monitoring and feedback program was enthusiastically supported by local (middle) management and it flourished. However, at the London and New York offices, the measurement program was only half-heartedly accepted by local management; as a consequence, it was quietly discontinued at those offices.[76]

**3** *A high level of employee participation.* Evidence from various settings supports the finding that the involvement and participation of employees is vital for the successful design and implementation of a performance measurement program.[77] With professional white-collar employees, it is especially important that participation occur, and early on.

**4** *Begin with success.* The initial strategy should be to try to begin the measurement program within parts of the organization where there is a good chance of achieving positive results—"winners." Given demonstrated successes, the credibility of the program increases, and this facilitates expansion to more complex and recalcitrant segments of the organization.

**5** *Build a critical mass.* Unless a critical mass is attained, the program is unlikely to be sustained. Accordingly, the measurement program must be diffused throughout a significant part of the organization.

**6** *Task force and charter.* In order to build a critical mass, design and implementation of the performance measurement system ought to be the responsibility of an *ad hoc* group of employees that "signals its 'clout' by its composition."[78] The task force, steering committee, or council should be chartered to represent top management in the development of a system within prescribed guidelines.

**7** *Information and communication.* From the very beginning, the task force should advertise its constructive intent. "Spelling out its mission, it should spread the word to lower management and the operating staff that no revolutionary 'new order' impends. It should establish communications with a labor union . . . it should take advantage of company newspapers or other in-house media to tell its story."[79] Additionally, the task force might designate some individuals as liaison people throughout the organization, and might conduct briefings, demonstrations, and send out announcements.

**8** *Training a cadre of users.* It is important that a sizable staff of auxiliaries exists to support the system. In this quest, each segment of the organization should be "seeded" with people who are trained in the use of the system. They will enable the system to work during the postdevelopment phase, and they will serve as advocates.

**9** *Initial development.* After a "debugging" period, performance measurement should be undertaken on a trial basis. To indicate the trial nature of the first installation, the system should explicitly be labeled as "first generation," suggesting that changes will occur.

**10** *Instructions and recommendations.* Before the task force is disbanded, an instruction manual should be written for users. The manual should describe the general nature of the system (i.e., the structure, data sources, purposes) and the measurement process per se (i.e., procedures, periodicity, forms, reports, staffing). Also, the task force should report on early results and offer recommendations.

**11** *Subsequent reviews.* Line managers should be responsible for reporting results of the program periodically. Having line managers do the reporting provides recognition and perhaps a feeling of accomplishment; it may also increase the psychological ownership and commitment of line managers. Reviews should be addressed to high-level administrators. A major issue should be identifying ways of obtaining the cooperation of first-level line managers in making the system "a way of life with the people they supervise."[80]

## SUMMARY

Judgmental performance measures are generally used because comprehensive, objective performance measures are unavailable. While some objective indicators do exist, they tend to be deficient, measuring only component aspects of job performance. A few studies, however, have compared judgmental and objective measures of job performance; they indicate that judgmental performance measures can correlate highly with more objective measures.

A great deal of research has been conducted concerning the development and validation of judgmental performance appraisal systems. Reviewing much of the literature, the first part of this chapter addressed four issues: the design of a performance measurement instrument, the evaluation process, characteristics of the rater, and the performance appraisal interview. Suggestions were offered in connection with each topic.

In light of recent court decisions and (sometimes contradictory) laws, ten guidelines were identified that represent the basic minimum requirements of a valid and defensible performance measurement system. Suggestions were also offered regarding implementation. Key steps include obtaining management support, encouraging employee participation, achieving initial successes, and diffusing the intervention throughout the organization.

## NOTES

1   Frank E. Saal, Ronald G. Downey, and Mary A. Lahey, "Rating the Ratings: Assessing the Psychometric Quality of Rating Data," *Psychological Bulletin,* 88 (1980), 419.

2   Frank J. Landy and James L. Farr, "Performance Rating," *Psychological Bulletin,* 87 (1980), 72; also see Donald H. Brush and Lyle F. Schoenfeldt, "Management Performance Appraisal: Validation and Application," unpublished paper, Rensselaer Polytechnic Institute, 1981, p. 3.

3   W. B. Walker, in "Performance Appraisal: The Barrier to Pay for Performance," *Proceedings, National Meeting of the American Compensation Association* (1978), p. 43.

4   Donald H. Brush and Lyle F. Schoenfeldt, "Management Performance Appraisal," p. 4.

5   Frank E. Saal, Ronald G. Downey, and Mary A. Lahey, "Rating the Ratings," p. 426.

6   Alan H. Locher and Kenneth S. Teel, "Performance Appraisal—A Survey of Current Practices," *Personnel Journal,* 56, No. 5 (May 1977), 245–247, 254. A more recent survey (1979) revealed that 50 percent of responding companies used ratings as the primary performance appraisal technique, and 78 percent used both ratings

and narrative evaluations. Apparently, narrative evaluations are becoming more widely used, especially for high-level jobs. See Kenneth S. Teel, "Performance Appraisal: Current Trends, Persistent Progress," *Personnel Journal,* 59, No. 4 (Apr. 1980), 296–301, 316.

**7** Frank J. Landy and James L. Farr, "Performance Rating," p. 72.

**8** For a thorough review of these processes, see the excellent review article by Jack M. Feldman, "Beyond Attribution Theory: Cognitive Processes in Performance Appraisal," *Journal of Applied Psychology,* 66 (1981), 127–148.

**9** For a comprehensive discussion and critique of the fine points distinguishing these techniques from one another see Gary P. Latham and Kenneth N. Wexley, *Increasing Productivity through Performance Appraisal* (Reading, Mass.: Addison-Wesley, 1981).

**10** Jack M. Feldman, "Beyond Attribution Theory," p. 144.

**11** Frank J. Landy and James L. Farr, "Performance Rating," pp. 82–89.

**12** John M. Ivancevich, "A Longitudinal Study of Behavioral Expectation Scales: Attitudes and Performance," *Journal of Applied Psychology,* 65 (1980), 139–140.

**13** Jack M. Feldman, "Beyond Attribution Theory," p. 144.

**14** John M. Ivancevich, "Behavioral Expectation Scales," pp. 139–146.

**15** Gary P. Latham and Kenneth N. Wexley, "Behavioral Observation Scales for Performance Appraisal Purposes," *Personnel Psychology,* 30 (1977), 266–267.

**16** Donald H. Brush and Lyle F. Schoenfeldt, "Management Performance Appraisal," passim.

**17** Frank J. Landy and James L. Farr, "Performance Rating," pp. 87–89.

**18** Gary P. Latham and Terence R. Mitchell, "Behavioral Criteria and Potential Reinforcers for the Engineer/Scientist in an Industrial Setting," *JSAS Catalogue of Selected Documents in Psychology,* 6, No. 3 (1976), Ms. 1316, p. 83.

**19** H. John Bernardin and Patricia C. Smith, "A Clarification of Some Issues Regarding the Development and Use of Behaviorally Anchored Rating Scales," paper presented at the 40th Annual Meeting of the Academy of Management (Detroit), 1980, p. 6.

**20** Derick W. Brinkerhoff and Rosabeth Moss Kanter, "Appraising the Performance of Performance Appraisal," *Sloan Management Review,* 21 (Spring 1980), 4.

**21** Herbert H. Meyer, Emanuel Kay, and John R. P. French, Jr., "Split Roles in Performance Appraisal," *Harvard Business Review,* 43, No. 1 (1965), 123–129. However, more recent research indicates that the inclusion of salary-related matters in the performance appraisal interview can have a positive effect due to the provision of more information and the energizing effects of salary discussion. Hence, it may be a mistake to "outlaw" the discussion of salary in performance appraisal interviews. See J. Bruce Prince and Edward E. Lawler III, "The Impact of Discussing Salary Action in the Performance Appraisal Meeting," unpublished paper, Univ. of Southern California, 1982, pp. 18–22.

**22** Daniel R. Ilgen and William A. Knowlton, Jr., "Performance Attributional Effects on Feedback from Superiors," *Organizational Behavior and Human Performance,* 25 (1980), p. 441.

**23** Derick W. Brinkerhoff and Rosabeth Moss Kanter, "Appraising the Performance of Performance Appraisal," p. 12. Moreover, evidence indicates that evaluations conducted to determine possible rewards are more stringent than evaluations conducted to determine possible penalties. See Michael C. Gallagher, "More Bias in Performance Evaluation?" *Personnel,* 55 (July–Aug. 1978), 35–48.

**24** W. B. Walker, "Performance Appraisal," pp. 43–44.

**25** William J. Bigoness, "Effect of Applicant's Sex, Race, and Performance on Employers' Performance Ratings: Some Additional Findings," *Journal of Applied Psychology,* 61 (1976), 80–84.

**26** Gene W. Dalton, "Motivation and Control in Organizations," in *Motivation and Control in Organizations,* ed. Gene W. Dalton and Paul R. Lawrence (Homewood, Ill.: Irwin-Dorsey, 1971), pp. 1–35; also see V. F. Ridgway, "Dysfunctional Consequences of Performance Measurements," *Administrative Science Quarterly,* 1 (1956), 240–247; also see Peter M. Blau, *The Dynamics of Bureaucracy* (Chicago: Univ. of Chicago Press, 1955).

**27** Harry Levinson, "Appraisal of *What* Performance?" *Harvard Business Review,* 54 (July–Aug. 1976), 30–36, 40, 44, 46, 160.

**28** Jack M. Feldman, "Beyond Attribution Theory," p. 144; also Gary P. Latham and Kenneth N. Wexley, *Increasing Productivity,* p. 96.

**29** Jack M. Feldman, "Beyond Attribution Theory," p. 144.

**30** Derick W. Brinkerhoff and Rosabeth Moss Kanter, "Appraising the Performance of Performance Appraisal," p. 13; also see Patricia Linenberger and Timothy J. Keaveny, "Performance Appraisal Standards Used By the Courts," *Personnel Administrator,* 26 (May 1981), 91–94.

**31** In this regard Brinkerhoff and Kanter, have written: "Managers who are powerless tend to act in domineering, controlling, and often punishing ways. They tend to reward mediocrity rather than talent, because talent is too threatening. . . . Finally, powerless raters, who tend to be rules-minded and see their own jobs in terms of 'putting in time' rather than performance, are less likely to evaluate subordinates accurately. With their nit-picking approach to supervision, they lack the motivation to carry out the performance appraisal process with sufficient care to facilitate employee development" ["Appraising the Performance of Performance Appraisal," *Sloan Management Review,* 21 (Spring 1980), 10–11. Copyright © 1980 by the Sloan Management Review Association. All rights reserved. Reprinted by permission.].

**32** Alan L. Patz, "Performance Appraisal: Useful But Still Resisted," *Harvard Business Review,* 53 (May–June 1975), 77. Copyright © 1975 by the President and Fellows of Harvard College; all rights reserved.

**33** Jack M. Feldman, "Beyond Attribution Theory," expressed this idea rather cogently: "the organization must establish an atmosphere in which valid evaluations have some positive consequences for both the evaluator and the evaluatee. The best evaluation system imaginable will be useless unless its consequences are meaningful. If, for example, a poor performing employee must be given a positive evaluation so he can be transferred, the evaluation system is meaningless. Likewise, if a reward system is so structured that the consequences of a very positive and a merely adequate evaluation are identical, the time spent developing an accurate, unbiased, highly differentiating system has been largely wasted" (p. 145). See also Susan Resnick and Monty Mohrman, "An Appraisal of Performance Appraisal: Summary Results of a Large Scale Study," unpublished report, Univ. of Southern California, 1981, pp. 43–44.

**34** Robert C. Ford and Kenneth M. Jennings, "How to Make Performance Appraisals More Effective," *Personnel,* 54 (Mar–Apr. 1977), 51–56.

**35** Derick W. Brinkerhoff and Rosabeth Moss Kanter, "Appraising the Performance of Performance Appraisal," p. 11.

**36** Felix M. Lopez, *Personnel Interviewing: Theory and Practice,* 2nd ed. (New York: McGraw-Hill, 1975), chapter 12. Relatedly, Alan L. Patz, "Performance Appraisal," quotes one manager's lament: "I've gone over this . . . three or four times with Ted, and I don't know why he doesn't understand it" ("Performance Appraisal," p. 78).

**37** Robert I. Lazer, "Performance Appraisal: What Does the Future Hold?" *Personnel Administrator,* 25 (July 1980), 70–71.

**38** Frank J. Landy and James L. Farr, "Performance Rating," pp. 74–76; H. John Bernardin and Robert L. Cardy, "Cognitive Complexity in Performance Appraisal: It Makes No Nevermind," paper presented at the 41st Annual Meeting of the Academy of Management (San Diego), 1981.

**39** Kurt Kraiger and J. Kevin Ford, "A Meta-Analysis of Ratee Race Effects in Performance Ratings," *Journal of Applied Psychology,* 70 (1985), 56–65; also see Frank J. Landy and James L. Farr, "Performance Rating," pp. 74–76.

**40** Ibid.; Abraham K. Korman, *Organizational Behavior* (Englewood Cliffs, N.J.: Prentice-Hall, 1977), p. 359.

**41** Abraham K. Korman, *Organizational Behavior,* p. 359.

**42** Gary P. Latham and Kenneth N. Wexley, *Increasing Productivity through Performance Appraisal,* p. 105.

**43** Ibid., pp. 107–118. In connection with the need for rater training, Latham and Wexley have written: "At the present time, few organizations incorporate training that will reduce rating errors in their performance appraisal system. They assume incorrectly that the careful construction of the appraisal instrument will obviate the need for training raters. This type of thinking is a mistake! Despite attempts to build sophisticated appraisal instruments . . . that are resistant to errors . . . evaluators continue to make errors when observing and evaluating employees" (*Increasing Productivity,* pp. 99–100).

**44** John Leo, "Memory: The Unreliable Witness," *Time,* 5 Jan. 1981, p. 89.

**45** Jack M. Feldman, "Beyond Attribution Theory," pp. 142–145.

**46** H. John Bernardin and Patricia C. Smith, "Behaviorally Anchored Rating Scales," p. 3.

**47** Jack M. Feldman, "Beyond Attribution Theory," pp. 135–141.

**48** Derick W. Brinkerhoff and Rosabeth Moss Kanter, "Appraising the Performance of Performance Appraisal," pp. 7–9.

**49** Robert I. Lazer, "Performance Appraisal," p. 69; Cynthia D. Fisher, "Transmission of Positive and Negative Feedback to Subordinates: A Laboratory Investigation," *Journal of Applied Psychology,* 64 (1979), 533–540.

**50** Douglas T. Hall and Edward E. Lawler III, "Unused Potential in Research and Development Organizations," *Research Management,* 12 (1969), 339–354; also Douglas T. Hall, *Careers in Organizations* (Santa Monica, Calif.: Goodyear, 1976), pp. 68, 155.

**51** For evidence consistent with this interpretation see Susan Resnick and Monty Mohrman, "An Appraisal of Performance Appraisal," pp. 10–12; also Ronald J. Burke and Eugene Deszca, "Supervisor-Subordinate Communication Experiences in Managing Job Performance: Two Blind Wisemen Describing an Elephant!" *Proceedings, ASAC Conference* (Montreal), 1980, p. 246.

**52** Tony Celluci and Mike Lombardo, "A Survey of Managerial Performance Appraisal Practices," *Center for Creative Leadership Bulletin,* 5 (June 1978), 3. Similarly, in the large-scale survey (with more than 2000 respondents) described by Resnick and

Mohrman, the mean duration of the performance appraisal interview was 55 minutes according to managers and only 36 minutes according to subordinates ("An Appraisal of Performance Appraisal," p. 12).

**53** Felix M. Lopez, *Personnel Interviewing.*

**54** Mortimer R. Feinberg, *Effective Psychology for Managers* (Englewood Cliffs, N.J.: Prentice-Hall, 1965), pp. 165–166.

**55** Robert I. Lazer, "Performance Appraisal," p. 69.

**56** Harry Levinson, "Management by Whose Objectives?" *Harvard Business Review,* 48 (July–Aug. 1970), 125–134.

**57** Along these lines, Gary P. Latham and Kenneth N. Wexley, *Increasing Productivity,* compare the performance appraisal interview to seat belts: "Most people believe they are necessary, but they don't like to use them" (p. 2).

**58** Information related to these eleven factors comes primarily from the following two sources: Ronald J. Burke, William Weitzel, and Tamara Weir, "Characteristics of Effective Employee Performance Review and Development Interviews: Replication and Extension," *Personnel Psychology,* 31 (1978), 903–919; and Wayne F. Nemeroff and Kenneth N. Wexley, "An Exploration of the Relationships between Performance Feedback Interview Characteristics and Interview Outcomes as Perceived by Managers and Subordinates," *Journal of Occupational Psychology,* 52 (1979), 25–34. Secondarily, pertinent information has been provided by the following: Herbert H. Meyer, Emanuel Kay, and John R. P. French, Jr., "Split Roles in Performance Appraisal"; Derick W. Brinkerhoff and Rosabeth M. Kanter, "Appraising the Performance of Performance Appraisal"; "The Issue of Feedback: How Do You Know How Well You Are Doing?" *Center for Creative Leadership Bulletin,* 5 (June 1978), 1–8; and Milan Moravec, "How Performance Appraisal Can Tie Communication to Productivity," *Personnel Administrator,* 26 (Jan. 1981), 51–54.

**59** Wayne F. Nemeroff and Kenneth N. Wexley, "Interview Characteristics and Interview Outcomes," p. 25.

**60** Wayne F. Nemeroff and Kenneth N. Wexley, "Interview Characteristics and Interview Outcomes"; Susan Resnick and Monty Mohrman, "An Appraisal of Performance Appraisal," pp. 10–20; also Ronald J. Burke and Eugene Deszca, "Supervisor-Subordinate Communication Experiences."

**61** Wayne F. Nemeroff and Kenneth N. Wexley, "Interview Characteristics and Interview Outcomes."

**62** Center for Creative Leadership, "The Issue of Feedback," pp. 2–5.

**63** D. W. Ball, "Failure in Sport," *American Sociological Review,* 41 (1976), 732–733. This account originally appeared in Jim Bouton's book *Ball Four* (New York: Dell, 1971), pp. 17–18.

**64** Gary P. Latham and Kenneth N. Wexley, *Increasing Productivity,* p. 32.

**65** Ibid., p. 48; Charles R. Klasson, Duane E. Thompson, and Gary L. Luben, "How Defensible Is Your Performance Appraisal System?" *Personnel Administrator,* 25 (Dec. 1980), 79; also Donald H. Brush and Lyle F. Schoenfeldt, "Management Performance Appraisal," p. 3.

**66** Gary P. Latham and Kenneth N. Wexley, *Increasing Productivity,* p. 80.

**67** Charles R. Klasson, Duane E. Thompson, and Gary L. Luben, "Your Performance Appraisal System," p. 80.

**68** Ibid., p. 81.

**69** Jack M. Feldman, "Beyond Attribution Theory," pp. 128, 142.

**70** For illustrations of validation procedures, see Donald H. Brush and Lyle F. Schoenfeldt, "Management Performance Appraisal"; also see Gary P. Latham and Terence R. Mitchell, "Behavioral Criteria and Potential Reinforcers."

**71** Charles R. Klasson, Duane E. Thompson, and Gary L. Luben, "Your Performance Appraisal System," pp. 81–82.

**72** Many of the guidelines for implementation were suggested by Irving H. Siegel in *Company Productivity: Measurement for Improvement* (Kalamazoo, Mich.: Upjohn Institute, 1980), pp. 45–53.

**73** Ibid., pp. 47–48. Also see Lawrence Rout, "White-Collar Workers Start to Get Attention in Productivity Studies," *Wall Street Journal,* 7 Aug. 1979, p. 19, in connection with the importance of top management support; also see Selma J. Mushkin and Frank H. Sandifer, *Personnel Management and Productivity in City Government* (Lexington, Mass.: Lexington Books, 1979), p. 45.

**74** Gary P. Latham and Kenneth N. Wexley, *Increasing Productivity,* pp. 199–200.

**75** Beth Sulzer-Azaroff, "Behavioral Ecology and Accident Prevention," *Journal of Organizational Behavior Management,* 2 (1978), 19.

**76** Stephen A. Allen, "Aer Lingus—Irish (B)," case #9-477-640 (Boston: Intercollegiate Case Clearing House, 1976), pp. 1–20.

**77** See Marvin E. Mundel, *Measuring and Enhancing the Productivity of Service and Government Organizations* (Tokyo: Asian Productivity Organization, 1975), p. 226; also Selma J. Mushkin and Frank H. Sandifer, *Personnel Management and Productivity,* p. 45.

**78** Irving H. Siegel, *Company Productivity,* p. 48.

**79** Ibid., p. 49.

**80** Gary P. Latham and Kenneth N. Wexley, *Increasing Productivity,* p. 201.

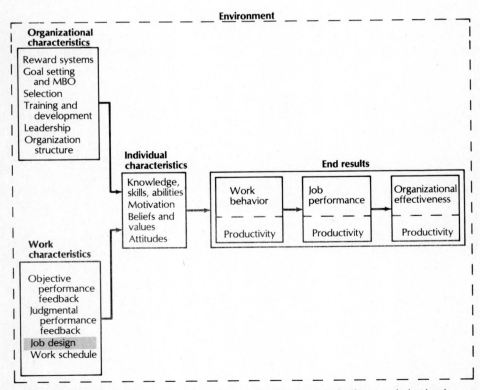

Conceptual framework of the determinants of productivity in organizations—a behavioral science approach.

# CHAPTER 11

# JOB DESIGN

For the past two decades, job design has been one of the most widely used behavioral science interventions. Programs incorporating various modifications have surfaced with such labels as job enrichment, work redesign, autonomous work groups, quality of work life, job restructuring, and so forth. Yet productivity improvement results have not been particularly impressive so far. Indeed, one of the leading exponents of job design based on behavioral science has commented that despite the high level of interest, "job enrichment seems to be failing at least as often as it succeeds."[1]

The present situation, consequently, is something of an anomaly: job design programs based on behavioral science have been widely implemented but they have also been problematic in regard to productivity. Of course, the popularity of a program is not sufficient justification for its continued use; nor is a history of problems sufficient reason for its discontinuance. Before drawing any conclusions about the utility of job design interventions for improving productivity, it is important to (1) review concepts and implementing procedures and (2) examine evidence of the efficacy of such interventions. After a brief historical overview, these two issues are considered in turn. Subsequent topics include (3) requisite conditions and constraints on job design interventions based on behavioral science, (4) a review of the efficacy of job design interventions based on work simplification, and (5) the explication of a third approach to job design, including evidence pertinent thereto.

## A HISTORICAL PERSPECTIVE

Around 350 B.C., Plato in his *Republic* argued for the advantages of task specialization. In his words,

Which would be better—that each should ply several trades, or that he should confine himself to his own? He should confine himself to his own. More is done, and
done better, and more easily when one man does one thing according to his capacity
and at the right moment. We must not be surprised to find that articles are made
better in big cities than in small. In small cities the same workman makes a bed, a
door, a plough, a table, and he often builds a house too. . . . Now it is impossible that
a workman who does so many things should be equally successful in all. In the big
cities, on the other hand . . . a man can live by one single trade. Sometimes he practices only a special branch of a trade. One makes men's shoes, another women's, one
lives entirely by the stitching of the shoe, another by cutting the leather. . . . A man
whose work is confined to such a limited task must necessarily excel at it.[2]

In 1776, Adam Smith noted in *The Wealth of Nations* that an individual
working alone could make at most twenty pins a day. However, by dividing
the work, which consisted of eighteen separate tasks, among ten workers, it was
possible to produce twelve pounds of pins a day—approximately 48,000 pins
or 4800 per worker.[3] Smith believed that specialization would not only increase
skill and dexterity, but also reduce the time spent changing operations and
accelerate the development of improved methods.[4]

Task specialization, standardization, and work simplification are three of
the key implementing concepts of what is now called the classical approach to
job design. Not only have these principles demonstrably contributed to greater
efficiency and uniformity of output, they have also been cost-effective. By paying people for the specific level of skill utilized, employers can hire workers
more economically; and by hiring people to perform narrowly defined jobs,
training and development costs can be held to a minimum. Industrial engineers, building on these concepts, have developed and employed techniques
such as time and motion study and elemental standard times. Hackman and
Oldham have labeled the classical approach to job design *Route 2*. (Route 1
will be described shortly.) In their view, Route 2 is characterized by first
designing jobs and then finding or fitting people to the jobs.[5]

According to some observers, the widespread application of Route 2 implementing concepts has led to a crisis among today's workers. Many of the workers whom Yankelovich characterizes as the "New Breed" may indeed have
expectations fundamentally incompatible with the Route 2 approach to job
design.

Other observers, though, assert that there is no real "crisis," except perhaps
in the eye of the beholder. Support for this position is provided by national
surveys that report no significant decline in job satisfaction during the past two
decades. Actually, the level of job satisfaction remains quite high: more than
80 percent of all employees are reportedly satisfied with their jobs.[6] One explanation for this finding is that workers attempt to select jobs that are consistent
with their values. Some workers see their jobs primarily as means to other
ends, rather than as ends in themselves. Those who see work as a means to
desired ends (such as financial gain) are likely to opt for the highest-paying
reasonably secure job available. In contrast, those who see work as a valued

end in itself may denigrate (and turn down) unfulfilling jobs, possibly choosing to do volunteer work instead.[7] From this perspective it is not surprising that different groups of workers view different aspects of their jobs as most important. In a 1974 national survey, workers rated the importance of twenty-three different job facets (the major categories being financial rewards, challenge, available resources, relations with coworkers, and comfort). Blue-collar workers most often rated "good pay" as "very important"; "interesting work" was in fifth place. In contrast, the facet most often rated "very important" by white-collar workers was "interesting work"; "good pay" was in seventh place.[8] People may adjust, it would appear, to nonstimulating work, extracting "surprisingly rich meanings."[9] And some employees prefer nonchallenging work because it allows them freedom to socialize or daydream without impairing their productivity.[10]

A new approach to job design emerged in the 1960s, grounded in the writings and research of behavioral scientists. This approach advocated designing jobs to fit people rather than vice versa, an approach which Hackman and Oldham have called *Route 1*. While the classical approach emphasized efficiency and the application of the "hard" sciences and engineering know-how, the behavioral approach saw individual growth and development as essential to achieving organizational effectiveness in the long run.

Two of the earliest concepts associated with the behavioral approach to job design were job enlargement and job enrichment. Job enlargement refers to adding tasks to a job so that the variety of activities is increased, e.g., bookkeepers can be asked to post accounts receivable as well as accounts payable entries. In job enlargement, the new tasks are on a par with the original ones in regard to difficulty and responsibility. Job enlargement therefore, has been referred to as "horizontal loading." Job enrichment involves increasing the difficulty or responsibility of the tasks that comprise a job, thereby raising the level of skill required to perform effectively. In an enriched job the individual may be responsible for organizing, planning, and controlling his or her own work, not just for carrying it out—hence the notion of "vertical loading."

The job characteristics model formulated by Hackman and Oldham in 1975 has received a great deal of attention from researchers and managers interested in job design. The model holds that four beneficial effects may result from well-designed jobs: (1) internal work motivation (feelings of satisfaction from performing well or dissatisfaction from performing poorly), (2) organizational commitment, as manifested by low turnover and absenteeism, (3) work satisfaction, and (4) performance quality (see Figure 11-1). Clearly, organizations stand to gain if employees experience a high level of internal work motivation, because this represents a "built-in" reward and punishment system. The advantages of low absenteeism, low voluntary turnover, and high-quality performance are obvious, and to the extent that work satisfaction increases, the quality of employee work life is improved.

Internal work motivation and the other effects are seen as occurring only if three psychological states exist: meaningfulness (the job is seen as inherently

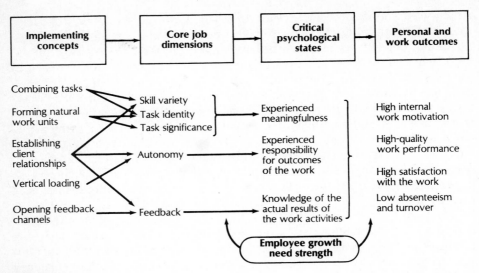

**FIGURE 11-1**
The Hackman and Oldham job characteristics model. (*J. R. Hackman, G. Oldham, R. Janson, and K. Purdy; © 1975 by the Regents of the University of California. Adapted from California Management Review, volume XVII, no. 4, p. 62 by permission of the Regents.*)

worthwhile), responsibility (the person feels that he or she influences how well the job is performed), and knowledge of results (the person knows what was accomplished). These three psychological states are seen as dependent in turn upon five job characteristics: variety (the number and level of skills utilized), identity (the worker completes a whole or identifiable piece of work), significance (the impact of the job on other people such as coworkers and customers), autonomy (the opportunity to make decisions), and feedback (information about job performance). Hackman and Oldham have identified five implementing concepts that can influence job characteristics: vertical loading, combining tasks (similar to horizontal loading), establishing client relationships, forming natural work units, and opening feedback channels. The application of these implementing concepts is illustrated in the next section.

## ROUTE 1 IMPLEMENTING CONCEPTS

*Combining tasks.* The job enrichment experiment at Indiana Bell Telephone vividly illustrates this concept. Compiling telephone directories initially involved twenty-one separate steps which were handled in an assembly-line fashion (e.g., checking assorted pages from various directories for accuracy). Subsequently, workers were given their own books to compile, creating an identifiable piece of work out of what was formerly an ongoing series of unidentifiable tasks.[11]

*Establishing client relationships.* Customarily, keypunch operators at The Travelers Insurance Companies were given work by assignment clerks who had received it from various users (clients). If questions arose, the supervisor communicated with the client, and then transmitted the information to the operators or to the assignment clerks. The job redesign program involved having keypunch operators receive work directly from clients and consult with clients directly regarding questions.[12]

*Opening feedback channels.* To the extent that job design changes incorporate the measurement and feedback of performance data, they encompass the intervention discussed in Chapters 9 and 10. (One possible difference might be noted: job design focuses on feedback provided by the work itself, as distinct from feedback provided by the supervisor.) Hackman underscores the importance of feedback and describes a method of opening up feedback channels:

> Tradition and established procedure in many organizations dictate that records about performance be kept by a supervisor and transmitted up (not down) the organizational hierarchy. Sometimes supervisors even check the work and correct errors themselves. The worker who made the error never knows it occurred and is therefore denied the very information that could enhance both internal work motivation and the technical adequacy of his performance. In many cases, it is possible to provide standard summaries of performance records directly to the workers. This would give the employees personally and regularly the data they need to improve their effectiveness.[13]

*Forming natural work units.* In the stock investment and transfer department of a large investment firm, 130 clerical employees were organized by function. Work was assigned in an arbitrary fashion by each functional supervisor. The change consisted of creating thirteen 10-person work teams. Each team was given responsibility for handling all functions relating to a specific set of clients.[14]

*Vertical loading.* At Buick's factory number 81 in Flint, Michigan, workers had little decision-making authority; they pretty much followed orders from supervisors. The change consisted of granting workers the authority to adjust machine settings, reject faulty raw materials, and even to stop the assembly line if a problem was evident. Of course, the increased authority was accompanied by increased responsibility.[15]

These five implementing concepts represent the most widely recognized, but not the only, mechanisms associated with job design interventions based on behavioral science. In broad terms, job design interventions specify "the contents, methods, and relationships of jobs in order to satisfy technological and organizational requirements as well as the social and personal requirements of the job holders."[16]

Pertinent to the social and personal requirements of job holders, in recent years much attention has been devoted to *quality of work life* (QWL) efforts. Although QWL programs may contain a job design component, they typically are more far-reaching in scope. While definitions and practices vary, QWL is generally seen as incorporating a philosophy of management that enhances the dignity of all workers,[17] that introduces changes in an organization's culture (i.e., finding new ways to identify and solve problems),[18] and that improves the physical and emotional well-being of employees (e.g., providing opportunities for growth and development).[19] Given the open-endedness of QWL, it is not surprising to find that more than a dozen different types of interventions have been classified under this rubric, including changes in work schedules (reviewed in Chapter 12), provision of training (see Chapter 6), participatory decision making and quality circles (Chapter 7), introduction of Scanlon and other gainsharing pay plans (Chapter 3), and modifications in organization structure (Chapter 8). Thus, in light of the diversity of interventions that are called QWL, the present chapter examines only those QWL projects that focused primarily on job design changes.

## ROUTE 1 INTERVENTIONS: AN EMPIRICAL REVIEW

The results of thirty-two experiments (reported in a lesser number of studies) are presented in Table 11-1. Studies were included in this review only if they provided a clear indication of the impact of job design on either productivity or production quality. Studies using performance ratings or dollar savings as the criterion variables were excluded. Positive results are probably overrepresented in this (as in all) reviews because journals are not given to publishing negative results. George Strauss has noted another complicating factor: "frequently reports are written by the very consultants who introduced job restructuring—hardly unbiased observers."[20]

Thirty experiments provided a clear indication of the impact of job design on productivity. The median result was an increase in productivity of 6.4 percent. (This result excludes 2 experiments in simulated work settings which yielded changes in productivity of 0 percent and −1 percent).[21] Since in 11 (out of 30) cases results were negative or zero, the present findings are not inconsistent with Hackman's observation that job design interventions do not reliably improve productivity. Indeed, Hackman suggests that increases in work quantity have only tended to occur when (1) productivity was very low to begin with because employees were really "turned off," and (2) hidden inefficiencies existed in the prior work system.[22]

Of the 30 interventions, 8 utilized all 5 implementing concepts, another 8 interventions used 3 or 4 of the implementing concepts, and 14 employed only 1 or 2 of the implementing concepts. Apparently, the more implementing concepts employed, the more positive the effect: median increases in productivity were 10.3 percent, 7.7 percent, and 2.5 percent, respectively.

In 13 of the 30 experiments, feedback channels were opened, and in 8 cases *objective* feedback was provided pertinent to measured outputs or error rates. In these 8 experiments productivity increases ranged from 2.7 percent to 81.7 percent—the median result being an increase of 17.2 percent.[23] In contrast, 17 job design interventions were conducted that did *not* open feedback channels; in these studies the median result in terms of productivity change was 0.0 percent.

In 21 cases the effects of job design on work quality are cited. The median result was an improvement (error reduction, typically) of 28 percent. This finding is consistent with Hackman's observation that the quality of work performed generally improves as a result of job design.[24] Performance feedback, however, again appears to be a particularly important implementing concept. Twelve experiments reporting the effects of job design on work quality did *not* incorporate the opening of feedback channels; in these interventions the median improvement in work quality was 12.9 percent.

In connection with the impact of job design on absenteeism, 13 studies provided some information, but only 9 provided a clear indication of the effect. In these studies, the median result was a decrease in absenteeism of 14.5 percent. Four of these studies did *not* open feedback channels, and the median result was a change in absenteeism of 0.0 percent. All in all, the evidence suggests that job design interventions can modestly reduce absenteeism.[25]

In 24 experiments the impact of job design on employee satisfaction was reported; in 20 cases the effect was positive, a "success rate" of over 80 percent. Yet, although satisfaction with *work* typically increases, job design generally has little positive effect on satisfaction with such other job facets as pay, security, coworkers, or supervision. Indeed, enrichment of the work sometimes prompts decreases in satisfaction with pay and supervision. Employees may feel underpaid in light of added responsibilities, and supervisors may interfere with the increased autonomy workers may expect to receive.[26]

The experiment at the Social Security Administration involving some fifty low-level clerical employees vividly illustrates what can happen when jobs are enriched psychologically but not financially. Although no promises were made prior to job enrichment concerning changes in pay rates as responsibility or productivity increased, the employees apparently came to expect pay increases. And when promotions and pay increases were not forthcoming, many employees were angry and bitter; they resented doing other people's work and not getting any tangible rewards for it.[27] The authors of the study commented, "It was not that they were indifferent to the work itself; they clearly preferred interesting to dull work. But . . . the extrinsic rewards came first. . . . many employees mentioned that they took jobs in this agency because of the security, the higher pay, and the superior benefits. . . . They were quite willing, if not anxious, to have more interesting tasks but only on the condition that some practical benefits would result."[28]

## DURABILITY AND SIDE EFFECTS

Another pertinent issue is the durability of the effects of job design interventions. Although job changes may endure, evidence suggests that the results and reactions to job changes may not. For instance, in the well-designed field experiment reported by Greene, productivity increased by an average of 10.3 percent during the 14-month study period. The trend, however, was unfavorable; output was up 14.2 percent after 5 months, but only 4.7 percent at the end of the experiment. Further, while the error rate declined by 15.5 percent on the aver-

**TABLE 11-1**
EFFECTS OF JOB DESIGN INTERVENTIONS ON PRODUCTIVITY, WORK QUALITY, AND ABSENTEEISM

| Study number and year | Setting and sample | Implementing concepts employed | Impact on productivity | Impact on work quality[a] | Impact on absenteeism[b] |
|---|---|---|---|---|---|
| 1 1957[c] | Hospital equipment manufacturer; 14 production workers | VL | −11% | +32% | NR |
| | Hospital equipment manufacturer; 43 production workers | CT<br>VL | −6% | +75% | NR |
| 2 1969[d] | AT&T; 40 long lines framesmen | CT<br>ECR<br>NWU<br>VL | −1% | +25.8% increase in percentage of work completed on time | No change |
| 3 1971[e] | Bankers Trust; typists | CT<br>VL | +108% | No change | NR |
| 4 1971[f] | AT&T; 40 typists | CT<br>ECR<br>OFC<br>VL | +20% (approx.) | +70% | NR |
| 5 1971[g] | AT&T; 18 auditing clerks | CT<br>ECR<br>VL | NR | +80% | NR |
| 6 1971[h] | Employment training center; 48 workers | CT | No significant change | Declined significantly | NR |
| 7 1971[i] | Mfg. co.; electronic products; 70 inspectors and quality analysts | CT<br>VL | +70% (approx.) | +50% | NR |
| 8 1971[j] | U.S. Internal Revenue Service; 44 tax examiners | CT<br>ECR<br>NWU<br>VL | No change | NR "improved" | NR |

| # | Year | Description | Code | | | |
|---|------|-------------|------|---|---|---|
| 9 | 1971[k] | PPG Industries; 92 twist-frame operators | CT | +12% | NR | NR |
| 10 | 1973[l] | Philips N.V.; mfg. employees | CT | No change | No change | NR |
| | | Philips N.V.; several thousand mfg. employees | VL | No change | "Slight improvement" | NR |
| | | Philips N.V.; TV assemblers | VL | +10% | Small (10%) improvement | NR |
| 11 | 1973[m] | Saab-Scania; engine assembly plant | All 5 | No change (slightly lower) | Improved | NR |
| 12 | 1973[n] | Volvo; 1500 auto assembly workers | All 5 | No change | Improved | Higher |
| 13 | 1973[o] | AT&T; 39 telephone operators | CT / VL | No change | No change | Lower |
| 14 | 1973[p] | Chase Manhattan Bank; clerical employees | All 5 | NR | +13% | NR |
| 15 | 1974[q] | General Electric Co.; mfg. employees | CT / OFC | +81.7% | +50% | NR |
| 16 | 1974[r] | Large insurance company; 40 keypunch operators | All 5 | +10.6% | +35.3% | −24% |
| 17 | 1974[s] | General Foods Corporation; production employees | All 5 | +25% (10–40%) | +80% | Reduced |
| 18 | 1975[t] | Swedish machine tool company; mfg. employees | CT / VL | +5% | NR | No change |
| 19 | 1975[u] | Large bank; stock transfer department; 23 clerical employees | NWU | No change (probably declined) | No change (probably declined) | No change |
| 20 | 1975[v] | Travelers Insurance Cos.; 98 keypunch operators | All 5 | +31.5% | +35% | −24% |

**TABLE 11-1**
EFFECTS OF JOB DESIGN INTERVENTIONS ON PRODUCTIVITY, WORK QUALITY, AND ABSENTEEISM (*Continued*)

| Study number and year | Setting and sample | Implementing concepts employed | Impact on productivity | Impact on work quality[a] | Impact on absenteeism[b] |
|---|---|---|---|---|---|
| 21 1975[w] | Bankers Trust Company; clerical employees; 3 departments | All 5 | +9.5% | +28% | NR |
| 22 1976[x] | U.S. Social Security Admin.; approx. 50 clerical employees | CT NWU OFC VL | +23.5% | NR | −5% |
| 23 1977[y] | AT&T; 10 telephone repair persons and installers | CT VL | +5.3% | NR | −42% |
| 24 1978[z] | Approx. 90 production workers | CT | +7.5% | No change | NR |
| 25 1979[aa] | Insurance company; 75 clerical employees | CT ECR VL | +24.4% | Improved | NR |
| 26 1979[bb] | Manufacturing company; electric welding systems | CT NWU VL | +5% | +46% | NR |
| 27 1979[cc] | Large government agency; 36 clerical employees | CT NWU OFC VL | +2.7% | NR | −35% |
| 28 1981[dd] | Investment bank; 130 clerical employees | ECR NWU OFC | +10.3% | +15.5% | −5% |
| 29 1981[ee] | Large company; word processing center | All 5 | +14.5% | +23.8% | Lower |

*Note:* CT = combining tasks; ECR = establishing client relationships; NWU = forming natural work units; OFC = opening feedback channels; VL = vertical loading; NR = not reported.

[a]Measured in terms of reduction in error *rate* (100% maximum), unless otherwise noted. Hence, a decrease in the percentage defective from, for example, 8% to 4% would be reported as an improvement in quality of 50%.

[a]Measured in terms of reduction in the absence *rate* (100% maximum).

[b]Louis E. Davis, "Job Design and Productivity: A New Approach," *Personnel*, 33 (1957), 423–427.

[c]Robert N. Ford, *Motivation through the Work Itself* (New York: American Management Association, 1969), pp. 51–60, 211–256.

[d]William W. Dettelback and Philip Kraft, "Organization Change through Job Enrichment," *Training and Development Journal*, 25 (Aug. 1971), 2–6.

[e]Robert Janson, "Job Enrichment in the Modern Office," in *New Perspectives in Job Enrichment*, ed. John R. Maher (New York: Van Nostrand, Reinhold, 1971), pp. 91–112.

[f]Ibid.

[g]Ronald C. Bishop and James W. Hill, "Effects of Job Enlargement and Job Change on Contiguous but Nonmanipulated Jobs as a Function of Workers' Status," *Journal of Applied Psychology*, 55 (1971), 175–181.

[h]John R. Maher and Wayne B. Overbagh, "Better Inspection Performance through Job Enrichment," in *New Perspectives in Job Enrichment*, ed. John R. Maher (New York: Van Nostrand, Reinhold, 1971), pp. 79–89.

[i]H. M. F. Rush, *Job Design for Motivation* (New York: The Conference Board, 1971), pp. 46–55.

[j]Ibid., pp. 67–70.

[k]William F. Dowling, "Job Redesign on the Assembly Line: Farewell to Blue-Collar Blues?," *Organizational Dynamics*, 2, No. 2 (1973), 53–55.

[l]Ibid., pp. 55–58.

[m]Ibid., pp. 58–60.

[n]Edward E. Lawler III, J. Richard Hackman, and Stanley Kaufman, "Effects of Job Redesign: A Field Experiment," *Journal of Applied Social Psychology*, 3 (1973), 49–62.

[o]Louise A. McNulty, "Job Enrichment: How to Make it Work," *Supervisory Management*, 18 (Sept. 1973), 7–15.

[p]E. M. Glaser, *Improving the Quality of Worklife . . . And in the Process, Improving Productivity* (Los Angeles: Human Interaction Research Institute, 1974), pp. 106–112.

[q]Robert Janson, "Job Enrichment Trial—Data Processing Department Analysis and Results in an Insurance Organization," paper cited in E. M. Glaser, *Improving the Quality of Worklife*, pp. 115–123.

[r]Lyman D. Ketchum, "Humanizing of Work," paper cited in E. M. Glaser, *Improving the Quality of Worklife*, pp. 57–69.

[s]Lars E. Bjork, "An Experiment in Work Satisfaction," *Scientific American*, 232 (Mar. 1975), 17–23.

[t]Linda L. Frank and J. Richard Hackman, "A Failure of Job Enrichment: The Case of the Change That Wasn't," *Journal of Applied Behavioral Science*, 11 (1975), 413–436.

[u]J. Richard Hackman, Greg Oldham, Robert Janson, and Kenneth Purdy, "A New Strategy for Job Enrichment," *California Management Review*, 17, No. 4 (1975), 57–71.

[v]W. Philip Kraft and Kathleen L. Williams, "Job Redesign Improves Productivity," *Personnel Journal*, 54 (1975), 393–397.

[w]Edwin A. Locke, David Sirota, and Alan D. Wolfson, "An Experimental Case Study of the Successes and Failures of Job Enrichment in a Government Agency," *Journal of Applied Psychology*, 61 (1976), 701–711.

[x]M. Segal and D. B. Weinberger, "Turfing," *Operations Research*, 25, No. 3 (1977), 367–386.

[y]William A. Pasmore and Donald C. King, "Understanding Organizational Change: A Comparative Study of Multifaceted Interventions," *Journal of Applied Behavioral Science*, 14 (1978), 455–468.

[z]Robert Janson, "Work Redesign: A Results-Oriented Strategy That Works," *S.A.M. Advanced Management Journal*, 44 (Winter 1979), 21–23.

[aa]Ibid., p. 23.

[bb]Christopher Orpen, "The Effects of Job Enrichment on Employee Satisfaction, Motivation, Involvement, and Performance: A Field Experiment," *Human Relations*, 32 (1979), 189–217.

[cc]Charles N. Greene, "Some Effects of a Job Enrichment Program: A Field Experiment," *Proceedings, 41st Annual National Meeting of the Academy of Management* (1981), pp. 281–285.

[dd]Ian Rolland and Robert Janson, "Total Involvement as a Productivity Strategy," *California Management Review*, 24, No. 2 (1981), 44–45.

age, errors were reduced by 21.2 percent after 6 months, and by only 7.2 percent at the end of the study.[29] A study by Maher and Overbagh also reported declines in performance and morale (in two of three groups) 1 year after the experiment began. Additional job design changes were made, resulting in an increase in performance and satisfaction.[30] A third experiment showed production rates declining in one of two experimental groups during a 6-month study period.[31] These few examples underscore Hackman and Oldham's concern that the "pressing problem [with job design interventions] may be what to do *next* to keep people challenged and interested in their work. For as people become accustomed to personal growth and learning on the job, what was once a challenge may eventually become routine, and ever more challenge may be required to keep frustration and boredom from setting in."[32] Alternatively, if employees become accustomed to job design changes which are accompanied by promotions and/or pay increases, they may want additional job design changes for these reasons.

Several additional effects may result from job design interventions. First, by increasing variety the organization obtains a more widely skilled and more flexible work force. It is sometimes argued that by having employees work on tasks where they are needed, rather than where they are assigned, bottlenecks can be reduced and productivity increased.[33] Second, the use of vertical loading may provide managers more time to manage proactively (i.e., with an emphasis on shaping the future) and thus less time need be spent responding to crises and conflicts. In this regard, one study concluded that by shifting significant responsibilities to subordinates, job enrichment improved the whole process of supervisory development. Subordinates became accustomed to responsibility, making them more ready for promotion, and supervisors' time was directed away from production toward planning, controlling, and development.[34] Third, the costs of coordination may be lowered through a reduced need for supervisors and inspectors; however, these savings may be offset by increases in other costs, e.g., training, or newly designed or additional equipment.

## SUMMARY OF EFFECTS

In assessing the efficacy of job design interventions based on behavioral science, it is notable that opinions differ sharply. In one of the more balanced assessments, Hackman stated:

> Although it is now generally recognized that work redesign is not a panacea for all organizational ills, it remains difficult to arrive at a "bottom line" estimate of the costs and benefits of job changes. Simple reports of improvements in job satisfaction are not likely to significantly warm the hearts of cost-conscious line managers; and . . . simple measures of production quantity or labor costs are inappropriate when used as the sole measure of the effects of work redesign. . . . What [are] the ultimate costs of "extra" supervisory time? Or of redundant inspectors? Or of absenteeism, soldiering, or sabotage? Until we become able to assess the effects of work

redesign on such outcomes, it will continue to be difficult to determine unambiguously whether or not work redesign "pays off" in traditional economic coin.[35]

In view of the mixed results to date, it may be useful to determine if there are factors which reliably affect the likelihood of a successful job design intervention. These factors (preconditions and constraints), deserve attention because they may enable the practitioner to know *in advance* whether or not a job design intervention is likely to work in a given setting.[36]

## ROUTE 1 INTERVENTIONS: SOME PRECONDITIONS AND CONSTRAINTS

More than a dozen preconditions and constraints have been discussed in the job design literature; unfortunately, in many cases little or no empirical validation has been provided. Nevertheless, these factors are described below, and the limited empirical evidence is reviewed.

### Accurate Diagnosis

It is widely agreed that job design should only be undertaken after a careful diagnosis indicates the existence of a problem regarding work satisfaction, internal work motivation, organizational commitment, or performance quality. If one or more of these problems exists, it is useful to determine (1) whether jobs are deficient in terms of motivating potential, and if so (2) which specific core dimension(s) is (are) in need of improvement.[37] All too often, though, job design interventions are undertaken without adequate diagnosis. Consider the following scenario. An executive returns from a seminar convinced that job design is a "neat idea," "the way to go," etc. Shortly thereafter, a program is begun. Experiencing only mixed success, the executive concludes that job design is yet another seemingly good idea that "just doesn't work in the real world."[38]

### Real Job Changes

Several instances of job design failures have been attributed to the introduction of minor, cosmetic job changes. Sometimes because of inertia or fear, managers may merely add "window dressing" to make jobs look different, rather than actually change what people *do* on their jobs.[39] Hackman and Oldham call this phenomenon the "small change."[40] As an example, the stock transfer department of a large bank manifested many signs of job enrichment: offices were rearranged and jobs were renamed—but the jobs themselves remained virtually unchanged. The program was unsuccessful. One manager concluded, "We tried job enrichment and it failed."[41] Consistent with the "small change" problem is the finding, mentioned previously, that the more implementing concepts employed in a job design intervention, the more positive the impact in terms of productivity.

### Technological Constraints

An organization's technology can constrain job design interventions in three ways: (1) the technology may limit the opportunity for increasing employee discretion (e.g., a machine-paced assembly line), (2) the technology may be too costly to alter, and (3) the technology may be extremely efficient, thereby more than compensating for the possible motivational advantages of job redesign. With respect to the first obstacle, Hackman and Oldham have commented that "any effort to redesign work in a technology that permits little employee discretion is probably doomed to failure from the outset because of the mechanics of the system itself."[42] The second and third obstacles relate to the economies of mass production. As Dowling has written,

> Take the case of manufacturing a pair of man's pants in a garment factory. Give the job to one man and he will take half a day; divide the work among many people on a line with each one using advanced technical equipment, and it takes one man-hour to produce a pair of trousers. The future of job redesign is not bright in a pants factory.[43]

### Personnel System Constraints

A variety of human resource management practices may potentially conflict with intended job design changes. Significant problems may emerge if personnel department practices are rigid in connection with job descriptions, performance appraisal instruments, selection and placement procedures, training programs, and, of course, compensation plans.[44] As Lee Dyer has noted, ". . . while increased psychic satisfaction at work may initially be seen by employees as adequate compensation for participating in [a job design program], advocates should be aware that this feeling is likely to be short-lived. Eventually workers come to feel that their sustained efforts should result in a sharing of the monetary gains resulting from cost-savings and increased productivity."[45] (Certainly, the job design intervention at the Social Security Administration bears out this contention.) And job design programs involving vertical loading or increased variety will likely make demands on the training function. Before embarking on a job design program, it is important to think about the implications for various personnel functions, as well as possible impacts on the organization's structure and communication practices.

### Organizational Controls and Operating Systems

Control system devices such as budgets, cost accounting systems, and production and quality control reports, must mesh with job design changes. If, for example, a financial control system requires that employees not interact with vendors (to avoid possible theft or fraud), the system precludes some job design changes. The provision of feedback directly to the person performing the work may conflict with feedback procedures already in place.[46] And some job design changes can create difficulties in coordination between units. In one case of job design failure, customer account clerks were given increased autonomy in scheduling their own work and setting their own pace. As a consequence, the unit's work output became less uniform and less predictable, causing delays in the work performed by the data processing unit. The result was slower customer service and increased friction between the two units.[47]

### Bureaucratic Climate

To the extent that an organization is characterized by centralized decision making and formalized rules and procedures, the work environment will be relatively inhospitable to innovation in general and job design changes in particular. Consistent with this view, Pierce, Dunham, and Blackburn found a significant interaction between job design and organization climate: employees responded more favorably to complex jobs when they were performed in non-bureaucratic (organic) as compared to bureaucratic organizations.[48] More concretely, a good example of how bureaucratic practices can "creep" into and undermine job design activities has been provided by Hackman. Organizational planners in a manufacturing company following standard company practice wrote detailed step-by-step descriptions of newly designed jobs. These descriptions were then sent to the employees who were told they would have more responsibility and autonomy in getting the work done. Hackman concluded that, "expecting to achieve a flexible, employee-oriented work system with rigid, bureaucratic procedures that operate strictly from the top down is unrealistic."[49]

### Union Cooperation

The quasi-official position of the AFL-CIO (as presented in the *Federationist*), has been to view the entire job design movement with considerable skepticism. Job enrichment has been seen as a form of manipulation and speedup, an attempt to direct attention away from the more important issues (such as pay, job security, and safety), and a veiled attempt to dump collective bargaining obligations.[50] One of the most outspoken and skeptical union leaders, William Winpisinger, offered the following observations when he was vice president of the Machinists Union:

> On the basis of fairly extensive experience as a union representative, I find it hard to picture management enriching jobs at the expense of profits. In fact I have a strong suspicion that "job enrichment" may be just another name for "time-and-motion" study.... Job enrichment is a stopwatch in sheep's clothing.... If you want to enrich jobs, enrich the pay check. The better the wage, the better the job satisfaction.[51]

Reflecting a more enthusiastic view, Irving Bluestone, a former president of the United Auto Workers (UAW), offered the following assessment of the typical worker's reaction to job enrichment: "While his rate of pay dominates his relationship to his job, he can be responsive to the opportunity for playing an innovative, creative, and imaginative role in the production process."[52] Consistent with this view, the UAW has participated with General Motors in an extensive QWL program for more than a decade. And while the UAW was once one of very few unions to view job design favorably, in the past few years several major unions have participated in such programs.[53] Indeed, some union officials are now declaring that the time has come for "a limited partnership—a marriage of convenience" with management to work for increased productivity by such means as job design programs.[54]

While there is a trend toward increased union acceptance of job design programs, the actual level of enthusiasm varies considerably from one union (or local) to another. It is, however, indisputable that a successful job design intervention requires good union-management relations and a spirit of cooperation. In a climate of mistrust, *any* attempt at job design may be countered with union resistance, compensation disputes, and jurisdictional boundary disputes.[55] It is important for management to anticipate probable union demands (e.g., increased pay for increased responsibility, no lost jobs) and to discuss such relevant issues with the union representative before implementation is begun. Yet, the negotiation of planned job changes is sometimes a "formidable task" in itself.[56] The challenge is to make job design a win-win proposition, and therefore a goal of both management and the union.

### Top Management Support

The initial success and subsequent survival of a job design intervention depends in large part on the sustained commitment of top management.[57] Consider the following two examples of job design failures. In one company a vice president was counted on (alone) to protect a fledgling project from "meddling" by others, who favored different approaches to improving organizational effectiveness. When the vice president was away for several months attending a management development program, his temporary replacement terminated the job enrichment activities and substituted a program more to his liking.[58] In the second case, a high-level executive agreed to sponsor a job enrichment program without really understanding that the intended changes would initially create a good deal of uncertainty in the organization. When he began hearing complaints from some of his subordinates about the "chaos" the project was causing, he concluded that he had been misled and withdrew his support from the project.[59]

Enduring top management support in implementing a job design project is important because changes may not proceed quickly or painlessly. Indicative of this, in one moderately successful job design intervention, the aftermath of job changes produced the following situation:

> It was not an easy period. The workers were going through a time of intense learning, not only of new operations but also of new social relations. . . . The mood was often

one of irritability and tension as the men pressed to maintain the rate of production.[60]

Yet "a great many managers are sure to latch on to one type of program or another . . . for a *fast fix* of a floundering operation; these people will be lucky if they do not do their organizations serious injury."[61] Job design programs, rather than yielding a short burst of productivity, are more likely to produce an initial decline as people learn new skills and assume new responsibilities. There is a need for vision, commitment, and risk taking on the part of those responsible for initiating a job design program.[62]

### Supervisory Support

In the rush to improve the jobs held by rank-and-file employees, problems may emerge in connection with supervisory cooperation.[63] For example, the personnel manager of a large electronics firm asserted that the biggest problem his organization had to overcome when job enrichment was undertaken was "changing the attitudes of supervisors." In his words, "The real problem wasn't so much in finding ways to enrich the lower level jobs as in challenging the assumptions the supervisors had about the *people* who performed these jobs. . . . Until we did some intensive organizational development with the supervisors we had little hope of succeeding in job enrichment."[64] Supervisors are often unwilling to impoverish their own jobs to enrich those of their subordinates.

There is (limited) evidence that a job design intervention will increase productivity only if the supervisors who implement it *believe* that increased productivity, not just changes in attitude, will result.[65] Training, involvement, and the commitment of line managers prior to the initiation of a job design program are essential to success. Also, it may be a lot easier to obtain the commitment of top-level managers—who may never have to get involved themselves—than it is to obtain the commitment of middle-level managers and supervisors.[66]

As lower-level jobs are enriched, the jobs of supervisors and middle managers should also be enriched, with forethought and participation. New skills may be required in dealing collaboratively with subordinates and in training subordinates to perform new tasks. Certainly more structure will be needed than such simple injunctions as "manage proactively," or "develop your subordinates."

### Readiness of Individuals

The success of a job design intervention depends in part on the *ability* and *desire* of employees to handle enriched jobs. Enriched work requires new skills; but because situations vary so greatly, there is no single test to determine whether individuals are capable of handling more challenging jobs.[67]

More than two dozen studies have addressed the issue of the desire to perform enriched work, by far the most thoroughly researched constraint or pre-condition pertinent to job design interventions. The basic thrust of this research has been to test the hypothesis that job enrichment works "best" (in regard to satisfaction and performance) when there is a good match between the person and the job, e.g., when an enriched job is given to a person with a strong desire for enriched work. Several different indicators of the desire for an enriched job have been examined. At the individual (psychological) level of analysis, most of the relevant studies have measured (1) growth need strength, (2) adherence to the Protestant work ethic, (3) higher-order need strength, or (4) need for achievement. Additionally, a number of group (sociological) indicators have been examined, such as (1) urban vs. rural employment location, (2) urban vs. rural current residence, and (3) urban vs. rural childhood residence. In general, there has been greater support for the person-job match (congruence) hypothesis using psychological compared to sociological indicators of the desire for enriched work. However, support for the hypothesis has not been particularly impressive.[68] More recent research has shown that the most promising indicator of the desire to perform enriched work is simply the individual's response to the direct, straightforward question, "Do you want greater job enrichment, and if so how?"[69]

Nevertheless, differences in the desire to perform enriched work are not a particularly important factor affecting the success of a Route 1 job design intervention. Longitudinal research indicates that enrichment tends to strengthen the desire for an enriched job. Indeed, Orpen has written that ". . . employees may respond quite favorably to enrichment even though they may initially have appeared to be the 'wrong' kind of employee."[70] Further, research has found that job characteristics alone are more than ten times as important in determining job reactions than the match between job characteristics and desired job characteristics: job characteristics accounted for up to 38 percent of the variability in job satisfaction, whereas the match between job characteristics and desired job characteristics (JC $\times$ DJC) accounted for less than 3 percent of the variability in job satisfaction.[71]

Two additional issues might be raised in connection with individual readiness for enriched jobs. First, evidence suggests that *job* tenure (not organizational tenure) may be related to reactions to job redesign. Research indicates that after 15 years on a given job, people become generally "immune" to differences in job characteristics—that is, their reactions appear to be rather muted to enriched features.[72] Many employees apparently find it "stultifying" to perform essentially the same tasks, year after year, merely applying the knowledge or learning acquired in the first year or two. Under these conditions an individual is likely to coast along, or get frustrated and not do anything beyond the routine.[73] The practical implication is that organizations should not allow job incumbents to get "stale" on the job, or vice versa.

Second, it should be noted that jobs can be too enriched as well as too impoverished. Human growth and performance require an optimal level of challenge. A job too easy or too meaningless, demotivates an employee; a job too hard, involving too much responsibility or risk, creates anxiety, frustration, or anger.[74] Studies have repeatedly shown that role overload, i.e., requiring an individual to do more than he or she possibly can in the time available, can have serious consequences to health.[75]

## Contextual Satisfaction

A small body of research has accumulated which indicates that satisfaction with other aspects of the job besides the work itself (pay, supervision, promotion opportunities, and coworkers) can also influence the success of job design interventions. When contextual satisfaction is low, implementation of job design changes should be done with caution, or perhaps delayed until contextual satisfaction is improved.[76] It would appear, however, that of the four components of contextual satisfaction, satisfaction with coworkers and, to a lesser extent, satisfaction with supervision are the most important for the success of a job design intervention. Interpersonal difficulties in the work environment (e.g., hostility, conflict) can materially hinder the implementation of job design changes.[77]

## Miscellaneous Complicating Factors

Numerous additional factors have been identified in the literature as possibly affecting the success of job design interventions. Detrimental factors are as follows:

- High turnover during the early phase of job design, resulting in new work group members who may not be adequately committed to the project's success[78]
- High turnover in the parent organization, causing top management to be reluctant to invest in the development of skills[79]
- Inadequate monitoring of the project's success, which may render an evaluation inconclusive[80]
- A mechanical, "cookbook" approach to implementation, i.e., excessive dogmatism[81]
- A physical layout where employees lack privacy (have high visibility, exposure), which may interfere with attempts to increase autonomy[82]
- Environmental turbulence which draws attention away from the job design intervention, possibly even causing it to be "put on the back burner"[83]

Positive factors are as follows:

- Project is initiated in a small plant (less than 100 employees)[84]
- Plant where trial is initiated is geographically remote, hence there likely will be more autonomy and less interference[85]
- Plant where trial is initiated produces a new product or uses a new technology, creating few ties to historical job patterns[86]

Perhaps the best way to summarize the discussion of preconditions and constraints is to let two of the most prominent exponents of Route 1 job design interventions speak for themselves. In 1975, Hackman wrote as follows:

> Redesigning a job often appears seductively simple, and some managers underestimate how much time and effort a project can take. In practice, job redesign is a rather challenging undertaking, requiring a good deal more energy than do most organizational development activities. . . . There are many reasons that it is hard to redesign jobs.[87]

More recently, Hackman and Oldham (1980) concluded:

> To redesign work halfheartedly or to use flawed change processes is, in most cases, to assure failure. And it is *hard* to do work redesign well.[88]

Certainly, the present review of preconditions and constraints is consistent with these comments. There is an ominous number of potential pitfalls that threaten the success of a Route 1 job design intervention. And as the unfavorable factors in a given situation add up, a job design project is almost certain to fail.[89] Compounding the problem, it would appear that only those organizations that are already well managed are likely to meet the conditions required for successful Route 1 job design.[90]

It may not be entirely fortuitous, therefore, that Route 1 interventions have been less and less frequently reported over the past two decades. A look at Table 11-1 bears out this claim. Of the 32 experiments examined, 3 were published before 1971, 21 were published in the 5 years from 1971 to 1975, and only 8 were published in the 9-year period from 1976 to 1984. This, of course does not deny the potential utility of job design; however, it may reflect the difficulty of doing it successfully.[91]

Opinions vary markedly on the future of Route 1 job design interventions. While some commentators are optimistic, Hackman and Oldham are not: "Our view, based on the choices that we now see being made, is that we are moving with some vigor down Route Two toward work simplification. That direction, moreover, seems unlikely to change in the foreseeable future for at least two reasons. . . . We know *how* to operate according to Route Two rules. . . . Route Two is more consistent with the behavioral styles and values of both employees and managers in contemporary organizations."[92]

The view of this writer is that organizations will continue to go down both Routes 1 and 2, but that a more promising direction is Route 3. While not dead ends, Routes 1 and 2 are less than optimal for achieving both employee growth and satisfaction, and organizational productivity. However, before describing Route 3, it is useful to review some of the recent results of Route 2 interventions.

## ROUTE 2 INTERVENTIONS: AN EMPIRICAL REVIEW

At the risk of oversimplifying matters somewhat, the distinction between Routes 1 and 2 might be viewed as follows. Broadly speaking, Route 1 represents an attempt to increase work *motivation* by making jobs more intrinsically satisfying to perform; Route 2 represents an effort to increase job-specific *ability* via work simplification and specialization. The former approach, clearly, has been a lot more popular during the past two decades. Whereas more than thirty Route 1 job design interventions have been reported in various published sources, only a few Route 2 interventions have been reported. But prior to reviewing the effects of Route 2 interventions, the disparity in popularity between the two approaches warrants comment.

Several explanations have been advanced for the relatively greater interest in Route 1 interventions. First, Route 1 reflects a more socially attractive value orientation. Most people prefer to view man as seeking personal fulfillment, meaning, and self-esteem through work, rather than as seeking (coveting) external rewards such as pay.[93] This predilection is certainly understandable among behavioral scientists, considering that they themselves have chosen careers that provide intrinsically rewarding work.[94] In a few instances, it would appear that this value orientation has led to biased reporting. For example, in *Work in America,* a book written by a task force assembled by the U.S. Department of Health, Education, and Welfare, substantial productivity improvements were reported as resulting from job enrichment at Texas Instruments. But *Work in America* neglected to mention that job enrichment was coupled with an 80 percent increase in pay and benefits. As Fein noted: "The omission of this pay data is strange, since the data appear prominently in the report from which the HEW task force obtained the case material."[95]

A second reason for the attractiveness of Route 1 job design is that it holds out the promise of increasing productivity without necessarily increasing expenses. Certainly the provision of psychic benefits to workers in exchange for increased productivity is highly cost-effective. Third, Route 1 interventions are entirely consistent with the popular theories espoused by Maslow, McGregor, Argyris, and Herzberg. These humanistic psychologists made a persuasive case for the existence of innate tendencies toward human growth and self-actualization. However, accumulating evidence suggests that this perspective may be somewhat simplistic: people have multiple needs (besides growth), and the intensities of these needs differ from individual to individual and over time.

Perhaps for these reasons very few examples of work simplification or industrial engineering (Route 2) job design interventions have been reported in the literature during the past two decades. Only five cases have been located, and they are reviewed next.

Clair Vough has described the extensive work simplification program undertaken at IBM's Electric Typewriter Division. All employees were given 15 hours of training, including information about the principles of motion economy, and the preparation of work-process flowcharts. Vough noted, "The slogan that emerged from the work-simplification classes was *Work Smarter, Not Harder.* Our aim was a speedup of production, not a speedup of human beings."[96] Coupled with the work simplification program was a cost-saving plan whereby individuals who contributed useful suggestions received a cash award based on the first year's dollar savings.

IBM's work simplification program produced a total savings in hours of eliminated work nearly double the hours invested in training (122,000 hours saved per year vs. 65,000 hours of training). However, the impact in terms of productivity (hours saved as a fraction of total hours worked) amounted to an annual increase of only 0.35 percent. Thus, benefits appear to have been meager, notwithstanding Vough's assertion that work simplification was the single behavioral program most responsible for the 65 percent increase in productivity in the division.[97]

A second example of a Route 2 intervention is provided by Hornbruch, a management consultant who acknowledges an intellectual debt to such classical job designers as Taylor, Gantt, Gilbreth, Bedaux, and Urwick. The Continental Illinois National Bank and Trust Company established an industrial engineering team of twelve recent college graduates, and the team was given the charge of "eliminating unnecessary work and streamlining the remaining work."[98] Early on, the team concluded that the entire managerial corps, some 400 people, should be trained in the techniques of industrial engineering. Top management entirely supported this effort. Managers who were uncooperative were relocated in the organization and "replaced by managers schooled in the principles and practices of scientific management."[99] As a result of the program, productivity reportedly increased in several areas of the organization. For instance in connection with check processing, an operation that involved 1550 employees working three shifts, several techniques were employed: work simplification, standardized instructions, the use of part-timers to increase staff flexibility, cross-training (a Route 1 practice), and vestibule training that allowed people to learn and practice "motion patterns" prior to employment. The effect of these changes was an increase in productivity of 9 percent.[100]

Route 2 job design was also implemented in the AM International division of Addressograph Multigraph Corporation. Elemental standard times were developed for all operations, from which the optimal method and sequence of operations for assembling a new copying machine were determined. In the new plant where this method of job design was employed, productivity was roughly double the level of the old plant where this product had been assembled: total assembly time was 16.1 hours compared to 32.0 hours.[101]

A fourth example of a Route 2 intervention involved the bookkeeping department of a franchise operation. At the outset, each of the 28 bookkeepers was responsible for performing five major tasks: (1) preparation of monthly statements (which entailed checking monthly revenue reports and lease and equipment contracts), (2) mailing monthly bills and, if necessary, reminder notices, (3) posting payments received to the franchisee's account, (4) payment of bills related to the franchisee's account, and (5) reconciliation of the monthly statement. Not only were there several tasks to perform, each bookkeeper was responsible for approximately 25 accounts. The job design intervention consisted of splitting the job in half, having some bookkeepers responsible for receivables and others responsible for payables, for statement preparation, and reconciliation. It was thought that this change would create greater expertise in each function and hence improve efficiency. It was also anticipated that the change would reduce the time required to train new book-keepers and that it would improve morale, since greater efficiency would reduce the pressure of deadlines. After three years, (1) only 6 of the original 28 bookkeepers remained with the company, (2) the turnover rate was especially high among new bookkeepers, few staying as long as 6 months—hence *total* training costs were higher, (3) the number of errors increased substantially as did the number of customer complaints, (4) overtime expense increased by roughly 150 percent, and (5) morale declined substantially. Apparently, the job design changes resulted in a loss of self-esteem among the bookkeepers: they no longer saw themselves as full-charge bookkeepers responsible for servicing specific accounts, but accounts payable (or receivable) clerks. Another factor is that they received less performance feedback after the change, since they were only responsible for part of a franchisee's transactions, and only half of the bookkeepers had the opportunity to see if the statements checked out. Thus, although hard productivity data were not available, it is pretty clear that pro-ductivity declined.[102]

The work simplification program undertaken at Intel Corporation is a fifth example of a Route 2 job design intervention. Although Intel is a young, rap-idly growing high technology company, its administrative procedures were also growing rapidly. For instance, if (prior to 1979) an engineer wanted to order a $2.79 mechanical pencil, processing the order required 12 sheets of paper and 95 administrative steps. Under the direction of Joseph Nevin, the person at Intel responsible for battling the expanding bureaucracy, office productivity increased by more than 30 percent. Within 2 years the company achieved an annual savings of $2.5 million, largely due to the elimination of 153 jobs. It is important to note, though, that, *jobs* were cut, *employees were not.* Intel had promised at the outset that it would not fire any permanent employee whose job was eliminated.[103]

The basic steps that Intel employed were as follows. First, rudimentary pro-ductivity and quality indices were established for the department under study. Second, a small team of managers and employees from that department, along with Nevin, met to examine each administrative procedure—methodically and in meticulous detail. Huge flow-process charts, spanning three walls of a conference room, were used to show each step in the current procedure, e.g., a yellow triangle indicated that a piece of paper was to be filed. Third, as a result of the detailed analysis of work methods, unnecessary operations were elimi-nated, others combined, and the remaining work was rationally ordered.

As a consequence many administrative functions were streamlined, e.g., the number of steps needed to hire a new employee was reduced from 364 to 250, the number of copies made by the accounts payable department was reduced by 29,700 per month, and an order for a $2.79 mechanical pencil was processed with 1 sheet of paper and only 8 steps. These efficiencies eliminated many jobs.

The accounts payable department was able to cut its staff from 71 to 51 employees, the employment office from 32 to 20, and the personnel records office from 14 to 7. Importantly, the quality and quantity of work performed improved. For example, before the intervention the personnel records department finished 72 percent of its work on time; after the changes, 92 percent.[104] According to Nevin, the employees were more satisfied after the changes because they were no longer performing activities that were a pointless waste of time. In his words, "People feel better not doing dumb things."[105]

Summing up the results of the five Route 2 case studies, two conclusions seem warranted. First, it appears that the impact on productivity is highly variable: in four cases productivity increased (by approximately 100 percent, 30 percent, 9 percent, and 0.5 percent), and in one case productivity clearly declined. Second, although the sample is too small to yield a statistically reliable finding, the median productivity increase of 9 percent suggests that Route 2 job design interventions may be at least as effective as Route 1 interventions.

## ROUTE 3 JOB DESIGN

Because Route 1 points in the direction of increased job scope and internal control, and Route 2 points in the direction of work simplification and external control, the two approaches appear antithetical. However, the distinction may represent a false dichotomy. To the extent that job design interventions can combine elements of both approaches, managers need not choose between Routes 1 and 2. Examples of interventions that combine features of Routes 1 and 2 (Route 3 interventions) are described below. Initial indications point to the superiority of this approach compared to Routes 1 or 2.

How can jobs be both enriched and simplified? Two ways have been used in practice. The first method has been to combine elements of job enrichment with increased external control; the second method has been to simplify jobs first, subsequently increasing both internal and external controls. The first approach is illustrated by the implementing concept of *total responsibility.* This concept is different from vertical loading in that it represents more than *increased* responsibility—the job incumbent is not just allowed to make more decisions. Further, the concept entails more than combining tasks or providing feedback. The goal is neither to maximize job scope (à la Route 1) nor to minimize the number of operations performed (à la Route 2), but to assign responsibility and accountability for a delineated unit of work *and* ensure via external monitoring that the work is performed satisfactorily. In a sense it combines the best of both approaches, an expanded job and increased management control.

Because the term total responsibility is Vough's, perhaps it is best to let him clarify the concept. Consider how Vough would apply total responsibility in a hotel setting.

Every day, every occupied hotel room is visited by a chambermaid who cleans up, changes the towels, and so on. If a faucet drips, that's not her business. If the TV set focuses poorly, that's for the house engineer to worry about (but the engineer doesn't know the set doesn't work unless an annoyed guest complains, which few do, so the next guest is also annoyed). How is the chief housekeeper, the maid's "end-of-line inspector," to know that a light bulb doesn't work, that a tub stopper is missing, that the thermostat is out of whack? She just takes a moment to check that the maid has been there and has cleaned up. *Who is in charge of the room?* Nobody. This simple responsibility is sliced up into functions—and the real responsibility falls between the cracks. That is why some of the world's largest and most expensive hotels leave their guests feeling cheated—and why an inexpensive, family-run motel often makes a guest feel he's visited someone's well-kept home.

If the manager of a large hotel or motel were to adopt the IBM Office Products approach to total responsibility, here's how he would do it: He would assign a chambermaid permanently to a wing or group of rooms; no switching around from day to day. She would be *totally in charge* of those rooms—in effect acting manager of a small hotel. She would be accountable to her top manager for any customer complaints about plumbing that doesn't work, a TV set that won't tune, curtains that won't pull, beds that sag. When she calls the plumber and he doesn't come, *she* should complain to her manager, because her neck is on the line.[106]

Thus, total responsibility entails (1) having employees assume complete responsibility for the quality and quantity of their own work, and (2) designing units of work which allow management to monitor this performance. The first aspect of total responsibility parallels what many Japanese companies do. Consider the similarities among the following three comments by Vough, Kazuo Iwama of Sony Corporation, and Gary Carlson, an electrician at a Buick plant that increased employee responsibility.

We can no longer afford to have people checking other people. This expensive practice in no way insures good quality. It dilutes effort and confuses the operators, who find themselves caught up in a game of "beat the inspector."[107]

I have no intention of criticizing American manufacturers, but take Zenith or RCA factories, where each worker's job on the line is clearly set and defined. He need only follow his specified function. If an incomplete component reaches his place on the line, it's not his responsibility, so he won't be blamed for the defect; it's management's responsibility.[108]

In the old system, the worker would put out bad parts because foremen were always pressing to make the schedule. They felt it was up to a quality inspector to find the bad parts. Now, we are quality inspectors, too.[109]

The second key aspect of total responsibility is the importance of establishing accountability. According to Vough: *"When something goes wrong and you don't know whose fault it is, the project is badly organized."*[110] Robert Janson, a management consultant in job design, echoes this view: for maximum control, management should identify all those points in the production process where there is a complete unit of work or subassembly, preferably something that can be tested.[111]

Although the hotel illustration is only hypothetical, Vough has provided several actual examples of the application of total responsibility. One application involved the packing function. Initially it was done by five people who filled boxes. However, products too often arrived at destinations dented or damaged, and it was impossible to identify who was at fault. Subsequently, the packing manager assigned each packer a specific set of shipping locations. Stated Vough, "I told the manager, 'Next time it happens, if you don't know who to fire, you've got to go.' That was the end of the trouble."[112]

A second, and less punitive, example concerned the parts department. Before the implementation of total responsibility, when a shipment arrived from a vendor, the first person (or persons) available was (were) supposed to break open the boxes, make entries on inventory cards, and put the stock away in the proper bins. Similarly, when requisitions were received, whoever happened to get the order was supposed to fill it. The job was considered one of the most boring in the plant, accuracy of records was a big problem, and too often inventory of a part fell below the reorder level, causing costly production slowdowns. "Nobody really cared, except the harried manager—and he had no way to make his *people* care."[113]

The total responsibility solution changed the situation dramatically. The manager divided the stockroom into sections, with one person responsible for each section and everything that happened in it: putting the stock away, the accuracy of records, promptness in filling orders, maintaining ample stock, and so forth. According to Vough, "the old problems disappeared. Morale and interest in the job improved, and the men began competing to have the best-running, best-looking, most accurate section in the stockroom. Each man was his own manager."[114]

A second approach to Route 3 job design involves work simplification combined with increases in internal and external control. A Citibank program of the early 1970s illustrates this approach. Notwithstanding the presence of huge computers and some 10,000 backroom employees, there were extensive delays, numerous errors, and poor responsiveness in terms of correcting errors. Robert White, the person responsible for the job design intervention, concluded that the employees were neither lazy nor incompetent, rather the system was the problem. Jeremy Main described the situation vividly in a *Fortune* article. Some 10,000 employees

> were scattered along a huge pipeline that passed each transaction through many hands. The backroom was organized by function: all check encoding was done in one place, all computer entries in another. Responsibility was lost, errors couldn't be corrected. White first simplified the work, eliminating all the superfluous steps he could find. Then he completely reorganized the backroom, replacing the functional divisions with small work stations equipped with small computers. Each group was responsible for a particular type of transaction . . . and one person often performed all the steps required. Errors could be found quickly; responsibility was clear. Service improved, the backroom staff was cut a resounding 40%. . .[115]

Thus, through a combination of work simplification (incorporating most of the Route 2 implementing concepts), job enrichment (incorporating all five implementing concepts), external monitoring, and improved office technology, productivity was increased by 67 percent.

Although Route 3 interventions have yielded both increased internal work motivation and increased external control, apparently all five core job dimensions have not been modified equally. The emphasis seems to have been on increasing responsibility and feedback; relatively smaller changes seem to have occurred in identity, significance, and variety. This observation is consistent with Griffin's study which examined relationships between job dimensions and productivity. Over a 1-year interval, two dimensions were found to be strongly related to productivity (feedback and autonomy); two dimensions were only weakly related (variety and identity); the fifth job dimension (significance) was not examined.[116]

## SUMMARY

Results of more than thirty job enrichment (Route 1) interventions support Hackman's conclusion that failures are almost as frequent as successes: the median impact on productivity has been 6.4 percent. Although some notable successes have been recorded, they are infrequent. Evidently, job enrichment is hard to do well; there are numerous preconditions and constraints that can jeopardize such a program.

A very small number of work simplification (Route 2) job design studies have been reported. While the median productivity effect (9 percent) is promising, the small number of studies makes this finding statistically unreliable.

A third approach to job design has been identified—Route 3—an approach that combines features of Routes 1 and 2. The limited evidence is encouraging and suggests that job design interventions in the future will likely resemble the Route 3 approach, incorporating such features as (1) increased (or total) responsibility over a limited area of work, (2) increased external measurement and control of the work performed, and (3) increased technological sophistication. Certainly these characteristics are compatible with jobs as frequently envisioned in the "office of the future."

## NOTES

1 J. Richard Hackman, "Is Job Enrichment Just a Fad?," *Harvard Business Review,* 53, No. 5 (1975), 130.

2 Claude S. George, Jr., *The History of Management Thought* (Englewood Cliffs, N.J.: Prentice-Hall, 1968), p. 15.

3 Adam Smith, *The Wealth of Nations* (New York: The Modern Library, 1937), pp. 4–5.

4 Jon L. Pierce, "Job Design in Perspective," *Personnel Administrator,* 25, No. 12 (1980), 67.

5 J. Richard Hackman and Greg R. Oldham, *Work Redesign* (Reading, Mass.: Addison-Wesley, 1980), pp. 260–266.

6 Robert P. Quinn, Graham L. Staines, and Margaret R. McCullough, *Job Satisfaction: Is There a Trend?* Manpower Research Monograph No. 30 (Washington, D.C.: U.S. Department of Labor, 1974), pp. 3–8. Since 1971 the percentage of sat-

isfied workers has actually exceeded 90 percent. See Andrew D. Szilagyi, Jr., and Marc J. Wallace, Jr., *Organizational Behavior and Performance,* 3d ed. (Glenview, Ill.: Scott, Foresman, 1983), p. 69.

7 George Strauss, "Job Satisfaction, Motivation, and Job Redesign," in *Organizational Behavior: Research and Issues,* ed. George Strauss, Raymond E. Miles, Charles C. Snow, and Arnold S. Tannenbaum (Madison, Wis.: Industrial Relations Research Association, 1974), pp. 28–33; also see J. Richard Hackman and Greg R. Oldham, *Work Redesign,* pp. 9–12.

8 Robert P. Quinn, Graham L. Staines, and Margaret R. McCullough, *Job Satisfaction,* p. 16.

9 George Strauss, "Job Satisfaction, Motivation, and Job Redesign," p. 31.

10 William E. Reif and Fred Luthans, "Does Job Enrichment Really Pay Off?," *California Management Review,* 15, No. 1 (1972), 33; also see "5 of 6 U.S. Auto Workers Dislike Swedish System," *New York Times,* 23 Dec. 1974, pp. 25, 31.

11 Robert N. Ford, "Job Enrichment Lessons from AT&T," *Harvard Business Review,* 51, No. 1 (1973), 97.

12 J. Richard Hackman, Greg Oldham, Robert Janson, and Kenneth Purdy, "A New Strategy for Job Enrichment," *California Management Review,* 17, No. 4 (1975), 67–69.

13 J. Richard Hackman, "Work Design," in *Improving Life at Work: Behavioral Science Approaches to Organizational Change,* ed. J. Richard Hackman and J. Lloyd Suttle (Santa Monica, Calif.: Goodyear, 1977), pp. 139–140.

14 Charles N. Greene, "Some Effects of a Job Enrichment Program: A Field Experiment," *Proceedings, 41st Annual National Meeting of the Academy of Management* (1981), pp. 281–282.

15 Thomas C. Hayes, "At G.M.'s Buick Unit, Workers and Bosses Get Ahead by Getting Along," *New York Times,* 5 July 1981, pp. F4–5.

16 Louis E. Davis, "The Design of Jobs," *Industrial Relations,* 6, No. 1 (1966), p. 21.

17 Howard C. Carlson, "A Model of Quality of Work Life as a Developmental Process," in *Trends and Issues in OD: Current Theory and Practice,* ed. W. Warner Burke and Leonard D. Goodstein (San Diego, Calif.: University Associates, 1980), p. 83.

18 Craig Lundberg, "Toward Comprehensive Organizational Reform: A Framework for Examining Quality of Work Life Applications and Effects," *Proceedings, 19th Annual Meeting of the Eastern Academy of Management* (1982), pp. 136–139.

19 Edward E. Lawler III, "Strategies for Improving the Quality of Work Life," *American Psychologist,* 37 (1982), 487.

20 George Strauss, "Job Satisfaction, Motivation, and Job Redesign," p. 46.

21 Denis D. Umstot, Cecil H. Bell, Jr., and Terence R. Mitchell reported a decline in productivity (of 1 percent) in their study "Effects of Job Enrichment and Task Goals on Satisfaction and Productivity: Implications for Job Design," *Journal of Applied Psychology,* 61 (1976), 379–394; similarly, Sam E. White and Terence R. Mitchell reported an impact on productivity of 0 percent in their study "Job Enrichment versus Social Cues: A Comparison and Competitive Test," *Journal of Applied Psychology,* 64 (1979), 1–9.

22 J. Richard Hackman, "Work Redesign and Motivation," *Professional Psychology,* 11 (1980), 449–450.

23 The one field experiment where objective feedback had only a minor effect on productivity (+2.7 percent) was flawed. Although productivity data were supposed to

be posted publicly, the researcher observed that, "many of the work units failed to do so regularly, thereby leading to more imprecise and infrequent feedback. It is noteworthy, in this respect, that the average change in employee perceptions of feedback was smaller than the average changes in the perceptions of the other core job characteristics following enrichment" [Christopher Orpen, "The Effects of Job Enrichment on Employee Satisfaction, Motivation, Involvement, and Performance: A Field Experiment," *Human Relations,* 32 (1979), 214].

24 J. Richard Hackman, "Work Redesign and Motivation," p. 449.

25 In a less positive vein, Hackman concluded that job design interventions have had "no clear effect" on absenteeism (Ibid., p. 450).

26 Ibid., p. 449.

27 Edwin A. Locke, David Sirota, and Alan D. Wolfson, "An Experimental Case Study of the Successes and Failures of Job Enrichment in a Government Agency," *Journal of Applied Psychology,* 61 (1976), 709–710.

28 Ibid., p. 710.

29 Charles N. Greene, "Some Effects of a Job Enrichment Program," p. 284.

30 John R. Maher and Wayne B. Overbagh, "Better Inspection Performance through Job Enrichment," in *New Perspectives in Job Enrichment,* ed. John R. Maher (New York: Van Nostrand, Reinhold, 1971), pp. 86–87.

31 H.M.F. Rush, *Job Design for Motivation* (New York: The Conference Board, 1971), pp. 46–55.

32 J. Richard Hackman, and Greg R. Oldham, *Work Redesign,* pp. 261–262. Interestingly, in an earlier work, Hackman argued that the effects of job design changes would be particularly enduring. He wrote, "Moreover, after jobs have been changed, the structure of the new tasks reinforces the changes that have taken place. One need not worry much about the kind of backsliding that occurs so often after training or attitude modification activities. The stimuli that most powerfully affect how a person behaves on the job are the ones that come from the job itself. And once those stimuli are changed, they are likely to stay that way—at least until the job is once again redesigned." See, "Is Job Enrichment Just a Fad?," *Harvard Business Review,* 53, No. 5 (1975), 138.

33 Edwin A. Locke, David Sirota, and Alan D. Wolfson, "Successes and Failures," p. 708.

34 W. Philip Kraft and Kathleen L. Williams, "Job Redesign Improves Productivity," *Personnel Journal,* 54 (1975), 397.

35 J. Richard Hackman, "Work Redesign and Motivation," p. 450.

36 David Sirota and Alan D. Wolfson, "Pragmatic Approach to People Problems," *Harvard Business Review,* 51, No. 1 (1973), 120–128; also Edwin A. Locke, David Sirota, and Alan D. Wolfson, "Successes and Failures," p. 701.

37 A comprehensive diagnostic framework and instrumentation are provided in J. Richard Hackman and Greg R. Oldham, *Work Redesign,* especially chapter 5 and the appendixes.

38 Ibid., pp. 109–110.

39 J. Richard Hackman, "Is Job Enrichment Just a Fad?" p. 131.

40 J. Richard Hackman and Greg R. Oldham, *Work Redesign,* p. 121.

41 Linda L. Frank and J. Richard Hackman, "A Failure of Job Enrichment: The Case of the Change That Wasn't," *Journal of Applied Behavioral Science,* 11 (1975), 433; also J. Richard Hackman, "Is Job Enrichment Just a Fad?," p. 131.

42 J. Richard Hackman and Greg R. Oldham, *Work Redesign,* p. 122.

**43** William F. Dowling, "Job Redesign on the Assembly Line: Farewell to Blue-Collar Blues?" *Organizational Dynamics,* 2, No. 2 (1973), 61.

**44** Wayne F. Cascio, *Applied Psychology in Personnel Management* (Reston, Va.: Reston Publishing, 1978), pp. 360–366.

**45** Lee Dyer, "Implications of New Theories of Work for the Design of Compensation Systems," *Proceedings of the 28th Annual Winter Meeting of the Industrial Relations Research Association* (1975), p. 161. Along these lines, Raymond E. Miles has noted that the pay of enriched jobs seldom fully reflects the added responsibilities: "Token pay increases may accompany job redesign, but over time members are likely to consider these token payments just that." See Miles' article, "Compensation, Organization Structure, and Control: Toward a Balance," *Proceedings, 1983 Spring Meeting of the Industrial Relations Research Association,* p. 143. Similarly, James O'Toole, in assessing the many cases in which job enrichment failed, concluded: "Another mistake was that the reformers expected workers to be more productive but not to share in the gravy. They assumed that intrinsic, psychic rewards were everything and that workers were not interested in such vulgar considerations as money." In "Thank God It's Monday: Work Incentives That Work," *Newsday,* 8 June 1980, p. 5 (Ideas).

**46** J. Richard Hackman and Greg R. Oldham, *Work Redesign,* pp. 124–126.

**47** J. Richard Hackman, "Is Job Enrichment Just a Fad?," pp. 131–132.

**48** Jon L. Pierce, Randall B. Dunham, and Richard S. Blackburn, "Social Systems Structure, Job Design, and Growth Need Strength: A Test of a Congruency Model," *Academy of Management Journal,* 22 (1979), 223–240.

**49** J. Richard Hackman, "Is Job Enrichment Just a Fad?," p. 133. For another case of climate incongruence see Paul S. Goodman, "Why Productivity Programs Fail: Reasons and Solutions," *National Productivity Review,* 1 (Autumn 1982), 379.

**50** George Strauss, "Job Satisfaction, Motivation, and Job Redesign," p. 45; William Serrin, "Companies Widen Worker Role in Decisions," *New York Times,* 15 Jan. 1984, p. 20.

**51** Michael Putney, "Work & Enjoy It, Inc.," *The National Observer,* 17 Mar. 1973, p. 16.

**52** Richard Walton, "Quality of Work Life Activities: A Research Agenda," *Professional Psychology,* 11 (1980), 488.

**53** Charles G. Burck, "Working Smarter," *Fortune,* 15 June 1981, pp. 70–71.

**54** Ibid., p. 70.

**55** Wayne F. Cascio, *Applied Psychology,* p. 366.

**56** J. Richard Hackman, "Is Job Enrichment Just a Fad?," p. 131. Illustrative of this point, in the case study reported by Lars E. Bjork ["An Experiment in Work Satisfaction," *Scientific American,* 232 (Mar. 1975), 19–21], preliminary discussions took more than a year. The (twelve) workers and the union refused to cooperate without a guarantee that pay would not be adversely affected if output declined.

**57** Paul S. Goodman, "Why Productivity Programs Fail," pp. 373–380.

**58** J. Richard Hackman, "Is Job Enrichment Just a Fad?," p. 131.

**59** Ibid.

**60** Lars E. Bjork, "Experiment in Work Satisfaction," p. 21.

**61** Charles G. Burck, "Working Smarter," p. 73, italics added.

**62** J. Richard Hackman and Greg R. Oldham, *Work Redesign,* p. 250.

**63** J. Richard Hackman, "Work Redesign and Motivation," p. 452.

**64** H.M.F. Rush, *Job Design for Motivation,* p. 25.

**65** Albert S. King, "Expectation Effects in Organizational Change," *Administrative Science Quarterly,* 19 (1974), 221–230. However, it would seem that supervisory expectations may be a necessary but not a sufficient condition for productivity improvement via job enrichment. Although the supervisors expected productivity gains in the study reported by Christopher Orpen ("Effects of Job Enrichment," p. 213), no gains materialized.

**66** Charles G. Burck, "Working Smarter," p. 73, cites the pertinent comments of Rosabeth Moss Kanter: "I find it's easy to get top executives on board. They like to be intellectual, they're impressed by professors, they're intrigued by concepts, they tend to be moved by examples of how other companies are doing it. They say, 'This is wonderful, let's do it a level below.' But to me that group down below is much more difficult. They'll have to pay the price."

**67** J. Richard Hackman and Greg R. Oldham, *Work Redesign,* p. 117.

**68** John B. Miner, *Theories of Organizational Behavior* (Hinsdale, Ill.: Dryden Press, 1980), pp. 260–261.

**69** David J. Cherrington and J. Lynn England, "The Desire for an Enriched Job as a Moderator of the Enrichment-Satisfaction Relationship," *Organizational Behavior and Human Performance,* 25 (1980), 139–159. Consistent with this finding is the earlier research by John P. Wanous, "Who Wants Job Enrichment?," *S.A.M. Advanced Management Journal,* 41 (Summer 1976), 15–22.

**70** Christopher Orpen, "Effects of Job Enrichment," p. 211.

**71** Gordon E. O'Brien and Peter Dowling, "The Effects of Congruency between Perceived and Desired Job Attributes upon Job Satisfaction," *Journal of Occupational Psychology,* 53 (1980), 124–127.

**72** Ralph Katz, "Job Longevity as a Situational Factor in Job Satisfaction," *Administrative Science Quarterly,* 23 (1978), 204–223; also see Ralph Katz, "The Influence of Job Longevity on Employee Reactions to Task Characteristics," *Human Relations,* 31 (1978), 703–725; and Ralph Katz, "Job Enrichment: Some Career Considerations," in *Organizational Careers: Some New Perspectives,* ed. John Van Maanen (New York: Wiley, 1977), pp. 133–147.

**73** Sigmund G. Ginsburg, "The High Achiever's Job Satisfaction," *Personnel Administrator,* 26, No. 1 (1981), 81.

**74** Edgar H. Schein, "Increasing Organizational Effectiveness through Better Human Resource Planning and Development," *Sloan Management Review,* 19, No. 1 (1977), 10, 14. One study found that about 40 percent of all employees are resistant to job enrichment, particularly those nearing retirement or without a college education. See Donald C. Collins and Robert R. Raubolt, "A Study of Employee Resistance to Job Enrichment," *Personnel Journal,* 54 (1975), 232–235, 248.

**75** Stephen M. Sales, "Organizational Role as a Risk Factor in Coronary Disease," *Administrative Science Quarterly,* 14 (1969), 325–336.

**76** Greg R. Oldham, J. Richard Hackman, and Jone L. Pearce, "Conditions Under Which Employees Respond Positively to Enriched Work," *Journal of Applied Psychology,* 61 (1976), 402. Also, the longitudinal research by Christopher Orpen, "Effects of Job Enrichment," pp. 189–217, supports the conclusion that contextual satisfaction moderates reactions to job design changes. Complicating matters somewhat, Orpen found that job enrichment increases contextual satisfaction; hence the variables are dynamically interrelated.

**77** John B. Miner, *Theories of Organizational Behavior,* p. 260.

**78** Paul S. Goodman, "Why Productivity Programs Fail," pp. 375, 378.

**79** Wayne F. Cascio, *Applied Psychology,* p. 359.

**80** Paul S. Goodman, "Why Productivity Programs Fail," p. 380; also J. Richard Hackman, "Is Job Enrichment Just a Fad?," pp. 132–133, 137.

**81** Wayne F. Cascio, *Applied Psychology,* p. 360.

**82** Comments of Greg R. Oldham at symposium on personnel practices, 42nd Annual Meeting of the Academy of Management (New York City), 1982.

**83** Paul S. Goodman, "Quality of Work Life Projects in the 1980s," *Proceedings, 1980 Spring Meeting of the Industrial Relations Research Association,* p. 491.

**84** Michael Beer and James W. Driscoll, "Strategies for Change," in *Improving Life at Work: Behavioral Science Approaches to Organizational Change,* ed. J. Richard Hackman and J. Lloyd Suttle (Santa Monica, Calif.: Goodyear, 1977), pp. 395–396.

**85** Ibid.

**86** Ibid.

**87** J. Richard Hackman, "Is Job Enrichment Just a Fad?," p. 131.

**88** J. Richard Hackman and Greg R. Oldham, *Work Redesign,* p. 250, italics in original.

**89** John B. Miner, *Theories of Organizational Behavior,* p. 258.

**90** As Hackman and Oldham, *Work Redesign,* p. 250, have commented, "What we may have, then, is yet another case in organizational life where the rich get richer, and the poor—if they try to make the leap—are likely to fail."

**91** In this regard, Wayne F. Cascio, *Applied Psychology,* p. 367, noted: "If behavioral approaches to designing work are ever to become powerful tools for organizational improvement, the challenge of implementation will have to be met with the meticulous and diligent attention it deserves."

**92** J. Richard Hackman and Greg R. Oldham, *Work Redesign,* pp. 266–268.

**93** Indeed, for centuries money has consistently had "bad press," and people who possess it have often been described in unflattering terms, e.g., being "loaded," "filthy rich," or having "piles" of it.

**94** Along these lines, see Mitchell Fein, "Job Enrichment: A Reevaluation," *Sloan Management Review,* 15, No. 2 (1974), 79. Fein cites a report indicating that Leonard Woodcock, president of the UAW was "very outspoken in his denunciation of government officials, academic writers and intellectuals who contend that boredom and monotony are the big problems among assembly workers." According to Woodcock, "a lot of academic writers . . . are writing a lot of nonsense."

**95** Mitchell Fein, "Job Enrichment," p. 74.

**96** Clair F. Vough, *Productivity: A Practical Program for Improving Efficiency* (New York: Amacom, 1979), p. 53.

**97** Ibid., p. 42.

**98** Frederick W. Hornbruch, Jr., *Raising Productivity: Ten Case Histories and Their Lessons* (New York: McGraw-Hill, 1977), p. 173.

**99** Ibid., p. 174.

**100** Ibid., pp. 178–184.

**101** Ibid., p. 161.

**102** This case has been disguised to protect the anonymity of the focal organization; the facts, though, are essentially correct.

**103** Jeremy Main, "How to Battle Your Own Bureaucracy," *Fortune,* 29 June 1981, pp. 54–58; also see Keith A. Bolte, "Intel's War for White-Collar Productivity," *National Productivity Review,* 3 (Winter 1983–84), 47–50, 52–53.

**104** Jeremy Main, "Battle Your Own Bureacracy," p. 58. As the supervisor commented, before the changes personnel records was "a most disorganized, unbelievably unproductive department."

**105** Personal communication, 1 June 1982.

**106** Clair F. Vough, *Productivity,* pp. 93–94, italics in original.

**107** Ibid., p. 83.

**108** "How the Japanese Manage in the U.S.," *Fortune,* 15 June 1981, p. 98.

**109** Thomas C. Hayes, "At G. M.'s Buick Unit, Workers and Bosses Get Ahead by Getting Along," *New York Times,* 5 July 1981, p. F4.

**110** Clair F. Vough, *Productivity,* p. 85.

**111** Robert Janson, "Work Redesign: A Results-Oriented Strategy That Works," *S.A.M. Advanced Management Journal,* 44 (Winter 1979), 24.

**112** Clair F. Vough, *Productivity,* p. 85.

**113** Ibid., p. 97, italics in original.

**114** Ibid.

**115** Jeremy Main, "Battle Your Own Bureaucracy," p. 56.

**116** Ricky W. Griffin, "Task Attributes and Long-Term Employee Productivity," *Proceedings, 41st Annual National Meeting of the Academy of Management* (1981), pp. 176–180.

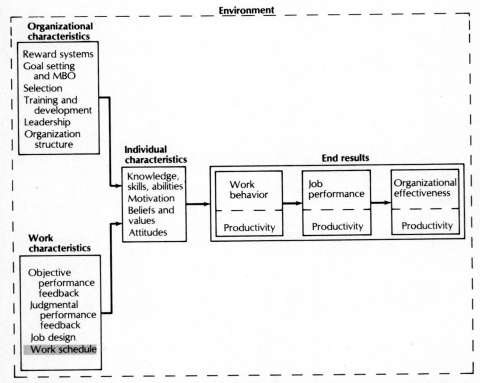

Conceptual framework of the determinants of productivity in organizations—a behavioral science approach.

# CHAPTER 12

# ALTERNATIVE
# WORK SCHEDULES

A recent development in the world of work is the growing adoption of alternative work schedules. Defined as any variation in the requirement that all permanent full-time employees in an organization adhere to the same, fixed, 5-day workweek, alternative work schedules have figured prominently in efforts to improve the quality of work life. The two most common forms, by far, have been the compressed workweek and flexible work hours. Several other innovations are (1) the use of permanent part-time employees, (2) job sharing, (3) "mini shifts" for jobs requiring intense effort, (4) extended vacations, (5) sabbaticals, and (6) phased retirement. These latter alternatives, however, have received limited application and little research attention. The present discussion, therefore, focuses exclusively on the compressed workweek and flexible work hours. The compressed workweek is reviewed in regard to trends in application, potential advantages, potential disadvantages, evidence of effectiveness, factors influencing effectiveness (boundary conditions), and future prospects. Then the flexible work hours literature is examined with respect to the same six issues. After a brief summary of the two sets of productivity results, suggestions are offered for implementation.

## THE COMPRESSED WORKWEEK (CWW)

The CWW involves scheduling the normal 36- to 40-hour workweek in fewer than 5 days, the most common form being the 4-day, 40-hour workweek (called the "four-forty"). There are, of course, numerous variations.[1]

## Trends in the Application of the CWW

In the early 1970s the CWW had "a meteoric rise to fame and public attention."[2] In 1970 only about 40 companies had a CWW plan in use; by 1972 some 2000 companies had implemented such a plan; and by 1973 an estimated 3000 companies had tried the CWW, and companies were converting to the CWW at a rate of about 150 per month.[3] Evidently 1973 marked the year of peak interest in the CWW. By 1975 a *Wall Street Journal* article reported that "industry's love affair with the 'four-forty' had clearly cooled." Company executives reportedly were not pleased with the results.[4] Indeed, a survey found that nearly one-third of the organizations that had adopted the CWW discontinued its use shortly thereafter.[5] While adoptions apparently increased during the 1970s, the rate of growth leveled off. In the late 1970s it was estimated that some 1.1 million Americans worked under a CWW;[6] the participation rate for all U.S. employees was estimated at 2.7 percent in 1980.[7]

## Possible Advantages of the CWW

The following potential benefits have been thought to accrue to employees and organizations from adoption of the CWW:

1 Increased leisure time, allowing employees to enjoy the nonwork aspects of life more fully
2 Reduced commutation costs
3 Lower setup and washup costs
4 Reduced absenteeism, because employees have more time available for personal matters and loss of a day's pay is more costly
5 Higher performance quality and quantity
6 More efficient use of plant and equipment if a second (3-day) mini shift is employed
7 Increased opportunity for employees to obtain a second job (i.e., to "moonlight") if so desired
8 An easy-to-implement intervention[8]

## Possible Disadvantages of the CWW

A review of the literature suggests the following potential problems:

1 External communications may suffer to the extent that vendors and customers are unable to contact particular employees.
2 Internal communication may decline, especially if the organization remains open 5 days a week.
3 Overtime may be hard to schedule, even if required for an urgent task.
4 It may be too costly, or impossible, to set up a second (3-day) shift.
5 Performance quality and quantity may decline if employees become fatigued toward the end of a 10-hour day.

**6** There may be "slippage" in the actual hours worked due to fatigue and/ or boredom.

**7** Increased moonlighting may exacerbate the problems associated with fatigue.

**8** Single parents may find that the extended workday interferes with non-work responsibilities.[9]

### Effectiveness Evidence

Almost all of the research to date on the CWW has been "highly impressionistic" to use the late William Glueck's term. His extensive literature review reported twenty anecdotal and ten "rigorous" accounts of the effects of the CWW.[10] However, even the "rigorous" reports are problematic because most relied on perceptions of productivity. Unfortunately, perceived changes in productivity often reflect attitudes about the intervention (i.e., whether the respondents want the program to be continued or discontinued), rather than actual changes.[11] The present review consequently examines only those studies which reported objective evidence of effectiveness.

Table 12-1 provides objective data concerning the effects of the CWW on productivity and absenteeism. Five studies reported evidence regarding productivity, with results ranging from a decrease of approximately 4.5 percent to an increase of 3.1 percent. The median result was a change of 0.0 percent. Five studies reported absenteeism data: in two cases absenteeism declined, in one case it increased, and in two cases there was no change. Hence, the median result was no change in absenteeism.

Surveys of employee attitudes have generally shown more positive results. Glueck found that job attitudes improved in 12 out of 18 studies, and Ronen and Primps reported that job satisfaction improved in 5 out of 9 (more rigorous) studies.[12] Yet even these results may be misleading because there is evidence that improvements in attitudes may not endure: "initially the results are positive. Later, the results return to prior levels or decline relative to the 5-40 pattern. Perhaps there is a 'Hawthorne Effect' in the early stages of the change."[13] Indeed, the adoption of the CWW has been followed frequently by disenchantment and declining enthusiasm over time.[14]

### Boundary Conditions

Several variables may affect the success of CWW interventions. The CWW is most likely to yield positive results when (1) the work is not physically or mentally taxing;[15] (2) the organization can operate with a 4-day workweek, or business permits hiring a mini shift;[16] (3) many of the employees are young and without family responsibilities;[17] and (4) many jobs are low-level, offering little intrinsic satisfaction (and, hence, the 4-day week may result in a perceived upgrading of status and responsibility, or alternatively, allow employees to "get

**TABLE 12-1**
EFFECTS OF THE COMPRESSED WORKWEEK (CWW) ON PRODUCTIVITY AND ABSENTEEISM

| Study number and year | Setting and sample | Impact on productivity | Impact on absenteeism |
|---|---|---|---|
| 1  1971[a] | Small manufacturing company | +3.1% | +35% (hours lost)<br><br>+4.9% (absence occurrences) |
| 2  1973[b] | Port Authority of N.Y. and N.J.; two departments | "No discernible trend" | NR |
| 3  1973[c] | Pharmaceutical company; 131 employees, various occupations | NR | −10% |
| 4  1974[d] | Industrial products company; 210 operative employees | NR | No change |
| 5  1975[e] | Accounting division of large multinational corporation; 474 clerical employees and supervisors | No significant change | NR |
| 6  1975[f] | Fabric mfg. company; 167 sewing employees | −1.1% | NR |
| 7  1977[g] | Industrial products company; 191 operative employees | NR | No change |
| 8  1984[h] | Midwestern plant; mfr. of business equipment; 559 operative workers and supervisors | −4½% (approx.) | −68% |

*Note:* NR = not reported
[a]Gilbert V. Steward and John M. Larsen, "A Four-Day, Three-Day per Week Application to a Continuous-Production Operation," *Management of Personnel Quarterly,* 10 (1971), 13–20.
[b]Louis J. LaCapra, "Trying Out the Four Day Work Week," *Public Personnel Management,* 2 (1973), 216–220.
[c]Walter R. Nord and Robert Costigan, "Worker Adjustment to the Four-Day Week: A Longitudinal Study," *Journal of Applied Psychology,* 58 (1973), 60–66.
[d]John M. Ivancevich, "Effects of the Shorter Workweek on Selected Satisfaction and Performance Measures," *Journal of Applied Psychology,* 59 (1974), 717–721.
[e]James G. Goodale and A. K. Aagaard, "Factors Relating to Varying Reactions to the 4-Day Workweek," *Journal of Applied Psychology,* 60 (1975), 33–38.
[f]Eugene J. Calvasina and W. Randy Boxx, "Efficiency of Workers on the Four-Day Workweek," *Academy of Management Journal,* 18 (1975), 604–610.
[g]John M. Ivancevich and Herbert L. Lyon, "The Shortened Workweek: A Field Experiment," *Journal of Applied Psychology,* 62 (1977), 34–37.
[h]Charles N. Greene, "Effects of Alternative Work Schedules: A Field Experiment," *Proceedings of the 44th Annual National Meeting of the Academy of Management,* 1984, pp. 269–273.

it over with" sooner).[18] The CWW also may enhance job satisfaction to the extent that it results in an enriched job. If employees work four out of five workdays, it is likely that task variety and autonomy will increase as people "cover" for each other and supervisors take days off as scheduled. (In one study, however, only 14 percent of the supervisors took their regularly scheduled day off.)[19]

**Future Prospects**

All factors considered, there is no evidence that the CWW improves productivity. Work quality may decline because of fatigue, some employees will find the long hours objectionable, and the plan may reduce customer service. Unit costs, moreover, may increase if there is slippage in the hours worked, or if the 4-40 becomes a bargaining point for a 4-38. In light of these actual and potential problems, and the meager and possibly transitory behavioral and attitudinal effects that have been demonstrated, the future of the CWW does not appear very promising.

## FLEXIBLE WORK HOURS (FWH)

In broad terms, FWH is a system of scheduling work which allows employees some choice about when they will work. Typically, there are hours when all full-time employees must work (the "core" hours) and hours when employees can exercise some discretion (the flexible hours). For example, at the Sandoz, Inc., plant in East Hanover, New Jersey, all employees must work during the core hours of 9:30 A.M. to 12:00 NOON and 2:00 P.M. to 4:00 P.M. The earliest possible starting time is 7:30 A.M., and the latest allowable stopping time is 6:00 P.M., yielding a 10½-hour "band width." Although Sandoz has a 37½-hour workweek, employees are allowed to work as many as 8 hours a day, "banking" up to 2½ hours per week. After 3 weeks of 8-hour workdays, the employee can take an extra day off with pay.[20] (Employees are not allowed to bank more than 2½ hours per week, as this would require paid overtime in accordance with the Fair Labor Standards Act; similarly, employees can only bank ½ hour per day, as the Walsh-Healey Act would require paying overtime for a longer day.) Companies with a 40-hour workweek typically only allow employees to choose when they will start (and stop) work each day.

In all FWH plans there are seven key features that can vary:

**1** The band width
**2** The core hours
**3** The flexible hours
**4** The length of the workweek
**5** Whether banking is permitted
**6** The variability of work schedule permitted
**7** The role of the supervisor[21]

The first five features have already been described. Schedule variability refers to whether employees are allowed to determine their starting and stopping times daily or weekly (giving advance notice) or monthly, etc. Supervisory roles can vary from (1) granting the supervisor no influence over individual work schedules to (2) allowing the supervisor to override a subordinate's schedule in cases of significant "organizational need" to (3) requiring that subordinates and supervisors negotiate schedules in advance to (4) requiring prior supervisory approval of a work schedule.

In light of the seven key features which can vary in FWH plans, it is not surprising that more than 100 different variants have emerged in practice.[22] The four most common plans have been (1) staggered group hours (e.g., the accounting department starts at 8:30, purchasing at 9:00), (2) staggered individual hours (the individual establishes a work schedule in advance), (3) flexible workdays (the individual determines his or her own work schedule daily, subject to certain limitations, e.g., core hours), and (4) flexible hours (the individual works the contracted number of hours whenever he or she wishes during the band width). Some companies allow a choice of one or more plans. For instance, at IBM's 14,000-employee unit in San Jose, California, employees can choose among three FWH plans, as well as the standard fixed-hour workday.[23]

### Trends in the Application of FWH

The first known implementation of FWH occurred in a West German aerospace company in 1967. In 1969, there were an estimated ten companies in West Germany using FWH; by 1974 there were 3000 companies in West Germany with FWH; and by 1977 some 20,000 West German companies had FWH.[24] FWH plans were also rapidly adopted in other West European countries. By 1975, an estimated 30 percent of the French work force and 40 percent of the Swiss work force worked under FWH, as did roughly 25 percent of the Austrian work force by 1979.[25]

In the United States the adoption of FWH was energetic, but less rapid than in Europe for reasons discussed below. It began with the introduction of FWH at Control Data Corporation in 1972. By 1974 roughly 4 percent of the U.S. work force was under FWH, by 1978 the figure rose to 8 percent, and by 1980 it reached 10 to 12 percent.[26] As Simcha Ronen noted in *Flexible Working Hours,* "however slow the United States has been in considering flexitime, it is clear that the idea is gaining acceptance in the private sector at an accelerating rate."[27]

As might be expected, the adoption rate of FWH has varied depending upon industry and occupation. Industries with high proportions of employees participating in FWH (in 1978) included insurance and finance (19.3 percent), utilities, transportation, and communication (17.1 percent), and wholesale and retail trades and services (14.4 percent).[28] High participation rates generally have been concentrated in high-level white-collar occupations, e.g., managers, professional and technical employees, and sales people. Further, the rate of adoption of FWH has been twice as rapid among clerical (low-level white-collar) employees compared with craft workers.[29] Not surprisingly, therefore, a survey of FWH users revealed that in only 7 percent of such organizations were half or more of the participating employees members of a union, and in only 17 percent of the cases were as many as 10 percent of the participating employees union members.[30] Thus, although there has been growing application of FWH, the trend has largely reflected a white-collar phenomenon.

## Possible Advantages of FWH

The literature on FWH has produced a prodigious list of potential benefits. For simplicity of presentation, these benefits have been classified into two groups, depending upon whether the primary beneficiary is the individual or the employing organization. Listed first, are the potential benefits to employees.

**1** Minimizes stresses resulting from work-nonwork conflicts. Some examples are: it aids single parents who must be breadwinners, homemakers, and parents; it makes it easier for employees to take care of personal matters, or to improve their education; it minimizes the problems experienced by dual-career couples by facilitating the coordination of schedules; and in general it offers an opportunity for a better balance between work, family, and personal life demands.

**2** Reduces travel time and travel costs. By allowing travel at off-peak hours, this can potentially save up to one hour a day. (However, if public transportation is used, there may be no savings, and possibly an increase, in travel time during off-peak hours.)[31]

**3** Reduces the daily stress of getting to work on time. Clearly it takes some pressure off an employee to know that he or she does not have to arrive at a specific time.

**4** Allows the employee to begin work when he or she arrives. It is not necessary for the individual to waste personal time waiting around for the "starting bell."

**5** Increases employee feelings of personal control, autonomy, and trustworthiness, and it may enhance the sense of well-being. It may provide a "new measure of self-respect for employees at every level."[32]

**6** Allows more *daytime* participation in nonwork activities. This may be advantageous to the extent that individuals have more energy during the daytime, and recreational facilities are more readily available.

It is notable that unlike FWH, the CWW does not provide individuals with three of the above-mentioned advantages (items 3–5), because the CWW is merely a rearranged fixed-hour work schedule. Continuing the list of potential advantages, the focus now turns to the ways in which organizations may benefit from FWH.

**1** Increases work motivation and productivity. Because employees are working hours when they feel more like working, fewer people are just "killing time." Relatedly, it has been argued that FWH may help in matching the employee's work schedule to his or her "body clock" or "bioclock." Hence, it is no longer necessary for the "late starter" to sit around from 8 A.M. to 9 A.M. in a semisomnolent stupor.[33]

**2** Improves working conditions, and hence productivity, in two ways. First, workers who arrive early, or who leave late, may benefit from more uninterrupted "quiet time." Second, some difficult projects can be completed more efficiently in one long day, compared with conventional work hours.

**3** Improves customer service insofar as it extends the hours the organization is able to serve customers.

**4** Substantially reduces tardiness. With FWH, the required starting time will coincide with the time the person arrives at work (provided the employee arrives prior to the core time). As an employee noted, "It's hard to be late when you have a two-hour leeway."[34] Additionally, FWH eliminates the common practice of having the supervisor reprimand late employees—an activity which frequently leads to feelings of anger, embarrassment, guilt, fear, and pity—but not necessarily to improved punctuality.[35]

**5** Reduces overtime costs. This benefit is particularly likely to obtain if employees schedule their work to coincide with peak loads or if managers are able to assign last-minute work to those employees who are working late hours by choice—e.g., a letter can be typed at 5 P.M. by a typist who works until 6 P.M.[36]

**6** Reductions in turnover, absenteeism, and grievances may result from higher levels of employee morale.

**7** Facilitates recruitment of superior employees. Because FWH is an attractive policy to many people—a welcome development to individuals not accustomed to this prerogative—the organization may be able to screen more job applicants.[37]

**8** Enables the organization to hire more women and handicapped workers, due to the increased flexibility it affords employees.

**9** Reduces sick leave and personal leave costs. Employees need not have "imaginary illnesses" in order to handle personal matters during working hours. As one plant manager put it: "With the advent of flexitime, our firm is no longer subsidizing dental appointments. The need to run and pay a bill, usually resulting in an extended lunch hour, is no longer time lost by the company."[38] Instead, time not worked is made up by the employee.

**10** Increases the skills of employees. FWH often leads to some cross-training of employees so they can "cover" for each other.[39]

**11** Improves external communication in some cases. Due to an earlier starting time, companies on the west coast may experience improved communication with parties on the east coast.

**12** Improves the accuracy of performance evaluations. Supervisors are less concerned about punctuality, and possibly more attentive to the more important aspects of job performance.[40]

### Possible Disadvantages of FWH

From the perspective of the individual employee, potential disadvantages include the following:

**1** Employees have to make up for lost time. As noted previously, the employee who is unavoidably late for work still has to work the required number of hours. Similarly, FWH may result in a loss of absence privileges, or an elimination of short work breaks. One union official summed it up this way: "Workers who used to get a couple of hours off during the day, with pay, to visit a doctor, are no longer paid for those hours; with Flexitime, if you take a couple of days off because of a death in the family, you have to work 2 extra days to make up for the time you lost."[41]

**2** Reduces substantially the opportunity to earn overtime pay. As the same union official commented: "There is no such thing as overtime with Flexitime."[42]

**3** Increases the surveillance of employees. In order to keep track of actual hours worked, a time clock may be introduced (or reintroduced), or employees may be required to sign in and out. Supervisors may be overly conscientious in monitoring employee work hours. The net result may be increased conflict and employee resentment.

**4** Unwanted job enrichment may occur. Some employees may not want the additional responsibility, autonomy, or variety that typically accompanies FWH.

**5** Creates resentment among employees who are excluded from participation in FWH. Jobs that provide internal services are often excluded from FWH, since understaffing can be very detrimental (such jobs include elevator operators, telephone operators, security guards, health and safety staff). Additionally, resentment may arise among those employees who formerly had exclusive claim to the prerogative of choosing their own work hours.[43]

Continuing the discussion of potential disadvantages, the following are possible drawbacks from the organization's perspective:

**1** Spreads the staff too thin at times, causing inadequate staffing and supervision of employees. This may especially be a problem during the early or late working hours. One manager commented: "On many days I need help in getting material together to respond to inquiries that arrive in the afternoon. But many of our employees choose to work early hours and that means they start getting ready by 3:00 to leave at 3:30. If you were here at 3:30 you'd see them marching out. It's trouble finding someone to do any work that I need done after that hour. Clerks ask me why I don't solve the problem by preparing materials for them to work on earlier in the day. My answer is that the event requiring attention didn't break then. I can't predict what is going to happen. A lot of work in the communications field involves responding to emergencies."[44]

**2** Increases overhead costs because of the longer hours of operation. Not only may there be an increase in utility and internal service expenses, but FWH may also entail capital outlays for time-monitoring equipment.

**3** Creates problems in connection with internal communication and coordination. For example, it will be more difficult to schedule meetings, and it will be harder to conduct training sessions. People may not be around when they are needed. Consider this comment: "The new excuse around here is called *flex-out*. Once and a while I need a particular employee in a hurry. If I can't find that person, I naturally ask another worker where he or she might be. More than half the time I get the answer that the guy or gal has flexed out. It used to be that if I couldn't find an inventory clerk, they would tell me the person was in the restroom. Flex out is a better excuse. You can be gone away from your work station longer."[45]

**4** Creates problems with respect to external communication and customer service. Clients or vendors may be unable to contact appropriate personnel during noncore hours. Consequently, coworkers and secretaries may have to take more messages.

**5** Requires changes in the personnel manual. Not only must new policies be articulated, but to the extent that jobs are altered, changes may be required in job descriptions and performance evaluation procedures.

**6** Substantially increases the difficulty of the supervisor's job. Supervisors will have to plan and coordinate activities far more carefully to ensure adequate coverage—especially since some employees will opt to "flex out" when the work load promises to be the heaviest, or when Friday afternoon arrives.[46] Illustrative of the increased need for supervisory planning, consider what happens if some employees arrive at 7:00 A.M. and no work has been planned for them; nothing may get done until the supervisor arrives.[47] Additionally, many supervisors find they have to work longer hours as the work day is expanded. In this regard one supervisor commented: "The company policy doesn't state in black and white that a supervisor cannot work flexible hours. But it might as well. I know of no supervisor who takes advantage of the policy. We have the opposite of flextime. If we want to do an honest job of supervising our employees, we have to work longer hours."[48] Moreover, supervisors may experience a reduction in employee cooperation, or encounter employee abuse of the system—e.g., employees may punch in or sign in for each other, or simply not put in a full day's work. Further, given the loss of authority and control (i.e., to demand and obtain attendance at specified times), supervisors will need to adopt a more participative approach to managing. Some, threatened by the loss of stability and power, will have difficulty adjusting and perform less effectively.[49]

**7** Creates potential problems in labor relations. It is not unlikely that there will be strong union opposition to any changes in contractual agreements affecting overtime compensation or work conditions.[50]

**8** Represents a nearly irrevocable commitment. That is, it is very difficult, if not impossible, to discontinue FWH—regardless of the effectiveness evidence—due to its popularity among employees. "Experimenting with flexible hours is like stepping on a moving sidewalk . . . [it] just keeps on going."[51]

### Effectiveness Evidence

Most of the research to date on FWH has been of very poor quality, consisting largely of anecdotal and impressionistic accounts, rather than objective data such as physical productivity measures. Most "studies" have merely consisted of descriptive, nonempirical evaluations which have often concluded, "We tried it and we liked it."[52] Indicative of this situation, a recent survey of 78 organizations that adopted alternative work schedules reveals that only 9 of the organizations obtained objective effectiveness evidence; and only 4 of the 78 organizations used the effectiveness information to undertake a formal evaluation of the program.[53] Although only a small *proportion* of the extant studies contains objective productivity results, the number of such reports is fairly sizable. Table 12-2 presents a survey of these reports.

Twenty studies have provided data concerning the impact of FWH on objectively measured productivity. In 10 cases there were positive results, the increases ranging from 2 percent to 12 percent, and in 10 cases results were either inconclusive or negative. The median result was an increase in productivity of roughly 1 percent.[54]

In total, 20 studies have reported the effects of FWH on absenteeism: 10 examined the effects in terms of overall absenteeism, and 10 reported results in terms of various component forms of absenteeism (e.g., sick leave days used, unpaid absence days, short-term absences, full-day absences, and so forth). With respect to the more inclusive criterion, overall absenteeism, results ranged from no change to a reduction in absenteeism of 71 percent. The median result was a decrease of 5.3 percent. A somewhat less impressive finding was generated by a nation-wide survey of 987 organizations. The survey asked personnel managers to indicate which of 34 absenteeism control methods their organizations employed (e.g., progressive discipline, daily attendance

**TABLE 12-2**
EFFECTS OF FLEXIBLE WORK HOURS (FWH) ON PRODUCTIVITY AND ABSENTEEISM

| Study number and year | Setting and sample | Impact on productivity | Impact on absenteeism |
|---|---|---|---|
| 1 1976[a] | Berol Corporation; 7 locations; various occupations | No change | −50% |
| 2 1976[b] | State Street Bank; 4 departments; largely clerical employees | No change | No change |
| 3 1977[c] | Metropolitan Life Insurance Co.; 5 departments; 246 clerical employees | No "clear-cut impact" | No significant change in short-term absences |
| 4 1978[d] | SmithKline Corporation; sample of 100 employees | NR | −50% (paid absences) −20% (single-day absences) |
| 5 1979[e] | U.S. Department of Labor, Office of Accounting | +3% | NR |
| 6 1980[f] | Mutual of New York; 22 clerical employees | +2.9% | −7.6% |

**TABLE 12-2**
EFFECTS OF FLEXIBLE WORK HOURS (FWH) ON PRODUCTIVITY AND ABSENTEEISM
(*Continued*)

| Study number and year | Setting and sample | Impact on productivity | Impact on absenteeism |
|---|---|---|---|
| 7  1980[g] | Control Data Corporation, aerospace and microcircuit divisions; 386 managerial and nonmanagerial employees | "Slightly favorable trend" | NR |
| 8  1981[h] | County welfare agency; 353 employees | +3.0% | −29.9% (paid absences) −143.9% (unpaid absences) |
| 9  1981[i] | Government agency; 64 clerical employees | −4.6% | NR |
| 10  1981[j] | U.S. Social Security Admin., Bureau of Data Processing; 350 employees | +12% | −3% (approx.) |
| 11  1981[k] | U.S. Department of the Interior, U.S. Geological Survey; 2230 employees | +10% | −7% (sick leave) |
| 12  1981[l] | U.S. Office of Personnel Management, Bureau of Policy and Standards; 240 employees | Inconclusive results | No significant change |
| 13  1981[m] | Library of Congress; 150 employees | +10.5% | −43% (sick leave usage) |
| 14  1981[n] | Navy Finance Center; Cleveland, Ohio; 64 employees | NR | −50% (sick leave usage) |
| 15  1981[o] | Navy Finance Office; Long Beach, California; 55 employees | No change | No change |
| 16  1981[p] | U.S. Army Computer Systems Command; Fort Belvoir, Virginia; 82 employees | NR | No change (sick leave) |
| 17  1981[q] | U.S. Army Tank Automotive Command; Michigan; 400 employees | +2% | −29% (sick leave usage) |
| 18  1981[r] | U.S. Information Agency; 33 employees | +5% | No change (short-term absences) No change (sick leave usage) |
| 19  1981[s] | First National Bank of Boston; 125 employees | +10% | No change |
| 20  1981[t] | Occidental Life Insurance Co.; 700 employees | No change | −21% (full-day absences) |

**TABLE 12-2**
EFFECTS OF FLEXIBLE WORK HOURS (FWH) ON PRODUCTIVITY AND ABSENTEEISM
(*Continued*)

| Study number and year | Setting and sample | Impact on productivity | Impact on absenteeism |
|---|---|---|---|
| 21  1981[u] | Pitney Bowes, Inc.; 220 employees | No conclusive indication | −16% |
| 22  1982[v] | Large multinational corp.; approx. 250 secretaries, technicians, and draftsmen | NR | −71% |
| 23  1982[w] | State government agency; 12 data entry operators | No significant change | NR |
| 24  1984[x] | Eastern plant; mfr. of business equipment; 455 operative workers and supervisors | +2½% (approx.) | −56% |

*Note:* NR = not reported.

[a]Simcha Ronen, *Flexible Working Hours* (New York: McGraw-Hill, 1981), pp. 174–175, 184, 194; "Berol Corporation Applies Flexitime in Four Countries," Work in America Institute's *World of Work Report,* July 1976, p. 8; David Robison, ed., *Alternative Work Patterns: Changing Approaches to Work Scheduling* (Scarsdale, N.Y.: Work in America Institute, 1976), pp. 27–29.

[b]Donald J. Petersen, "Flexitime in the United States: The Lessons of Experience," *Personnel,* 57, No. 1 (1980), 24; Simcha Ronen, *Flexible Working Hours,* pp. 182, 189, 195.

[c]Virginia E. Schein, Elizabeth H. Maurer, and Jan F. Novak, "Impact of Flexible Working Hours on Productivity," *Journal of Applied Psychology,* 62 (1977), 463–465.

[d]John R. Hinrichs, *Practical Management for Productivity* (New York: Van Nostrand Reinhold, 1978), pp. 133–134; Simcha Ronen, *Flexible Working Hours,* p. 195. (Whereas Hinrichs reported a decrease in single-day absences of 20%, Ronen reported the reduction to be 14%; the former result is used in this review.)

[e]Pam Silverstein and Jozetta H. Srb, *Flexitime: Where, When, and How?* (Ithaca, N.Y.: Cornell University, 1979), pp. 20–22.

[f]Donald J. Petersen, "Flexitime in the United States," p. 25.

[g]Ibid., p. 26.

[h]Jay S. Kim and Anthony F. Campagna, "Effects of Flexitime on Employee Attendance and Performance: A Field Experiment," *Academy of Management Journal,* 24 (1981), 729–741. This study reported data for both experimental and control groups; hence effectiveness results were computed by subtracting changes in the control from changes in the experimental group. Thus, the reduction in unpaid absences of 143.9% (!) resulted from a decrease of 45.7% in the experimental group and an increase of 98.2% in the control group. (Only long-term absences were examined for the purposes of this review. This was because what the authors called short-term absence—an absence of less than two hours' duration—really corresponds to a measure of lateness.)

[i]Christopher Orpen, "Effect of Flexible Working Hours on Employee Satisfaction and Performance: A Field Experiment," *Journal of Applied Psychology,* 66 (1981), 113–115.

[j]Simcha Ronen, *Flexible Working Hours,* pp. 126, 141.

[k]Ibid., pp. 128, 143.

[l]Ibid., pp. 126, 141.

[m]Ibid., pp., 127, 142.

[n]Ibid.

[o]Ibid.

[p]Ibid., pp. 128, 143.

[q]Ibid.

[r]Ibid.

[s]Ibid., pp., 176, 184, 194.

[t]Ibid., pp. 179, 186, 195.

[u]Ibid., pp. 180–181, 187, 195.

[v]V. K. Narayanan and Raghu Nath, "A Field Test of Some Attitudinal and Behavioral Consequences of Flexitime," *Journal of Applied Psychology,* 67 (1982), 214–218.

[w]David A. Ralston, "The Employees May Love Flextime, But What Does It Do for the Organization's Productivity?" paper presented at the 42nd Annual National Meeting of the Academy of Management, 1982, p. 9.

[x]Charles N. Greene, "Effects of Alternative Work Schedules: A Field Experiment," *Proceedings of the 44th Annual National Meeting of the Academy of Management* (1984), pp. 269–273.

records kept by supervisors). The absenteeism rate among the 207 organizations using FWH was 4.5 percent; in contrast, the absenteeism rate among the 780 nonusers of FWH was *lower,* at 4.3 percent.[55] Interestingly, the impact of FWH on the various specific component indicators of absenteeism has generally been more positive, the median result being a decrease of 21 percent. This latter result, however, pertains only to specific partial indicators—indicators that may have been selected and reported because of their favorability. Hence, some skepticism may be warranted in interpreting the findings for partial absenteeism indicators.

The impact of FWH on attitudes has generally been quite positive: typically 75 to 95 percent of all respondents have approved of the change or have indicated no interest in returning to fixed work hours. (In one setting it was reported that everyone was pleased with FWH, except one person who was described as "only an old grouch anyway.")[56] Similarly, about 85 percent of respondents have said that their job satisfaction (or morale) had improved as a result of FWH. Ronen, in a review of 27 studies, found that job attitudes improved in 26 cases.[57] These findings, however, may be a bit misleading. In a recent study in which work satisfaction was measured before and after FWH—but in which *no reference was made to the possible impact of FWH*— there was no change in work satisfaction. The authors commented,

> ... other flexitime research has frequently made reference to flexitime in the process of gathering data. In other words, employees knew that flexitime was the topic under investigation. Given that flexitime is a desirable company policy for employees because it does facilitate travel, reduce interrole conflict, and increase a sense of being in control in the work setting, it is quite understandable to find employees reporting that they like it more than they dislike it. Flexitime is valued in this case not because it enhances work satisfaction, per se, but because it makes working a little bit easier. Thus, questionnaires used to gather employee attitudes about flexitime will yield favorable results if the link to flexitime is made obvious. When the link to flexitime is not salient, the traditional [positive] relationship may not occur.[58]

### Boundary Conditions

A number of variables have been identified in the literature as factors that may affect the success of FWH. These are:

*Compatible technology.* The task or technology should "fit" (be appropriate) if FWH is to prove successful. A suitable setting would be where individuals work independently on isolated work modules (e.g., an R&D laboratory). FWH is also likely to prove successful in cases where expansion occurs in the number of hours a shared physical resource (e.g., a computer facility) can be used.[59] In contrast, unfavorable settings would seem to be those involving (1) sequential tasks (e.g., an assembly line with add-on or checking functions), (2) functionally narrow or fragmented work necessitating a high degree of internal communication and coordination, (3) a multiple-shift, or 24-hour operation, or (4) an internal service department requiring continual readiness.[60] In view of these limiting conditions, it is not surprising that the application of FWH has been greater in white-collar than in blue-collar jobs. Moreover, when applied to both white- and blue-collar employees in the same organization, the impact has been more favorable among the former: reductions in overtime were 60 percent greater in one study, and 100 percent greater in another.[61]

*Organizational flexibility.* If it is necessary that a given work unit be fully staffed at all times, it may be necessary to "borrow" employees from other units. The cross-training of employees, therefore, may be a necessary condition for the successful implementation of FWH.[62]

*Support of involved parties.* It is important that union representatives and top management grant their imprimaturs. The commitment of first-level managers is probably of even greater importance, since they will deal with most of the difficulties of making FWH work.

*Employee characteristics.* Several individual difference variables may function as predisposing (rather than as necessary) boundary conditions: while they may not be crucial, they may improve the chances for success. Success is more likely if employees are young, part of dual-career families (or single parents), are receptive to increased responsibility and variety (i.e., they have high growth need strength), and if they place great value on convenient work schedules.[63] Additionally, to the extent that employees live in highly-populated, traffic-congested areas, the benefits of FWH will be enhanced.

*Clear and appropriate objectives.* FWH should be introduced only if the explicit purpose is an improvement in the quality of work life. If management expects an improvement in productivity, disappointment will likely ensue, and this may lead to discontinuance. Evidence indicates that only 15 percent of adopting organizations have implemented FWH with the expectation that productivity would improve.[64]

## Future Prospects

Two recent trends point toward continued growth in the application of FWH. First, a large segment of today's work force consists of highly educated young people who have expectations that go beyond a good salary and job security. Many of these people (the "new breed") want jobs that engage their skills and potential abilities; they want diversity, change, and the opportunity to make choices; and they expect a certain measure of autonomy at work and flexibility on the part of supervisors.[65] A concomitant goal of the new breed is the opportunity for increased leisure time: indeed, many are willing to trade a pay increase for increased time off.[66] And related to the growing leisure ethic is the desire for more immediate gratification: "Instead of focusing on the future and considering the present as a preparatory stage, younger people tend to emphasize the present and concentrate on experiencing the here and now."[67] FWH can help integrate the goals of younger workers (the largest age cohort in American history) with those of employing organizations.

A second important trend has been the dramatic growth in the number of working women. Whereas the conventional family used to consist of a male breadwinner and a nonworking housewife, by 1977 only 14 percent of all families fell into this category. Women were working in 49 percent of all families, and 72 percent of all employed women held full-time jobs.[68] Not only has there been growth in the proportion of two-paycheck families, the increased incidence of women holding high-level (e.g., professional or managerial) jobs has led to a rapid increase in dual-career families—where both husband and wife are highly job-involved.[69] Jerome Rosow, of the Work in America Institute, has commented,

> *the multiworker family is becoming the answer to inflation and rising expectations for 50% of U.S. families.* Obviously, then, working hours must become more flexible to adjust to the needs of multiworker families. In light of the rising work participation of women, *time schedules must be accommodated* to the problems of child care and childrearing. Work institutions must recognize the dual roles of working wives and working mothers who must meet the competing demands of work and home life.[70]

Many U.S. corporations have already had their consciousnesses raised in connection with the need for FWH. It has been predicted that the proportion of employees working under FWH will grow from roughly 12 percent (in 1980) to 25 percent in 1990.[71] The 1980s "may be the decade in which Americans free themselves from the tyranny of the time clock."[72]

It is interesting to question why it will have taken more than two decades to reach a 25 percent participation rate in the United States versus only one decade in some European countries. One factor is the labor shortage in western Europe (accompanied by a high incidence of imported labor) which provided an impetus to attract a relatively untapped source of labor, housewives. High levels of traffic congestion, and the high cost of gasoline also contributed to the attractiveness of FWH. Also, FWH quickly became an ideological issue in Europe around which labor organizations rallied. The following statement, from a 1973 meeting of the International Labor Organization, typifies this commitment:

> Life has become too regimented, too impersonal, too monotonous, too frenzied and altogether too limiting and too restrictive to the present generation of Europeans. How can we reintroduce into European societies a greater measure of freedom, a greater respect for human dignity, and a fuller measure of personal responsibility, without doing away with the minimum of discipline and order that are essential for continued stability and prosperity? [The answer: FWH.][73]

In contrast, the labor movement in the United States has generally viewed FWH with disinterest or skepticism, presumably reflecting concern about loss of overtime pay and jobs. Finally, the fact that in the United States the initial experimentation with alternative work schedules centered around the CWW may have slowed adoption of FWH for three reasons. First, the CWW posed a threat to organized labor: it could lead to relaxation of overtime laws or, at the minimum, changes in contractual agreements. Second, the CWW diverted attention away from FWH. Third, the general lack of enthusiasm for the CWW may have spilled over to dampen interest in other innovative work schedules, including FWH.

## SUMMARY

The present review of the two most prominent alternative work schedules has yielded the following findings. With respect to objectively measured productivity, the CWW and FWH have produced median improvements of 0 percent and 1 percent, respectively. In terms of impact on absenteeism, the CWW yielded a median result of no change; FWH reduced overall absenteeism by 5.3 percent, and (selected) component measures by 21 percent. Regarding the impact on employee attitudes, positive effects were obtained in 60 percent of the CWW studies and roughly 95 percent of the FWH studies. Results, therefore, have been generally superior for FWH compared to CWW interventions. Not surprisingly, the discontinuance rate has been almost five times as high for the CWW compared to FWH: nearly one-third of the CWW interventions were discontinued versus 5 percent to 8 percent of the FWH interventions.[74] Clearly, FWH is the superior approach.

However, the primary benefit resulting from FWH is an improvement in the quality of work (and nonwork) life; the evidence indicates that on the whole there is no improvement in productivity, and only a modest reduction in overall absenteeism. The following summary assessment seems on target: "Flexible work hours may have more advantages than disadvantages for work organizations as a means of improving the quality of working life, especially as it is a system that is relatively inexpensive to introduce."[75] It is likely that as employee interest in FWH grows, employers will be forced either to justify their opposition or to adopt such a program.[76]

Organizations planning to implement FWH may want to consider a number of issues before adopting such a plan. Fixed work schedules have a long history of custom and practice; hence, there will probably be some resistance to change. Certainly, changing work schedules is not a decision to be taken lightly, especially since, for all practical purposes, the decision may be an irrevocable one—even if demonstrably unsuccessful from the organization's perspective. It is important, therefore, that prior to implementation (1) a feasibility study be undertaken, possibly by an ad hoc committee, to examine work patterns and staffing requirements; (2) work flows be plotted by time of day; and (3) union representatives be contacted for their views. Management should be clear as to *why* it is considering the adoption of FWH: some objectives are more realistic than others.

If FWH appears to be feasible, it is important that its implementation be planned carefully. As mentioned previously, there are seven parameters that need to be considered in the design of a FWH plan. It should be decided, for example, whether banking of hours will be allowed. Careful consideration should be given to legal and contractual obligations.[77] Attention should also be paid to the mechanics of keeping track of hours worked: e.g., will employees be required to punch a time clock? will special monitors be purchased? will employees be required to sign in and out? Additionally, it is important to plan for an evaluation of FWH. Effectiveness criteria should be identified in advance, and (if possible) baseline measurements obtained. In short, management should not proceed impulsively. As one insurance company executive put it: "Just don't decide that next week in your company or government office you'll install some sort of flexible hours program."[78]

Several suggestions might be made in connection with the initial phase of the implementation process. Implementation is likely to be successful to the extent that top management visibly and enthusiastically supports the change. One way to convey this support is by having high-level line executives conduct orientation meetings. At such meetings the advantages and disadvantages of FWH should be explicitly identified—i.e., there should be a balanced presentation. Employees should be encouraged to express their concerns, a limited number of employees should attend each orientation meeting, and program parameters should be communicated clearly, repeatedly, and in writing. It is particularly important that orientation meetings be held with first-line supervisors, since they will have to handle most of the ensuing problems. Their commitment is crucial to the success of FWH. Management also should continue to consult with union representatives to insure against misconceptions. The coordination of these efforts may require the appointment of a FWH project director, someone responsible for overseeing all aspects of implementation.

The intervention might be labeled an "experiment" or a "pilot test" initially. By doing so, the costs associated with failure (and perhaps the likelihood of failure) may be reduced. It may also be advantageous to conduct the initial test at a remote location, one with low visibility, or in a setting where employees are customarily given considerable autonomy.[79]

Another way to reduce risks is to increase the amount of flexibility employees are allowed in stages, as experience warrants: e.g., a gradual lengthening of the band width, or the addition of a banking provision. It will also be useful, as the program is under way, to hold meetings with first-line supervisors to discuss problems associated with the new role requirements and to provide feedback to supervisors so they can adjust their behavior accordingly.[80] Finally, it is important to obtain extensive evaluation evidence from the trial run so that a sound basis exists for expanding or discontinuing the program.

## NOTES

1 In continuous process (24 hours a day, 7 days a week) operations, it is often advantageous to schedule 12-hour work shifts, the workweek consisting of alternating 3- and 4-day schedules. See James A. Breaugh, "The 12-Hour Work Day: Differing Employee Reactions," *Proceedings of the 42nd Annual National Meeting of the Academy of Management* (1982), pp. 277–281. Perhaps the most extreme form of

schedule is the one used by river boat pilots who work 30 days and are off 30 days. See William F. Glueck, "Changing Hours of Work: A Review and Analysis of the Research," *The Personnel Administrator,* 24 (Mar. 1979), 44.

2 Jules Asher, "Flexi-Time, Four-Day Weeks Thrive Despite Recession," *APA Monitor,* 6 (Apr. 1975), 5.

3 John M. Ivancevich and Herbert L. Lyon, "The Shortened Workweek: A Field Experiment," *Journal of Applied Psychology,* 62 (1977), 34 (for estimated adoptions as of 1972); Alvar O. Elbing, Herman Gadon, and John R. M. Gordon, "Flexible Working Hours: It's About Time," *Harvard Business Review,* 52, No. 1 (1974), 18 (for estimated adoptions in 1970 and 1973); and James G. Goodale and A. K. Aagaard, "Factors Relating to Varying Reactions to the 4-Day Workweek," *Journal of Applied Psychology,* 60 (1975), 33 (for the estimated monthly adoption rate in 1973).

4 Pam Silverstein and Jozetta H. Srb, *Flexitime: Where, When, and How?* (Ithaca, N.Y.: Cornell University, 1979), p. 10.

5 Jules Asher, "Flexi-Time," p. 5; also see Eugene J. Calvasina and W. Randy Boxx, "Efficiency of Workers on the Four-Day Workweek," *Academy of Management Journal,* 18 (1975), 605.

6 William F. Glueck, "Changing Hours," p. 45.

7 *New York Times,* 10 Apr. 1982, p. 30.

8 William F. Glueck, "Changing Hours," p. 45; also Simcha Ronen and Sophia B. Primps, "The Compressed Work Week as Organizational Change: Behavioral and Attitudinal Outcomes," *Academy of Management Review,* 6 (1981), 68–73.

9 William F. Glueck, "Changing Hours," p. 45; Jules Asher, "Flexi-Time," p. 5; and James G. Goodale and A. K. Aagaard, "Varying Reactions," pp. 33–38. Interestingly, Glueck points out that a century ago, when 10- and 12-hour work days were commonplace, workers alternated between intense periods of work and periods of idleness—i.e., there was plenty of "socializing and song" (Glueck, p. 45).

10 William F. Glueck, "Changing Hours," pp. 46–47, 66–67.

11 In connection with this issue see William D. Hicks and Richard J. Klimoski, "The Impact of Flexitime on Employee Attitudes," *Academy of Management Journal,* 24 (1981), 340. In one study involving alternative work schedules, objective measurements of productivity showed no real changes; however "subjective feelings and opinions" provided wide agreement that productivity had improved. See Pam Silverstein and Jozetta H. Srb, *Flexitime,* p. 18. Similarly, at SmithKline Corporation, 93 percent of the workers thought that productivity had improved because of an alternative work schedule; however only 32 percent of the supervisors thought that productivity improved. See Donald J. Petersen, "Flexitime in the United States: The Lessons of Experience," *Personnel,* 57, No. 1 (1980), 27.

12 William F. Glueck, "Changing Hours," p. 46; and Simcha Ronen and Sophia B. Primps, "Compressed Work Week," pp. 66–67.

13 William F. Glueck, "Changing Hours," p. 46.

14 Alvar O. Elbing, Herman Gadon, and John R. M. Gordon, "Flexible Working Hours," p. 18. For instance John M. Ivancevich and Herbert L. Lyon, "The Shortened Workweek," concluded that, "The long-term impact . . . [revealed by the 25-month data] suggests that conversions to the 4-40 workweek may not be as beneficial as has previously been claimed" (p. 36).

15 Myron D. Fottler, "Employee Acceptance of a Four-Day Workweek," *Academy of Management Journal,* 20 (1977), 660–661; also William F. Glueck, "Changing

Hours," pp. 46–47; also see Simcha Ronen and Sophia B. Primps, "Compressed Work Week," pp. 71–72.

16 William F. Glueck, "Changing Hours," p. 47.
17 Simcha Ronen and Sophia B. Primps, "Compressed Work Week," p. 73; also William F. Glueck, "Changing Hours," p. 46.
18 Myron D. Fottler, "Employee Acceptance," pp. 661–666; Simcha Ronen and Sophia B. Primps, "Compressed Work Week," pp. 68–72.
19 James G. Goodale and A. K. Aagaard, "Varying Reactions," p. 37.
20 Simcha Ronen, *Flexible Working Hours* (New York: McGraw-Hill, 1981), p. 181.
21 Robert T. Golembiewski and Carl W. Proehl, Jr., "A Survey of the Empirical Literature on Flexible Workhours: Character and Consequences of a Major Innovation," *Academy of Management Review,* 3 (1978), 838–840.
22 John W. Newstrom and Jon L. Pierce, "Alternative Work Schedules: The State of the Art," *The Personnel Administrator,* 24 (Oct. 1979), 21.
23 M. Gerstel, "Flexible Work Hours Equal More Productive Employees," *Electronic Business,* 7 (Mar. 1981), A28, 30.
24 Alvar O. Elbing, Herman Gadon, and John R. M. Gordon, "Flexible Working Hours," pp. 18–19; Pam Silverstein and Jozetta H. Srb, *Flexitime,* p. 6.
25 Jules Asher, "Flexi-Time,", p. 5; Pam Silverstein and Jozetta H. Srb, *Flexitime,* p. 6; William H. Glueck, "Changing Hours," p. 62.
26 John W. Newstrom and Jon L. Pierce, "Alternative Work Schedules," p. 21; James O'Toole, "Thank God It's Monday: Work Incentives That Work," *Newsday,* 8 June 1980, p. 5 (Ideas); Phil Farish, "Pair Potpourri," *Personnel Administrator,* 26 (June 1981), 10; Damon Stetson, "Work Innovations Improving Morale," *New York Times,* 20 Sept. 1981, p. 53. Consistent with the historical pattern, it was estimated that in 1977, 5.8 percent of U.S. employees worked under FWH (see Donald J. Petersen, "Lessons of Experience," p. 21).
27 Simcha Ronen, *Flexible Working Hours,* p. 172.
28 Stanley D. Nollen and Virginia H. Martin, *Alternative Work Schedules. Part 1: Flexitime* (New York: Amacom, 1978), p. 1. Similarly, a Conference Board study (Information Bulletin No. 92) found that FWH was employed by 15 percent of banking organizations and by 34 percent of insurance companies. See Harriet Gorlin, *Personnel Practices II: Hours of Work, Pay Practices, Relocation* (New York: The Conference Board, 1981), p. 12.
29 Phil Farish, "Pair Potpourri," p. 10.
30 Stanley D. Nollen and Virgina H. Martin, *Alternative Work Schedules,* p. 12.
31 Georgia Dullea, "Workers Find 'Flexitime' Makes for Flexible Living," *New York Times,* 15 Oct. 1979, p. B14; William F. Glueck, "Changing Hours," p. 62; Pam Silverstein and Jozetta H. Srb., *Flexitime,* pp. 38–39; Simcha Ronen, *Flexible Working Hours,* p. 59.
32 Alvar O. Elbing, Herman Gadon, and John R. M. Gordon, "Flexible Working Hours," p. 155.
33 Simcha Ronen, *Flexible Working Hours,* pp. 58–59, 68.
34 Pam Silverstein and Jozetta H. Srb., *Flexitime,* p. 13.
35 Simcha Ronen, *Flexible Working Hours,* pp. 59–60.
36 Ibid., pp. 72–73.
37 Pam Silverstein and Jozetta H. Srb, *Flexitime,* p. 39. The organization may also be able to tap new labor sources, e.g., women with young children.
38 Talmar E. Curry, Jr., and Deane N. Haerer, "The Positive Impact of Flexitime on Employee Relations," *Personnel Administrator,* 26 (Feb. 1981), 63–64.

**39** Pam Silverstein and Jozetta H. Srb, *Flexitime,* p. 39.

**40** Virginia E. Schein, Elizabeth H. Maurer, and Jan F. Novak, "Supervisors' Reactions to Flexible Working Hours," *Journal of Occupational Psychology,* 51 (1978), 336.

**41** Simcha Ronen, *Flexible Working Hours,* p. 238.

**42** Ibid.

**43** Ibid., pp. 65, 76–77.

**44** Andrew J. DuBrin, *Contemporary Applied Management* (Plano, Tex.: Business Publications, Inc., 1982), p. 199.

**45** Ibid., p. 202.

**46** Donald J. Petersen, "Lessons of Experience," p. 29; Robert T. Golembiewski, Carl W. Proehl, Jr., and Ronald G. Fox, "Is Flexi-Time for Employees 'Hard Time' for Supervisors? Two Sources of Data Rejecting the Proposition," *Journal of Management,* 5 (1979), 254.

**47** Andrew J. DuBrin, *Contemporary Applied Management,* p. 207.

**48** Ibid., p. 202. Along these lines, another manager commented that first-level supervisors "absorb the scheduling problems associated with these systems, which is clearly added work and . . . [they often] feel as though they have to be on the job when the first worker appears and until the last leaves. If these first line supervisors are feeling put upon . . . then all subordinates will probably pay the price" (in Simcha Ronen, *Flexible Working Hours,* p. 76).

**49** Simcha Ronen, *Flexible Working Hours,* p. 224; also see Robert T. Golembiewski, Carl W. Proehl, Jr., and Ronald G. Fox, "Hard Time," pp. 242, 248–249. Golembiewski et al. concluded, however, that the required "behavioral and attitudinal changes are within the competencies of most supervisors" (p. 248).

**50** Simcha Ronen, *Flexible Working Hours,* pp. 231–233. Indeed, as the president of the American Federation of Government Employees stated, "Our primary concern is that none of the rights American workers have fought for over the years, including the right to overtime pay after an eight hour day, be sacrificed in any effort to extend the scope of existing flexitime experiments" (in Simcha Ronen, *Flexible Working Hours,* p. 231).

**51** Alvar O. Elbing et al., "Flexible Working Hours," p. 154. And one supervisor has commented, "Just try taking F-T away and see what happens" (in Golembiewski et al., " 'Hard Time,'" p. 254).

**52** John W. Newstrom and Jon L. Pierce, "Alternative Work Schedules," p. 22.

**53** Ben Burdetsky and Marvin S. Katzman, "Evaluation of Alternative Work Pattern Applications," unpublished paper, George Washington University, 1981, pp. 1–11.

**54** It might be noted that the present review has excluded a study of computer programmers by Ralston (Table 12-2, study no. 23) that measured productivity in terms of an objective input (hours of computer time used), rather than an objective output. Had this study been included, however, the median impact on productivity would have remained the same, 1 percent. Another review, by Stanley D. Nollen, in "Does Flexitime Improve Productivity?" *Harvard Business Review,* 57, No. 5 (1979), reported that although the median increase in *subjectively perceived* productivity was 48 percent (p. 12), observed increases in objectively measured productivity ranged from 5 to 14 percent, and such increases could be expected to occur one-third to one-half of the time (p. 18)—yielding an average increase of slightly under 4 percent.

**55** Dow Scott and Steve Markham, "Absenteeism Control Methods: A Survey of Practices and Results," *Personnel Administrator,* 27 (June 1982), 73–76, 81.

**56** Robert T. Golembiewski et al., " 'Hard Time,'" p. 243.

57 Simcha Ronen, *Flexible Working Hours,* pp. 137–139, 152, 192–193, 202–203.

58 William D. Hicks and Richard J. Klimoski, "The Impact of Flexitime," p. 340.

59 David A. Ralston, "The Employees May Love Flextime, but What Does It Do for the Organization's Productivity?" paper presented at the 42nd Annual National Meeting of the Academy of Management, 1982, p. 11.

60 Alvar O. Elbing et al., "Flexible Working Hours," pp. 20, 22, 24, 28; William F. Glueck, "Changing Hours," p. 63; Jay S. Kim and Anthony F. Campagna, "Effects of Flexitime on Employee Attendance and Performance," *Academy of Management Journal,* 24 (1981), pp. 739–740; Donald J. Petersen, "Lessons of Experience," pp. 22, 29–31; Pam Silverstein and Jozetta H. Srb, *Flexitime,* p. 40; Robert T. Golembiewski et al., " 'Hard Time,' " p. 252.

61 Simcha Ronen, *Flexible Working Hours,* p. 73.

62 Cary B. Barad, "Flexitime under Scrutiny: Research on Work Adjustment and Organizational Performance," *Personnel Administrator,* 25 (May 1980), 74. Pertinent to this issue, Hercules, Inc. terminated its FWH and CWW programs in June 1982, after eight years of experience with these programs. The company's public affairs director offered the following explanation: "The message very simply is that we have to control costs. Times are very difficult" (*New York Times,* 10 Apr. 1982, p. 29).

63 Boas Shamir, "A Note on Individual Differences in the Subjective Evaluation of Flexitime," *Journal of Occupational Psychology,* 53 (1980), 215–217.

64 Stanley D. Nollen, "Does Flexitime Improve Productivity?" p. 18.

65 Jerome M. Rosow, "Changing Attitudes to Work and Lifestyle," in *Alternative Work Patterns: Changing Approaches to Work Scheduling,* ed. David Robison (Scarsdale, N.Y.: Work in America Institute, 1976), pp. 5–8; James O'Toole, "Thank God It's Monday," p. 5 (Ideas); Daniel Yankelovich, "The New Psychological Contracts at Work" *Psychology Today,* 11, No. 12 (1978), 46–50; Patricia A. Renwick and Edward E. Lawler III, "What You Really Want from Your Job," *Psychology Today,* 11, No. 12 (1978), 53–65, 118.

66 Regarding the desire for increased leisure, a U.S. Department of Labor survey found that 28.6 percent of American workers said they would forgo a 10 percent pay increase for a shorter work day; 43.5 percent said they would forgo the pay raise for longer weekends; and 65.6 percent were willing to trade increased pay for an extended vacation. Perhaps even more impressive are the results of an experimental program conducted in Santa Clara, California, in 1976. Employees were allowed to trade a pay *cut* for extra time off. More than 17 percent of the employees traded pay cuts of 5, 10, or 20 percent for an extra 2, 4, or 8 weeks of vacation time. See Maureen McCarthy, "Trends in the Development of Alternative Work Patterns," *The Personnel Administrator,* 24 (Oct. 1979), 33.

67 Simcha Ronen, *Flexible Working Hours,* p. 4.

68 See Clark Kerr, "Introduction: Industrialism with a Human Face," in *Work in America: The Decade Ahead,* ed. Clark Kerr and Jerome M. Rosow (New York: Van Nostrand Reinhold, 1979), p. xvi. It is notable that in 1960, 30 percent of all families consisted of a male breadwinner and a nonworking housewife.

69 Lyn Rosensweig, "The Dual-Career Couple: Its Impact on the Organization," unpublished masters thesis, Baruch College, 1981, pp. 1–6.

70 Jerome M. Rosow, "Changing Attitudes," pp. 7–8 (italics in original).

71 Kim Anderson, " 'Flextime' Grows, but Not on LI," *Newsday,* 21 July 1981, p. 37. And according to Nollen, by 1990 it is "within the realm of reasonable possibility" that 50% of all U.S. workers will work under FWH (in Anderson, p. 37).

**72** Jerome M. Rosow as quoted in Damon Stetson, "Work Innovations Improving Morale," *New York Times,* 20 Sept. 1981, p. 53. As William A. Emerson, Jr., put it in "Punctuality is the Thief of Time," *Newsweek,* 16 Dec. 1974: ". . . time. I know I can't take it with me, so I think I'll spend it on myself" (p. 13).

**73** Pam Silverstein and Jozetta H. Srb, *Flexitime,* p. 5.

**74** A discontinuance rate of 8 percent was mentioned in Stanley D. Nollen and Virginia H. Martin, *Alternative Work Schedules,* p. 44; a discontinuance rate of 5 percent was noted in the *National Productivity Review,* 1 (Spring 1982), 244.

**75** Christopher Orpen, "Effect of Flexible Working Hours on Employee Satisfaction and Performance: A Field Experiment," *Journal of Applied Psychology,* 66 (1981), 115.

**76** Pam Silverstein and Jozetta H. Srb, *Flexitime,* p. 45.

**77** A comprehensive discussion of legal issues, by an attorney specializing in employment law, is provided in Simcha Ronen, *Flexible Working Hours,* Chapter 18, pp. 277–304.

**78** Pam Silverstein and Jozetta H. Srb, *Flexitime,* p. 23.

**79** John R. Hinrichs, *Practical Management for Productivity* (New York: Van Nostrand Reinhold, 1978), p. 136.

**80** Simcha Ronen, *Flexible Working Hours,* pp. 223–228; Robert T. Golembiewski et al., " 'Hard Time,'" pp. 248–249, 252–257.

PART # FOUR

## TOWARD
## ORGANIZATIONAL
## ACTION

# CHAPTER 13

# THE IMPLEMENTATION OF PLANNED CHANGE IN ORGANIZATIONAL SETTINGS

This chapter presents a prescriptive (normative) model pertinent to implementing planned change. Before describing the model, however, it is useful to review what has been accomplished thus far, and to outline what remains to be done. In light of this broad overview, the rationale for the present discussion should be clear.

Part One provided two perspectives on productivity: a societal-level analysis of factors influencing productivity, and treating these factors as givens, a conceptual framework of some of the determinants of organizational productivity. Parts Two and Three examined in detail ten behavioral science techniques that have figured prominently in efforts to improve productivity in work organizations. For each technique an attempt was made to determine the magnitude, reliability, and durability of the impact on productivity, as well as boundary conditions affecting results. Additionally, suggestions for implementation were offered in connection with each type of intervention.

Each of the ten interventions represents, of course, a specific type of planned organizational change. Part Four expands on the issue of application by first providing a normative model for implementing planned change, in general (Chapter 13). The concluding chapter summarizes productivity results and offers suggestions pertinent to organizational diagnosis and the establishment of a productivity department.

## THE TWO SIDES OF CHANGE: ADAPTATION AND ADJUSTMENT

It is virtually a truism that organizations must be able to adapt to a changing environment if they are to survive. Changes in technology, consumer tastes, government regulations, the costs of various inputs (e.g., raw materials, energy, capital), and the values and competencies of prospective employees, are but some of the threats to organizational existence. The magnitude of the threat resulting from the accelerating rate of technological change and the knowledge explosion was dramatically underscored by Toffler in his 1970 best seller, *Future Shock*. If the last 50,000 years of human existence were divided into lifetimes of approximately 62 years each, there would have been 800 such lifetimes. Of these, 650 would have been spent in caves; electricity would have been used in two lifetimes; petroleum would have been used in only the present (800th) lifetime; and the computer, of course, would have been used in less than half of the most recent lifetime.[1]

The practical consequence of turbulence is that most companies or divisions of major companies find they must undertake moderate organizational changes at least once a year and major changes every 4 or 5 years.[2] Yet, according to a Conference Board report, "reorganization is usually feared because it means disturbance of the status quo. . . . [Hence], needed reorganization is often deferred, with a loss of effectiveness and an increase in costs."[3]

The process of adaptation to external events creates tension with respect to internal adjustment. Often an organization's members will object to enacted or proposed changes: they (or at least many of them) may entirely refuse to cooperate; they may ignore parts of the intended change; they may follow the letter but not the spirit of the new law, "going through the motions" while deliberately allowing mistakes to be made; or they may comply, but with deep resentment, possibly complaining to managers, coworkers, customers, suppliers, or anyone who will listen. Reactions of this nature are often called "resistance to change." Of course, reactions will vary across individuals: some individuals may be neutral or indifferent; others may be enthusiastic. In short, "change leads to consternation for some [people], indignation for others, shock for still others, and hope for a few."[4]

## REACTIONS TO CHANGE

Many hypotheses have been advanced to explain the varying reactions to change, and a formidable list of explanatory variables has been generated, including:

1 Fear of the unknown, or inadequate information
2 Fear of being unable to learn new skills (or the embarrassment of being slow to learn)
3 Threats to expertise or to power
4 Threats to pay and perquisites
5 Reduction in social interaction
6 Personality characteristics (e.g., dogmatism)
7 Lack of participation in the change process
8 Increase in job responsibilities

**9** Decrease in job responsibilities

**10** Organizational climate (e.g., trust, openness, authenticity, risk-taking propensity)

Unfortunately the (laundry) list of possible explanations for differing reactions to change is virtually endless. But rather than attempting to list all the possible reasons why an organization's members might be favorably or unfavorably disposed toward a change, it might be more fruitful to examine a more parsimonious conceptual scheme.

Reactions to change depend largely on two factors: (1) the *substance* or content of the change and (2) the *process* by which the change is planned and implemented. Borrowing from Chester Barnard's inducements-contributions model, it is hypothesized that reactions to change are positively related to changes in inducements (benefits) and negatively related to changes in contributions: employees resist changes (both for substantive and process-related reasons) to the extent that (1) actual or anticipated inducements are reduced, (2) actual or anticipated required contributions are increased, and (3) benefits are reduced *and* required contributions increased. Viewed in this manner, employee reactions to change depend upon whether the terms of the inducements-contributions exchange are perceived to be favorably, unfavorably, or immaterially altered.

People are involved in various exchange relationships: with friends, family, employers, civic and political associations, and so forth.[5] At work, the competencies the individual has developed determine to a large extent the terms of the exchange, and these competencies often result from extensive investments in time and energy. Hence, changes that minimize the utility of old skills, or require the acquisition of new skills, may be resisted even when the changes benefit the organization. In this regard, Renato Tagiuri cites the case of the admirals of the U.S. Navy who were opposed to the introduction of the continuous-aim gun mounting—a change that offered a 2000 percent improvement in naval gun fire effectiveness. In Tagiuri's words, "for the Ordnance Admirals the continuous-aim gun mounting was not just a technical innovation: It potentially affected their entire way of life."[6]

Or consider the case of Dr. Ignaz Semmelweis. In 1848 he discovered that when physicians washed their hands in a solution of chlorinated lime, the incidence of mortality among women after childbirth fell from 18 percent to 1 percent. Yet, Dr. Semmelweis's colleagues in Vienna rejected this suggestion; and they also rejected him—within a year he was dismissed from the clinic where he practiced medicine. Why the resistance to change? According to Jay Hall, because it threatened an important status symbol, the surgical smock. (A heavily smeared smock was a visible sign of professional importance.)[7]

The moral of these two cases is clear. People often consciously choose to ignore valid and useful information, or they reject constructive changes. Often this resistance reflects self-serving motives: people may have vested interests that are threatened. Sometimes the resistance reflects provincialism: e.g., the "not invented here" (NIH) syndrome. Paraphrasing Gellerman: Who's against change? Anyone who has to sacrifice something to achieve it—and that includes nearly everyone.[8]

## A NORMATIVE MODEL FOR IMPLEMENTING PLANNED CHANGE

Writing in 1513, Niccolò Machiavelli offered the following observation about the implementation of planned change:

> It must be considered that there is nothing more difficult to carry out, nor more doubtful of success, nor more dangerous to handle, than to initiate a new order of things.[9]

In the past few decades, though, advances have been made in the implementation of planned change as a result of systematic analysis of case studies and the application of deductive reasoning.

Although many theories and concepts have been advanced regarding how to effect planned change, the normative model described here is based largely on the work of Gene Dalton.[10] However, while the empirical basis for Dalton's six-factor model consisted of six case studies, the present eight-factor model is based on published reports of numerous instances of planned change.[11] The eight factors are reviewed next.

### Felt Need

The existence of internal tension or pain—i.e., a felt need—is a precondition for effective change in human systems at any level of analysis (intrapersonal, interpersonal, organizational). Where there is no pain, there is no problem; where there is no problem, there is no action.[12] Clearly, the optimal time to intervene in an organizational setting is when sufficient tension exists in the system to motivate members to seek alternative methods (or solutions).

In the absence of felt need, the organization's members should be informed about existing problems, and the costs of not changing should be emphasized. Also, if possible, increased pressure for change might be brought to bear from external sources. Initially, changes should be centered around visible problems and deficiencies, those that are evident to virtually all organizational participants.[13] It is important that a felt need for change extend to those managers who must authorize the expenditure of resources required to undertake a change program.

### Visible Top Management Support

Few ideas are as widely accepted as the notion that visible top management support is critical to the successful achievement of planned change.[14] Rather than reviewing case studies supportive of this view, it is more instructive to examine some of the reasons *why* such support is so important.

The support of a respected and trusted source increases the confidence of organizational members that a proposed change will be successful.[15] Somewhat akin to the "placebo effect," the imprimatur of a respected authority figure raises optimism, and expectations of success tend to be self-fulfilling.[16]

A second, related explanation is that visible top management support is needed to overcome the inertia and fear of failure that pervade middle management ranks in many organizations. Middle managers often greet proposed changes with caution, passivity, and skepticism (although these reactions may not be expressed overtly). Senior management must provide the enthusiastic support and commitment needed to nourish a fledgling change effort.[17]

Another explanation is that top managers serve as role models for other organizational members. Tubbs and Widgery reported the case of a company which spent $50 million on capital improvements, an investment which yielded an increase in productivity of less than 1 percent after 2 years. Subsequently, a behavioral intervention was undertaken which resulted in a 7.7 percent increase in productivity after 2 years and a cost savings of $7 million. A key feature of this successful intervention was that top managers taught others by setting an example. As Tubbs and Widgery concluded: "Most important to the success of any organizational improvement effort is the support of the person at the top—not in word, but in deed."[18]

The three previously mentioned reasons for the utility of visible top management support can also be conceptualized in terms of the application of three sources of power: expertise, legal authority, and personal attractiveness. Top management support can also entail the application of two less subtle sources of influence: rewards and penalties. Top management can signal, explicitly or implicitly, its willingness to reward or punish members in accordance with their cooperation.[19] Although there is evidence that coercive power contributes positively to the success of change efforts, coercion can cause resentment and should be used judiciously, and in conjunction with other power bases.[20] One possible dysfunctional consequence of the use of coercion is a decline in organizational trust: "Obeying a distorted golden rule, people do to others what they perceive is being done to them."[21]

Summing up, for a change program to be effective it is crucial that top management signal its strong commitment to the change, via both word and deed. A change program needs as sponsors those managers whose departments are most directly affected. As further evidence of management's commitment to a change effort, an external change agent may be retained to provide assistance. It is, however, important for change agents, whether external or internal, to recognize that although many managers may express an interest in effecting change, few will be willing to act on that interest. George Huber has explained this phenomenon as follows:

> Many who assumed that such assistance was forthcoming have been disappointed. . . . The powerful person who was counted on saw either that other prob-

lems were more demanding of attention or that influence would be best saved for use in another battle. There are always other battles.[22]

### Gradual Clarification

Organizational changes threaten the nature, and even the existence, of an employee's exchange with the organization. Consequently, on hearing about an impending change, the individual is likely to wonder how the change will affect his or her work (and nonwork) situation. As one management consultant has observed, the bottom line for everyone is "What will it mean for me? Will I be better off?"[23] Of course, an almost limitless number of specific questions are likely to come to the person's mind: will new competencies be needed, and if so, what amounts of time and energy will be needed to acquire them; will the change affect the career prospects of the individual's supervisor (employees often advance in organizations in tandem); will the influence or composition of the individual's work group be affected; and so forth.

In light of the many questions that employees will want answered, managers should provide advance information (warnings) about planned change and communicate frequently and fully. While initial statements should be general (e.g., there is a need for improved control over expenses), gradually the specific features of a change should be made clear (e.g., supervisors should prepare monthly reports of deviations from standards).[24]

Illustrative of the importance of gradual clarification is the case of a retail company that decided to switch from manual to computerized credit records in two branch offices. In one branch the manager informed all her employees about the impending changes, even those employees in departments that would not be affected. As the change progressed, she continued to keep employees informed and focused on operating details. The other branch manager decided not to tell her employees about the change until the week of the changeover; she did not want to upset them. When they found out, however, they were shocked and visibly upset. Three months after the changeover an evaluation study found that the change was progressing smoothly in the first branch but that the second branch was in turmoil. Many employees had resigned; those who remained had difficulty adjusting; cooperation and satisfaction were low; and performance was poor.[25]

Clearly, it is important that all employees be given information about forthcoming changes. To be sure, if management fails to communicate about change, the information vacuum will be filled by informal (and possibly less accurate) channels, such as the grapevine.[26]

As time goes by the behavioral implications of planned change should become increasingly clear to all participants. That is, employees should learn exactly what is to be done differently. Yet, determining the behavioral ramifications of a change is the most difficult component of the change process:

> Movement toward increasingly specific goals, while seeming the most obvious, is . . . probably the dimension on which most change efforts flounder. General goals, often

widely and genuinely shared, too frequently die for the lack of the crucial idea as to how the first few concrete steps can be taken.[27]

"Excellence," for example, is a worthy pursuit, but what specifically should people *do* to achieve it?

### Facilitation and Support

One step that minimizes resistance to change is to assist employees in acquiring required new skills. Instruction or formal training might be provided, possibly coupled with time and energy equivalents—e.g., relieving individuals of some preexisting duties or relaxing deadlines. Managers also can provide emotional support by listening empathetically, by recognizing (rather than denying) an employee's feelings, and by being patient. Such actions allow some seemingly big problems to dissipate with the passage of time.[28]

Relatedly, the gradual introduction of changes can facilitate acceptance. "Massive change: massive anxiety: massive resistance."[29] Managers, therefore, should attempt to introduce changes in steps, maximizing stability around each temporary phase of the change process.[30]

Yet managers often are too impatient to proceed in steps. Illustrative of this problem is the Dashman Company case, one of the best-known case studies ever published. Shortly after assuming his new position, Mr. Post issued a directive to all twenty (previously autonomous) purchasing executives: "Hereafter, each of the purchasing executives in the several plants of the company will notify the vice-president in charge of purchasing [Mr. Post] of all contracts. . ." Six weeks into the peak buying season, Mr. Post had received no notices.[31] While there are many possible explanations for this remarkable management failure—indeed, Mr. Post's behavior is contrary to all eight guidelines of the normative model described here—it is clear that the intended change was unaccompanied by facilitation or support. Although from a technical perspective changes may be possible, and doable in short order, the behavioral aspects of change often require time-consuming concomitant actions.[32]

### Altering Component Subsystems

Organizations are systems that tend toward equilibrium. Adaptive and maintenance mechanisms tend to cause small changes to be "ironed out" (a process called homeostasis), yielding a steady state.[33] Moreover, inertia tends to persist even if past practices have not proven particularly successful. Organizations sometimes get "locked into" belief systems and practices that are no longer adequate solutions to problems; ironically, ineffective solutions are often clung to all the more closely in times of adversity. In other words, organizations often behave neurotically.

It follows conceptually, (and it has been demonstrated empirically) that attempted changes in organizations are more likely to "take hold" if they encompass several relevant subsystems rather than just one. Thus, to the extent that appropriate changes occur in all three major determinants of organizational effectiveness—organizational, work, and individual characteristics—changes are more likely to prove effective.

Evidence indicates that it is important that changes occur in social relationships, because relationships sustain patterns of interaction and work behavior.[34] Where social relationships are altered (e.g., by changing job assignments or work schedules) behavioral changes are facilitated.[35] In the absence of changes in social relationships there will be little support and reinforcement for intended changes.

In a broader vein, change programs that alter only structural (organizational) characteristics or only technological (work) characteristics are generally less effective than those which alter both structure and technology.[36] It is important to ascertain why this has been the case. One plausible explanation is that change programs that alter multiple subsystems are more likely to be institutionalized. Unless changes are incorporated within formal operational procedures they are highly vulnerable to extinction.[37] In practical terms, this means that merely training supervisors to delegate authority to subordinates, for example, may prove ineffective if not combined with changes in other subsystems. If, however, changes are also made in formal job responsibilities (e.g., job descriptions are changed), along with changes in various organizational practices (e.g., in MBO criteria, feedback reports, and in reward systems), it is more likely that delegation actually will occur. In the absence of institutionalization, intended changes tend to become "back burner" items for many organizational members. Largely ignored, the intended changes gradually fade into organizational oblivion (and fall off the stove).

### Increased Self-Esteem

Reactions to change, and the effectiveness of change efforts, tend to be favorable to the extent that changes heighten an employee's sense of self-esteem.[38] The self-esteem of employees can be affected by the manner in which change is introduced (the change process) and the content of the change. Four illustrations of the impact of the change process on self-esteem are provided below.

In the case of the Dashman Company, the new vice president chose not to meet or even talk with the purchasing executives to discuss an organizational problem; instead he sent out a form letter instructing them to change their procedures. Clearly, the metacommunication (the message about the relationship between the parties) demeaned the purchasing executives. In essence, they were told that their ideas and opinions were unimportant (indeed, the letter began, "Hereafter. . ."); further, it was implicitly communicated that Mr. Post was now the boss, that they were to do as told, and so forth. Apparently the process by which the change was introduced lowered (or threatened) the self-esteem of the individuals who were expected to carry out the change.

A second illustration of the potential role of self-esteem in the implementation of planned change is provided by Guest's study of an automobile assembly plant. Prior to the arrival of the new production manager, the plant was the least efficient one in the division and there was abundant evidence of unsatisfactory performance. The new production manager, in his first meeting with all the supervisors, stated candidly that plant Y had a bad reputation. He said he had heard that many members of the work group were incapable of doing their jobs. He continued: "I am willing to prove that this is not so, and until shown otherwise, I personally have confidence in the group." After 3 years the plant was the most efficient one in the division.[39]

A third example of the potential impact of self-esteem on the effectiveness of planned change is provided by the classic case of the Lamson Company. Management decided to construct a radically new type of distillation tower, one incorporating technology unlike that in the existing towers. Because the successful operation of the new tower was of "vital importance," management canvassed the entire facility to identify only "outstanding" workers to operate the new tower. The select group was given special training, and the members "made many suggestions for improvements to eliminate some of the bugs" that showed up in the equipment in the early stages. Many of the suggestions were adopted, and some of the men felt they were "even doing engineering work." Management was pleased with the operating results in the new unit. Presumably, among the contributing factors were the recognition and respect paid to employees, which in turn led to enhanced feelings of self-esteem.[40]

A fourth, and final example of the role of self-esteem in the change process is provided by the famous Relay Assembly Test Room experiment conducted at the Western Electric Company's Hawthorne works. Dalton interpreted the causes of the persistent increases in productivity observed over a 2-year period:

> . . . the treatment the women were given seems almost perfectly designed to increase their sense of self-esteem. A new supervisor who was promoted to department chief became the test observer and he treated them very differently from their previous supervisor. The observer and the experimenters made every effort to obtain the women's whole-hearted cooperation for each change, consulting them about each change and even canceling some changes which did not meet with their approval. The women's health, well-being, and opinions were the subject of genuine concern. . . . the experimenters created conditions which gave the women a greater sense of importance and worth.[41]

The content of a change, along with the process, can also affect self-esteem, reactions to change, and the effectiveness of a change effort. To the extent that a change increases psychological, social, or extrinsic rewards, employees are likely to feel increased self-esteem. In the four illustrations just cited, it can be seen that the content of the changes also likely affected self-esteem. In the Dashman Company the purchasing executives experienced a reduction in responsibility and autonomy, and they resisted the change. In the automobile plant the opposite was the case: the employees experienced and expressed increased feelings of competence, and some reportedly hoped to be promoted. In the Lamson Company, the new job assignments were physically, socially, and psychologically more satisfying; consequently, the employees were unanimously opposed to going back to the old distillation towers, even on a part-time basis. In the Relay Assembly Test Room, the women received a great deal of attention, they became part of a cohesive work group, and they earned increased pay as productivity improved.

## Participation

There is abundant evidence that employee participation in the change process improves reactions to change and the effectiveness of planned change efforts. Some writers have characterized the impact of participation in terms of the difference between commitment and compliance.[42]

In general, successful changes involve a change agent who, with top management support, engages "several levels of the organization in collaborative, fact-finding, problem-solving discussions to identify and diagnose current organization problems. . . . For all successful changes, the [process] is essentially the same—a large number of people collaborate to invent solutions that are of their own making and which have their own endorsement."[43] In contrast, failure tends to result where there is no sharing of influence via the joint participation of managers and subordinates in decision making.[44]

A review of research on the effects of participation came to the following four conclusions.

1 Participation in decisions sharply increases the acceptance of decisions. This is most dramatic where changes from traditional habits or beliefs are involved. . .

2 The process of participation affects the attitudes only of those actively consulted; those who stand outside the process apparently aren't influenced.

3 Participation in inconsequential decisions doesn't affect general attitudes.

4 The effects of participation may be mediated by personality. Those with an authoritarian orientation and low need for independence react positively where little participation is used.[45]

Why does participation work? First, participation allows individuals to have a sense of "psychological ownership" which in turn helps them to internalize a change.[46] Second, participation, especially in the early stages of a change, allows individuals to protect their own interests, resources, and power bases.[47] Certainly, these two reasons for the effectiveness of participation are entirely consistent with the (second and third) conclusions above.

Kotter and Schlesinger have provided an excellent illustration of the effective use of participation:

The head of a small financial services company . . . created a task force to help design and implement changes in his company's reward system. The task force was composed of eight second- and third-level managers from different parts of the company. The president's specific charter to them was that they recommend changes in the company's benefit package. They were given six months and asked to file a brief progress report with the president once a month. After they had made their recommendations, which the president largely accepted, they were asked to help the company's personnel director implement them.[48]

Two aspects of this case are noteworthy: (1) the president allowed adequate time for the exploration of issues for problem solving and (2) the president obtained the involvement of line managers. In contrast, many executives mistakenly move too quickly and involve too few people, even though they may lack the information needed to design and implement successfully a given change.[49] Also, had a consultant, or the personnel department, been given total responsibility for the change, it is less likely that middle management would have felt much commitment to the plan; certainly it would not have been "their baby."

Along these lines, in recent years considerable attention has been paid to the consensus-seeking approach employed by many successful Japanese companies. For example, at Hitachi, where the informal process of consensus building (*nemawashi*) precedes the formal documentation of decisions (*ringi*), it may take months for management to make a decision. But afterward, there is rarely any backbiting or sabotage.[50] A similar approach to decision making has recently been introduced at Westinghouse Corporation. One manager's reaction: "We spend a lot of time trying to get a consensus, but once you get it, the implementation is instantaneous. We don't have to fight any negative feelings."[51]

Although participation generally improves reactions to change, two cautions should be noted. Managers ought not use participation as a ploy—e.g., trying to get people to think they have a say when they really have not. This type of manipulation, sometimes called "psychological participation," is eventually seen through and resented. Another, perhaps more subtle, form of manipulation is to invite an influential person to participate in a decison-making group simply to gain that person's tacit endorsement. Because the person's ideas are not sought, merely his or her public affiliation with the change effort, this practice (co-optation) is steeped in tokenism and deceit. Also, it should be noted that not all individuals want to participate in making decisions; some people simply are not interested. When Honda attempted to involve low- and middle-level managers in the decision-making process the response was, "We'll do whatever you decide."[52]

### Preserving Exchange Favorability

Organizational members are very sensitive to possible adverse developments resulting from changes (e.g., reductions in benefits and/or increases in required contributions). Accordingly, it is sometimes necessary for managers to provide additional benefits to employees to facilitate the acceptance of intended changes—metaphorically speaking, to give with one hand while taking away with the other: "change should be designed and implemented in such a way as to minimize power loss and maximize power gain by those affected by the change."[53]

Illustrative of this concept is the way in which the New York Sanitation Department introduced the use of side-loading (two-worker) trucks in place of rear loading (three-worker) trucks. Although management asserted that it had the right to implement the change without consulting the union, management sought a "quick and peaceful resolution" of the matter.[54] Accordingly, the matter was brought before an impasse panel. The panel rendered a decision after considering the advantages and disadvantages of the change to both parties. Eight advantageous features of the change from the workers' perspective were noted, most having to do with improved safety.[55] Offsetting these advantages was one (big) disadvantage: although workers would have to walk less, they would load more. Consequently, the panel recommended that workers on side-loading trucks be paid a shift differential of $11. One year later it was calculated that the cost of collecting 1 ton of garbage had declined by 17 percent (from $35 to $29 a ton) after paying the shift differential. Also, in light of the reduction in the number of workers needed to collect garbage, workers could be assigned other jobs and there was a reduction in the backlog of uncollected refuse left overnight.[56] The overall first-year savings was $7.2 million, and this resulted from the replacement of less than one-quarter of the back-loading trucks. Subsequently both parties agreed to extend the use of side-loading trucks to the entire sanitation department. Although the shift differential was raised to $12.50 to $15, depending on the size of the truck, it was anticipated that the total annual productivity saving would approximate $25 million. Mayor Koch called the new agreement "revolutionary."[57]

Clearly, the preservation of exchange favorability is particularly appropriate when there is going to be a significant loss (of any kind) to employees as a result of a change and when employees have the power to impede or prevent the change from being successful. However, although the use of "sweeteners" is an easy way to reduce resistance, it can be expensive: "Once a manager makes it clear that he will negotiate to avoid major resistance, he opens himself up to the probability of blackmail."[58]

## SUMMARY

The normative model presented here identifies eight factors which influence reactions to change, and ultimately the effectiveness of change efforts. Although most of the research to date on planned change has not directly tested the model, the evidence (from some 400 cases) is generally consistent with the model.

The one study that has most closely approximated a direct test of the model employed a correlational design to examine 77 reported change cases. Managers' reports of change characteristics, process dynamics (e.g., manifest resistance), and outcomes (e.g., performance and satisfaction) were obtained. Although the dimensions of the change characteristics examined did not correspond exactly to those in the present normative model, a number were conceptually very similar. Focusing solely on the dimensions that were similar, positive relationships were found between the following change characteristics and performance (in order of descending importance): visible top management support, felt need, gradual clarification (and communication), and coercive power.[59] Clearly, this study underscores the importance of top management support.

One final issue deserves added emphasis. An accumulating body of evidence indicates the importance of changing the multiple subsystem determinants of organizational effectiveness—tasks, organizational practices, and people. Concomitantly, there is growing skepticism about the utility of change programs which focus on altering the attitudes and/or behaviors of people without also changing work characteristics or organizational practices (which are needed to institutionalize changes). For example, James Lee recommends that managers avoid all theories that suggest that employees can, by conscious design, undergo major changes in their work behavior. A superior approach is to alter tasks so that behavior in the desired direction is produced:

> If a particular manager needs to learn to delegate more of his work but glues himself to his operation, his superior officer can give him specific tasks that take him physically away from his operation before sending him to management seminars on "how to delegate."[60]

Along these lines, Amitai Etzioni has concluded that behavioral changes via the education and enlightenment approach are hard to come by. The assumption embedded in many change programs, says Etzioni, is that "if you go out there and get the message across, persuade, propagandize, explain, campaign—people will change."[61] Yet, such approaches have been demonstrably unsuccessful in getting people to use seat belts, avoid unwanted pregnancies, curb drug abuse, stop smoking, avoid venereal disease, etc. Etzioni asserts:

> What is becoming increasingly apparent is that to solve social problems by changing people is more expensive and usually less productive than approaches that accept people as they are and seek to mend not them but the circumstances around them. . . . Applying cost-effectiveness measurements to efforts to cut down the horrendous toll on American highways—59,220 Americans were killed in 1970—the HEW study noted that driver education saves lives at the cost of $88,000 per life . . . [in contrast] seat belts [cost] a mere $87. Yet we continue to stress driver education as the chief preventative measure.[62]

While people-focused interventions are effective in changing cognitions and attitudes, they are not as successful as other methods in changing behavior: multiple subsystem approaches which change tasks, organizational practices, and social relationships are superior to those that seek to change people directly.[63]

## NOTES

1 Alvin Toffler, *Future Shock* (New York: Random House, 1970), p. 15.
2 John P. Kotter and Leonard A. Schlesinger, "Choosing Strategies for Change," *Harvard Business Review,* 57, No. 2 (1979), p. 106. Also see Stephen A. Allen, "Orga-

nizational Choices and General Management Influence Networks in Divisionalized Companies," *Academy of Management Journal,* 21 (1978), 354–356.

3 Cited in John P. Kotter and Leonard A. Schlesinger, "Choosing Strategies," p. 106.

4 Gene E. Hall, Susan F. Loucks, William L. Rutherford, and Beulah W. Newlove, "Levels of Use of the Innovation: A Framework for Analyzing Innovation Adoption," *Journal of Teacher Education,* 26, No. 1 (1975), 5. It should be noted, however, that resistance to change does not always arise solely out of concern for personal interests. At times resistance is prompted by genuine (and possibly valid) concerns about organizational effectiveness.

5 Renato Tagiuri, "Notes on the Management of Change: Implications of Postulating a Need for Competence," in *The Administrator: Cases on Human Aspects of Management,* ed. John D. Glover, Ralph M. Hower, and Renato Tagiuri, 5th ed. (Homewood, Ill.: Richard D. Irwin, 1973), pp. 201–203. Also see George J. McCall and J. L. Simmons, *Identities and Interactions* (New York: Free Press, 1966), and Peter M. Blau, *Exchange and Power in Social Life* (New York: Wiley, 1964). Michael Argyle has likened the negotiation that occurs in social encounters to the haggling that pervades a rug bazaar. See his book, *The Psychology of Interpersonal Behaviour* (Baltimore, Md.: Penguin Books, 1967), p. 42.

6 Renato Tagiuri, "Notes," p. 204.

7 Jay Hall, "Dr. Semmelweis and the Problem of Learned Ignorance," *Data Forum,* 2 (Spring 1983), 1, 8.

8 Saul W. Gellerman, "Who's Against Productivity?" *The Conference Board Record,* 10 (Sept. 1973), 43.

9 John P. Kotter and Leonard A. Schlesinger, "Choosing Strategies," p. 106.

10 Gene W. Dalton, "Influence and Organizational Change," in *Organization and People: Readings, Cases and Exercises in Organizational Behavior,* ed. J. B. Ritchie and Paul Thompson (St. Paul, Minn.: West Publishing, 1976), pp. 363–387. Originally published in Arant R. Negandhi, ed., *Modern Organizational Theory* (Kent, Ohio.: Kent State University Press and the Comparative Administration Research Institute, Kent State University), pp. 343–372.

11 David G. Bowers, "OD Techniques and Their Results in 23 Organizations: The Michigan ICL Study," *The Journal of Applied Behavioral Science,* 9 (1973), 21–43 (23 cases); Gene W. Dalton, "Influence and Organizational Change" (6 cases); "Dashman Company" (Boston: HBS Case Services, 1947) No. 9-642-001, also published in John D. Glover et al., *The Administrator,* pp. 499–500 (1 case); William N. Dunn and Fredric W. Swierczek, "Planned Organizational Change: Toward Grounded Theory," *The Journal of Applied Behavioral Science,* 13 (1977), 135–157 (67 cases); Saul W. Gellerman, "Who's Afraid of Productivity?" (6 cases); Cyrus F. Gibson, "A Methodology for Implementation Research," in *Implementing Operations Research/Management Science,* ed. Randall L. Schultz and Dennis P. Slevin (New York: American Elsevier Publishing, 1975), pp. 53–73 (1 case); Michael Goodwin, "Pact is Near on Adding 2-Man Garbage Crews," *New York Times,* 15 Oct. 1981, pp. A1, B8, and Joyce Purnick, "2-Man Garbage Crews Agreed On for the City," *New York Times,* 20 Apr. 1982, pp. A1, D22 (1 case); Larry E. Greiner, "Patterns of Organization Change," *Harvard Business Review,* 45, No. 3 (1967), 119–130 (18 cases); John R. Hinrichs, *Practical Management for Productivity* (New York: Van Nostrand Reinhold, 1978) (12 cases); William A. Hultgren, "Capital Productivity: Control Data's Successful Asset Reduction Program," *National Productivity Review,* 1 (Spring 1982), 173–182 (1 case); Masayoshi Kanabayashi, "Honda's

Accord: How a Japanese Firm Is Faring on Its Dealings with Workers in U.S.," *Wall Street Journal,* 2 Oct. 1981, pp. 1, 25 (1 case); John P. Kotter and Leonard A. Schlesinger, "Choosing Strategies" (9 cases); Carole A. Lambert and Richard E. Kopelman, "An Instance of Planned Change (A)" (Boston: HBS Case Services, 1981) No. 9-481-714 (1 case); Carole A. Lambert and Richard E. Kopelman, "An Instance of Planned Change (B)" (Boston: HBS Case Services, 1981) No. 9-481-715 (1 case); "Lamson Company" (Boston: HBS Case Services, 1948) Nos. 9-449-003 to 9-449-007, also published in John D. Glover et al., *The Administrator,* pp. 5–7 (1 case); Jeremy Main, "Westinghouse's Cultural Revolution," *Fortune,* 15 June 1981, pp. 74–93 (1 case); Arlyn J. Melcher, "Participation: A Critical Review of Research Findings," *Human Resource Management,* 15, No. 2 (1976), 12–21 (9 cases); Danny Miller and Peter H. Friesen, "Structural Change: Quantum Versus Piecemeal-Incremental Approaches," *Academy of Management Journal,* 25 (1982), 867–892 (164 cases); Lawrence M. Miller, *Behavior Management* (New York: Wiley, 1978) (11 cases); William A. Pasmore and Donald C. King, "Understanding Organizational Change: A Comparative Study of Multifaceted Interventions," *The Journal of Applied Behavioral Science,* 14 (1978), 455–468 (1 case); Thomas H. Patten, Jr., "Pay Cuts: Will Employees Accept Them?" *National Productivity Review,* 1 (Winter 1981–82), 110–119 (25 cases); Jerry I. Porras, "The Comparative Impact of Different OD Techniques and Intervention Intensities," *The Journal of Applied Behavioral Science,* 15 (1979), 156–178 (35 cases); John R. Schermerhorn, Jr., "Managerial Ingredients of Successful Planned Change in Hospitals," *Proceedings, 40th Annual National Meeting of the Academy of Management* (1980), pp. 32–36 (77 cases); Stewart L. Tubbs and Robin N. Widgery, "When Productivity Lags, Check at the Top: Are Key Managers Really Communicating?" *Management Review,* 67, No. 11 (1978), pp. 20–25 (1 case). It should be noted that the total number of cases (473) probably includes some double counting; the number of independent cases likely exceeds 400, nonetheless.

12 Harry Levinson, comments during invited address before the New York Metropolitan Association for Applied Psychology, Feb. 15, 1979.

13 Frederick S. Lane, "Higher Education," in *Productivity Improvement Handbook for State and Local Government,* ed. George J. Washnis (New York: Wiley, 1980), p. 1178; also see John S. Thomas, "So. Mr. Mayor, You Want to Improve Productivity. . .," in *Managing State and Local Government: Cases and Readings,* ed. Frederick S. Lane (New York: St. Martin's Press, 1980), p. 410.

14 This view has been advanced by such organization development researchers and writers as Argyris, Beckhard, Blake and Mouton, Dalton, Greiner, and many others.

15 Gene W. Dalton, "Influence and Organizational Change," p. 369.

16 Ezra Stotland, *The Psychology of Hope* (San Francisco: Jossey-Bass, 1969). For an examination of what happens in the absence of hope see Martin E. P. Seligman, *Helplessness: On Depression, Development, and Death* (San Francisco: W. H. Freeman, 1975).

17 John S. Thomas, "So, Mr. Mayor," p. 414; John R. Hinrichs, *Practical Management,* pp. 178, 182.

18 Stewart L. Tubbs and Robin N. Widgery, "When Productivity Lags," p. 25.

19 Recall, for instance, the application of coercive power in connection with the work simplification program at the Continental Illinois National Bank & Trust Company (mentioned in Chapter 11). Uncooperative middle managers were replaced by those who were more receptive to the change effort.

20 John R. Schermerhorn, Jr., "Managerial Ingredients," p. 35. Relatedly, John P. Kotter and Leonard A. Schlesinger, "Choosing Strategies," have cautioned that "forcing change on people can have too many negative side effects over both the short and long term" (p. 113).

21 Louis B. Barnes, "Managing the Paradox of Organizational Trust," *Harvard Business Review,* 59, No. 2 (1981), 115.

22 George P. Huber, *Managerial Decision Making* (Glenview, Ill.: Scott, Foresman, 1980), p. 219.

23 Daniel D. Cook, "Labor Faces the Productivity Challenge," *Industry Week,* 9 Mar. 1981, p. 64.

24 Gene W. Dalton, "Influence and Organizational Change," pp. 371–372.

25 Keith Davis, *Human Behavior at Work: Organizational Behavior,* 6th ed. (New York: McGraw-Hill, 1981), pp. 214–215.

26 Norman Sigband, "Proaction . . . Not Reaction for Effective Employee Communications," *Personnel Journal,* 61, No. 3 (1982), 190.

27 Gene W. Dalton, "Influence and Organizational Change," pp. 383–384.

28 Greg Davis and R. J. Bullock, "Resistance to Change: Models and Implications for OD," paper presented at the 41st Annual National Meeting of the Academy of Management, 1981, p. 7.

29 Renato Tagiuri, "Notes," p. 207.

30 Ibid. Tagiuri also notes the comment by Alfred North Whitehead, "The art of progress is to preserve order amid change, and to preserve change amid order" (p. 208). Also see Greg Davis and R. J. Bullock, "Resistance to Change," pp. 5–7.

31 "Dashman Company."

32 See Ronald G. Capelle, *Changing Human Systems* (Toronto: International Human Systems Institute, 1979), p. 135; also see James A. Lee, "Behavioral Theory vs. Reality," *Harvard Business Review,* 49, No. 2 (1971), 157. In Lee's words, "if a major organizational change is sought, top management should double the behavioral scientist's estimate of the time required, and triple its own."

33 Daniel Katz and Robert L. Kahn, *The Social Psychology of Organizations* (New York: Wiley, 1966), especially Chapter 2. Regarding the conservative (homeostatic) nature of organizations, John D. Rockefeller III commented in *The Second American Revolution* (New York: Harper & Row, 1973), "An organization is a system with a logic of its own, and all the weight of tradition and inertia. The deck is stacked in favor of the tried and proven way of doing things and against the taking of risks and striking out in new directions" (p. 72).

34 Gene W. Dalton, "Influence and Organizational Change," pp. 372–376.

35 Ibid. Indeed, Dalton points to the dramatic behavioral changes that often result from membership in a "total institution," e.g., a convent or a military organization, where individuals experience a complete change in social relationships.

36 Frank Friedlander, "The Facilitation of Change in Organizations," *Professional Psychology,* 11 (1980), 525; also see William N. Dunn and Fredric W. Swierczek, "Planned Organizational Change," p. 147; also Danny Miller and Peter H. Friesen, "Structural Change." However, Jerry I. Porras, "OD Techniques and Intervention Intensities," did not find support for this proposition (p. 167).

37 John R. Hinrichs, *Practical Management,* pp. 178–183.

38 Gene W. Dalton, "Influence and Organizational Change," pp. 376–379.

39 Ibid., pp. 367, 377.

40 "Lamson Company."

**41** Gene W. Dalton, "Influence and Organizational Change," p. 379. (The term "women" has been substituted for the term "girls" which appeared in the original.)

**42** John P. Kotter and Leonard A. Schlesinger, "Choosing Strategies," p. 110; also William N. Dunn and Fredric W. Swierczek, "Planned Organizational Change," especially pp. 148–149.

**43** Larry E. Greiner, "Patterns of Organizational Change," pp. 125, 128. Copyright © 1967 by the President and Fellows of Harvard College; all rights reserved.

**44** Ibid., p. 125. There is (limited) evidence that failure results from adopting the other extreme approach to planned change—management delegating total responsibility for decision making to subordinates.

**45** Arlyn J. Melcher, "Participation: A Critical Review of Research Findings," *Human Resource Management,* 15, No. 2 (1976), pp. 19–20. Copyright © 1976 John Wiley & Sons, Inc. Reprinted by permission.

**46** Larry E. Greiner, "Patterns of Organizational Change," p. 128; also Gene W. Dalton, "Influence and Organizational Change," pp. 379–383.

**47** Greg Davis and R. J. Bullock, "Resistance to Change," pp. 8–9.

**48** John P. Kotter and Leonard A. Schlesinger, "Choosing Strategies," p. 109. Copyright © 1979 by the President and Fellows of Harvard College; all rights reserved.

**49** Ibid., p. 113.

**50** Tozo Hikichi, "Japan's Management Structure & Worker Support." invited address at an Arthur Andersen & Co. sponsored conference, "Productivity: The Japanese Formula" (New York), Oct. 13, 1981.

**51** Jeremy Main, "Westinghouse's Cultural Revolution," p. 93. Similarly, in the successful change effort described by Stewart L. Tubbs and Robin N. Widgery, "When Productivity Lags," "It was agreed that there should be a consensus for the program, and a go/no-go philosophy was followed at each level of management" (pp. 21–22). Also, it is interesting to note that in the case reported by Carole A. Lambert and Richard E. Kopelman, "An Instance of Planned Change (A)," an important change was implemented immediately, after little discussion—certainly no consensus was achieved—and considerable resistance arose. In contrast, in the companion case, "An Instance of Planned Change (B)," a nearly identical change was implemented in a similar organizational setting, but only after 18 months of extensive discussion; subsequently, the change was widely accepted. Perhaps, therefore, the choice is between an initial, "up-front" investment in time and a later, possibly greater, investment.

**52** Masayoshi Kanabayashi, "Honda's Accord," p. 25.

**53** Greg Davis and R. J. Bullock, "Resistance to Change," p. 9.

**54** Matthew A. Kelly, "Opinion and Recommendations in the Matter of the Impasse between the City of New York Department of Sanitation and the Uniformed Sanitationmen's Association, Local 831, I.B.T.," 10 Dec. 1980, pp. 5–6.

**55** For example, one advantage was described as follows: "Side loading virtually eliminates the hazard of being injured, crippled or even killed as has not infrequently been the case over the past 30 years or so when loaders at the rear of the truck have been run into by an oncoming vehicle especially at night and during wet, icy and stormy conditions" (p. 7).

**56** Clyde Haberman, "Regan Sees 'Major' Advance in Two-Man Garbage Trucks," *New York Times,* 21 Mar. 1982, p. 48.

**57** Joyce Purnick, "2-Man Garbage Crews," pp. A1, D22.

**58** John P. Kotter and Leonard A. Schlesinger, "Choosing Strategies," p. 110.

**59** John R. Schermerhorn, Jr., "Managerial Ingredients," p. 33. Indicative of the relative magnitudes of association with performance, beta coefficients were as follows: visible top management support, .30; felt need, .25; gradual clarification (and communication), .23; coercive power, .15.

**60** James A. Lee, "Behavioral Theory vs. Reality," p. 157.

**61** Amitai Etzioni, "Human Beings Are Not Very Easy to Change After All," in John D. Glover et al., *The Administrator,* p. 221. This article originally appeared in *Saturday Review,* 3 June 1972, pp. 45–47; © 1972 Saturday Review magazine. Reprinted by permission.

**62** Amitai Etzioni, "Human Beings," pp. 222–223.

**63** William A. Pasmore and Donald C. King, "Understanding Organizational Change," pp. 462–467. Also see Rensis Likert, *The Human Organization: Its Management and Value* (New York: McGraw-Hill, 1967), p. 77.

# CHAPTER 14

# TOWARD A PRACTICAL PROGRAM FOR PRODUCTIVITY IMPROVEMENT

This, the concluding chapter, deals with organizational action directed toward productivity improvement. Three major topics are discussed in this regard.

Given the primary focus of this book, examining the efficacy of ten prominent technologies used to improve productivity, the chapter begins with a summary of empirical findings. Results are examined in terms of the average magnitude of productivity improvement and the durability of this effect.

Of course, the improvement in productivity that results from the application of a given technology depends in large part on the appropriateness of the intervention, the fit between the intervention and existing organizational, work, and individual characteristics. Accordingly, the issue of diagnosis is discussed in some detail.

Implementation of a productivity improvement program requires more than good intentions. Individuals must be assigned specified responsibilities for planning, organizing, coordinating, and following up on productivity-related activities. One way to influence these activities is through the creation of the role of productivity manager (or director of productivity). The book concludes with a description of how such a role might function in a work organization.

## SUMMARY OF RESULTS: WHAT HAS WORKED AND WHAT HAS NOT

Table 14-1 summarizes the empirical evidence regarding the effects of ten prominent behavioral science interventions on productivity. Results are examined in terms of the magnitude and durability of effects, and an impact index

**TABLE 14-1**
EFFECTS ON PRODUCTIVITY OF TEN BEHAVIORAL SCIENCE INTERVENTIONS

| Intervention | Impact | | |
|---|---|---|---|
| | Magnitude[a] | Durability[b] | Composite |
| **Organizational characteristics** | | | |
| 1 Reward systems | | | |
|    Output-based individual plans | 4 | 2 | 6 |
|    Group gainsharing plans | 4 | 2 | 6 |
| 2 Goal setting | 3 | 1 | 4 |
| 3 Management by objectives (MBO) | 2 | 2 | 4 |
| 4 Selection | | | |
|    Tests | 3 | 3 | 6 |
|    Biographic data | 2 | 3 | 5 |
|    Realistic job preview | 1 | 2 | 3 |
| 5 Training and development | 3 | 2 | 5 |
| 6 Leadership | | | |
|    Participation | 1 | 2 | 3 |
| 7 Organization structure | | | |
|    Decentralization | 3 | 2 | 5 |
| **Work characteristics** | | | |
| 8 Performance feedback | | | |
|    Objective indicators | 3 | 2 | 5 |
| 9 Job design | | | |
|    Job enrichment | 2 | 1 | 3 |
|    Work simplification | 2 | 2 | 4 |
| 10 Alternative work schedules | | | |
|    Compressed workweek (CWW) | 1 | 1 | 2 |
|    Flexible work hours (FWH) | 1 | 1 | 2 |

[a]Magnitude categories are as follows: very high (4) > 15%; high (3) = 10 to 15%; moderate (2) = 5% to 10%; low (1) = 0% to 5%.
[b]Durability estimates are categorized as follows: long = 3; moderate = 2; short = 1.

has been created that incorporates both indicators. (Because the durability scores are based on less data and are considerably more subjective than the magnitude scores, only three levels of durability are identified compared with four levels of magnitude.)

In terms of the locus of the change effort, interventions that alter organizational characteristics have generally been superior in all three effectiveness indicators (magnitude, durability, and the composite impact index) to those interventions that primarily affect work characteristics. The two most effective interventions have been reward systems (output-based) and employee selection devices (tests). Three of the least effective interventions have been job design (job enrichment), alternative work schedules, and leadership changes (participation). Ironically, these latter approaches to productivity improvement have received a great deal of attention: many writers and behavioral scientists have argued for using job enrichment and participation to improve organizational effectiveness.

## ORGANIZATIONAL DIAGNOSIS

As noted previously (in Chapter 2), evaluating the effectiveness of different approaches to productivity improvement by examining results across studies, necessitates making a number of assumptions. A crucial assumption is that a given intervention is warranted in the situation in which it is applied: there is no need to strengthen organizational or work characteristics that are already quite satisfactory. Yet a common criticism of some organizational behavior consultants is that they tend to view their subspecialties (e.g., management development, job redesign) as providing useful techniques for improving the functioning of all organizations—or worse yet—as providing solutions for all organizational problems. As Paul Thayer has commented: "We go around willy-nilly applying our solution to every organization that will let us, without the careful diagnosis needed . . . sometimes [we] go back to the original problem and wonder how they and especially we, ever thought the solution would fit the problem."[1]

There is wide agreement that organizations should avoid totally prepackaged organizational improvement interventions—those that offer universalistic solutions (panaceas).[2] As Mayford Roark has put it: "Beware the man who knows the answers before he understands the question."[3]

Although it is possible for a productivity improvement intervention to prove successful in the absence of an organizational diagnosis (just as it is possible for someone to provide the correct answer without listening to the question), the likelihood of successful action is obviously greater if based on diagnostic information: "In order to cope with reality, one must know what reality is."[4]

### Criteria for Assessing the Adequacy of an Organizational Diagnosis

In light of the importance of an organizational diagnosis as the basis for improvement activity, the question arises as to the criteria for judging the adequacy of a given diagnostic procedure. Three criteria are of paramount importance. First, the diagnostic procedure should produce valid data, not artifactual or spurious outgrowths of particular measurement methods or observers. When managers rely solely on casual observations to make inferences about their own organizations, the inferences may be of doubtful validity.[5]

Yet it is not uncommon for managers to disparage sources of diagnostic information other than their own perceptions. Frequently it is argued: "Any good manager knows what his people are thinking. That's what we get paid for."[6] Unfortunately, managers are not always successful in "reading peoples' minds." Illustrative of this problem, a large wood products company decided to administer climate surveys in two divisions. One of the divisions was uniformly seen as being well-managed, as enjoying excellent employee relations, and possessing a good organizational climate—which corporate managers frequently referred to as "The Osage Advantage." The other division was seen as having severe employee relations problems. To the complete surprise of top management, the division seen as having "The Osage Advantage" (not the actual name) scored the same as or *lower* than the division seen as plagued with problems on many important characteristics. Presumed differences in employee attitudes were not confirmed, and the "Osage Advantage," like the Emperor's new clothes, was not evident. Although corporate management, assuming the results to be a foregone conclusion, was initially reluctant to conduct a climate survey, the data from the first two divisions led them to embrace the systematic collection of diagnostic information.

A second criterion for gauging the adequacy of a diagnostic procedure is the extent to which it is based on valid theory. Observations should be guided by theorized networks of variables that are logically and empirically interrelated. In the absence of valid theory, data collection resembles a "fishing expedition"; and the interpretation of results is problematic, since relationships can only be "explained" after the fact. The centrality of theory is indicated in Alderfer's definition of organizational diagnosis: "a process based on behavioral science theory for publicly entering a human system, collecting valid data about human experiences with that system, and feeding that information back to the system to promote increased understanding of the system by its members."[7]

A third criterion for assessing the adequacy of an organizational diagnosis is comprehensiveness. If a diagnosis does not examine all relevant factors, inferences about functioning may be inaccurate and action plans inappropriate. Consider the experience of a New England paper mill.

> The diagnosis indicated that productivity was down, morale was low, conflicts were apparent between individuals and units. In light of this information, team building was selected as the appropriate change action. The change agent worked with skill, but little improvement was noticed. One day a visiting engineer listened to the mill machinery and commented, "It sounds like your major drive shaft is out of line." Following this lead, the drive shaft was examined, found to be faulty, and replaced. Productivity immediately jumped, accompanied by feelings of satisfaction and improved morale. Conflicts dropped. Someone then asked... "Why did we do all that team building when what was needed was a new drive shaft?"[8]

## Who Should Do the Diagnosis?

The importance of valid, theory-based, and comprehensive diagnostic information raises the question of who should conduct the diagnosis. Three approaches have been adopted: reliance solely on individuals who are not part of the organization, reliance solely on organization members, and reliance on the joint efforts of outsiders and insiders. The weight of opinion clearly favors the third approach, because it combines the benefits of the first two. Outsiders, typically lacking vested interests to protect, are more likely to be trusted than are insiders; hence greater disclosure of relevant information should result, yielding a more accurate diagnosis: "All individuals have vested interests in organizations. Even if individuals did not press their own interests, other members of the system would be unable to accept a consultant relationship from a peer, and the complete insider would be rendered ineffective as a result."[9] Further, because an outsider does not have to worry about "living" with the members of an organization, there is less need to conform to norms or "buy into" myths.

However, one of the problematic features of using an outsider to perform a diagnosis is that the outsider can easily be prevented from understanding crucial aspects of a system's functioning.[10] The outsider may not be sensitive to shared beliefs, myths, anxieties, and their underlying logics. In liaison with knowledgeable insiders, though, they can more clearly identify these unique, symbolic aspects of organizational life.[11] Moreover, the informed insider can help by pointing out some of the specific political realities (e.g., coalitions and conflicts) which are a prominent part of organizational life.[12] By incorporating information about the myths, symbols, and politics—the nonrational aspects of organizational behavior—an organizational diagnosis can be more insightful and functional.

The outsider-insider team can employ several methods for obtaining diagnostic information. Three of the most prominent methods are observations, interviews, and questionnaire surveys. The advantages and disadvantages of these sources of information are reviewed next.

**Observations**

The observation of people at work can add importantly to the diagnostic process in two ways. First, observed patterns of behavior provide a basis for hypothesis formulation and subsequent hypothesis testing concerning the organization. Second, during the feedback process examples of behavioral observations add to the richness and complexity of interpretations. Certainly such examples help capture some of the uniqueness of a given organization.[13]

Yet many organizational behavior consultants are apparently reluctant to employ observation as part of the diagnostic process. It has been suggested that some highly trained, young consultants are "so caught up in esoteric charts, graphs and jargon that they . . . no longer can look at people as people but merely as objects which will fill out multi-paged questionnaires suitable for pumping into electronic memory banks."[14]

One of the most accurate gauges of employee attitudes and the general health of an organization is the "lightheartedness quotient"—operationally defined as the proportion of employees who laugh or smile. This measure, which can be obtained during the first few minutes of an on-site visit, is a good place to start an organizational diagnosis. An obvious sign of good mental health in children and adults is their ability to laugh. "If the people in a business office are distant and cold with one another, you're looking at a disturbed organization."[15]

While it is not being suggested that observational data should be the sole basis for an organizational diagnosis, certainly such information can contribute importantly to the diagnostic process. It should be recognized, however, that observational techniques when applied on a systematic basis, are a costly source of information, requiring high levels of skill and training. Systematic observation of an ongoing social system requires knowing how to classify acts, knowing the appropriate amount of detail to record, and knowing how to distinguish one event sequence from the next. Moreover, if observers are outsiders, they will be "unaware of the double, hidden, and mutually understood meanings of particular phrases, behaviors, actions and cues."[16]

### Interviews

Although employees may have many useful ideas about organizational problems and possible remedies, their ideas usually will not be evident by observation, and they may not be provided by a questionnaire survey. Many people dislike writing. A. A. Imberman, a management consultant, noted, "In 30 years of consulting experience and face-to-face interviews with about 500,000 hourly workers—blue collar and white collar—I have found there is a gold mine of information in their comments."[17] Illustrative of the potential utility of conducting interviews are the following two sets of comments. The first is from a bank employee, the second from an insurance company employee.

> You want to know why so many trainees leave the bank after a year or so? Look at the Management Training program we're in. Take this part of the program where you are a spreader for six months. It takes about a week to learn all there is to know about this job; after that it is just boring repetition. They treat an advance in this program like such a big deal, but it is usually just a progression of boring steps. . . . If you wear a pressed suit and a clean white shirt every day for three years and don't display any more imagination than a cow, you will be a success in this management program. That's why no more than about 10% stick it out. And then the bank president wonders why he hasn't been able to retain more. He's never asked anybody why, except maybe the executive vice president, who doesn't know any more about it than the president.[18]

> What can be done about the supply department? The supplies are ordered once a week from Central, but you never get what you order. If you are Number One, you get it all, but the other branches don't get equal treatment. Here's what happens. You need 5,000 premium notice envelopes so you order that number, but the supply department cuts the quantity right in half. So you learn fast that you have to double what you need in order not to run out. The point is, this whole scheme is silly. Look in there. We're sitting with all sorts of extra envelopes, stationery, clips, typewriter ribbons and what not, just because we can't trust the supply department to give us what we need when we need it. So we hoard. Multiply that by the number of

branches in this region and you will have some idea of the large amount of idle money tied up in supplies.[19]

Clearly these comments substantiate Imberman's assertion that most hourly workers "are not helpless nobodies, but men and women with hopes and agonies and concerns—among which the state of the company is one of the most pressing."[20] The remarkable candor of these comments probably reflects both Imberman's competence as an interviewer and his role as an outsider.

Interviews are a good source of information about possible problems; they may yield hypotheses for subsequent examination, and they provide a richness of detail and concreteness to an organizational diagnosis. However, interview data may be somewhat deficient when used as the *sole* basis for diagnosing organizational functioning and providing feedback to key executives.

The high reliance placed on interviews by the American Productivity Center has led to some criticism. Reportedly, the APC's approach to productivity consulting begins by interviewing all employees in an organization. Then the consultants write a brief report outlining the physical and managerial impediments to improved productivity. But according to an oil company executive on loan to the APC, "All the APC tells you is, 'Yup, you've got a productivity problem.' In other words, it isn't anything you don't already know."[21]

Although the diagnostic information obtained may be valid, interview data are problematic when used as the sole basis for assessment and feedback. Interview (and observational) data (1) do not transcend the consultant (like hearsay evidence, they are subject to possible distortions or biases), (2) are relatively qualitative in form, (3) typically represent only a limited amount of data, (4) are hard to interpret insofar as there are no normative (i.e., average) scores, and (5) fail to capitalize on the confidence people usually have in computer-printed outputs.[22] Evidence indicates that "hard headed" executives, ordinarily the most resistant to diagnostic feedback and change suggestions, are the feedback recipients most likely to be influenced by computerized printouts.[23]

### Questionnaire Surveys

During the past two decades questionnaire surveys increasingly have been used in organizational settings. Although surveys are sometimes used as an instrument for change per se, their primary value lies in their use as a diagnostic tool, indicating the changes that are needed. All told, ten potential benefits have been identified as possibly resulting from the use of surveys. These benefits are reviewed next, followed by a discussion of several potential drawbacks.

**1** *Identify current problems.* Many if not most of the problems identified by a survey will be known to managers. (If this were not the case, the face validity of surveys would be highly suspect.) Sometimes, however, unexpected results emerge from organizational surveys. The case of the "Osage Advantage" is one example; another case involved a large clerical unit.

From occasional employee comments and complaints, management expected the survey to show an overworked and underpaid workforce. But when opinions from all its employees were taken into account (not just the most vocal), a very different picture emerged. In fact, overall, the employees felt well paid and secure in their jobs. But there were strong indications that people were not being stretched to their full capabilities—and they wanted to be. . . . Thus, the survey provided management with an opportunity to take steps toward creating a more challenging, more productive climate.[24]

**2** *Anticipate future problems.* In addition to identifying current problems, surveys can also serve as an early warning device, enabling management to recognize potential problems and correct them before they mushroom.[25] By identifying employee concerns at a relatively early stage, surveys allow management to maintain organizational "well being," rather than having to fight emergent "illnesses."[26]    Evidence that survey data function as a leading indicator of organizational effectiveness has been reported by Likert. He found only slight, insignificant relationships between survey data on organizational practices and concurrent measures of organizational effectiveness. However, after a time lag of 1 year, correlations were substantial ($r = .50$), and after a 2-year lag correlations were even stronger ($r = .70$).[27] By obtaining data about today's managerial practices and work characteristics, managers will be in a position to predict tomorrow's organizational effectiveness and they will be better able to influence the day after tomorrow's organizational effectiveness.

**3** *Prioritize problems.* In any organization, members will have many ideas about problems and opportunities for improvement. But which are the crucial problems, the important problems, and the relatively trivial problems? It is commonplace for surveys to identify an organization's greatest weaknesses (and strengths) and to report results in order of magnitude of deviation. Two approaches are widely used: (1) scores on all items are compared against norms developed from comparable organizations; (2) scores on all items are compared against scores from different parts of the same organization (e.g., across divisions). Extensive normative bases exist for some surveys.[28]

**4** *Comprehensiveness.* Questionnaire surveys (often referred to as "attitude surveys") were used originally simply to assess employee morale. Currently, though, surveys are used to measure various aspects of organizational, work, and individual characteristics as well as end-result variables. Instruments with demonstrated psychometric adequacy exist to measure a wide variety of phenomena, ranging from reward system responsiveness to technical obsolescence.[29]

**5** *Basis for evaluating improvement efforts.* If a questionnaire survey is administered more than once, the resulting longitudinal data may be useful in assessing the effectiveness of improvement efforts. For example, a mining firm headquartered in New York City used the Hay climate survey for four consecutive years: "Repeat surveys served as the vehicle for evaluating the effectiveness of newly-instituted performance appraisal and planning systems, as well as for assessing modifications to the compensation program. Detailed longitudinal and subunit analyses revealed significant improvements in climate consistent with the company's change efforts."[30]

**6** *Improve employee relations.* The very act of conducting a questionnaire survey signals a concern about employees' views. And to the extent that changes result from a survey, the message is that management respects the opinions of employees, is sensitive to their goals, and seeks to improve the quality of their working lives. Clearly such implicit messages should enhance employee relations.

Evidence indicates that companies conducting questionnaire surveys have a lower incidence of strikes (24 percent in one survey experienced a strike during the prior 6 years) compared to companies that do not conduct surveys (48 percent in the same survey experienced a strike during the prior 6 years).[31] Two explanations might be advanced: (*a*) surveys allow a firm's management to identify problems at an early stage and to respond effectively, and (*b*) companies with better labor relations are more likely to conduct surveys. It is not clear which explanation is more correct.

**7** *Improved work group communication.* After the results of a survey have been tabulated, it is commonplace for a manager to meet with his or her work group to discuss the work group's data. (Several years ago, a small survey indicated that such feedback meetings occur in roughly 65 percent of the organizations that conduct surveys.)[32] The survey data provide a natural vehicle for addressing process-related issues which ordinarily never might be discussed, given conventional norms and the press of substantive problems. Such feedback meetings serve as a safe forum, and possibly a catalyst, for the upward communication of employee concerns and problems.[33] Although the immediate supervisor may be physically proximate to the work group, this alone does not assure open communication.[34] Moreover, to the extent that the sharing of data produces an open exchange of divergent views, increased trust is likely to develop in the work group.[35]

**8** *Managerial training.* The questionnaire survey process can serve as an indirect means of management training. Insofar as managers participate in the process of developing questions, interpreting results, conducting feedback sessions, and planning improvement activities, they are likely to improve their skills and develop new insights.[36]

**9** *Increasing the value of noncash benefits.* A questionnaire survey can be used to design and evaluate employee benefit plans more effectively. As noted previously (in Chapter Three), organizations typically use an ad hoc approach to employee benefits: benefits are thrown together piecemeal, nonsystematically, and largely in response to external events or current fads. In contrast, a survey can assess employee valuations of a wide variety of possible benefits and benefit packages. Recently one company asked employees to assess how much they would be willing to pay (using their own money) for each of 55 different benefits. A cost-benefit ratio was computed for each option, based on actual costs compared to the amounts employees said they would spend using their own money. The optimal fixed benefit plan—where all employees received the same package—was worth almost $200 more to each employee than the plan that was in effect.[37]

**10** *Guide intervention activities.* Diagnostic information concerning an organization's strengths and weaknesses can increase the likelihood that appropriate interventions will be undertaken:

> For constructive change to occur, there must exist an appropriate correspondence of the treatment (action, intervention) with the internal structural and functional conditions of the entity for which change is intended. Since by definition these internal conditions *pre*-exist, this means that treatments *must* be selected, designed and varied to fit the properties of the client entity.[38]

Surveys allow an identification of the properties of the client entity.

Of course, there are also some potential drawbacks associated with the use of questionnaire surveys. These are reviewed next. The five potential problems identified, however, are not entirely unique to questionnaire surveys: they reflect some of the problems associated with any attempt to diagnose and improve organizational effectiveness.

**1** *Reactivity.* Because surveys are a relatively intrusive data gathering technique, there is the potential for influencing employee attitudes or behaviors. Dissatisfactions which previously did not exist may be created, or low-level concerns may be intensified. In colloquial terms, surveys may "stir things up."[39] Accordingly, resistance to participation in surveys is sometimes verbalized as follows: "I don't want anyone 'messing' around with my people. If you start asking questions you may raise doubts and create problems where none exist."[40]

Although it has been argued that surveys can only heighten concerns, not create new ones,[41] the validity of this claim has not been demonstrated empirically. Research is also needed on the extent to which questionnaire items sensitize, or perhaps desensitize, individuals to different types of issues. Until this issue is resolved, it is hard to say whether potentially troublesome topics should be confronted or avoided.

In a sense the issue of reactivity represents a real dilemma for the diagnostic questionnaire survey. If results provide evidence that a suspected problem exists, critics will carp that surveys "only tell us what we already know." On the other hand, should unexpected results emerge, detractors may attribute the problems to reactivity saying, "there were no signs of trouble until the pollsters went around stirring things up among the few troublemakers we have in this organization."[42] Thus, at the extreme this is a no-win situation.

**2** *Raised expectations.* A second concern is that the conduct of a survey may raise expectations that management will improve things. Sometimes managers will ask, "If the survey identifies problems, won't we be forced to do something to solve the problems?" Perhaps the best answer is yes and no. Certainly it would be inadvisable to conduct a survey if management intended to do nothing, the only motive being idle curiosity.[43] However, employees will not expect management to solve *all* problems identified; but they will (reasonably) expect action on some problems.[44]

**3** *Indeterminacy of required interventions.* Another problematic aspect of the survey process is the role of judgment in determining corrective actions. Often there are two or more interventions that might be employed to deal with a problem; consequently, survey-based organizational improvement programs need to contain elements of both science and art. Of course, this limitation applies to all diagnostic methods in organizational behavior. Nevertheless it is a problem that warrants recognition.

**4** *Creation of conflicts.* Any process that proposes to examine and possibly change organizational practices inevitably will create a certain degree of tension. Although the survey process in general may be beneficial to an organization, there can be no assurance that all members will gain status or power: indeed, some people may fare less well as a result of the changes that result.

**5** *Costs and benefits.* A fifth potential drawback of questionnaire surveys is that the costs incurred may exceed the benefits derived. Increasingly, however, diagnostic surveys are seen as highly cost effective, provided that they meet a number of logical conditions.[45] These include a sound theoretical model, demonstrated psychometric adequacy, the availability and involvement of knowledgeable resource persons, the provision of comprehensive data feedback, and the inclusion of questions dealing with things that management can change.[46] Indeed, a review of 37 survey feedback projects found that when most of these conditions were met (12 cases) all interventions led to "positive change"; however, when half or more of these conditions were not met, the proportion of successes dropped to only 12 percent.[47] This finding underscores the importance of the methods used in conducting a questionnaire survey, a topic discussed later in this chapter. First, though, several examples of successful diagnostic surveys are reviewed.

### Diagnostic Questionnaire Surveys: Some Successful Applications

**1** Based on the findings of questionnaire surveys, Union Carbide Corporation instituted new training programs and redesigned jobs, increasing the responsibility of blue-collar workers. The result: "In just three months, productivity soared by 25%; the amount of finished goods passing inspection jumped from 60% to 80% and absenteeism dropped from 5% to 3%."[48]

**2** A questionnaire survey was administered in a nationwide retail organization with an exceptional record of growth and profitability. The survey results indicated significant relationships between perceived managerial practices and (*a*) store profits, (*b*) store turnover (of employees), and (*c*) store morale. It was found that lean staffing was not producing greater profitability but overworked and disenchanted employees who could neither run a store effectively nor provide nor receive adequate training. Additionally, it was found that training was importantly related to low turnover and high profits.

Management convened a task force to review the survey results and develop action recommendations. Twenty-eight specific recommendations were eventually adopted, with time frames ranging from 1 month to 1 year. Although it was reportedly "too soon to determine the quantitative impact of the new policies and programs," turnover had seemingly "begun to trend downward."[49]

3 A questionnaire survey was administered to 345 clerical employees in a large manufacturing company. Turnover had averaged about 30 percent, compared with 20 percent in other large companies in the same area. Not surprisingly, it was found that terminators had lower satisfaction scores than nonterminators. Based on the survey data, management instituted various changes in organizational policies. A follow-up survey again showed that satisfaction was significantly related to turnover. But more important, the turnover rate was reduced from 30 percent to 12 percent. Given cost accounting estimates of $1000 to hire and train a new worker, the reduction in turnover alone translated into an increase in productivity of approximately 3 percent.[50]

4 A survey-based organizational improvement program was initiated in a large plant employing more than 6000 people. Questionnaire responses from 240 managers served as the basis for departmental feedback sessions focusing on both task and relationship problems. Over a two-year period productivity increased by 7 percent, attitudes improved, absenteeism declined (previously it had been increasing), and a cost savings of $7 million was achieved. In contrast, 2 years before the survey program was begun, some $50 million was spent on new tools and equipment, an expenditure that yielded an increase in productivity of less than 1 percent.[51]

5 Although not really a field experiment, an analysis was performed of the financial impact of job attitudes. It was found that the intrinsic satisfaction scores of 160 bank tellers were significantly related to absenteeism and turnover, and that intrinsic motivation was significantly related to job performance (teller balancing shortages). Based on cost accounting estimates it was concluded that a 15 percent increase in satisfaction scores of the bank tellers would yield a potential annual savings of $125,160—or $782 per teller.[52] Thus, a moderate (15 percent) improvement in job attitudes would have likely improved productivity by approximately 6 percent.

### Conducting a Survey-Based Organizational Diagnosis

A great deal of knowledge exists concerning the development and and validation of questionnaire scales, the design and administration of surveys, the analysis and interpretation of survey data, and the application of such information to organizational improvement. However, the present discussion is limited to identifying a number of principles useful in conducting a diagnostic survey.

As is the case with virtually all planned organizational improvement efforts, the imprimatur of top management and the support of middle and lower level managers are crucial.[53] This support "involves more than just a management decision to allow a survey to be conducted. . . . The decision to survey should reflect management's commitment to administer the program professionally and to view the results—even if critical—in a constructive manner."[54]

Generally speaking, the greater the participation of employees in the survey process, the greater the receptivity to change: "Participation undercuts opposition and objection. . . . Involving persons or groups in the design of a project or policy ensures their support. Their hand leaves its imprint not only on the design but on them. They see it as a good plan—workable, after all, they recommend it."[55] It follows, therefore, that organizations should survey the views of *all* employees, even though a smaller number of responses may be entirely sufficient to produce statistically reliable results. All employees should feel that their opinions are valued, and the results should be based on everyone's opinion—and therefore credible to the nonstatistician. Further a 100 percent sample helps in providing feedback about each work unit.[56]

The integrity of the survey process requires careful attention to ensuring the confidentiality of all responses and the anonymity of responding individuals— at least as far as management is concerned. Participants should know in advance that their responses will be shown to managers and nonmanagers only in the form of grouped data. Certainly, "if the collection of data is surrounded by mistrust, anxiety, or suspicion, the data may be of little value for diagnostic, motivational or planning purposes."[57] One approach is to collect completed questionnaires in a sealed box and then to have a local mailing committee forward the forms to an independent organization for tabulation.

When results are fed back there is a tendency for some managers to play the game "Guess Who Said That."[58] Consequently, percentage breakdowns should not be provided when the sample comprises fewer than fifteen people; means should not be provided if the sample is smaller than ten people. Potentially even more troublesome is the feeding back of responses to open-ended questions. As a general rule it is advisable that all comments be reworded, because peculiarities of expression may allow a manager to identify, or mistakenly identify, a survey respondent: "Even a well-intentioned manager may be tempted in such an instance to act vindictively or in a biased manner. To the extent that managers are encouraged to take action against people rather than their problems, the survey has failed."[59] It would seem that the loss of some accuracy in reporting is a small price to pay for preserving the integrity of the survey process.

The major benefits of a diagnostic survey begin when the data are returned to individuals in the organization and problem solving begins. Research and experience indicate that significant changes occur only when meetings are held to work with the data. Although a formal feedback report can be a useful document, it is not a substitute for involving the organization's members in working with the data.

Typically, work groups only meet to discuss substantive ("out-there") issues: process-related ("here-and-now") issues are too threatening. However, survey feedback provides a vehicle for dealing with managerial and behavioral concerns; it legitimates the discussion of process-related issues. Hence change results both from the content of the data and the process of using survey data to identify and solve problems.[60]

As a general rule, organizations should report the results of surveys to employees, no matter how negative the results. And survey results should be reported fully to top management. Dunham and Smith offer the following admonition: "The cardinal rule in reporting survey results to top executives is to summarize the results so they can be understood, but to present them so candidly that they cannot be misunderstood. This takes knowledge and technical competence and often a great deal of courage! . . . To be less than candid, however, is to do a disservice to employees, management, and the organization."[61]

The presentation of results to any group is made easier by the use of a conceptual framework. One way to begin is by presenting information about the overall favorability of organizational, work, and individual characteristics; afterward, specific strengths and weaknesses can be addressed. This approach builds on an easily understood perspective—rather than an extensive "laundry list" of variables. When survey findings are presented in the form of an ad hoc collection of scores, the findings are typically received with indifference, because to the recipients such information is largely uninterpretable.[62]

Although disseminating survey results, interpreting and diagnosing problems, and conducting problem-solving discussions may be necessary conditions for organizational change, they are not sufficient in themselves. The crucial condition is the *institutionalization of mechanisms for ensuring that action plans are developed and carried out.* In the absence of formal arrangements that require these activities, managers will tend to ignore, if not forget, such activities. Ongoing responsibilities will take precedence over what may be seen as a one-shot phenomenon. Thus the important action-taking stage cannot be left to chance. What is needed, to use Ted Mills' phrase, is an architecture of permanence.

Finally, as noted previously, survey feedback by itself has demonstrated only limited and temporary effects.[63] In fact in one study, just providing feedback but not doing anything else (a practice that some people inelegantly refer to as "dump and run"), produced less favorable results than not providing any feedback at all.[64] Thus, survey feedback alone is a very limited tool for organizational improvement.[65] However, used as a diagnostic device, and coupled with interventions that directly affect organizational and work characteristics, the combined effects can be substantial and enduring.

## ESTABLISHING A PRODUCTIVITY DEPARTMENT

One way to institutionalize the use of diagnostic information as a basis for organizational change is by establishing a productivity department. The role of productivity manager and the creation of productivity departments are rapidly emerging phenomena on the corporate scene in the United States. In 1982 there were an estimated 300 companies that employed high-level productivity managers in corporate or division staffs. In comparison, an exhaustive national search uncovered just three such companies in 1975.[66] Further evidence of the rapid emergence of the role of productivity manager is provided by the history of the American Productivity Management Association (APMA), an organization dedicated to sharing productivity improvement ideas and to monitoring the evolving function of productivity manager. Founded in 1980, by 1981 it had 80 corporate members, and by 1983 the 200 corporate members had aggregate revenues exceeding $450 billion.[67]

Although the role of productivity manager has rapidly gained organizational acceptance, the topic of productivity still evokes little interest in the public at large. Many managers and elected officials are reluctant to talk about productivity, for fear of putting people to sleep.[68] Yet to many in the field of personnel and labor relations, the issue of productivity is far from dull. Indeed the term "productivity" often evokes strong negative reactions. Consider the following comments, reflective of reactions in the private and public sectors, respectively:

> The whole concept of productivity is often a loaded topic for employees and unions. Workers tend to think. . . "reduce costs, cut head count". . .So when management talks "productivity," unions hear "lost jobs," more often than not.[69]

> The very term "productivity improvement" implies criticism of present methods. . . . Unfortunately, the mere mention of the word productivity is often sufficient to stir thoughts of budget cuts and layoffs.[70]

In recent years, however, recognition has grown that productivity improvement is essential for protecting jobs, curbing inflation, improving the competitiveness of exports, conserving natural and human resources, and of course, improving the standard of living. Indicative of this awareness, Douglas Fraser, president of the United Automobile Workers, has told the rank and file that "producing more efficiently is an absolute necessity if we are not to lose our markets and our jobs."[71] Equally to the point, construction trade union leaders recently wrote their members: "If you want to work part time, get a job outside the construction industry. Protect your job and your future by cutting out absenteeism and low productivity."[72] Furthermore, signs of growing sympathy for productivity improvement have become evident in the trucking, airline, steel, and tire industries—all extremely troubled industries facing threats of massive job losses. Thus, it appears that Gordon Bloom's 1972 prophecy has come to pass. Interest in productivity improvement has emerged only by default—because it has become evident to all parties that their goals cannot be achieved without it.

Concomitantly, there have been more and more calls by all parties—labor, management, and government—for adoption of the four C's in labor relations: cooperation, collaboration, consultation, and compromise.[73] Consequently, there has been movement toward harmony in labor relations, rather than combative hostility; and toward establishing a "win-win" partnership, instead of "outmoded adversarial antagonisms."[74] In short, there has been a growing emphasis on increasing the value of goods and services produced, rather than a concern for divvying up the pie. As Edward Siebert of Grumman Aerospace put it: "All of this adversarial stuff that goes on in some industries is bad news. That's the biggest difference between the U.S. and Japan."[75]

### The Organizational Productivity Department: Six Desiderata

Because the productivity department is a relatively recent phenomenon, little research has been conducted concerning the determinants (or even the correlates) of productivity department effectiveness. The present discussion, therefore, relies heavily on opinions and descriptive accounts of current practices.[76]

**An Influential Director**   The director of a productivity department should be an organizational "heavyweight." Virtually all corporate productivity departments operate in a staff capacity.[77] With limited functional authority, coupled with (typically) a small staff and modest budget, the director of productivity must be knowledgeable and persuasive to be effective. Ideally, the productivity director should be able to adopt a multidisciplinary approach to productivity improvement, encompassing knowledge of the behavioral sciences, industrial engineering, operations management, and office technologies.[78] In addition, useful areas of competence include accounting, budgetary planning and control, and systems analysis. The productivity director also should have strong organizational skills, i.e., be "politically savvy," and have solid relationships with influential organizational members.

Most corporate productivity directors have had significant line experience. At American Hospital Supply Corporation, for example, the vice president, productivity management, was formerly manager of a key $600 million operating unit. He commented: "By putting me in this position, rather than some staff person, the company made it clear to everyone from the beginning that the program was to be taken seriously."[79] At Grumman Aerospace, Ed Siebert became corporate productivity director after 37 years of progressively responsible experience with the company. With this background, Siebert (in his words) knew "how the business was run, and how to get things done." Moreover, he knew "where the snakes were and which rocks not to lift."[80]

Consistent with these two examples of productivity directors, a 1980 survey by APMA identified the following characteristics of productivity managers (not necessarily productivity directors): median experience, 19 years; median salary, $67,500.

Not only should the productivity director be personally influential, it is widely agreed that the role needs a good deal of organizational influence.[81] Frequently the productivity director reports directly to the corporate president or chief operating officer.[82]

Because productivity is in part determined by economic and market considerations (e.g., economies of scale, growth in demand), competitive advantage is a highly relevant consideration. Managing productivity, therefore, should not be divorced from strategic decision making concerning product or service features.[83] "Adopting productivity programs without [due consideration of the] competitive context is like playing Russian roulette: the results range from nil to disaster. Doing the wrong things efficiently is not productive."[84]

**Top Management Sponsorship** An effective productivity department requires forceful, continuing, and visible support from top management. At the minimum, this should include issuing a policy statement indicating support for the productivity improvement effort; establishing appropriate organizational mechanisms for implementing such an effort; and the provision of adequate funding.[85] As an executive at U.S. Steel has observed: "We are finding that spoken and written words do not convince employees. They form their opinions by observing management decisions and actions."[86]

A review of twelve *successful* productivity improvement efforts found that only seven of the programs were still in operation after 3 years. Six of the seven ongoing programs had received a "continuing strong management push"; in contrast, only one of the five discontinued programs had received management's continuing support.[87]

The primary obstacle to implementing a productivity improvement program based on behavioral science is internal organizational politics. As Saul Gellerman has observed:

> Organizations that want to change, can. But by itself, productivity is not a sufficiently moving cause to create that desire. Important yes—even vital perhaps; but moving, no. There is no sex-appeal, no pizazz, no charisma in productivity. It needs help . . . what makes or breaks a productivity program is the *power* of its advocates. . . . Most organizations are not democracies: the opinions that move them are concentrated in a small group of top and middle managers. But neither are they dictatorships: they respond with considerable inertia to what their leaders command. A productivity improvement program—or for that matter, any change—that fails to take account of these realities is doomed.[88]

The support of the chief executive officer is particularly crucial in connection with the establishment of an effective productivity management department. Many, if not most, line managers will be rather passive and noncommittal regarding productivity improvement programs. They will be willing to review proposals, but few will aggressively search for or implement solutions. The CEO must supply the enthusiasm and leadership needed to sustain a productivity department.[89] And this enthusiasm should be manifested in ways that are public and relatively irrevocable. To the extent that both of these conditions are met, line managers are likely to commit themselves to improving productivity.[90] As Richard McNabb, of the Machinery & Allied Products Institute, noted, "when big corporations appoint a productivity manager, I think what they're doing is making a statement that productivity within the company is a high-priority issue."[91] In brief, top management must provide the enabling mandate to ensure an "architecture of permanence."[92]

**Long-Term Perspective** Capturing the loyalty and commitment of hundreds or thousands of individuals in an organization, so that they direct their energies toward a common set of goals is an extremely difficult undertaking.[93] It takes long-term thinking, consistency, and staying power. Because it takes years to change skills, attitudes, and behaviors in an organization, "the lack of long-range planning in human resources is frequently disastrous."[94] Improving productivity demands more than a "quick-fix," gimmick-of-the-month mentality.[95] As one productivity manager commented: "This company, and this country, didn't jump into a productivity slump. We worked our way into it slowly over a long period of time, and we are going to have to work our way out of it in about the same way."[96]

An important rationale for establishing a productivity department is to avoid the problems associated with crash programs and one-shot efforts.[97] Productivity improvement requires a longer range perspective than ordinary tasks, for two reasons. First, to repeat Gellerman's observation, "Who's against productivity? Anyone who has to sacrifice something to achieve it—and that includes nearly everyone."[98] Second, because productivity improvement efforts often take months of persistent effort before they pay off, they are at a disadvantage in competing for management attention. Many managers, procrastinating about productivity improvement efforts, will attend instead to activities important to everyday operations.[99] And when the organization's environment is turbulent, or where there are internal exigencies, productivity improvement activities are especially likely to be ignored.[100] A productivity department, therefore, can only be effective if managers are convinced of its durability.[101]

**A Critical Mass** According to Fran Tarkenton, of the Performance Management Companies, "Far too many companies are not getting maximum value from their investment of time and money in a variety of so-called 'productivity improvement' programs because they are usually isolated or uncoordinated activities."[102] By establishing an organizational productivity department, it is possible to cumulate and coordinate productivity improvement efforts under a single umbrella, i.e., to achieve a critical mass. Relatedly, Leon Skan, of APMA, has noted that in "most large companies, managers have gotten into the habit of expecting productivity improvements to come from some big breakthrough. This must change so that these people begin looking for all the little ways of improving productivity and working on these, and keep working on them."[103] The productivity department, potentially, can coordinate and motivate efforts designed to achieve a series of "little successes."

It is probably advisable to install productivity programs along a number of fronts simultaneously, rather than to focus efforts exclusively on a single, insular project: the chances of success are increased using a "shotgun approach rather than a rifle shot."[104] If this view is generally correct, it follows that the productivity department should orchestrate a variety of productivity improvement efforts.

A productivity department's effectiveness will be enhanced if successful interventions are extended to significant segments of the organization, following the dictum, "diffuse or die."[105] After evidence of a successful implementation is available, the program should be initiated elsewhere, provided that local managers are receptive.[106] Demonstrated successes will increase credibility and facilitate further adoptions: to be sure, it is important to achieve a high batting average.

**Institutionalization of Changes**   Virtually all planned organizational change efforts are likely to fade into oblivion in the absence of incorporation into ongoing operating, control, and reward systems. The viability of a productivity department, therefore, rests upon its ability to institutionalize changes. Several mechanisms might be employed. First, line managers might be required to formulate written productivity goals and measures, and be held accountable for achieving productivity results.[107] (The productivity department, of course, would be available to assist in this process.) Second, productivity improvement efforts and results should be incorporated into managerial performance appraisal and reward systems. Third, productivity management should be incorporated into budgeting, organizational planning, and resource allocation processes. More specifically, the productivity department might be given an active role in the capital budgeting process, evaluating project proposals in terms of productivity improvements as well as financial outcomes. And line managers might be required to provide status reports (to higher-level line executives) that contain productivity data on ongoing projects. Knowing that reports will pinpoint responsibility and (perhaps) be circulated to all interested parties will likely motivate follow through on productivity improvement projects. As Leon Skan put it: "What firms must do if they are really serious about improving productivity is to build the concept into their management systems and keep it there."[108] In contrast, productivity management programs that are outside the management mainstream have generally failed to achieve meaningful results.[109]

**Preparedness for Resistance**   Although it is attractive to view organizations as rationally structured systems, operating on logical principles, and populated by individuals working toward shared objectives, this view is somewhat uto-pian. It must be recognized that organizations are political arenas in which individuals battle for power and influence to achieve personally valued ends.[110] Consequently, many seemingly beneficial change efforts are thwarted by the political activities of organizational members who are seeking to enhance or protect their own power bases (and to eliminate those of potential rivals).[111] Some of the tactics managers can use to sabotage change efforts under the guise of advancing organizational well-being include: stalling to deenergize a project; bogging a project down with demands for more information; and attempting to discredit the change agent.[112]

An awareness of the politics of implementation is beneficial for a couple of reasons. First, it may represent a form of stress innoculation. There is evidence that "forewarned is forearmed."[113] Second, and more concretely, the director of productivity might well be advised to assess his or her own unit's power bases, and to build implementation strategies around them. A number of pos-sible political tactics are:

1 Alignment with powerful others
2 Development of trade-offs with client subunits
3 Design of interventions that initially entail little risk (e.g., focusing on research)
4 Expanding and publicizing initial successes
5 Linking up with already approved and noncontroversial programs
6 Keeping a low profile in the face of adversity

Political "maneuvers" clearly raise ethical issues and possibly personal moral dilemmas. A case can be made, however, for political sensitivity and development of the skills underlying the politics of implementation. At a min-imum, one can choose among those tactics that are morally acceptable.[114]

Resistance to change may also take the form of overt objections. In such cases the productivity manager must be able to respond promptly and effec-tively, providing compelling arguments to overcome objections.[115] Resistant managers will offer ingenious reasons why a particular productivity improve-ment program is unnecessary or lacking in merit; for instance,

1 This is similar to the program we tried a few years ago. And everyone knows that one didn't work.
2 It's a good idea, but we don't have the resources to implement it.
3 We're already doing it, in our own way.
4 Of course, we're always looking for improvements, but meanwhile we're doing the best we can.

Such objections may merely be defensive reactions, not reasoned positions. Accordingly, it is important to press for facts and the identification of real problems; one should not give up and accept the *status quo* until it is shown that improvements are impossible.[116] The productivity department representative should communicate expectations that a program is worthwhile, and that it can be made workable.[117] In the absence of this kind of enthusiastic support, little innovation is likely to be attempted.

### The Organizational Productivity Department: A Mission Statement

A number of functions can be identified as comprising the possible mandate of a productivity department. Briefly, a productivity department might pursue the following related objectives.[118]

**1** *Survey opportunities.* The productivity department might conduct a systematic, comprehensive, and theory-based diagnosis of organizational, work, and individual characteristics. On the basis of this diagnosis, the major strengths and weaknesses of the organization could be identified, leading to action planning, implementation, and evaluation. Institutionalization of this process should be part of the mandate.

**2** *Disseminate information.* Although productivity improvement is fundamentally a line responsibility, a productivity department can play a useful role by providing information and ideas about how to do it.[119] Toward this end a productivity newsletter might be published, and a council of productivity coordinators established, comprised of representatives from various units of the organization. Meeting periodically to exchange information and ideas, the members might report on their own experiences with productivity improvement activities. The establishment of a council or steering committee can serve not only to provide useful ideas, but to build the psychological ownership needed for change to occur.[120] Or the productivity department might itself make presentations to the various departments, perhaps describing programs that have worked elsewhere. In short, the productivity department should strive to inform and stimulate improvement steps; it might also serve as a clearinghouse and resource on productivity improvement methods.

**3** *Coordinate efforts.* Some projects will be beyond the scope of a single organizational subunit (e.g., the integration of computer-aided design and computer-aided manufacturing; the implementation of quality circles). The productivity department can help organize such efforts, in essence serving as a project manager responsible for coordination. The capacity to introduce innovative efforts presumably can be enhanced by the provision of "seed money" to invest in meritorious productivity improvement projects.[121]

**4** *Abet productivity measurement.* In many organizations productivity is only a vague ideal, pursued and monitored only indirectly (e.g., via attention to such objectives as profits, ROI, market share, etc.). Managers, consequently, have often lacked consistent, operationally meaningful measures of productivity (and changes in productivity). Lacking a systematic way to measure productivity, they have been at a loss as to how to manage productivity.[122] The productivity department can assist subunits in developing relevant indicators of productivity, help monitor productivity trends for the company as a whole, and keep track of various micro measures of productivity (e.g., actual and projected improvements resulting from funded capital budget proposals).

**5** *Assure recognition of gains.* The productivity department can publicize the results of productivity improvement programs. One possible vehicle is a productivity newsletter. Departmental successes might be linked to token tangible reinforcers and social recognition. Although organizations appear to be reluctant to use social reinforcers—perhaps because American workers are seen as too sophisticated or too cynical—their low use should make them all the more valued.[123] For example, at Manufacturers Hanover Trust Company productivity successes are reported in an ad hoc publication, *Productivity Spotlight*. People also are recognized via posters, certificates, and award ceremonies. Since the company's productivity slogan is "You Are the Key to Productivity," recipients of some awards (appropriately) receive a gold-plated key.[124]

**6** *Compile productivity data.* The productivity department might generate a report that compiles the productivity efforts and achievements of the various departments. This report should be distributed widely, with copies going to high-level line executives.

**7** *Encourage productivity consciousness.* In broad terms, the productivity department might be a catalyst to get people thinking about and initiating actions to improve productivity. The need for productivity improvement should be part of the decision making process at every level of the organization.

### SUMMARY

This, the concluding chapter, has summarized the empirical evidence regarding the efficacy of ten prominent approaches to productivity improvement. Two of the approaches with greatest impact, generally speaking, are output-based reward systems and tests for selection purposes; two of the least effective (yet widely publicized) approaches are job enrichment and participative leadership. Of course, the particular type of intervention that will work best in a given setting depends on the situation: there are no sure-fire, cure-all panaceas; rather the "cure should fit the ailment."

Accordingly, emphasis was placed on the role of organizational diagnosis. While it is crucial to know what needs to be done, it is another (and far more difficult) matter to implement needed changes. In this regard the potential role and possible mandate of a productivity department were described.

Unfortunately, productivity improvement is unlikely to happen automatically or spontaneously. Productivity has to be planned and systematically pursued; it has to be managed.

### NOTES

**1** Dava Sobel, "Psychologists for Industry Say They've Oversold Themselves," *New York Times,* 2 Sept. 1980, p. C2. (Paul Thayer was formerly the president of the

Industrial and Organizational Psychology division of the American Psychological Association.) Thayer's observation calls to mind Abraham Kaplan's observation that "It comes as no particular surprise to discover that a scientist formulates problems in a way which requires for their solution just those techniques in which he himself is especially skilled." See Abraham Kaplan, *The Conduct of Inquiry: Methodology for Behavioral Science* (Scranton, Penn.: Chandler, 1964), p. 28.

2 Larry Greiner, "Red Flags in Organization Development," *Business Horizons,* 15 (June 1972), 23; Jay W. Lorsch, "Making Behavioral Science More Useful," *Harvard Business Review,* 57 (March–April 1979), 172–176; Don Hellriegel and John W. Slocum, Jr., "Assessing Organizational Change Models: Toward a Comparative Typology," in *Readings in Management,* ed. Max D. Richards, 6th ed. (Cincinnati: South-Western, 1982), pp. 516–517; John R. Hinrichs, *Practical Management for Productivity* (New York: Van Nostrand Reinhold, 1978), p. 183; Claudia H. Deutsch, "Productivity: The Difficulty of Even Defining the Problem," *Business Week,* 9 June 1980, pp. 52–53; James L. Gibson, John M. Ivancevich, and James H. Donnelly, Jr., *Organizations: Behavior, Structure, Processes,* 4th ed. (Dallas: Business Publications Inc., 1982), p. 545. In the words of Gibson et al., "Instead of a 'canned' approach in which the diagnosis and method are the same for different companies, a more 'tailored' approach to change is needed. That is, interventions which fit the particular problems of an organization are needed" (p. 545). Consistent with the conclusion that there is no one best solution to all organizational problems is research reported by Dennis Umstot: "An Empirical Study of Personality and Consultant Performance," *Proceedings, 41st Annual Meeting of the Academy of Management* (1981), pp. 130–133. Umstot found that highly rated consultants tended to be more open-minded, flexible, nondogmatic, spontaneous, and impulse expressive.

3 Mayford L. Roark, "Some Approaches to the Management of Change," *Proceedings, 1977 IFIP Congress,* p. 112.

4 Douglas McGregor, quoted by A. A. Imberman in "The Low Road to Higher Productivity," *The Conference Board Record,* 12 (Jan. 1975), 30.

5 J. Richard Hackman and Greg R. Oldham, *Work Redesign* (Reading, Mass.; Addison-Wesley, 1980), pp. 100–102.

6 Robert T. Golembiewski and Richard J. Hilles, *Toward the Responsive Organization: The Theory and Practice of Survey/Feedback* (Salt Lake City: Brighton Publishing, 1979), p. 3.

7 Clayton P. Alderfer, "The Methodology of Organizational Diagnosis," *Professional Psychology,* 11 (1980), 459.

8 William G. Dyer, "Selecting an Intervention for Organizational Change," *Training and Development Journal,* 35 (Apr. 1981), 62.

9 Clayton P. Alderfer, "Methodology," p. 461.

10 Ibid.

11 David M. Boje, Donald B. Fedor, and Kendrith M. Rowland, "Myth Making: A Qualitative Step in OD Interventions," paper presented at the 40th Annual National Meeting of the Academy of Management, 1980, pp. 9–12.

12 See for example, Cyrus F. Gibson, "A Methodology for Implementation Research," in *Implementing Operations Research/Management Science,* ed. Randall L. Schultz and Dennis P. Slevin (New York: American Elsevier Publishing, 1975), pp. 53–73.

13 Clayton P. Alderfer, "Methodology," p. 465.

14 Donald K. White, "Office Life: Smiles, Laughs a Good Sign," *The Industrial Psychologist,* 18 (May 1981), 21.

**15** Comments of Harry Levinson as reported by Donald K. White, "Office Life," p. 21.

**16** David G. Bowers and Jerome L. Franklin, *Survey-Guided Development: Data-Based Organizational Change,* rev. (La Jolla, Calif.: University Associates, 1977), p. 63.

**17** A. A. Imberman, "The Low Road," p. 30.

**18** Ibid.

**19** Ibid., p. 35.

**20** Ibid., p. 37.

**21** "The American Productivity Center's Slim Yield," *Business Week,* 3 Nov. 1980, p. 96.

**22** Bernard Bass and Enzo Valenzi, "Organizational Psychology: A Professional Application," *Professional Psychology,* 11 (1980), p. 472.

**23** Ibid.

**24** "Productivity Anonymous: What Your Employees Know Could Help You," *Hay Management Memo,* No. 321 (1979), pp. 1–2. Also see David Sirota and Alan D. Wolfson, "Pragmatic Approach to People Problems," *Harvard Business Review,* 51, No. 1 (1973), 125. As Sirota and Wolfson have observed, "management may think it knows what is happening, but it is frequently dead wrong."

**25** Wallace Martin, "What Management Can Expect from an Attitude Survey," *Personnel Administrator,* 26 (July 1981), 75; "From Results to Action: Translating Climate Surveys," *Hay Management Memo,* No. 310 (1978), p. 1.

**26** Randall B. Dunham and Frank J. Smith, *Organizational Surveys: An Internal Assessment of Organizational Health* (Glenview, Ill.: Scott, Foresman, 1979), p. 44.

**27** Rensis Likert, "Human Organizational Measurements: Key to Financial Success," in *Readings in Management,* ed. Max D. Richards, 6th ed. (Cincinnati: South-Western, 1982), p. 347. (This article originally appeared in the May 1971 issue of the *Michigan Business Review.*) Along these lines, survey data have also demonstrated predictive validity with respect to reward system practices. See Richard E. Kopelman, "Organizational Control System Responsiveness, Expectancy Theory Constructs, and Work Motivation: Some Interrelations and Causal Connections," *Personnel Psychology,* 29 (1976), 205–220.

**28** For example, the Institute for Social Research's Survey of Organizations (SOO) has been used by more than fifty organizations; the Hay Associates survey by more than sixty major corporations; and the Organizational Analysis Questionnaire (OAQ) has been used by more than one hundred organizations. The OAQ, developed by Behavioral Science Resources, prioritizes problems based on two considerations: their frequency of occurrence and criticalness.

**29** The OAQ, for example, measures seventeen dimensions of organizational characteristics, including teamwork, leadership, employee development, and goal setting.

**30** "From Results to Action: Translating Climate Surveys," *Hay Management Memo* No. 310 (1978), p. 1. Also see Randall B. Dunham and Frank J. Smith, *Organizational Surveys,* pp. 102–103, 126.

**31** Wallace Martin, "What Management Can Expect," p. 75.

**32** Ernest C. Miller, "Attitude Surveys: A Diagnostic Tool," *Personnel,* 55 (May–June 1978), 7.

**33** Randall B. Dunham and Frank J. Smith, *Organizational Surveys,* p. 126.

**34** William E. Dodd and Michael L. Pesci, "Managing Morale through Survey Feedback," *Business Horizons,* 20 (June 1977), 38.

**35** Louis B. Barnes, "Managing the Paradox of Organizational Trust," *Harvard Business Review,* 59, No. 2 (1981), 111–112.

**36** Randall B. Dunham and Frank J. Smith, *Organizational Surveys,* pp. 55, 126.

**37** Randall B. Dunham and Roger A. Formisano, "Designing and Evaluating Employee Benefit Systems," *Personnel Administrator,* 27 (Apr. 1982), 29–35.

**38** David G. Bowers, Jerome L. Franklin, and P. A. Pecorella, "Matching Problems, Precursors, and Interventions in OD: A Systematic Approach," *Journal of Applied Behavioral Science,* 11 (1975), 393.

**39** "Productivity Anonymous: What Your Employees Know Could Help You," p. 2.

**40** William G. Dyer, "When is a Problem a Problem?" *Personnel Administrator,* 23 (June 1978), 70.

**41** Ibid.

**42** Robert T. Golembiewski and Richard J. Hilles, *Toward the Responsive Organization,* p. 188.

**43** Bonnie Goldberg and George G. Gordon, "Designing Attitude Surveys for Management Action," *Personnel Journal,* 57 (1978), 546, 549.

**44** "Productivity Anonymous: What Your Employees Know Could Help You," p. 2. In this regard it is notable that the survey program at Sears Roebuck requires that after the results are fed back to the work group, the manager initiates at least one concrete, tangible change in response to the survey results. (Frank J. Smith, comments at the American Psychological Association Workshop, "The Interpretation and Use of Survey Feedback in Organizational Settings," 1979.)

**45** Wendell L. French and Cecil H. Bell, Jr., *Organization Development: Behavioral Science Interventions for Organization Improvement,* 2d ed. (Englewood Cliffs, N.J.: Prentice-Hall, 1978), p. 156. In connection with cost-effectiveness, Robert T. Golembiewski and Richard J. Hilles, *Toward the Responsive Organization,* have commented that "surveys provide a convenient means of learning what is going on among the organizational legions . . . at a cost . . . that is minuscule compared to the potential yields of information and goodwill" (p. 1).

**46** David G. Bowers and Jerome L. Franklin, *Survey-Guided Development,* pp. 129–134; Robert T. Golembiewski and Richard J. Hilles, *Toward the Responsive Organization,* p. 11; and Bonnie Goldberg and George G. Gordon, "Designing Attitude Surveys," pp. 546, 549.

**47** David G. Bowers and Jerome L. Franklin, *Survey-Guided Development,* pp. 129–134.

**48** "Personnel Widens Its Franchise," *Business Week,* 26 Feb. 1979, p. 121.

**49** Bonnie Goldberg and George G. Gordon, "Designing Attitude Surveys," pp. 546–549.

**50** Charles L. Hulin, "Job Satisfaction and Turnover in a Female Clerical Population," *Journal of Applied Psychology,* 50 (1966), 280–285; also Charles L. Hulin, "Effects of Changes in Job Satisfaction Levels and Employee Turnover," *Journal of Applied Psychology,* 52 (1968), 122–126. (The conversion of salary or dollar savings to an estimate of change in productivity was done using the procedure described in Chapter 3, footnote 29.)

**51** Stewart L. Tubbs and Robin N. Widgery, "When Productivity Lags Check at the Top: Are Key Managers Really Communicating?" *Management Review,* 67 (Nov. 1978), 20–25.

**52** Philip H. Mirvis and Edward E. Lawler III, "Measuring the Financial Impact of Employee Attitudes," *Journal of Applied Psychology,* 62 (1977), 1–8.

**53** Wallace Martin, "What Management Can Expect," p. 76; Andrew D. Szilagyi and Marc J. Wallace, Jr., *Organizational Behavior and Performance,* 3d ed. (Glenview,

Ill.: Scott, Foresman, 1983), p. 574; also David Sirota and Alan D. Wolfson, "Pragmatic Approach," p. 127.

**54** Randall B. Dunham and Frank J. Smith, *Organizational Surveys: An Internal Assessment of Organizational Health* (Glenview, Ill.: Scott, Foresman, 1979), p. 61. Copyright © 1979 Scott, Foresman. Reprinted by permission.

**55** Gerald R. Salancik, "Commitment is Too Easy!" *Organizational Dynamics,* 6 (Summer 1977), 74.

**56** Robert T. Golembiewski and Richard J. Hilles, *Toward the Responsive Organization,* p. 52; Randall B. Dunham and Frank J. Smith, *Organizational Surveys,* pp. 65–66.

**57** David A. Nadler, *Feedback and Organization Development: Using Data-Based Methods* (Reading, Mass.: Addison-Wesley, 1977), p. 11. Golembiewski and Hilles, *Toward the Responsive Organization,* discuss at great length whether respondents should or should not be identifiable. They note three primary advantages of preserving anonymity: higher response rate, reduced falsification of data, and minimization of the likelihood of managerial retribution. They also note two advantages to being able to identify respondents: (1) survey data can be matched with information from personnel files (e.g., performance ratings) and (2) by obtaining longitudinal panel data it is possible to examine individual change scores. Golembiewski and Hilles recommend a compromise, Respondents can be asked to volunteer identifying information (e.g., last four digits of mother-in-law's phone number) that will only be seen by an independent researcher. In one study some 71 percent of respondents volunteered identifying information (p. 216).

**58** Randall B. Dunham and Frank J. Smith, *Organizational Surveys,* p. 88.

**59** Ibid., p. 100. Copyright © 1979 Scott, Foresman. Reprinted by permission.

**60** David A. Nadler, *Feedback,* pp. 49, 150, 152.

**61** Randall B. Dunham and Frank J. Smith, *Organizational Surveys,* p. 108. Copyright © 1979 Scott, Foresman. Reprinted by permission.

**62** David G. Bowers and Jerome L. Franklin, *Survey-Guided Development,* pp. 8, 91; David A. Nadler, *Feedback,* p. 165.

**63** John M. Nicholas, "The Comparative Impact of Organization Development Interventions On Hard Criteria Measures," *Academy of Management Review,* 7 (1982), 535–536, 540.

**64** Edward J. Conlon and Kenneth L. Hamilton, "Leadership Style and Propensity to Communicate Survey Feedback Data: An Empirical Investigation," paper presented at the 13th Annual National Meeting of the American Institute for Decision Sciences (Boston), 1981, p. 15.

**65** David A. Nadler, *Feedback,* pp. 10, 171.

**66** Marta Mooney, "Organizing for Productivity Management," *National Productivity Review,* 1 (1982), 141.

**67** Peter J. Lemonias and Brian L. Usilaner, "Productivity Management: A Neglected Approach for Reducing Federal Government Costs," *National Productivity Review,* 3 (1984), 146.

**68** Jeremy Main, "Why Government Works Dumb," *Fortune,* 10 Aug. 1981, p. 147.

**69** John R. Hinrichs, *Practical Management for Productivity* (New York: Van Nostrand Reinhold, 1978), p. 182. Along these lines, Daniel D. Cook in his article, "Labor Faces the Productivity Challenge," *Industry Week,* 9 Mar. 1981, quotes a United Rubber Workers of America official as stating: "We've agreed to lots of productivity programs in the past, and just about every time we wound up getting shafted by management." Hence, according to Cook, "When management asks for a union's cooperation to improve productivity, most workers have learned to anticipate working faster—for less pay. And, down the road, they've suspected a plant closing. To labor, productivity has long been a dirty word" (p. 61).

**70** John S. Thomas, "So, Mr. Mayor, You Want to Improve Productivity. . .," in *Managing State and Local Government: Cases and Readings,* ed. Frederick S. Lane (New York: St. Martin's Press, 1980), pp. 411, 426.

**71** A. H. Raskin, "Can Management and Labor Really Become Partners?" *Across the Board,* 19 (July–Aug. 1982), 16.

**72** Carla O'Dell, "Labor-Management Cooperation: A Renewable Resource," *The Productivity Letter,* 1 (Jan. 1982), 6 (published by the American Productivity Center). In this vein, Peter Drucker has noted that labor leaders increasingly accept the view that "The worker's welfare depends on capital formation and productivity—even in the short run. The two largely determine how many jobs there will be, how secure they can be and how well paid they can be" (in "Are Unions Becoming Irrelevant?" *Wall Street Journal,* 22 Sept. 1982, p. 30). Yet changing the attitudes of workers is a slow process. In the same article Drucker cited one union leader who stated that "It is our proudest boast that the total wage package in our industry is some 30 percent to 40 percent higher than the average wage package in American manufacturing. But would there be record unemployment in our industry—approaching the levels of the depression—if that 30 percent to 40 percent had been put into plant modernization instead of wages and benefits? I know that all my colleagues in the union leadership ask themselves this question. But no one dares come out with it into the open—he wouldn't last 10 minutes if he did" (Ibid.).

**73** Carla O'Dell, "Labor-Management Cooperation." Also, at the conference, "Current Directions in Productivity—Evolving Japanese and American Perspectives" (New York City), Mar. 1982, three speakers (E. Douglas White, Egils Milbergs, and Ted Mills) all reported a trend toward labor-management cooperation.

**74** Reports of effective labor-management cooperation have become increasingly commonplace: e.g., Arnold S. Judson, "New Strategies to Improve Productivity," *Technology Review,* 78 (July–Aug. 1976), 65 (Esso Petroleum); Phil Farish, "Pair Potpourri," *Personnel Administrator,* 27 (Sept. 1982), 18 (Jones and Laughlin); "Former UAW Counsel Tells Managers: Drop Adversarial Roles, Work With Unions," *ASPA Resource,* Aug. 1982, p. 7 (Ford Motor Company).

**75** Personal communication, 15 Jan. 1982.

**76** One hopes that in the future organizational behavior researchers will conduct empirical investigations concerning the productivity management function.

**77** Leon Skan, personal communication, 22 Jan. 1982. (Leon Skan is the executive director of the American Productivity Management Association.)

**78** Marta Mooney, "Organizing," p. 147.

**79** Marta Mooney, "Productivity Improvement at American Hospital Supply Corporation," *National Productivity Review,* 2 (1983), 311.

**80** Personal communication, 15 Jan. 1982.

**81** Marta Mooney, "Organizing," p. 144; also Peter J. Lemonias and Brian L. Usilaner, "Productivity Management," pp. 145–154, came to this conclusion based on their survey of thirteen successful productivity management programs (six in the private sector, seven in the public sector); also see Jon English and Anthony R. Marchione, "Productivity: A New Perspective," *California Management Review,* 25 (Jan. 1983), 58–59, 62–63.

**82** Y. K. Shetty, "Key Elements of Productivity Improvement Programs," *Business Horizons,* 25 (Mar.–Apr. 1982), 16–17.

**83** John Dutton and Annie Thomas, "Managing Organizational Productivity," *The Journal of Business Strategy,* 3 (Summer 1982), 40–44.

**84** Stephen Moss, "A Systems Approach to Productivity," *National Productivity Review,* 1 (1982), 274.

**85** Y. K. Shetty, "Key Elements," p. 16; also Peter J. Lemonias and Brian L. Usilaner, "Productivity Management," p. 147.

**86** *National Productivity Review,* 2 (Winter 1982–83), 86.

**87** John R. Hinrichs, *Practical Management,* pp. 171–174, 178–182.

**88** Saul W. Gellerman, "Who's Against Productivity?" *The Conference Board Record,* 10 (Sept. 1973), 43.

**89** John S. Thomas, "So, Mr. Mayor," p. 414.

**90** Gerald R. Salancik, "Commitment," pp. 64–68.

**91** "Organizing for Productivity," *Industry Week,* 9 Feb. 1981, p. 58.

**92** Ted Mills, comments at conference, "Current Directions in Productivity—Evolving Japanese and American Practices," (New York City), Mar. 1982.

**93** Wickham Skinner, "Big Hat, No Cattle: Managing Human Resources," *Harvard Business Review,* 59, No. 5 (1981), 108–109.

**94** Ibid., p. 112.

**95** John R. Hinrichs, "Avoid the 'Quick-Fix' Approach to Productivity Problems," *Personnel Administrator,* 28 (July 1983), 40–43; also see Edmund J. Metz, "Managing Change: Implementing Productivity and Quality Improvements," *National Productivity Review,* 3 (1984), 303–313.

**96** Marta Mooney, "Organizing," p. 143.

**97** Edmund J. Metz, "Managing Change," pp. 311–313; also John S. Thomas, "So, Mr. Mayor," p. 413.

**98** Saul W. Gellerman, "Who's Against Productivity?" p. 43.

**99** John S. Thomas, "So, Mr. Mayor," p. 415.

**100** John R. Hinrichs, *Practical Management,* p. 182. Also pertinent is the case study described by Cyrus F. Gibson, "Methodology," pp. 53–73.

**101** Patricia Schroeder, "The Politics of Productivity," *Public Personnel Management,* 9, No. 4 (1980), 242; Y. K. Shetty, "Key Elements," pp. 21–22; Edmund J. Metz, "Managing Change," p. 303; Peter J. Lemonias and Brian L. Usilaner, "Productivity Management," pp. 147–148.

**102** Ron Zemke, "Productivity Improvement Efforts Take on Broader Perspective," *Training/HRD,* 19 (Mar. 1982), 8.

**103** Marta Mooney, "Organizing," pp. 141–142. Similarly, John R. Hinrichs in, "What's Wrong With Traditional Productivity Improvement Programs," *Training/HRD,* 19 (Mar. 1982), 90, suggests that many small changes can add up to sizable productivity gains.

**104** John R. Hinrichs, *Practical Management,* p. 182.

**105** Ibid., p. 183; Paul S. Goodman, "Why Productivity Programs Fail: Reasons and Solutions," *National Productivity Review,* 1 (1982), p. 377.

**106** Saul W. Gellerman, "Who's Against Productivity?" p. 43.

**107** Peter J. Lemonias and Brian L. Usilaner, "Productivity Management," pp. 147–148.

**108** Marta Mooney, "Organizing," p. 144. In this vein, J. V. Riordan in "The Impact of the Recession on Productivity Programs," *National Productivity Review,* 2

(1983), wrote: "Today, total integration of productivity concepts in all management processes appears to be the cutting edge of productivity improvement" (p. 209).

**109** Peter J. Lemonias and Brian L. Usilaner, "Productivity Management," p. 146.

**110** Virgina E. Schein, "Examining an Illusion: The Role of Deceptive Behaviors in Organizations," *Human Relations,* 32 (1979), 288–290.

**111** Virginia E. Schein, "Political Strategies for Implementing Organizational Change," *Group and Organization Studies,* 2, No. 1 (1977), p. 43; also see Abraham Zaleznik, "Power and Politics in Organizational Life," *Harvard Business Review,* 48, No. 3 (1970), 47–60.

**112** Virginia E. Schein, "Examining an Illusion: The Role of Deceptive Behaviors in Organizations," p. 291.

**113** See Harold G. Kaufman, *Professionals in Search of Work: Coping with the Stress of Job Loss and Underemployment* (New York: Wiley Interscience, 1982), p. 210, for research on the "immunizing" effects of stress innoculation.

**114** Virginia E. Schein, "Political Strategies," pp. 46–47.

**115** John S. Thomas, "So, Mr. Mayor," pp. 414–415.

**116** Ibid., p. 415. Also see Patricia Schroeder, "Politics," pp. 238–239 for a good list of excuses.

**117** Gerald R. Salancik, "Commitment," pp. 77–78; John S. Thomas, "So, Mr. Mayor," pp. 414–415.

**118** The productivity department at Grumman Aerospace Corporation served as a model for many of the ideas in this section.

**119** "Organizing for Productivity," pp. 58, 60; Marta Mooney, "Organizing," p. 142.

**120** Edmund J. Metz, "Managing Change," p. 312.

**121** Marta Mooney, "Organizing," p. 147.

**122** Ibid., p. 142.

**123** One highly successful company, Herman Miller, Inc., makes extensive use of public recognition in connection with its Scanlon plan (e.g., there is a "Manager of the Year" award). In connection with this plan, the company has prepared a movie which this writer has shown several times to students (in New York City). It is interesting that initially students react by laughing at the scenes showing social recognition. However, when asked afterward whether they would like to work for Herman Miller if the company were located in New York City, roughly 75 percent respond affirmatively.

**124** Richard J. Lambert, "Productivity Awareness at Manufacturers Hanover Trust," *National Productivity Review,* 2 (1983), 300–306.

# NAME INDEX

# SUBJECT INDEX